PROTESTANT NONCONFORMIST TEXTS
VOLUME 3

This volume gathers and introduces texts relating to English and Welsh Nonconformity. Through contemporary writings it provides a vivid insight into the life and thought of the Methodists, Congregationalists, Baptists, Quakers, Unitarians and other groups that formed pieces in the diverse mosaic of the nineteenth-century chapels. Each aspect of Nonconformity has an introductory discussion, which includes a guide to the secondary literature on the subject, and each passage from a primary source is put in context.

PROTESTANT NONCONFORMIST TEXTS

Series editor: Alan P. F. Sell

This series of four substantial volumes is designed to demonstrate the range of interests of the several Protestant Nonconformist traditions from the time of their Separatist harbingers in the sixteenth century to the end of the twentieth century. It represents a major project of the Association of Denominational Historical Societies and Cognate Libraries. Each volume comprises a General Introduction followed by texts illustrative of such topics as theology, philosophy, worship and socio-political concerns. This work has never before been drawn together for publication in this way. Prepared by a team of twelve editors, all of whom are expert in their areas and drawn from a number of the relevant traditions, it provides a much-needed comprehensive view of Nonconformity told largely in the words of those whose story it is. The works will prove to be an invaluable resource to scholars, students, academics and specialist and public libraries, as well as to a wider range of church, intellectual and general historians.

Other titles in the series:

Protestant Nonconformist Texts Volume 1
1550 to 1700
Edited by R. Tudur Jones
with Arthur Long and Rosemary Moore

Protestant Nonconformist Texts Volume 2
The Eighteenth Century
Edited by Alan P. F. Sell
with David J. Hall and Ian Sellers

Protestant Nonconformist Texts Volume 4
The Twentieth Century
Edited by David M. Thompson
with J. H. Y. Briggs and John Munsey Turner

Protestant Nonconformist Texts
Volume 3

The Nineteenth Century

Edited by
DAVID BEBBINGTON

with
KENNETH DIX
and
ALAN RUSTON

WIPF & STOCK · Eugene, Oregon

Wipf and Stock Publishers
199 W 8th Ave, Suite 3
Eugene, OR 97401

Protestant Nonconformist Texts Volume 3
The Nineteenth Century
By Bebbington, David W. and Dix, Kenneth
Copyright©2006 by Bebbington, David W.
ISBN 13: 978-1-4982-1917-4
Publication date 2/3/2015
Previously published by Ashgate, 2006

Contents

Series Editor's Preface	xv
Acknowledgements	xvii
Abbreviations	xix
Introduction	1

Part I: Sermons

Introduction		13
I.1	Robert Hall on the Substitution of the Innocent for the Guilty, 1822	14
I.2	Adam Clarke on Happiness the Privilege of Every Real Christian, 1828	16
I.3	William Gadsby on the Acceptable Year and Day of Vengeance, 1842	17
I.4	C. H. Spurgeon on the Immutability of God, 1855	19
I.5	W. Morley Punshon on the Gospel, n.d.	21
I.6	Joseph Parker on the Gospel, n.d.	22
I.7	J. H. Thom on God a Spirit, n.d.	23
I.8	Alexander Maclaren on the Wells of Salvation, 1882	24
I.9	Hugh Price Hughes on Christ the Greatest of Social Reformers, 1889	26
I.10	R. F. Horton on the Living Christ, 1891	27

Part II: Theology

Introduction		31

Statements of Faith

II.1	Collingham Baptist Church Confession of Faith, c. 1801	33
II.2	The General Baptist New Connexion Catechism on God, 1805	35
II.3	Welsh Calvinistic Methodist Confession of Faith on God, 1823	36
II.4	Congregational Union Declaration, 1833	39
II.5	Quaker Testimony to the Authority of Christ in his Church, 1840	44
II.6	Unitarian Opinion, 1846	47
II.7	Evangelical Alliance Basis of Faith, 1846	49
II.8	Salvation Army Religious Doctrines, 1878	50
II.9	Baptist Union Declaratory Statement, 1888	51

Contents

II.10	Evangelical Free Church Catechism, 1899	52

Theologians

II.11	Andrew Fuller on Duty Faith, 1801	59
II.12	Edward Williams on Moderate Calvinism, 1809	60
II.13	Richard Watson on Arminianism, 1829	62
II.14	William Arthur on Entire Sanctification, 1856	63
II.15	James Martineau on the Incarnation, 1861 and 1864	64
II.16	R. W. Dale on the Atonement, 1878	65
II.17	W. B. Pope on Theology as a Science, 1880	67
II.18	A. M. Fairbairn on the Kingdom of God, 1893	68
II.19	P. T. Forsyth on God the Holy Father, 1896	69
II.20	J. S. Lidgett on the Fatherhood of God, 1897	70

Controversies and Issues

II.21	William Huntington on the Divine Law, 1804	72
II.22	William Steadman on Believer's Baptism, 1812	73
II.23	Robert Hall on Terms of Communion, 1815	74
II.24	Suffolk and Norfolk Strict Baptist Association Circular Letter, 1829	75
II.25	Isaac Crewdson's Resignation from the Quakers, 1836	77
II.26	Epistle from the Meeting for Sufferings, 1836	78
II.27	Samuel Davidson on Biblical Criticism, 1839	79
II.28	J. Angell James on the Postmillennial Hope, 1848	80
II.29	B. W. Newton on Premillennialism, 1850	81
II.30	John Harris on the Inspiration of the Scriptures, 1851	82
II.31	T. T. Lynch on the *Rivulet* Controversy of 1855–57	83
II.32	J. Howard Hinton's Critique of J. Baldwin Brown's *The Divine Life in Man*, 1860	84
II.33	James Wells and William Bidder on the Eternal Sonship of Christ, 1860	85
II.34	Leicester Conference on the Terms of Religious Communion, 1877	86
II.35	Samuel Cox on the Larger Hope, 1877	87
II.36	Charles Beard on the Person of Christ, 1881	89
II.37	C. H. Spurgeon on the Down Grade, 1887	90
II.38	R. F. Horton on Inspiration, 1888	91
II.39	John Clifford on the Social Gospel, 1888	92
II.40	D. W. Simon on Congregational Thought, 1891	93

Contents

Part III: Writings

Introduction 97

Philosophy and Apologetic
III.1   George Payne on Reason in Religion, 1828   98
III.2   Adam Clarke on the Being of God, 1829   99
III.3   Henry Rogers from *The Eclipse of Faith*, 1852   100
III.4   *The British Quarterly Review* on J. S. Mill, 1860   102
III.5   Thomas Cooper on the Moral Argument for God, 1875   102
III.6   A. M. Fairbairn on Mansfield College, Oxford, 1889   104
III.7   Hugh Price Hughes on Social Evolution, 1894   105

Science
III.8   *The Methodist Magazine* on Natural Theology, 1825   106
III.9   John Pye Smith on Science and Religion, 1839   107
III.10 John Clifford on Darwinian Evolution, 1882   108
III.11 W. H. Dallinger on the Creator, 1887   109

Other Non-Fiction
III.12 David Bogue and James Bennett, *History of Dissenters*, 1808   111
III.13 John Foster on the Aversion of Men of Taste to Evangelical Religion, 1819   111
III.14 John Kenrick on Christian Liberty, 1836   113
III.15 *The Inquirer*, 1842   114
III.16 Mary Ann Hearn (Marianne Farningham) on *The Christian World*, 1857   115
III.17 *The Methodist Times*, 1885   116

Fiction
III.18 George Eliot, *Adam Bede*, 1859   117
III.19 Margaret Oliphant, *Salem Chapel*, 1863   118
III.20 M. G. Pearse, *Daniel Quorm and his Religious Notions*, 1875   119
III.21 W. H. White, *Autobiography of Mark Rutherford*, 1888   120
III.22 W. H. Mills, *Grey Pastures*, on a Bazaar of c. 1890   121

Part IV: Worship

Introduction 125

General
IV.1   Hugh Bourne on the Camp Meeting Preacher, c. 1820   127
IV.2   Robert Hall as a Preacher, 1821   128
IV.3   Adam Clarke as a Preacher, 1833   129

Contents

IV.4	Edward Miall on the Reform of Worship, 1849	130
IV.5	William Trotter on Brethren Worship, c. 1850	131
IV.6	James Martineau's Call to Worship, 1862	132
IV.7	Saul Street Primitive Methodist Chapel, Preston, 1869	132
IV.8	R. W. Dale on Preaching, 1877	134
IV.9	A Strict Baptist View of Worship, 1879	135
IV.10	Gideon Congregational Church, Newfoundland Street, Bristol, 1880	136
IV.11	The Welsh *Hwyl*, c. 1880	137
IV.12	Caroline Stephens on Quaker Silent Waiting, 1891	138
IV.13	*The British Weekly* on Sermon Texts, 1896	139
IV.14	C. Silvester Horne and T. H. Darlow: Orders for Morning and Evening Service, 1897	140

Sacraments

IV.15	Adam Clarke on the Holy Communion, 1830	142
IV.16	Primitive Methodist Communion at Conference, 1841	143
IV.17	Baptist Noel on Believer's Baptism, 1849	144
IV.18	Catholic Apostolic Church Eucharist, 1850	144
IV.19	A Primitive Methodist Defence of Pouring in Baptism, 1862	146
IV.20	C. H. Spurgeon on the Real Presence, c. 1880	147

Music and Hymnody

IV.21	William Gadsby's Hymn of Praise to Christ, 1814	148
IV.22	Hymn on Revival from the Primitive Methodist Short Hymn Book, 1829	149
IV.23	J. C. Philpot on Singing in Worship, 1859	150
IV.24	Henry Allon on Church Choirs, 1870	151
IV.25	Presbyterian Views on Organs, 1856–70	152
IV.26	Salvation Army Regulations for Brass Bands, 1881	154
IV.27	W. G. Tarrant's Easter Hymn, c. 1890	155

Architectural Setting

IV.28	John Blackburn on the Gothic Style, 1847	156
IV.29	Philip Sambell on the Gothic Style, 1867	157
IV.30	Penmaenmawr Wesleyan Chapel, 1890	157
IV.31	John Wills on Duties of Caretakers, 1893	158

Part V: Spirituality

Introduction	163

Conversion

V.1	John Rippon on the Theology of Conversion, 1801	165

Contents

V.2	An Independent Conversion, 1804	165
V.3	A Particular Baptist Conversion, 1809	166
V.4	A Wesleyan Conversion, 1812	167
V.5	A General Baptist Conversion, 1820	168
V.6	A Quaker Conversion, c. 1830	169
V.7	J. Angell James on Faith, 1834	170
V.8	A Primitive Methodist Conversion, c. 1838	170
V.9	A Methodist Conversion, c. 1900	172

Experience

V.10	A Baptist View of the Baptism of the Holy Ghost, 1810	173
V.11	A Wesleyan Full Consecration to God, c. 1810	174
V.12	A Religion of Experience, 1834	175
V.13	A Congregationalist's Spiritual Encouragement, 1838	176
V.14	A Peculiar People Healing, c. 1875	177
V.15	Thomas Waugh on the Power of Pentecost, c. 1895	177

Activities

V.16	Opposition to a Baptist, c. 1805	179
V.17	Samuel Budgett's Business Policy, c. 1820	180
V.18	Helen Herschell on Family Prayer, c. 1840	180
V.19	Thomas Binney on the Best of Both Worlds, 1853	181
V.20	A Strict Baptist View of Emigration, 1853	182
V.21	Edmund Gosse, His Father and a Christmas Pudding, 1857	183
V.22	Caring for Orphans by Faith, 1867	184
V.23	Methodist Bible and Prayer Union Requests for Prayer and Praise, 1881	185

Death

V.24	A Wesleyan Death, 1803	187
V.25	A Quaker Death, 1823	188
V.26	A Congregationalist Death, 1824	189
V.27	A Letter of Consolation, 1839	190
V.28	A Huntingtonian Death, 1844	191
V.29	A Baptist Death, 1852	192
V.30	A Unitarian Memorial, 1862	193

Part VI: Chapel

| Introduction | | 197 |

Ministry

| VI.1 | Ministers and Secular Business, 1812 | 199 |
| VI.2 | Robert Vaughan on the Ministry, 1843 | 200 |

VI.3	The Wesleyan Ordination Service, 1848	201
VI.4	C. H. Spurgeon on the Ministry, 1876	202

Lay Leadership

VI.5	A Primitive Methodist Preachers' Plan, 1854	204
VI.6	A Baptist Deacon from 1858	206
VI.7	John Harvey on Local Preachers, 1864	206

Membership

VI.8	Calvinistic Methodist Rules of Discipline, 1801	208
VI.9	Application to Join a Congregational Church, 1829	210
VI.10	Church Membership at the Metropolitan Tabernacle, 1860	212
VI.11	Investigation into Bankruptcy of Sir Morton Peto at Bloomsbury Baptist Church, 1868	213
VI.12	Public Recognition of Wesleyan Members, 1878	214
VI.13	R. W. Dale on Church Membership, 1881	215
VI.14	Articles of War for Salvation Army Soldiers, 1882	216

Activities

VI.15	Wesleyan Conference Resolutions on Society Activities, 1821	218
VI.16	An Independent Sunday School Anniversary, c. 1825	219
VI.17	Hugh Bourne on Class Meetings and Love Feasts, 1829	220
VI.18	A Baptist on Church Meetings, 1835	222
VI.19	Northamptonshire Baptist Association Circular Letter on Prayer Meetings, 1842	223
VI.20	William Gadsby on Sunday Schools, 1843	225
VI.21	A Congregational Funeral, c. 1850	226
VI.22	A Brethren Bible Reading, c. 1850	227
VI.23	Plans for a Wesleyan Sunday School, 1856	228
VI.24	Preparation for a Christmas Tea Party, c. 1890	229

Part VII: Women

Introduction	233

Female Experience

VII.1	A Unitarian's Life (died 1828)	235
VII.2	A Wesleyan's Resolutions, 1853	236
VII.3	A Wesleyan's Revelation, 1853	237
VII.4	A Strict Baptist's Letter to Her Son, 1858	238
VII.5	A Primitive Methodist's Devotion and Culture (died 1891)	239

Marriage, Home and Children

VII.6	Mothers' Meetings, 1841	241

VII.7	A Bad Marriage, 1840s	242
VII.8	J. Angell James on Woman's Mission, 1852	243
VII.9	Child Care, 1850s	244
VII.10	A Woman Fulfilled (died 1892)	245

Leadership in the Church

VII.11	Hugh Bourne on the Ministry of Women, 1808	247
VII.12	William O'Bryan on the Punctuality of Female Preachers, 1822	248
VII.13	A General Baptist's Role, 1840s	249
VII.14	Catherine Booth on Female Ministry, 1859	250
VII.15	Quaker Women's Meetings, 1861	251
VII.16	Mission Preaching, 1875	252
VII.17	Wesleyan Deaconesses, 1890	253

Part VIII: Mission

Introduction	257

Home Mission

VIII.1	Report of the Lancashire Independent Association, 1812	259
VIII.2	Hugh Bourne on Camp Meetings, 1829	260
VIII.3	Charles Finney on Revivals, 1839	261
VIII.4	Manchester City Mission Operations, 1842–43	262
VIII.5	Unitarian Domestic Mission Station, 1859	263
VIII.6	Hugh Stowell Brown Lecturing to the Men of Liverpool, 1862	264
VIII.7	A Costermongers' Tea Meeting, 1863	265
VIII.8	Catherine Booth on Evangelistic Adaptability, 1883	267
VIII.9	Thomas Champness on Pioneer Evangelism, 1886	268
VIII.10	William White on Quaker Adult Schools, 1895	270

Overseas Mission

VIII.11	The Missionary Society Report, 1803	272
VIII.12	Robert Hall on the British and Foreign Bible Society, 1810	274
VIII.13	Ridley Herschell on the Jews, 1841	275
VIII.14	*The Juvenile Missionary Magazine*, 1844	277
VIII.15	Missionary Policy in India, 1858	278
VIII.16	George Richardson Urging Quaker Missionary Work, 1859	280
VIII.17	Frederick Trestrail on Native Churches, 1860	281
VIII.18	Wesleyan Missionary Controversy, 1890	285

Contents

Part IX: Public Issues

Introduction   291

Ecclesiastical Issues
IX.1	Unitarian Marriage Grievance, 1817	293
IX.2	Quaker Opposition to Tithes, 1832	294
IX.3	Baptist Disabilities, 1833	296
IX.4	Catholic Apostolic Church Great Testimony, 1837	298
IX.5	Edward Baines on Education Policy, 1843	300
IX.6	Dissenters' Chapels Act, 1844	301
IX.7	Edward Miall on Church Rates, 1851	303
IX.8	A Quaker Plea for Liberty of Conscience, 1856	304
IX.9	Prosecution of Primitive Methodists for Singing at an Interment, 1861	305
IX.10	Universities Tests Act, 1871	308
IX.11	Case for Disestablishment, 1894	309

Social Issues
IX.12	John Stephens on the Duties of the Poor, 1819	311
IX.13	Quaker Address on the Slave Trade, 1822	312
IX.14	William Knibb on Slavery, 1832	313
IX.15	A Primitive Methodist on Total Abstinence, 1846	314
IX.16	Peter M'Owan on the Sabbath, 1850	316
IX.17	Quaker Appeal against the Crimean War, 1854	317
IX.18	William Booth on the Way Out of Darkest England, 1890	318
IX.19	*The Methodist Temperance Manual*, 1895	320
IX.20	Samuel Keeble on Christian Socialism, 1896	322

Public Life
IX.21	Adam Clarke on Civil Government, 1830	324
IX.22	G. B. Browne on Parliamentary Reform, 1832	325
IX.23	West Riding Baptists on Civil Rights, 1843	326
IX.24	J. N. Darby against Voting, 1848	328
IX.25	Ann Gilbert against Women's Suffrage, 1849	329
IX.26	Agricultural Trade Unionists, 1872	330
IX.27	R. W. Dale on Political and Municipal Duty, 1884	331
IX.28	R. W. Dale on Christ and the State, 1891	333

Contents

Part X: Denominations

Introduction   339

Structures
X.1   The British and Foreign Unitarian Association, 1825   341
X.2   Wesleyan Conference against Agitation, 1835   342
X.3   Henry Allon on the Congregational Union, 1881   343
X.4   J. Guinness Rogers on a Congress of the Free Churches, 1890 345
X.5   Quaker Organisation, 1891   348
X.6   J. H. Rigg on Wesleyan Ecclesiastical Organisation, 1897   351

New Denominations
X.7   Methodist Unitarians, c. 1817   355
X.8   William O'Bryan on the Bible Christian Schism, 1815   356
X.9   Propositions Leading to the Wesleyan Methodist Association, 1835 357
X.10 Catholic Apostolic Catechism, 1843   359
X.11 Presbyterian Church in England Overture on Independence, 1844 362
X.12 Wesleyan Reformers' Resolutions, 1850   364
X.13 Primitive Methodist Organisation, 1864   366
X.14 Churches of Christ Principles, 1873   370
X.15 Free Church of England Declaration, 1876   372
X.16 The Cokelers, 1879   374
X.17 Fritchley Monthly Meeting of Friends Minute, 1881   375

Relations with the Church of England
X.18 Dan Taylor's Reasons for Dissenting from the Church of England,
      1805   378
X.19 J. C. Philpot's Resignation from Worcester College, Oxford, 1835 379
X.20 J. H. Newman on Dissent, 1836   381
X.21 James Hamilton on the Need for English Presbyterianism, 1850 382
X.22 Joshua Wilson on the Forthcoming Bicentenary of the Great
      Ejection, 1861   384
X.23 J. H. Blunt on the Future of Methodism, 1886   386
X.24 J. H. Rigg on the Oxford Movement, 1895   386
X.25 P. T. Forsyth on Established and Free Churches, 1896   388

Select Bibliography   391
Index of Persons   395

Series Editor's Preface

I had long felt the need of a series which would present texts from the history and thought of Protestant Nonconformity in England and Wales in such a way that the breadth of the Nonconformists' interests, the extent and variety of their activities, and the depth of their devotion from the days of the sixteenth-century Separatists onwards would become plain. When the Association of Denominational Historical Societies and Cognate Libraries was formally constituted on 23 October 1993, with the objective of sharing intelligence and facilitating co-operative scholarly activity across the several denominational boundaries, I formally proposed the preparation of a series of Protestant Nonconformist Texts to the membership.

There was unanimous agreement that a need existed which could, and should, be met. It was determined that the series should comprise four volumes covering the periods 1550–1700, the eighteenth century, the nineteenth century and the twentieth century; and that each volume should be in the hands of a coordinating editor assisted by two cooperating editors drawn from different church traditions. The secretaries of the member societies, with the guidance of their respective committees, nominated scholars who might be approached to serve as editors. I am pleased to say that within a month the twelve editors were mustered, and I am most appreciative of their enthusiasm for the task, and of the expeditious way in which they have carried it out. It is proper to make special and grateful mention of the late Reverend Professor R. Tudur Jones who, in addition to serving as the coordinating editor of the first volume – a task he completed within days of his sudden and much lamented death on 23 July 1998 – also cordially agreed to act as consultant on Welsh matters to the editors of all four volumes. The sudden death of the Reverend Dr Ian Sellers, a contributing editor of Volume II, has left a further significant gap in the ranks of scholars of English Nonconformity.

The editors were given a fairly free hand in the organization of their volumes: indeed, the nature of the materials has been permitted to suggest the layout of the several volumes. It is claimed that the order of each volume is clear and justifiable, even if in format one may differ slightly from another.

It is hoped that the series will prove helpful to students and interested readers, and that scholars may find it useful to have a checklist of sources which, though necessarily limited by considerations of space, is intended as an appetizer and a stimulus to further quarrying.

Above all, it is hoped that worthy tribute is here paid to those who, often at great personal cost, and in face of socio-political obstacles of various kinds, declared their faith and bore their witness. Indeed (to advert to realities, not to utter a lament), in a time of general apologetic caution, widespread doctrinal ignorance and apathy, fitful ecumenism, queried national institutions and overall numerical decline among the Protestant Nonconformists of England and Wales, it

Series Editor's Preface

may even be that forebears have something to teach those who inherit their mantle – and any others who may care to listen.

On behalf of my editorial colleagues I should like to thank Sarah Lloyd, Liz Pearce and all at Ashgate Publishing for their commitment to this project and for the care they have lavished upon it.

Alan P. F. Sell

Acknowledgements

The co-ordinating editor of this volume wishes to thank the very many people who gave generous assistance, including those who responded to a circular requesting suggestions of documents for inclusion: David Barton, Professor Clyde Binfield, Dr Brian and Faith Bowers, Simon Bright, Dr Russell Campbell, the Rev. Professor Grayson Carter, the Rev. Dr Gordon Catherall, the Rev. Dr David Cornick, Dr Neil Dickson, Dr Clive Field, Dr David Gowland, Dr Dorothy Graham, the Rev. Dr Timothy Grass, Howard Gregg, David J. Hall, Dr John Hargreaves, Dr Elaine Kaye, Dr Deryck Lovegrove, Ted Milligan, Susan Mills, Dr Peter Nockles, the Rev. Dr Henry Rack, the Rev. Dr Ian Randall, Dr Doreen Rosman, Professor Ted Royle, the late Dr Ian Sellers, the Rev. Dr Nigel Scotland, the Rev. Roger Standing, Dr Brian Stanley, the Rev. Dr David Thompson, the Rev. John Munsey Turner, Dr John Vickers, Professor Reg Ward and Dr Linda Wilson. I apologise that in many instances excellent suggested passages for inclusion have had to be left out for reasons of space and balance. In particular I want to express warm gratitude to Dr Timothy Larsen, whose willingness to search for obscure items was an invaluable resource.

My colleagues as co-operating editors in the preparation of this book, Dr Kenneth Dix and Alan Ruston, readily took responsibility for a proportion of the documents. I very much appreciate their contribution and expertise. Professor Alan Sell, the general editor of the series, gave guidance, support and many practical suggestions. I am grateful for his invitation to take on this volume. Members of the secretarial staff in the Department of History at the University of Stirling, Margaret Hendry, Annabelle Hopkins and Nicola Jeffress, and my mother-in-law, Margaret Lacey, did a great deal of work towards the completion of this project. I want to add a word of appreciation to my wife Eileen and daughter Anne for their tolerance of many second-hand bookshop trips over the years. Without these visits, the body of books on which this collection of texts primarily rests could not have been assembled.

David Bebbington
December 1998

Supplementary Note

The text, as the passage above suggests, was submitted to the intended publishers in December 1998. Although the text has not been altered in any material way since then, references have been updated to take into account significant recent publications. I am grateful to Ashgate for taking over responsibility for this book.

Acknowledgements

Publication of this volume has been made possible by a grant from the Scouloudi Foundation in association with the Institute of Historical Research.

DWB
April 2005

Abbreviations

Only two abbreviations have been used in this volume:

DEB *The Blackwell Dictionary of Evangelical Biography*, ed. D. M. Lewis, Oxford, 1995
DNB *The Dictionary of National Biography*, ed. Leslie Stephen and Sidney Lee, London, 1885–1901 (etc.)

Introduction

The nineteenth century was strikingly different from the eighteenth in England and Wales. Population, for one thing, was far higher. Whereas in the mid-eighteenth century there were roughly five and a half million people, in the mid-nineteenth there were nearly eighteen million. Industrialisation, though a much more gradual process than used to be supposed, changed how many people earned their livings. Already by the opening of the century manufacturing was not far short of agriculture as a source of national income. Towns and cities were rapidly expanding, so that in Lancashire, the county most drastically affected by the rise of industry, population density went up from 179 per square mile in 1750 to 253 per square mile by 1801. Insecurity of employment and urban squalor created suffering for many of the poorer classes, but the country as a whole became richer. New wealth as well as discontent among the poor was a potential challenge to the traditional social order based on landed property. The first industrial society in the world, with all the tensions of adjustment it created, had been born.

In this unfamiliar setting Protestant Nonconformity fared remarkably well. Between 1772 and 1851 its total of worshipping congregations multiplied tenfold. Its numbers more than kept pace with population growth. Whereas in 1715–18 Nonconformists formed about 6 per cent of the population, in 1851 they constituted some 17 per cent in England and no less than 45 per cent in Wales.[1] At the religious census of 1851, the only official return of worshippers ever undertaken in England, Nonconformists were shown to be not far short of half the churchgoing population. It was an astonishing achievement. A despised religious minority, formally relegated to the margins of national life, had turned into a vast social movement that looked set to overtake the established church in the affections of the people.

Our understanding of how this transformation took place has been greatly enhanced in recent years. The earliest research into nineteenth-century churchgoing suggested that the churches had never gained the allegiance of the industrial workers who flocked into the cities. In 1957 E. R. Wickham wrote that 'since the emergence of the industrial towns, the working classes, the labouring poor, the artisan class, as a class and as adults, have been outside the churches'.[2] Subsequent work provided evidence that Nonconformity did include in its ranks many of the skilled workers of early industrialisation, but since they formed a small and diminishing proportion of the working classes as a whole it was still believed that there was a gulf between the chapels and the industrial masses.[3] Then it was shown that places of worship sometimes reflected the social composition of the surrounding areas, so drawing in a significant number of factory workers.[4] The immensely painstaking research by Michael Watts has now established that the working people were actually present in the chapels in large numbers. In the great majority of counties in England and Wales, and in all the main Evangelical Nonconformist denominations, with the exception of the London Independents, the chapel worshippers were predominantly poor. Even in the towns the urban poor were strongly represented.[5] So it now seems clear that the older case was mistaken: Nonconformists were not drawn merely from the middle classes together with a few hangers on from lower down the social scale. The strength of Nonconformity at the middle of the nineteenth century was a consequence of its attractions to the people towards the bottom of the class structure.

The geographical spread of Nonconformity was as extensive as its social appeal. It was more flexible than the Church of England, hampered as it was by legal restrictions from the past, and so could respond to the needs of the rising urban-industrial society as well as to the call of the countryside. Thus in the north of England, where the greatest advances of industry took place, Methodism was able to become particularly strong. Alan Everitt has shown that in rural areas Nonconformity flourished in places of scattered or growing settlement, diverse landownership, absentee squires and parsons and poor provision of parish churches.[6] In such places, which shared many characteristics with the rising cities, the social influence of the landed elite could not be exercised to ensure loyalty to the Church of England. It has also been suggested that popular evangelists could capitalise on existing folk superstitions to draw country-dwellers into Nonconformity.[7] A vivid sense of the supernatural, it has now been pointed out, also survived in urban England into the twentieth century.[8] So conditions were favourable for the penetration of town and countryside by the message of the chapels.

Nonconformity could grow in part because it made its appeal to both sexes. A study of Congregational and Baptist churches has shown that women were in a majority, forming on average 61 per cent of the membership in the first quarter of the century and 68 per cent in the last quarter.[9] When the subject is attendance rather than membership, however, the evidence demonstrates that the gender balance was more equal. Certainly in London at the turn of the twentieth century, whereas women constituted 66 per cent of Anglican and 64 per cent of Roman Catholic attendances, they formed rather under 60 per cent of the attendance at Free Church services. Among the Primitive Methodists and the Quakers there were actually more men than their proportion in the population.[10] Men, especially in the working classes, seem to have been less eager to take upon themselves the responsibilities of membership, but they did come to chapel. Men were overwhelmingly the formal leaders, both ministerial and lay, of Nonconformist congregations, and yet women did occupy strategic roles. It is not surprising that by the end of the century Sunday school teachers, with their enormous success in bringing the young into the sphere of church life, were preponderantly female. Perhaps more surprising is their prominence in fund-raising: bazaars, for instance, were a female precinct. The experience of women, together with instances of their holding various positions of leadership, is sampled in Part VII of this volume, but many other passages illustrate their full participation in the Nonconformist way of life.

Introduction

The growth of Nonconformity was not merely a consequence of favourable circumstances in the early nineteenth century. It was primarily the effect of its metamorphosis under the influence of Evangelicalism. Not all branches of Nonconformity in the nineteenth century turned to Evangelical religion. Its advances were stoutly resisted by the Unitarians who sprang from Presbyterian roots, together with some of the original General Baptists and a range of newer sectarian groups including Swedenborgians, Mormons, Theosophists and Christadelphians. Although they were not wholly untouched by the missionary temper of the times, the Unitarians paid the price of remaining apart by shrinking in numbers while Evangelical Nonconformity expanded. Methodists of every variety, Congregationalists and most Baptists, together with several smaller bodies, all formed part of the sweep of popular Evangelical enthusiasm. They therefore shared a preoccupation with the atonement, the fulcrum of Evangelical theology. The doctrine of the cross crops up repeatedly in the extracts in this collection, appearing, for instance, where saving faith is defined as 'a belief that Christ really died for sinners' (Part V, document 7; hereafter such references are given in the form 'V.7'). Evangelicals also placed emphasis on the Bible, which explains why acceptance of the 'Divine Inspiration, Authority, and Sufficiency of the Holy Scriptures' stands first in the basis of faith of the Evangelical Alliance (II.7). Another characteristic of Evangelicals was their insistence that conversion of some kind is the essential entrance to the Christian life. That belief is illustrated here by the accounts of conversion given in the first section of Part V. Evangelicals holding these convictions were driven to activism. People needed to hear the message of the cross so that they could believe the Bible and be converted.[11] Hence Evangelical Nonconformity was inherently expansionist.

The missionary impulse gave rise to the societies dedicated to overseas evangelism founded from the 1790s onwards. Their work of planting the Christian faith abroad was ultimately another success story of extraordinary proportions. Although it is rightly recognised that global circumstances were propitious and that, after the initial stages, the gospel was spread primarily by indigenous evangelists, the achievement of thousands of obscure individuals in the chapels who put aside weekly pennies for the missionaries must not be obscured (Part VIII, second section). But mission was also undertaken at home. The sermon, so often in the nineteenth century designed to awaken sinners to repentance, was the primary method (Part I). Literature in abundance was disseminated in a period hungry for the printed word. Revivalism in its myriad expressions – the camp meeting, the anxious seat, the invitation tea meeting, the travelling gospel van – reinforced the more regular methods (Part VIII, first section). The willingness to adapt to the evangelistic possibilities of the age, an inventiveness commended by Catherine Booth, the wife of the founder of the Salvation Army (VIII.8), was one of the chief reasons for the gaining of new converts. Evangelical Nonconformity achieved expansion because it aimed to grow.

The activism of the chapels embraced philanthropic efforts to better the lot of the needy and increasingly spilled over into the public sphere. From the repeal of the Test and Corporation Acts in 1828 onwards, Nonconformists played a growing part in political affairs, both locally and nationally (Part IX). Frequently, and even when they were advocating an end to discrimination against themselves, the Evangelical note of principled denunciation of wrong was heard. The political campaigns of Nonconformity, so central to the evolution of Victorian Liberalism,[12] were rooted in the moral passion that flourished in the chapels. It was a temper, as has often been noticed, that was transmitted to the Labour Party of the twentieth century. The Evangelical spirit of the chapels did much to create the political culture of modern Britain.

If there was a contrast between the eighteenth and nineteenth centuries, there was also a distinction within the nineteenth between the earlier and later Victorian years. The growing prosperity of the country meant that ordinary households became more affluent. The average male urban worker gained more than 60 per cent in real wages between 1860 and 1900. The growth of the commercial sector of the economy led to greater wealth for the upper middle classes – the manufacturers and merchants – and to an increase in the size of the lower middle classes – the shopkeepers and clerks. There were greater opportunities for upward social mobility. The outward signs of respectability, that quintessential Victorian value, became easier to attain. More could afford to place an aspidistra in the parlour window.

Nonconformity, which enjoyed the support of many manufacturers, merchants, shopkeepers and clerks, was necessarily affected. Already in 1858, according to a critic, some wanted 'genteeler roads to heaven'.[13] The impact was clear on chapel buildings, which were increasingly built in the Gothic style, and in patterns of worship, which added organs, choirs and elements of liturgy (Part IV). As the disabilities of Nonconformists were removed one by one through Liberal legislation, so the sense of what it was to be a Dissenter from the established church faded. In particular the abolition in 1871 of the religious tests that excluded them from degrees in the ancient universities (IX.10) allowed some of the brightest sons of the chapels to be assimilated to the establishment, both spiritual and secular. There was a tendency, even among those who remained loyal to the faith of their fathers, to slacken their involvement in chapel life. The Wesleyans had to accept, for example, that membership did not necessarily mean weekly attendance at the class meeting for the exploration of spiritual experience (VI.12). Participation in the evangelistic outreach of the chapels began to seem less decorous. Was it good manners to challenge an acquaintance about the state of his soul? Something of the movement's backbone weakened.[14] Growth slowed, and, in the last quarter of the century, membership began to fall relative to population.

The effects of greater prosperity were felt in other ways too. From the 1870s the mass of the population enjoyed enough income to spend some of it on entertainment. The music hall became immensely popular; so did organised sport. The revolution in leisure posed a serious challenge to the chapels. They had a strategic choice. Either they could denounce the development as frivolity to be avoided by the serious-minded, and so risk alienating those who enjoyed such entertainment. Or else they could try to emulate the secular trend and provide leisure activities of their own, the danger here being that chapel life might itself be secularised in the process.[15] The former was the stance, for example, of the

Holinesss movement within Methodism, which stressed the imperative to deepen the spiritual life (V.15); the latter was the approach of General Booth, with his encouragement of brass bands within the Salvation Army (IV.26). The two tendencies united, however, in the common cause of the crusade against drink, which was diagnosed as the most dangerous element in popular leisure activities (IX.19). Both strategies, it seems, played a part in sapping Nonconformist strength.

At the same time intellectual changes were impinging on Nonconformist thinking. The preoccupations of the Enlightenment, which were associated with Evangelicalism as well as Unitarianism from their beginnings, were giving way in the nation at large to a taste for the romantic – the venerable, the immaterial and the felt. Unitarians, with their greater openness to the latest intellectual fashions, recast their theology in the new idiom (I.7). Evangelical Nonconformists, however, initially resisted the shift, which they associated – rightly – with another: a move away from the concentration on the atonement to a focus on the incarnation. In Anglican theology and the concerns of the wider society, Boyd Hilton has identified a transition in that direction around the 1860s.[16] A few Congregationalists followed suit (II.32, 34), but they formed only the liberal fringe of an orthodox Nonconformist community that was in general wedded to the synthesis of Evangelicalism with the Enlightenment that it had inherited.[17] The most significant doctrinal broadening was probably in eschatology: there was a decline in the prominence of hell, and some even entertained the hope that all would eventually be saved.[18] The impact of Darwinism was less than might be supposed, partly because it was assimilated without as much strain as is usually imagined (III.10, 11). The chief symptom of altered ways of thinking was a lessening of interest in any form of doctrine, the growth of the supposition that Christianity did not need intellectual articulation because it was a matter of life rather than propositions (II.40). So, despite the rapidly changing cultural context, the fundamental premises of most Nonconformist thinking were shifting only slowly.

The most stimulating hypothesis about the altered tone of Nonconformity between the middle of the century and its later years has been propounded by R. J. Helmstadter. His argument is that in the period from the 1830s to the mid-1880s Nonconformity had a coherent outlook based on a rugged individualism. The Evangelical theology of the chapels taught individual conversion; the great political aim, the removal of Dissenting disabilities, was part of the cause of individual liberty; the bourgeoisie dominating the movement displayed individual enterprise; and the social policy espoused in the chapels encouraged individual self-help. By the 1890s, the heyday of the Nonconformist Conscience, Helmstadter contends that all these characteristics had been transformed. Biblical criticism and moral criticism of doctrine had undermined Evangelicalism; the chief political aim was no longer personal freedom but a set of social goals; the waning of discrimination allowed the assimilation of the potential leaders to the national elite; and the welfare policies that were recommended depended on the activity of the state. It is the earlier period, Helmstadter claims, that deserves to be called the epoch of the Nonconformist Conscience because at that time the chapels possessed one that revealed a clear identity.[19]

The case has many strengths. At mid-century Nonconformists did generally uphold individual conversion, espouse an approximation to laissez-faire as their economic and social panacea and press causes of their own that harmonised with the principle of liberty. At its end, as extracts in this volume illustrate, many of them did turn to a social gospel that entailed state intervention to promote the welfare of the people (I.9, II.39, IX.20). Yet Helmstadter's argument exaggerates the extent of the transformation. The popular Evangelicalism of the pews did not disappear, and the social gospel, as most of its advocates insisted, was entirely compatible with the gospel for the individual. The apparently individualistic spirit of the earlier period was qualified by a deep-seated emphasis on responsibilities to the family, the chapel and the wider community. Evangelicalism itself encouraged mutual care, expressed, for example, in active philanthropy. Methodism, furthermore, did not endorse the political campaigns for the redress of grievances, let alone for disestablishment. So the Helmstadter hypothesis cannot be endorsed in its entirety because there was far more continuity between attitudes in the earlier and later years of Victoria's reign than he allows.[20]

The challenge of altering circumstances, however, was certainly addressed less successfully at the end of the century than in its first half. Rural Nonconformity began to struggle in the years of agricultural depression from the mid-1870s and, as suburbanisation advanced, down-town places of worship suffered from depleted congregations. The growth of alternative forms of social provision threatened some of the ways in which the chapels had appealed to the working classes. After 1870 the state filled the gaps in the existing schooling system so that the Nonconformist educational role was diminished. Professional social workers and welfare facilities such as public baths began to undermine the chapels as philanthropic agencies, a process that accelerated in the following century.[21] The large number of auxiliaries, institutions and buildings belonging to churches of all kinds was beginning to become a burden rather than a springboard for mission.[22] Although Nonconformists felt an increasing sense of their place in the public sphere, a development that was to culminate in the 1906 general election when more of their number sat in parliament than ever before or since, the overall influence of the chapels was perceptibly diminishing before the end of the nineteenth century. They might call themselves Free Churchmen as a sign that they had positive ideals and organise themselves in Free Church Councils (X.4), but before 1901 there were clear warnings of the absolute reduction in church membership figures that first became apparent five years later. Decline was to be the prevailing pattern of the twentieth century.

In order to show the richness of the Nonconformist part in nineteenth-century life, a topical arrangement has been chosen for this volume. Within each part, or section within a part, the passages are presented in chronological order. The book begins (Part I) with a selection of sermons because they were formative of the whole chapel ethos. Next comes theology, the distinctive beliefs of the Nonconformist communities. Within Part II, formal statements of faith, often longer than subsequent items in the collection, stand first, followed by a sample of the work of leading theologians and then by passages illustrating major debates of the century. Part III is more miscellaneous: it encompasses philosophy, which was far less distinguished in this century than in the previous one; science, which was more controversial; other non-fiction, including several periodicals (though others are illustrated elsewhere); and fictional accounts of chapel life. Part IV, on worship, includes specific sections on the sacraments, on music and hymnody and on architecture, and its opening general section incorporates accounts of preaching as opposed to the content of sermons given in Part I. Spirituality, the subject of Part V, is broadly defined. This part begins with narratives of conversion, illustrates individual religious experience, offers instances of the application of spirituality and ends with death-bed scenes.

Part VI is about the corporate life of the chapels. The ministry and the lay leadership that served the Nonconformist congregations are treated in two sections; conditions of membership and the activities that were the stuff of chapel communities follow in the other two. Because of the crucial role of women in the chapels, sometimes obscured in the standard primary sources, Part VII is devoted to their experience, home life and responsibilities. Women are nevertheless by no means excluded from other parts of the volume. The missionary impulse, at home and abroad, is illustrated in Part VIII, and the engagement with public issues, ecclesiastical, social and general, in Part IX. The tenth and final part covers the internal structure of denominations, concentrating in its second section on the principles that animated some of the bodies that were born during the century. The third section deals with relations between Nonconformity and the Church of England.

The aim has been to give an overall picture of Nonconformity, neglecting neither its ideas nor its social expressions. There has been a rough attempt to maintain a balance between the denominations, though in order to include some of the smaller ones the space allocated to the larger ones has necessarily been diminished. Even so not all the bodies that flourished in the nineteenth century have found a place. By and large these are denominations with earlier origins such as the Moravians and the Swedenborgians, but a number of new bodies on the fringe of Nonconformity have not been illustrated: the Mormons, Theosophists and Christadelphians are amongst them.[23] Several documents illustrate what was happening in Wales, but, because most of the sources are in Welsh, the coverage in this volume, which is confined to texts in English, is not proportionate to the strength of Welsh Nonconformity. Although many of the bodies regarded themselves as pan-British at the time, no documents from Scotland have been included; nevertheless several of the individuals quoted were originally from Scotland.

Another principle of selection has been to avoid duplicating the existing collections of source materials in this field. D. M. Thompson, *Nonconformity in the Nineteenth Century*, London, 1972, and John Briggs and Ian Sellers, *Victorian Nonconformity*, London, 1973, both contain extracts relating to many of the themes covered in this volume. For the Methodists, there is Rupert Davies *et al.*, ed., *A History of the Methodist Church in Great Britain*, vol. 4, London, 1988, roughly half of which consists of documents on the nineteenth century. Gerald

Parsons, ed., *Religion in Victorian Britain*, vol. 3, Manchester, 1988, is devoted to source material, though Nonconformity receives less than its fair share.

With the aim of trying to make this book as serviceable as possible, each passage has an introduction designed to place it in its context. There is always specification of the source of a document. In most cases there is also an indication of secondary works where further information on the subject may be found. Frequently there is reference to the *Dictionary of National Biography* or, if an individual is not included in that work, to the *Blackwell Dictionary of Evangelical Biography*. The absence of a mention of the latter does not mean that there is no relevant entry: indeed, in many cases this recent two-volume collection will be found invaluable for the period down to 1860. No references have been made to unpublished dissertations. Every part of the volume contains an introduction that alludes to each document that follows and also a list of the main relevant secondary literature.

C. H. Spurgeon, the greatest preacher of the nineteenth century, once laid down the principle that the students whom he trained for the Baptist ministry should 'continue in association with common humanity'.[24] They should live in ordinary homes during their college years so that they would not lose touch with everyday life. They must be rooted in the people. The movement they represented achieved that goal to a remarkable degree. Nineteenth-century Nonconformity identified closely with the masses of England and Wales. It nurtured their spirituality and structured their worship; it also gave them opportunities for communal life and shaped their public aspirations. Growing rapidly until it served nearly half the churchgoers in the land, Nonconformity enjoyed more success than before or since. Although its penetration of popular culture undoubtedly began to wane before the century was over, it remained a central and creative force to the end of Victoria's reign and beyond. It was still a vehicle through which the common people could embrace and express the Christian faith. The chapels of the nineteenth century form an instance of the thorough indigenisation of Christianity.

Notes

1. M. R. Watts, *The Dissenters*, vol. 2, Oxford, 1995, pp. 24–9.
2. E. R. Wickham, *Church and People in an Industrial City*, London, 1957, p. 215.
3. A. D. Gilbert, *Religion and Society in Industrial England: Church, Chapel and Social Change, 1740–1914*, London, 1976.
4. M. Smith, *Religion in Industrial Society: Oldham and Saddleworth, 1740–1865*, Oxford, 1994.
5. Watts, *Dissenters*, vol. 2, pp. 319–22.
6. A. Everitt, *The Pattern of Rural Dissent: The Nineteenth Century*, Leicester, 1972.
7. J. Obelkevich, *Religion and Rural Society: South Lindsey, 1825–1875*, Oxford, 1976, chap. 6. D. Clark, *Between Pulpit and Pew: Folk Religion in a North Yorkshire Fishing Village*, Cambridge, 1982.
8. S. C. Williams, *Religious Belief and Popular Culture in Southwark, c. 1880–1939*, Oxford, 1999, chap. 3.

Introduction

9. C. D. Field, 'Adam and Eve: Gender in the English Free Church Constituency', *Journal of Ecclesiastical History*, 44 (1993), pp. 63–79.
10. H. McLeod, *Religion and Society in England, 1850–1914*, Basingstoke, Hampshire, 1996, p. 67.
11. D. W. Bebbington, *Evangelicalism in Modern Britain: A History from the 1730s to the 1980s*, London, 1989.
12. E. F. Biagini, *Liberty, Retrenchment and Reform: Popular Liberalism in the Age of Gladstone, 1860–1880*, Cambridge, 1992.
13. *The Freeman*, 17 November 1858, p. 702.
14. J. Cox, *The English Churches in a Secular Society: Lambeth, 1870–1930*, New York, 1982, chaps 5, 7.
15. K. S. Inglis, *Churches and the Working Classes in Victorian England*, London, 1963, chap. 2.
16. B. Hilton, *The Age of Atonement: The Influence of Evangelicalism on Social and Economic Thought, 1785–1865*, Oxford, 1988, chaps 7, 8.
17. D. W. Bebbington, 'Gospel and Culture in Victorian Nonconformity', in J. Shaw and A. Kreider, eds, *Culture and the Nonconformist Tradition*, Cardiff, 1999.
18. M. R. Watts, *Why did the English stop going to Church?*, London, 1995.
19. R. J. Helmstadter, 'The Nonconformist Conscience', in G. Parsons, ed., *Religion in Victorian England*, vol. 4, Manchester, 1988.
20. D. W. Bebbington, *Victorian Nonconformity*, Bangor, Gwynedd, 1992, pp. 58–71.
21. Cox, *English Churches in a Secular Society*, chap. 6.
22. S. J. D. Green, *Religion in the Age of Decline: Organisation and Experience in Industrial Yorkshire, 1870–1920*, Cambridge, 1996.
23. J. E. Hutton, *History of the Moravian Church*, London, 1909. R. Hindmarsh, *Rise and Progress of the New Jerusalem Church in England, America and Other Parts*, ed. E. Madeley, London, 1861. V. B. Bloxham *et al.*, ed., *Truth will Prevail: The Rise of the Church of Jesus Christ of Latter-Day Saints in the British Isles, 1837–1987*, Solihull, West Midlands, 1987. W. S. Smith, *The London Heretics, 1870–1914*, London, 1967, pp. 145–64. B. R. Wilson, *Sects and Society*, London, 1967, chap. 12.
24. *Annual Paper descriptive of the Lord's Work connected with the Pastor's College, during the Year 1870*, London, 1871, p. 15.

PART I

SERMONS

Introduction

Preaching, like the pulpit in most chapels, was central in Nonconformity. The most popular form of publication in the early nineteenth century was the sermon. It was at once advice for living, a guidepost to heaven and a species of popular entertainment. The content varied enormously, for there were exposition and exhortation, speculation and instruction, warning and consolation – and very much else too. During the century the content altered with the decline of Calvinism in the Reformed communities and a general broadening of theology in almost all the denominations. Yet there was constancy in most Nonconformist bodies outside Unitarianism in proclaiming the common Evangelical faith. Sin and salvation were the staple themes of the pulpit.

There was also continuity in presentation. When, in 1869–70, the prominent metropolitan Congregational minister Alexander Raleigh lectured to trainees for the ministry on 'The Plan and Growth of a Sermon', he listed the standard sections as the exordium, introducing the discourse; the proposition, clearly stating its thrust; the proof, vindicating the case; and the conclusion, which was to be both 'personal and practical'.[1] There would have been little variation in the principles commended to students either before or afterwards. Yet style changed greatly during the century, and not in a single direction. In the early part of the century the driving imperative of the Evangelical Revival to save souls, reinforced by the preference of the Enlightenment for clarity, produced greater simplicity in diction and structure than had often been the case in the past. In the middle years of the century there was a tendency, especially in the more fashionable pulpits, to adopt a more elaborate form of rhetoric in keeping with the expectations raised in the wake of the romantic movement. This form of 'Pretty-ism',[2] however, came to be despised in the last years of the century. A crisper, more recognisably modern form of language was used in the pulpit instead. In the sample given below, the early phase is represented by Clarke (I.2), under Enlightenment influences, and Gadsby (I.3), who, though standing apart from much of the legacy of the Evangelical Revival, nevertheless showed a burning zeal for souls. The mid-century floridity is illustrated in Punshon (I.5) and Thom (I.7), and the later reaction to plainness in Hughes (I.9) and Horton (I.10).

The sample of ten preachers is confined to the abler occupants of the pulpit. The vast numbers of untrained lay preachers would have spoken in a very different manner, sometimes uncouthly but often powerfully. The denominational range includes one Strict Baptist (I.3), three mainstream Baptists (I.1, 4, 8), three Wesleyans (I.2,5,9), two Congregationalists (I.6,10) and a Unitarian (I.7). The theological range includes two men who tried to resist the doctrinal developments of the time (Gadsby, Spurgeon) and four who welcomed them in varying degree (Parker, Thom, Hughes and Horton). The others were more or less content with the form of the faith prevailing in their day, neither wanting to repudiate contemporary thought nor to accelerate its change.

Nineteenth-century Nonconformist sermons have been woefully under-studied. There is but one useful secondary work: H. Davies, *Worship and Theology in England*, vols 3 and 4, Princeton, New Jersey, 1961 and 1962; republished Grand Rapids, Michigan, 1996. For preaching in worship, see the first section of Part IV.

Notes

1. M. Raleigh, ed., *Alexander Raleigh*, Edinburgh, 1881, p. 203.
2. E. M. Champness, *The Life-Story of Thomas Champness*, London, 1907, p. 103.

Document I.1

Robert Hall on the Substitution of the Innocent for the Guilty, 1822

Robert Hall (1764–1831), Baptist minister successively at Bristol, Cambridge, Leicester and again at Bristol, was generally thought to be the ablest preacher of his day. Trained at Bristol Academy and Aberdeen University, he turned against the rational Dissent that initially attracted him and became an outspoken assertor of evangelical faith, especially in *Modern Infidelity Considered* (1800). Yet he also remained a convinced champion of religious liberty. See G. W. Hughes, *Robert Hall*, London, 1943; and DNB.

This extract is taken from his most celebrated sermon, 'On the Substitution of the Innocent for the Guilty' (1822), preached on Isaiah 53: 8. It offers, in copious and elegant language, a reasoned defence of a central evangelical tenet. The source is *The Works of Robert Hall, A.M.*, ed. O. Gregory, London, 1839, vol. 5, pp. 91–3. For Hall's pulpit style, see IV.2.

That the voluntary substitution of an innocent person, in the stead of the guilty, may be capable of answering the ends of justice, nothing seems more necessary than that the substitute should be of equal consideration, at least, to the party in whose behalf he interposes. The interests sacrificed by the suffering party, should not be of less cost and value than those which are secured by such a procedure. ...

In this view the redemption of the human race seemed to be hopeless; and their escape from merited destruction, on any principles connected with law and justice, absolutely impossible. For where could an adequate substitute be found? Where, among the descendants of Adam, partakers of flesh and blood, could *one* be selected of such preeminent dignity and worth, that *his* oblation of himself should be deemed a fit and proper equivalent to the whole race of man? to say nothing of the impossibility of finding there a spotless victim (and no other could be accepted). Who is there that ever possessed that prodigious superiority in all the qualities which aggrandize their possessor to every other member of the human family, which shall entitle him to be the representative, either in action or in suffering, of the whole human race? In order to be capable of becoming a victim, he must be invested with a frail and mortal nature; but the possession of such a nature reduces him to that equality with his brethren, that joint participation of meanness and infirmity, which totally disqualifies him for becoming a substitute. Here a dilemma presents itself, from which there seems no possibility of escape. If man is left to encounter the judicial effects of his sentence, his ruin is sealed and certain. If he is to be redeemed by a substitute, that substitute must possess contradictory attributes, a combination of qualities not to be found within the compass of human nature. He must be frail and mortal, or he cannot die a sacrifice; he must possess ineffable dignity, or he cannot merit as a substitute.

Such were the apparently insurmountable difficulties which obstructed the salvation of man by any methods worthy of the divine character; such the darkness and perplexity which involved his prospects, that it is more than probable the highest created intelligence would not have been equal to the solution of the question, *How shall man be just with God?*

The *mystery hid from ages and generations*, the mystery of *Christ crucified*, dispels the obscurity, and presents, in the person of the Redeemer, all the qualifications which human conception can embody as contributing to the perfect character of a substitute. By his participation of flesh and blood, he becomes susceptible of suffering, and possesses within himself the materials of a sacrifice. By its personal union with the eternal Word, the sufferings sustained in a nature thus assumed, acquired an infinite value, so as to be justly deemed more than equivalent to the penalty originally denounced.

His assumption of the human nature made his oblation of himself *possible*; his possession of the divine rendered it efficient; and thus weakness and power, the imperfections incident to a frail and mortal creature, and the exemption from these, the attributes of time and those of eternity, the elements of being the most opposite, and deduced from opposite worlds, equally combined to give efficacy to his character as the Redeemer, and validity to his sacrifice. They constitute a person who has no counterpart in heaven or on earth, who may be most justly denominated '*Wonderful*;' composed of parts and features of which, (however they may subsist elsewhere in a state of separation,) the combination and union, nothing short of infinite wisdom could have conceived, or infinite power effected. The mysterious constitution of the *person* of Christ, the stupendous link which unites God and man, and heaven and earth; that mystic ladder, on which *the angels of God ascended and descended*, whose foot is on a level with the dust, and whose summit penetrates the inmost recesses of an unapproachable splendour, will be, we have reason to believe, through eternity, the object of profound contemplation and adoring wonder.

Document I.2

Adam Clarke on Happiness the Privilege of Every Real Christian, 1828

Adam Clarke (c. 1760–1832) was the leading Wesleyan intellectual of the early nineteenth century. Coming from Ireland, he became a Methodist preacher in 1782 and for most of the rest of his career after 1795 was assigned to London so that he could take advantage of the scholarly facilities of the capital. Mastery of a wide range of ancient languages enabled him to compose an authoritative eight-volume commentary on the Bible (1810–25), though his rejection of the doctrine of the eternal Sonship of Christ caused controversy. Nevertheless he was elected president of the Methodist Conference in 1806, 1814 and 1822. See *An Account of the Infancy, Religious and Literary Life of Adam Clarke, LL.D., F.A.S., &c.*, London, 1833; I. Sellers, *Adam Clarke, Controversialist*, St Columb Major, Cornwall, 1976; and DNB.

The extract is taken from a sermon on Philippians 4: 4 entitled 'Genuine Happiness the Privilege of Every Real Christian in This Life' published in A. Clarke, *Discourses on Various Subjects*, vol. 1, London, 1828, pp. 233–7. The pervasive values of the Enlightenment (reason and religion, happiness itself) are striking, but, against some of its leading exponents, Clarke insists that true happiness depends on the spiritual state. For Clarke as preacher, see IV.3.

When the Apostle exhorts the Philippians to *rejoice*, I conceive that the term implies the same as *be happy*: and, as he exhorts them to *rejoice always*, then he must mean, *be constantly happy*: and, to be *constantly happy*, is to have *happiness* – or, to be in the *state of happiness* ...

If the present state be only the *threshold* of being, – if it be a state of probation, – if man, in the estimate of reason and religion, should be guided by *wisdom*; and true wisdom is that, which directs to the *best end*, by the use of the *most proper means*: then, that must be the *best end of man*, that has in view his *true blessedness in this life*, and his *eternal glorification* in the world to come. 'What shall we eat, what shall we drink, and with what shall we be clothed?' – in a word, how shall we acquire *animal gratification*? are enquiries with which the *Gentiles* may be endlessly exercised; but he who has the revelation of God should have higher objects of pursuit, and such as become an immortal spirit.

This is the subject on which St. Paul addresses the Christians at Philippi, and, through them, all, in every place, who profess the *Christian name*. He speaks to them of *spiritual* happiness, exhorts to its acquisition, and shews in what it consists.

I shall, therefore, give a definition of what I conceive true happiness to be ... It is *that state of mind in which the desires are all satisfied, by the full possession of that, which, for its own sake, is to be desired above all things, as containing in itself every thing that is suited to the nature, capacity, and wishes of an immortal spirit, with the rational conviction that this state may be permanent*; – and this, without circumlocution, I state to be, the *approbation of God in the conscience*; and the *image of God in the heart*. Where these are, there must be *happiness*: where these are permanent, there must be permanent happiness. The actual existence of these things, or the possibility of their attainment, I consider to be directly implied in the exhortation of the Apostle, Rejoice in the Lord always: and again I say, rejoice. He who can rejoice is so far happy: but no man can *rejoice*, even in the slightest degree, but from a *consciousness* of *happiness* at the time; and happiness implies perfect *satisfaction* or *contentment of mind*, from a gratification of its *wishes* and *desires*. And this necessarily implies these *two* things: – 1. *Actual possession* of that which gratifies or contents; and, 2. *Comfortable persuasion* that the possession shall be *continued*. For, 1. If a man *possess not* that which his soul has earnestly desired, and without which he could not be comfortable, he cannot have *rejoicing in himself*; and, 2. If he have not a well grounded hope, and full persuasion that this possession, and his consequent happiness, may be *continued*, – that none can deprive him of it, and that it cannot be lost but through his own fault, – he cannot *rejoice*. Hence, therefore, it is evident, that the *thing* that constitutes happiness must be so far in *possession*, as to leave no craving desire ungratified; and must be so sure in *prospect*, in reference to its *future continuance*, as to leave no anxious apprehension of *unavoidable* privation.

Document I.3

William Gadsby on the Acceptable Year and Day of Vengeance, 1842

William Gadsby (1773–1844) was a prominent Particular Baptist minister in Manchester from 1806 to 1844. He rejected the moral law as the believer's rule of life, the teaching of Fuller (see II.11), and open communionism (see II.23). He emphasised conversion as a deep conviction of sin followed by a Spirit-given illumination, in which the individual is entirely passive. With John Gadsby (his son) he commenced *The Gospel Standard* in 1835, to act as an organ for the more conservative Strict and Particular Baptists. See J. H. Philpot, ed., *The Seceders*, Vol. 2, London, 1932: B. A. Ramsbottom, *William Gadsby*, Harpenden, Hertfordshire, 2003; and DNB.

This extract is from *Sermons of William Gadsby with a Short Biography by B. A. Ramsbottom*, Harpenden, Hertfordshire, 1991, pp. 119–20, and is based on Isaiah 66: 2. It is conservative in content, showing a strong debt to seventeenth-century Calvinism, but displays great rhetorical vigour. The doctrines of particular election and substitution are in evidence.

'To proclaim the acceptable year of the Lord, and the day of vengeance of our God.' I shall endeavour, as God shall assist, to make a few remarks upon these two things:
    I.   'The *day of vengeance* of our God and the *acceptable year* of the Lord.'
    II.   The *proclamation* of them by the blessed Lord of life and glory.

I. Now we read in the Word of God of some solemn displays of God's vengeance and wrath; and yet our text speaks as if there were but one 'day of vengeance.' Why, was it not 'the day of vengeance' when he destroyed Sodom and Gomorrah? Was it not 'the day of vengeance' when he swallowed up Korah, Dathan, and Abiram, and all their company, and when they went down into the pit alive? Was it not a 'day of vengeance' when he hurled Satan and his adherents from their high-towering thrones, and sank them into 'blackness of darkness?' Was it not a 'day of vengeance' when he drowned the Egyptians in the Red Sea? And are not the damned in hell, devils and damned spirits feeling 'the day of vengeance' now? And yet, put it all together, it were as nothing compared to 'the day of vengeance' in our text. Therefore the Holy Ghost fixes upon this important subject as '*the* day of vengeance' that outstretches all the rest.

And what was it? The 'day,' when Divine Justice unsheathed its sword, and the wrath of that incensed Justice was poured with all it inflexible fury upon the God-man Mediator; when all the sins of the church, – heart sins, lip sins, sins however circumstanced, were gathered together, and put upon the Surety, and when the whole of the wrath due to the millions of God's elect was poured into the heart of their covenant Head, – the Lord Jesus Christ. That was '*the* day of vengeance' with a witness. Here Justice exacted its utmost mite, and made no abatement; and his solemn Majesty paid the debt to the full.

Sin may appear a trifling matter to you or me; we may be sufficiently hardened to laugh at it, to trifle with it; but it did not trifle with the Son of God. It broke his heart, it tortured his soul, and harrowed up his mind; and with all the majesty and glory of his infinite Godhead, he had but strength enough to bear up under the tremendous wrath that he had to endure for his people. This was 'the day of vengeance,' and here the wrath of God was poured out to the uttermost.

Neither did Divine Justice look upon sin as a trifling matter. If God the Father loved the people with an everlasting love (and he did), if he fixed his heart upon them in eternity, if he considered them his jewels, the crown of his glory, and yet this people could not possess the bliss he provided for them till Justice was satisfied in the Surety and sin was punished there, sin was not trifling thing in the eyes of God. The wrath of God poured upon devils and damned spirits is for their various transgressions; but here is the holy, the harmless, the innocent Lamb of God, the glory of heaven, and he for whom all things were created, he for whose pleasure all was made, standing as Surety for sinners; and though he was the Father's infinite delight, the people whose cause he had espoused must be set free, and the wrath of God must be poured upon him, as the Surety, and poured there to the uttermost. Thus Jehovah demonstrated his holy, his righteous indignation against sin, and it was 'the day of vengeance.'

Document I.4

C. H. Spurgeon on the Immutability of God, 1855

Charles Haddon Spurgeon (1834–92) is commonly regarded as the greatest preacher of the nineteenth century in the English-speaking world. He combined solid biblical teaching and a strong evangelistic aim with a lively style and a vivid wit. A follower of Andrew Fuller in theology, he was nevertheless heavily indebted to the older Puritan tradition and in the main outlines of his position remained Calvinistic. He was from 1854 minister of New Park Street Baptist Church, Southwark, which in 1862 moved to the Metropolitan Tabernacle. See P. S. Kruppa, *Charles Haddon Spurgeon*, New York, 1982; M. Hopkins, *Nonconformity's Romantic Generation: Evangelical and Liberal Theologies in Victorian England*, Carlisle, 2004; and DNB.

A weekly sermon was issued from January 1855: this extract is from the first in the series published in *The New Park Street Pulpit*, Vol. 1, London, 1956, pp. 2–3. It has the title 'The Immutability of God', and is based on Malachi 3: 6. As in all of his sermons, Spurgeon applies his exposition of scripture to the everyday life of his hearers, and to its eternal relevance.

I shall offer some exposition of my text, by first saying, that God is Jehovah, and he changes not *in his essence*. We cannot tell you what Godhead is. We do not know what substance that is which we call God. It is an existence, it is a being; but what that is, we know not. However, whatever it is, we call it his essence, and that essence never changes. The substance of mortal things is ever changing. The mountains with their snow-white crowns, doff their old diadems in summer, in rivers trickling down their sides, while the storm cloud gives them another coronation; the ocean, with its mighty floods, loses its water when the sunbeams kiss the waves, and snatch them in mists to heaven; even the sun himself requires fresh fuel from the hand of the Infinite Almighty, to replenish his ever-burning furnace. All creatures change. Man, especially as to his body, is always undergoing revolution. Very probably there is not a single particle in my body which was in it a few years ago. This frame has been worn away by activity, its atoms have been removed by friction, fresh particles of matter have in the mean time constantly accrued to my body, and so it has been replenished; but its substance is altered. The fabric of which this world is made is ever passing away; like a stream of water, drops are running away and others are following after, keeping the river still full, but always changing in its elements. But God is perpetually the same. He is not composed of any substance or material, but is spirit – pure, essential, and etherial spirit – and therefore he is immutable. He remains everlastingly the same. There are no furrows on his eternal brow. No age hath palsied him; no years have marked him with the mementoes of their flight; he sees ages pass, but with him it is ever *now*. He is the great I AM – the Great Unchangeable. Mark you, his essence did not undergo a change when it became united with the manhood. When Christ in past years did gird himself with mortal clay, the essence of his divinity was not changed; flesh did not become God, nor did God become flesh by a real actual change of nature; the two were united in hypostatical union, but the Godhead was still the same. It was the same when he was a babe in the manger, as it was when he stretched the curtains of heaven; it was the same God that hung upon the cross, and whose blood flowed down in a purple river, the same self-same God that holds the world upon his everlasting shoulders, and bears in his hands the keys of death and hell. He never has been changed in his essence, not even by his incarnation; he remains everlastingly, eternally, the one unchanging God, the Father of lights, with whom there is no variableness, neither the shadow of a change.

He changes not *in his attributes*. Whatever the attributes of God were of old, that they are now; and of each of them we may sing 'As it was in the beginning, is now, and ever shall be, world without end, Amen.' Was he *powerful*? Was he the mighty God when he spake the world out of the womb of non-existence? Was he the Omnipotent when he piled the mountains and scooped out the hollow places of the rolling deep? Yes, he was powerful then, and his arm is unpalsied now; he is the same giant in his might; the sap of his nourishment is undried, and the strength of his soul stands the same for ever. Was he wise when he constituted this mighty globe, when he laid the foundations of the universe? Had he *wisdom* when he planned the way of our salvation, and when from all eternity he marked out his awful plans? Yes, and he is wise now; he is not less skilful, he has not less knowledge; his eye which seeth all things is undimmed; his ear which heareth all the cries, sighs, sobs, and groans of his people, is not rendered heavy by the years which he hath heard their prayers. He is unchanged in his wisdom; he knows as much now as ever, neither more nor less; he has the same consummate skill, and the same infinite forecastings. He is unchanged, blessed be his name, in his *justice*. Just and holy was he in the past; just and holy is he now. He is unchanged in his *truth*; he has promised, and he brings it to pass; he hath said it, and it shall be done. He varies not in the *goodness*, and generosity, and benevolence of his nature. He is not become an Almighty tyrant, whereas he was once an Almighty Father; but his strong love stands like a granite rock, unmoved by the hurricane of our iniquity. And blessed be his dear name, he is unchanged in his *love*. When he first wrote the covenant, how full his heart was with affection to his people. He knew that his Son must die to ratify the articles of that agreement. He knew right well that he must rend his best beloved from his bowels, and send him down to earth to bleed and die. He did not hesitate to sign that mighty covenant; nor did he shun its fulfilment. He loves as much now as he did then; and when suns shall cease to shine, and moons to show their feeble light, he still shall love on for ever and for ever. Take any one attribute of God, and I will write *semper idem* on it (always the same.) Take any one thing you can say of God now, and it may be said not only in the dark past, but in the bright future it shall always remain the same: 'I am Jehovah, I change not.'

Document I.5

W. Morley Punshon on the Gospel, n.d.

William Morley Punshon (1824–81) was the most admired orator among the Wesleyans of the mid-Victorian years. His lectures as well as his sermons sold in large numbers. In 1868 he moved to Canada so that he could marry his deceased wife's sister, then prohibited in English law, but returned in 1873 on the death of his second wife. See F. W. MacDonald, *The Life of William Morley Punshon, LL.D.*, London, 1887.

The extract is from an undated sermon on Romans 1:16 published in the second series of *Sermons by the Rev. W. Morley Punshon*, London, 1884, pp. 21–4. It shows careful crafting in its calculated repetition and balanced phrasing, but, like most Methodist sermons of its day, it rises to a direct appeal to its hearers at the end.

Man is guilty – the Gospel speaks of pardon.
That we are guilty before God we need not stop to prove. The fall has impressed itself in evidences too countless to be doubted; and our observation of the iniquities of others, and our experience of our own, fasten upon us the conviction that as by nature we are the children of wrath, so by practice we are the children of disobedience; 'The wrath of God abideth upon us.' We are exposed to his displeasure, compared with which the concentrated indignation of the universe would be as the harmless anger of a child. From this wrath to come we are naturally unable to escape. Repentance will not avail us – it can neither recall the past, nor avert the future. Penances, however severe, cannot atone for transgression. Sacrifices of costliness cannot purchase the forgiveness of sin. Tears, shed for ages, cannot wash the leprous soul, nor quench the penal fires. The vain confidences fail us; the hail sweeps away the refuges of lies; but the Gospel of Christ comes to the aid of our hopelessness with its glorious message. *Pardon!* 'Let the echo fly the spacious earth around.' *Pardon!* Sound it in the ears of the sinful, that they may rejoice, and of the lost, that they may live. *Pardon!* Go into the sepulchre with it, that it may wake some Lazarus in his moral shroud; speak it high and clear, that it may rouse the failing strength, and fire the glazing eye. *Pardon – Pardon for the guilty! Pardon without money and without price. Pardon* for the guilty, for the lost, for all, for *you*. This is the Gospel of Christ. Call me fanatical, pity me as imbecile, brand me as mad; – 'I am not ashamed of the Gospel of Christ.' ...

Man is miserable – the Gospel makes him happy.
Misery and guilt are necessarily connected. The wicked are like the troubled sea which cannot rest. I need not, for my purpose, and I would not if I could, harrow up your feelings by a detail of the miseries of the world. I need not image the woe and wretchedness of toiling sons of want – pestilence impregnating the air with poison – war fertilizing the plains with blood. I need not unroof for your inspection the squalid habitations of poverty, nor bid you breathe the feculent air of

prisons, nor show you the marks on the brow of the hunger-born where the hoof of the fiend has trod. In the search for misery you need not go so far. You have only to enter the heart of the unpardoned sinner, and you find it nestling there: sin is uncancelled, and therefore misery broods. I appeal to you, sinner – is it not true? Your conscience slumbers sometimes, and you try to drown it in intemperance or company; but it is not dead – it is not dead – and ever and anon it dashes from your lips the untasted cup of pleasure, and appals you with the horrors of the life to come. I appeal to you, half-hearted and almost persuaded sinner – is it not true? You are halting between two opinions. You have too much religion to enjoy the world, and far too little to be happy in the church, and you are not happy; you know you are not happy. You have tried philosophy and pleasure, and taste and science, and even scepticism, and they are miserable comforters. Oh, I rejoice that I stand before you with the Gospel of Christ. Here is the balm – the vital and all-healing balm. The atonement which satisfied justice, can satisfy conscience too – the blood that took away the sin, shall allay the anxieties of the soul. Come to the cross. Come at once – come now. So shall you be enabled from heartfelt and exulting experience of its blessings to swell the full-voiced tribute, which by and by the ransomed universe shall render. 'I am not ashamed of the Gospel of Christ.'

Document I.6

Joseph Parker on the Gospel, n.d.

Joseph Parker (1830–1902) was Congregational minister in Banbury, Manchester and, from 1869, in London. There, at the City Temple, he maintained a celebrated preaching ministry, including the Thursday noonday service that attracted many eminent Londoners. He was chairman of the Congregational Union in 1884 and 1901 and president of the National Free Church Council in 1902. See J. Parker, *A Preacher's Life*, London, 1899; W. Adamson, *The Life of the Rev. Joseph Parker*, Glasgow, 1902; and DNB.

The extract is from an undated sermon on Matthew 9: 35 entitled 'What is the Gospel?' published in the posthumous *The Gospel of Jesus Christ*, London, 1903, at pp. 10–12. Its burden, that the expression of the gospel may vary even though its content is authentic, well illustrates the liberal tendency in Parker's Evangelicalism that formed a foil to Spurgeon's conservative version.

What, then, is The Gospel? Never does the substance of it require modification or amendment, but the statement of the Gospel admits of new phases and aspects as the generations come and go. For want of knowing this, many people have been thought to be heretical who have only been inventive; some have been supposed to have been apostates, who have been for the moment it may be the victims of their own ardent but reverent imagination. Always distinguish between the substance and the mere method of putting it. With the substance we are to take no liberties, that is the eternal and unchangeable quantity; but as to method, plan, process, there what liberty we have! ...

We may have become so accustomed to a kind of pulpit lullaby that, unless we hear it rising, falling, dying, and so running through all the gamut of its expression, we may think the Gospel is not being preached. Welcome variety of expression. The horticulturist is not afraid of variety in his garden; men are not afraid to throw the few simple notes of music into a million forms; yea, they glory in the multiplication of the combinations. Why should we imagine that God can be seen only in one colour, and from one standpoint, and in one set of words? Let us rejoice in the abounding imagination of men, in the difference between Paul and John, and James and Jude – now all love, now all flame, now burning like the volcano, and now flashing like a fountain of refreshment in the midst of the wilderness; it is not God's truth that has changed, it is God that is being illustrated and magnified in the gifts of His sons.

This Gospel, then, is good news, good news from God, good news about God. Good news should be set to good music. Good news should never be expressed by sour or reluctant lips; the whole life should tell out all the music of God's love in noble suffering, in heroic patience, in chivalrous construction of each other's conduct, in bearing one another's infirmities, in helping the helpless, in helping the blind man across the crowded thoroughfare. *That* may be an orthodoxy, and some metaphysical conjuring may be a trick which elicits nothing but Divine contempt.

Document I.7

J. H. Thom on God a Spirit, n.d.

John Hamilton Thom (1808–94), with James Martineau (see II.15) and J. J. Tayler, was one of the leading spirits of the generation of Unitarians who rejected the legacy of Joseph Priestley in favour of a faith showing a profound debt to the romantic temper of the nineteenth century. While acting as minister of Renshaw Street Chapel in Liverpool, he exercised a wider influence through his writings. See V. D. Davis, 'Memoir', in *A Minister of God*, London, 1901; the excellent R. K. Webb, 'John Hamilton Thom: Intellect and Conscience in Liverpool', in P. T. Phillips, ed., *The View from the Pulpit*, Toronto, 1978; and DNB.

The extract is from the first sermon in a posthumous collection, *A Spiritual Faith*, 2nd edn, London, 1908, pp. 9–11. The title is 'God is a Spirit'; the text is John 4: 24. Christianity, in Thom's view, is in course of development, a process that entails moving beyond theology and ecclesiasticism. The affinity with the transcendentalism of the American Unitarian W. E. Channing is very much apparent.

We know that everything evil in us is against the law of our own spirit – is unspiritual; that everything vindictive, unmerciful, careless of the well-being of others, is a contradiction to our own souls – a stain upon our inmost life. How utterly, therefore, must it be removed from the Spirit of God! Let a man think of God as an Infinite Spirit, and he will hold of Him no ungenerous, no distrustful, no unrighteous doctrines. Let a man refuse to believe of God whatever the Spirit of God does not commend to his own soul, and the weary burdens Fear or Theology has laid upon religion will fall away from faith, and leave God Himself to act upon us, as Spirit on spirit. It is neglect of *the inward Teacher* that has arrested spiritual progress, obstructed the natural developments of Christianity, prevented the highest truths upon these subjects flowing freely through the world, made religion a tradition, and the soul that should be taught of God a vassal to the Church.

Religion is the feeling of God Himself acting on the soul; theology is man's thought of God in a symbolized form: it is, therefore, unavoidable that it should present God in the intellectual image of Man. Theology is not God, but man's philosophy of God; and as a substitute for the teaching of the Holy Spirit, it is fatal to religion: it is to interpose the formulas of our own minds between us and the living Spirit.

I suppose the only meaning of religious life, if you define it by its essential difference from all other life, is a sense of being moved by God; and a sense of God is a sense of intercourse with an Infinite Spirit in any of the directions in which a pure spirit may reveal the perfections of His Being. As often as we are religious, the infinite Lord of Life is in communion with something in us that is kindred to Himself. We cannot enter those regions of life unless the Father draw us. Now, what are the elements of the Infinite *in us*? Everything that gives a sense of intercourse with a Spirit we know is not our spirit – for it is above us, and rebukes us, and prompts us, and invites us onwards, and sometimes speaks in peace that passeth understanding, and sometimes in judgment that we cannot disown, though it disowns us; and these divine openings in our nature are in love, desire for purity, thirst for righteousness, for truth and beauty. Consciousness of a heavenly Presence in the visible universe, the awe of conscience, the feeling of a holy Being whose eye is upon us, the sentiment of an immortal life, – in all these only the Infinite Spirit can nourish us; and Revelation has its end not in giving us God's teachings in human forms or words, but in helping us to place and keep our spirits in personal communion with Him, their inexhaustible Fountain. This, according to himself, is the truth that Christ came to give the world – truth not as a form of thought, but as the reality of spiritual life, which is intercourse with God: 'That all may be one, as Thou, Father, art in me, and I in Thee.'

Document I.8

Alexander Maclaren on the Wells of Salvation, 1882

Alexander Maclaren (1826–1910) was trained at Stepney Baptist College and became minister in Southampton (1846–58) and Union Chapel, Manchester (1858–1903). He was twice president of the Baptist Union, in 1875 and 1901. He disliked committees and organisations, pastoral work and preaching on special occasions, but was recognised throughout the English-speaking world as the supreme exponent of an expository ministry. See E. T. McLaren, *Dr. McLaren of*

Manchester, London, [1912]; D. Williamson, *The Life of Alexander Maclaren*, London, [1910]; and DNB.

This extract from a sermon based on Isaiah 12: 3, 'The Wells of Salvation', is taken from *The Secret of Power and Other Sermons*, London, 1882, pp. 217–19.

Consider, again, what is *the way of drawing* from the well of salvation.

It is not difficult to come to a right understanding of the act which answers to this part of the metaphor. People have given many answers to the question, If God be the fountain of salvation, how are we to get the water? If I may say so, pumps of all sorts have been tried, and there has been much weary working of arms at the handles, and much jangling of buckets and nothing brought up. The old word is true, with a new application to all who try in any shape to procure salvation by any work of their own: 'Thou hast nothing to draw with, and the well is deep.' But there is no need for all this profitless work. It is as foolish as it would be to spend money and pains in sinking a well in some mountainous country, where every hill-side is seamed with watercourses, and all that is needed is to put one end of any kind of wooden spout into the 'burn' and your vessels under the other. The well of salvation is an Artesian well that needs no machinery to raise the water, but only pitchers to receive it as it rises.

Christ has taught us what 'drawing' is. To the Samaritan woman He said, 'Thou wouldst have asked of him and he would have given thee living water.' So, then, Drawing is Asking. To the crowds in the Temple courts He said, 'Let him come unto me and drink.' So, then, Drawing is Coming. To the listeners by the Sea of Galilee He said, 'He that cometh to me shall never hunger; and he that believeth on me shall never thirst.' So Coming, Asking, Drawing, are all explained by Believing. To trust Christ is to come to Him. To trust Christ is to draw, and to trust Christ is to drink. Simple faith draws all God's goodness into the soul.

Now that faith which is thus powerful, must fix and fasten on a definite historical act. The faith which draws from the fountain of salvation is not a vague faith in generalities about God's goodness and the like, but it grasps God as revealed and becoming our salvation in the person and work of Jesus Christ. Nor is it a vague faith which has regard to Christ in his lovely character and perfect purity only, but one which lays hold on that great miracle of love perfected on the Cross where He bore our sins. In that wonderful discourse in which Christ proclaims Himself the Bread of Life, it is very instructive to note that He advances from the more general statement that life comes from eating of that bread which is Himself, to the more special and defined one, 'Whoso eateth my flesh and drinketh my blood hath eternal life.' Not merely Christ, but Christ crucified, is the food of our souls, the water of life. So then the drawing is faith, and that a faith which grasps the great sacrifice which Christ has made, as the channel whereby God's salvation comes to each thirsty lip and drooping soul.

Document I.9

Hugh Price Hughes on Christ the Greatest of Social Reformers, 1889

Hugh Price Hughes (1847–1902) was amongst the most charismatic religious figures of the last years of the nineteenth century, drawing attention to the pressing social problems of his day. The phrase 'The Nonconformist Conscience' is indelibly associated with his name. From 1886 he was superintendent of the West London Wesleyan Mission, in 1896 he was first president of the National Free Church Council and in the following year, after surmounting considerable opposition, president of the Wesleyan Conference. See [D. P. Hughes], *The Life of Hugh Price Hughes*, London, 1905; C. Oldstone-Moore, *Hugh Price Hughes: Founder of a New Methodism, Conscience of a New Nonconformity*, Cardiff, 1999; more critically, J. Kent, 'Hugh Price Hughes and the Nonconformist Conscience', in G. V. Bennett and J. D. Walsh, eds, *Essays in Modern English Church History*, London, 1966; and DNB.

The extract is from a characteristic sermon, 'Christ the Greatest of Social Reformers' on Luke 12: 15, published in *Social Christianity*, London, 1889, at pp. 53–6. The argument that Christ had improved the lot of women and the appeal to working men are typical; so is the combination of simple diction with unqualified superlatives.

We cannot be too frequently reminded that ancient society was founded upon utter contempt for man *as man*. It is the more necessary that we should insist upon this to-day, because there are some very gifted and sincere, though ill-informed writers, who try to persuade us, and especially try to persuade the young men and young women of our time, that Christianity is essentially a selfish religion, that Christianity has taught men to neglect their human duty, and to be absorbed in a selfish endeavour to escape from hell and to get to heaven. I do not deny that some very sincere Christians may have presented such a caricature of Christianity as that. But when we begin to investigate the question historically, we shall find that apart altogether from the influence of Jesus Christ upon our future. He has already done more for society in Europe than all the great reformers before Him; and that everything in the existing civilization of this country of which we have any right to be proud is due to Jesus Christ. He was the greatest social Reformer the world has ever seen. He did not only [do] more for heaven, but a great deal more for earth than was ever done before. If any of us have formed so mutilated a conception of His teaching as to imagine that the Christian ideal is to save our own souls and neglect our fellow-citizens, so much the worse for us.

Read your Bible with your eyes open, read history with your eyes open, and then you will see that however fearfully individual Christians may have neglected their duty, Jesus Christ came into this world to save human society as well as to save individuals. Indeed, you cannot effectually save the one without saving the other. I implore you to remember that when Christ came, man *as man* had no rights whatever; and if that was the case even with man, I need scarcely say it was much more the case with woman. There are some in the present day who even dare to tell us that Buddha was more illustrious than Christ. What has Buddha done for woman in comparison with what Christ has done for her? When Christ came, woman was regarded throughout the whole civilized world as a necessary evil, as a slave, as alternately the plaything and the plague of man; and if every man owes so much to Christ, every woman owes a great deal more. In the 'good old times' before Christ came, physical force was in the ascendant, and the result was that woman, having less physical strength than man, was everywhere degraded and enslaved.

And if women were infamously treated, much more were children. What has Buddha done for children? In every country where the influence of Buddha prevails, infanticide is practised and sanctioned. So it was in the Roman Empire and in Greece. Take the masterpiece of ancient literature, the ideal Republic of Plato, which is the special study of every classical scholar. Well, Plato, in his ideal Republic, makes provision, on a gigantic scale, for the murder of superfluous children. Let the men of Europe, and especially the working men of Europe, who have never had the opportunity of individual research, and who are in danger of being misled by the use of such words as 'republic' and 'freedom,' distinctly understand that when Jesus Christ, the greatest of all social reformers, came into this world, there was no protection for the weak, there was no comfort for the sorrowful, there was no effective restraint for the wicked.

Christ came, and the great Revolution began at once. They said of His disciples, soon after His crucifixion, that they were revolutionists, and that they turned the world upside down; and the impeachment was true. They were the greatest revolutionists the world has ever seen. They introduced into human society ideas which had never entered the head of man before, and the only pity is that their revolution has not gone a great deal further.

Document I.10

R. F. Horton on the Living Christ, 1891

Robert Forman Horton (1855–1934) was the first Nonconformist to attain a fellowship at Oxford, at New College in 1879. He created a stir by abandoning the university for the ministry, and from its foundation in 1884 until 1930 he served at Lyndhurst Road Congregational Church in north London. He was chairman of the Congregational Union in 1903 and president of the National Free Church Council in 1905. See R. F. Horton, *An Autobiography*, London, 1917; A. Peel and J. A. R. Marriott, *Robert Forman Horton*, London, 1937; and DNB.

The sermon extract shows a cultured confidence, but even more a personal, almost mystical, tone typical of Horton. It is taken from 'The Living Christ', in *Sermons delivered in Lyndhurst Road Church, Hampstead*, London, 1893, pp. 48–9.

And now, finally, I want to lead you up to the most important fact of all. Although, as I have tried to show you, the sheer historical testimonies to the Gospels are adequate, although, as I have hinted, the internal and the intrinsic tests of the Gospels put it beyond question that they are genuine, yet as a simple matter of fact our Christian faith does not depend exclusively on these Gospels. It depends upon the living Christ; upon an actual indubitable person. Thousands believed on Him – yes, savingly believed – before the Gospels were ever penned; thousands believe to-day who have no adequate knowledge of what these Gospels contain, and have scarcely known the record that they gave. The Christ who was conceived by Paul and preached throughout the Roman world as the transforming power which changed it into the Christian world, was not the Christ of any biography. Paul says he 'knew no man, not even Christ, after the flesh.' The Christ whom Paul preached does not rest, as the passage we have just read (1 Cor. xv. 1–8) shows us, upon the records of the Gospels. The Christ whom he preached was a living person; a person so real that men could come to Him, and coming to Him could believe on Him, could be saved by Him, could be changed from the very roots of their being upward, could be redeemed from sin, could overmaster the passions of a lifetime, could arise as new creatures in Him to go out in the world and manifest Him to others who do not believe.

And, to-night, dear friends – I say it in all humility – the Christ whom I preach to you, the Christ whom I try to preach from week to week in this pulpit, is a Person whom I know; the experience which I ask you to share is an experience which I have tested; it is not imaginary, but real. I ask you to find out whether it can be real for you. Christ is here; I do not mean in this book, but Himself in the spirit. In the spirit He pleads with you men and women who are made in His image, and He says 'Come unto me, and I will give you rest.' In the spirit you hear Him; in the spirit you can answer Him; in the spirit you can come to Him, and in the spirit you can find rest to your souls. What is recorded of His beautiful human life, and of His tragic death, may throw a lovely light upon His character, upon His aims and upon His wish to save; but it is not the record of Him, it is Christ Himself to whom you must come.

PART II

THEOLOGY

Introduction

The theology of the overwhelming majority of nineteenth-century Nonconformists was Evangelical. It emerges equally in the simple scripturalism of the General Baptist New Connexion catechism (II.2) and in the doctrinal affirmations of the more elaborate Congregational Union declaration (II.4). Particular aspects of Evangelical belief illustrated here include biblical inspiration (II.30) and the alternative eschatologies of postmillennialism (II.28) and premillennialism (II.29). The Unitarians, of course, stood apart from Evangelicalism (II.6, 15, 36); so, in some measure did high Calvinists (II.21, 33). Nor did denominations forget their distinctive convictions: believer's baptism for the Baptists (II.22) and Arminianism with entire sanctification for the Methodists (II.13, 14). Although most denominations inherited their confessional statements from an earlier age, the Welsh Calvinistic Methodists did draw up a full Confession of Faith (II.3), the Salvation Army registered a brief one (II.8) and the Wesleyans produced systematic theologians for the first time (II.13, 17). But the prevailing tone was Evangelical, as the titles of two bodies whose credal statements are presented here, the interdenominational Evangelical Alliance (II.7) and the National Council of the Evangelical Free Churches (II.10), bear witness.

The doctrinal issues that arose were therefore primarily related to the impact and erosion of Evangelical ways of thinking. In the early nineteenth century the Baptists assimilated the Evangelical impulse by modifying their thought (II.11, 1) and practice (II.23), but suffered schism in the process (II.24); the Congregationalists similarly adapted their doctrinal position (II.12); and the Quakers experienced an equivalent schism (II.25, 26, 5). In the later part of the century there were tensions as thinkers pushed at the boundaries of Evangelical belief: over biblical criticism (II.27), the language of worship (II.31), the fatherhood of God (II.32), the need for definition of faith (II.34) and universalism (II.35). Towards the end of the century there were efforts to accommodate Evangelicalism to newer trends of thought: over the atonement (II.16), biblical criticism (again) (II.38), social engagement (II.39), the kingdom of God (II.18) and the fatherhood of God (again) (II.20). And there were stout defences of the received faith, notably by C. H. Spurgeon (II.37), eliciting a Baptist denominational response (II.9), and, in a manner that took full account of contemporary intellectual trends, by P. T. Forsyth (II.19). The process of erosion was capably diagnosed at the time by D. W. Simon (II.40).

The Evangelical theological currents are discussed in D. W. Bebbington, *Evangelicalism in Modern Britain: A History from the 1730s to the 1980s*, London, 1989, and an excellent case study is W. B. Glover, *Evangelical Nonconformists and Higher Criticism in the Nineteenth Century*, London, 1954. Mark Hopkins illuminates the growing divergence of liberals from conservative Evangelicals among Congregationalists and Baptists in *Nonconformity's Romantic Generation: Evangelical and Liberal Theologies in Victorian England*, Carlisle, 2004. D. A. Johnson, *The Changing Shape of English Nonconformity, 1825–1925*, New York, 1999, argues for a successful adaptation of theology to modernity. In the nineteenth century itself R. W. Dale wrote a penetrating analysis in *The Old Evangelicalism and the New*, London, 1889. Wales is covered in outline in W. Evans, *An Outline of the History of Welsh Theology*, London, 1900, and a magisterial account of developments there at the end of the century is found in R. Tudur Jones, *Faith and the Crisis of a Nation: Wales, 1890–1914*, ed. R. Pope, Cardiff, 2004. There are studies of the thought of particular denominations: W. Strawson, 'Methodist Theology, 1850–1950', in R. Davies et al., ed., *A History of the Methodist Church in Great Britain*, vol. 3, London, 1983; R. Tudur Jones, *Congregationalism in England, 1662–1962*, London, 1962; J. H. Y. Briggs, *The English Baptists of the Nineteenth Century*, Didcot, Oxfordshire, 1994; and, for the Unitarians, R. K. Webb, 'John Hamilton Thom: Intellect and Conscience in Liverpool', in P. T. Phillips, ed., *The View from the Pulpit: Victorian Ministers and Society*, Toronto, 1978, and R. Waller, 'James Martineau: The Development of his Thought', in B. Smith, ed., *Truth, Liberty, Religion: Essays Celebrating Two Hundred Years of Manchester College*, Oxford, 1986.

Statements of Faith

Document II.1

Collingham Baptist Church Confession of Faith, c. 1801

Collingham consists of two villages, North and South, some five miles north of Newark in Nottinghamshire. The Baptist church there, dating from the seventeenth century, had originally been General, but in the late eighteenth century it became Particular. In accordance with traditional Dissenting practice, a church covenant was drawn up around the very beginning of the nineteenth century, and to it the following Confession of Faith was attached. Although it concludes abruptly, the document is complete. Its doctrine is Calvinistic, but there is evidence of Andrew Fuller's moderate version of Reformed teaching (see II.11) in the absence of double predestination in article 3.

The document is taken from a transcription from the Collingham church book in an appendix of F. M. W. Harrison, 'The Life and Thought of the Baptists of Nottinghamshire', unpublished University of Nottingham Ph.D. thesis, 1972. On the background, see W. L. Lumpkin, *Baptist Confessions of Faith*, Chicago, 1959.

The Confession of Faith

1st. of the Trinity in Unity

We believe there is one living and true God, without human Parts, Members or Passions: infinite eternal and unchangeable; the Creator and Preserver of all things both visible and invisible. And in this Godhead there are three persons possessing the same Nature and Attributes, equal in Glory, Power and Eternity. These Divine Persons before all Time entered into a sacred Covenant : to save a Remnant of Mankind from Misery to everlasting Happiness.

2nd. of the Holy Scriptures

We believe the Scriptures contained in the Old and New Testaments to be the infallible Word of God, being given by Divine Inspiration and revealing all things necessary to Salvation, the standard of all Doctrines, of all Experience, and of all Practice, being now complete, admitting of no Additions to be made to it, nor anything whatever to be taken from it.

3rd. of the Decrees of God

We believe that God from all Eternity by the infinitely wise and holy Council of His Will, did freely and immutably foreordain whatsoever comes to pass, yet so that He is neither the author of sin nor is any violence put on the will of the Creature. By his decree he fixed a Remnant of Mankind as the object of his familiar Love, to receive Grace in time and Glory in Eternity and having conferred this high and inestimable favour on this Remnant according to the Election of Grace, he left others in that state in which they were considered as fallen so that in consequence of their going on and continuing in Sin, they will become Monuments for the Glory of his Justice.

4th. of Christ the Mediator

We believe that it pleased God in his eternal Purpose to choose, ordain and appoint the Lord Jesus Christ, the second person in the Blessed Trinity to be the only Mediator between him and the fallen sinner. Into his hands the Elect were given that they might obtain salvation in and through him. In the fulness of time He assumed human Nature, being God and Man in Person, and this he did willingly and of his own free Choice. In this Nature he completely fulfilled the Holy Law and satisfied inflexible Justice. He died as a Ransom, Sacrifice and Atonement for his People, and in the same Nature he rose from the Dead, is gone into Heaven as the Head Representative and Intercessor of his people, and lives there to see all Effects of his Undertaking applied to them as stipulated in the Everlasting Covenant of Grace.

5th. of Justification

We believe that all Elect stand justified in the sight of God, and are delivered from Condemnation and Wrath, through the Righteousness of Jesus imputed, consisting of his active and passive obedience performed in their Room and Stead, and that all the Elect in due Time are brought to believe in Christ as the Lord their Righteousness, and to Experience Justification in their Consciences by Faith and enjoy Peace with God through the Mediator's Blood.

6th. of Providence

We believe that God who hath created all things by his Power and Wisdom, doth also by his superintending Hands, uphold, direct, dispose and govern all Creatures and all Events by his holy and wise Providence, for the Welfare of his people and to the praise and Glory of his name, according to the immutable Council of his Will.

7th. of the Fall

We believe that God having created Man did enter into a Covenant with him, called the Covenant of Nature, in which Life was promised on his Obedience but every kind of Death denounced on his Disobedience, he being seduced by the subtilty of Satan did wilfully transgress the Law of Creation and break the Covenant by eating the forbidden fruit.

Document II.2

The General Baptist New Connexion Catechism on God, 1805

The New Connexion of General Baptists, which had been established in 1770, was dominated by its founder, Dan Taylor (1738–1816), until his death. In 1806, while serving as minister of the General Baptist church in Whitechapel, Taylor published a catechism to expound the distinctive Evangelical Arminianism combined with Baptist practice that marked his denomination. Designed, like traditional catechisms in general, for training children in the faith, it adopted a pithy style, the answers all being phrased in the language of scripture with the biblical text annexed. On Taylor, see A. Taylor, *Memoirs of the Rev. Dan Taylor*, London, 1820; and DNB.

The extract consists of the two sections on the doctrine of God and is taken from Dan Taylor, *A Catechism*, 6th edn, London, 1805, pp. 5, 6.

SECT. II.
God the Creator and Preserver of all Things.

Q. 1. Can you tell me who made you?
A. The blessed God made me, and fashioned me. Psal. cxix. 73.
Q. 2. Did the blessed God make all things?
A. Yes; he created all things, and for his pleasure they are and were created. Rev. iv. 11.
Q. 3. And does he preserve you?
A. Yes; he holdeth our souls in life. Psa. lxvi. 9.
Q. 4. And does he preserve and uphold all things?
A. Yes; he preserveth them all. Neh. ix. 6.
Q. 5. Are our life and death, and health and sickness, all in the hand of God?
A. Yes; the Lord killeth and maketh alive: he bringeth down to the grave, and he bringeth up. I Sam. ii. 6.
Q. 6. Does the blessed God supply all your wants?
A. Yes; all our springs are in him. Psa. lxxxvii. 7.
Q. 7. And does he supply all creatures?
A. Yes; he satisfieth the desire of every living thing. Psal. cxiv. 16.

SECT. III.
The Perfections of God.

Q. 1. Is the blessed God a Spirit or Spiritual Being?
A. Yes; God is a Spirit; and they that worship him, must worship him in spirit and in truth. John iv. 24.
Q. 2. Is the blessed God every where present?
A. Yes; he is not far from every one of us. Acts xvii. 27.
Q. 3. And is God eternal?
A. Yes; from everlasting to everlasting he is God. Psal. xc. 2.
Q. 4. Is he also unchangeable?

A. Yes; with him is no variableness, neither shadow of turning. James i. 17.

Q. 5. And does he know all things?

A. Yes; his understanding is infinite. Psa. cxlvii. 5.

Q. 6. Is he a powerful Being?

A. Yes; he can do every thing. Job xlii. 2.

Q. 7. And is he a holy Being?

A. Yes; there is none holy as the Lord. 1. Sam. ii. 2.

Q. 8. And is he true and faithful?

A. Yes; God is not a man, that he should lie, nor the son of man, that he should repent. Num. xxiii. 11.

Q. 9. Is he also a just God?

A. Yes; he is a God of truth, and without iniquity, just and right is he. Deut. xxxii. 4.

Q. 10. And is he not also a God of goodness and love?

A. Yes; he is good to all, and his tender mercies are over all his works. Psa. cxiv. 9.

Document II. 3

Welsh Calvinistic Methodist Confession of Faith on God, 1823

The Methodists arising from the Evangelical Revival in Wales were largely Calvinistic. In the early years of the nineteenth century they gradually emerged as a denomination, and in 1823 published a Confession of Faith. The primary role in its preparation was taken by David Charles (1762–1834) – see DEB. The document appeals to scripture in its notes, but is strongly reasoned in its presentation. Section 1, on the being of God, is markedly coloured by natural theology; section 3, on God's decrees, is resolutely Calvinistic. Yet, after debates in the connexion over the previous decade, the Calvinism it professed was of a moderate variety.

The extracts are from *The History, Constitution, Rules of Discipline, and Confession of Faith of the Calvinistic Methodists or the Presbyterians of Wales*, Caernarvon, 1900, pp. 38–9 and 45–7. The footnotes, indicated by letters in the original, have been changed to numbers.

I. OF THE BEING OF GOD.

There is one God and only one true and living God. The light of nature in man proves the being of God. All nations acknowledge a God, or gods. Natural conscience, accusing or else excusing, proves the being of God, and man's responsibility to him for his actions.[1] The creation proves the being of God, as an effect proves that it had a cause. The creation could not have come into being of itself: it must have had a cause.[2] The being of man himself proves the being of God: forasmuch as one man is the offspring of another man, the first man must have existed; consequently, he must have had a Creator.

Theology

The order, beauty, adaptation, harmony, and consistence of the creation proves that a wise God gave it being, and upholds and governs all things.[3] All creatures answer purposes which they could not themselves have ordained or designed; it is evident, therefore, that one great Governor rules over all.[4] The terrible retributions that have befallen some of God's enemies in this world, and the terrors that have dismayed their consciences at death, after a life spent in denying God, prove his existence. ...

5. OF GOD'S DECREE.

God, from eternity, after the counsel of his own will, and for the manifestation and exaltation of his glorious attributes, decreed all that he would do in time and to eternity, in creation, in the government of his creatures, and in the salvation of sinners of the human race; yet so that he is not the author of sin nor constrains the will of his creature in its actions.[6] The decree of God depends not in the least upon the creature nor upon the foreknowledge of God himself; on the contrary, God knows that certain things will be, because he has decreed that they should be.[7] God's decree is infinitely wise,[8] and perfectly just;[9] eternal,[10] free,[11] comprehensive,[12] secret,[13] gracious,[14] holy,[15] good,[16] unchangeable,[17] and effectual.[18]

Notes

1. For *there is* one God. I *Tim.* ii. 5. I *am* the first and I *am* the last; *and* beside me *there is* no God. *Isa.* xliv. 5. For *when* the Gentiles, which have not the law, do by nature the things contained in the law, these having not the law, are a law unto themselves, &c. *Rom.* ii. 14, 15.
2. The heavens declare the glory of God; and the firmament sheweth his handy work, &c. *Psalm* xix. 1–3. For the invisible things of him from the creation of the world are clearly seen, being understood by the things that are made, *even* his eternal power and Godhead, so that they are without excuse. *Rom.* i. 20.
3. Lift up your eyes on high, and behold who hath created these things, that bringeth out their host by number; he calleth them all by names by the greatness of his might, for that *he is* strong in power; not one faileth. *Isa* xl. 26. Let them praise the name of the LORD: for he commanded, and they were created. He hath also stablished them for ever and ever: he hath made a decree which shall not pass. *Psalm* cxlviii. 5. 6. For this they willingly are ignorant of, that by the word of God the heavens were of old, and the earth standing out of the water and in the water. 2 *Peter* iii. 5.
4. The Lord hath prepared his throne in the heavens; and his Kingdom ruleth over all. *Psalm* ciii. 19. Yea, the stork in the heaven knoweth her appointed time; and the turtle and the crane and the swallow observe the time of their coming; but my people know not the judgment of the Lord. *Jer.* viii. 7; *Job* xxxix.
5. And Pharoah said. Who *is* the Lord that I should obey his voice to let Israel go? I know not the LORD, neither will I let Israel go. *Exod.* v. 2. And Pharoah sent, and called for Moses and Aaron, and said unto them, I have sinned this time: the Lord *is* righteous, and I and my people *are* wicked. *Exod.* ix. 27. And took off their chariot

wheels, that they drove them heavily; so that the Egyptians said, Let us flee from the face of Israel; for the Lord fighteth for them against the Egyptians. *Exod.* xiv. 25.
6. In whom also we have obtained an inheritance, being predestinated according to the purpose of him who worketh all things after the counsel of his own will. *Ephes.* i. 11. The LORD of hosts hath sworn, saying, Surely as I have thought, so shall it come to pass; and as I have purposed, *so* shall it stand, &c. *Isa.* xiv. 24–27. Declaring the end from the beginning, and from ancient times *the things* that are not *yet* done, saying, My counsel shall stand, and I will do all my pleasure, &c. *Isa.* xlvi. 10, 11. Seeing his days are determined, the number of his months *are* with thee; thou hast appointed his bounds that he cannot pass. *Job* xiv. 5. And brake up for it my decreed *place*, and set bars and doors. And said, Hitherto shalt thou come, but not further: and here shall thy proud waves be stayed. *Job.* xxxviii. 10, 11. He hath also stablished them for ever and ever: he hath made a decree which shall not pass. *Ps.* clxviii. 6. When he gave to the sea his decree, that the waters should not pass his commandment: when he appointed the foundation of the earth. *Prov.* viii. 29. Fear ye not me, saith the LORD: will ye not tremble at my presence, which have placed the sand *for* the bound of the sea, by a perpetual decree, that it cannot pass it: and though the waves thereof toss themselves, yet can they not prevail; though they roar, yet can they not pass over it? *Jer.* v. 22. When the Most High divided to the nations their inheritance, when he separated the sons of Adam, he set the bounds of the people according to the number of the children of Israel. *Deut.* xxxii. 8. And all the inhabitants of the earth *are* reputed as nothing: and he doeth according to his will in the army of heaven, and *among* the inhabitants of the earth: and none can stay his hand, or say unto him. What doest thou? *Dan.* iv. 35. Are not two sparrows sold for a farthing? and one of them shall not fall on the ground without your Father. But the very hairs of your head are all numbered. *Matt.* x. 29, 30. For to do whatsoever thy hand and thy counsel determined before to be done. *Acts* iv. 28. Known unto God are all his works from the beginning of the world. *Acts* xv. 18. And hath made of one blood all nations of men for to dwell on all the face of the earth, and hath determined the times before appointed, and the bounds of their habitations. *Acts* xvii. 26.
7. The lot is cast into the lap; but the whole disposing thereof *is* of the LORD. *Prov.* xviii. 33. And the vessel that he made of clay was marred in the hands of the potter: so he made it again another vessel, as seemed good to the potter to make *it*. Then the word of the LORD came to me, saying, O house of Israel, cannot I do with you as this potter? saith the LORD. Behold, as the clay *is* in the potter's hand, so *are* ye in mine hand. O house of Israel, &c. *Jer.* xviii. 4–10. Even so, Father; for so it seemed good in thy sight. *Matt.* xi, 26. My counsel shall stand, and I will do all my pleasure. *Isa.* xlvi. 10. Thou wilt say then unto me, Why doth he yet find fault? For who hath resisted his will? Nay but, O man, who art thou that repliest against God? Shall the thing formed say to him that formed *it*, Why hast thou made me thus? Hath not the potter power over the clay, of the same lump to make one vessel unto honour, and another unto dishonour? *Rom.* ix. 19–21.
8. O the depth of the riches both of the wisdom and knowledge of God! how unsearchable *are* his judgments, and his ways past finding out! *Rom.* xi. 33.
9. The Lord is righteous in all his ways, and holy in all his works. *Ps.* cxlv. 17.
10. According to the eternal purpose which he purposed in Christ Jesus our Lord. *Ephes.* iii. 11.
11. For he saith to Moses, I will have mercy on whom I will have mercy, and I will have

compassion on whom I will have compassion. So then *it is* not of him that willeth, nor of him that runneth, but of God that sheweth mercy. *Rom.* ix. 15, 16.

12. In whom also we have obtained an inheritance, being predestinated according to the purpose of him who worketh all things after the counsel of his own will. *Ephes.* i. 11.
13. The secret things *belong* unto the Lord our God; but those *things* which *are* revealed *belong* unto us and to our children for ever, that *we* may do all the words of this law. *Deut.* xxix. 29.
14. Who hath saved us, and called *us* with an holy calling, not according to our works, but according to his own purpose and grace, which was given us by Christ Jesus before the world began. 2 *Tim.* i. 9.
15. According as he hath chosen us in him before the foundation of the world, that we should be holy and without blame before him in love. *Ephes.* i. 4.
16. And we know that all things work together for good to them that love God, to them who are the called according to *his* purpose. For whom he did foreknow, he also did predestinate to be conformed to the image of his Son, that he might be the firstborn among many brethren. Moreover whom he did predestinate, them he also called: and whom he called, them he also justified: and whom he justified, them he also glorified. *Rom.* viii. 28–30.
17. But he *is* in *one mind*, and who can turn him? And *what* his soul desireth, even *that* he doeth. For he performeth *the thing that is* (*For the children* being not yet born, neither having done any good or evil, that the purpose of God according to election might stand, not of works, but of him that calleth). *Rom.* ix. 11.
18. Declaring the end from the beginning, and from ancient times *the things* that are not *yet* done, saying, My counsel shall stand, and I will do all my pleasure. *Isa.* xlvi. 10.

Document II.4

Congregational Union Declaration, 1833

At the formation of the Congregational Union of England and Wales in 1833 it was agreed to issue a Declaration of Faith. It was not a confession, because, as the preamble insists, the document was not binding on the churches, which remained entirely independent in polity. The second part consists of an exposition of that polity. The whole was drawn up by George Redford, Congregational minister at Worcester (see DNB), and then revised in minor ways by a small committee. The theology of the Declaration is the moderate Calvinism that prevailed in the denomination. As R. W. Dale (see II.16) points out, its sacramental doctrine is much lower than what Independents had professed in the seventeenth century. Dale offers a critical appraisal in his *History of English Congregationalism*, London, 1907, pp. 699–709.

The whole of this document is reprinted from A. Peel, *These Hundred Years: A History of the Congregational Union of England and Wales, 1831–1931*, London, 1931, pp. 69–74.

DECLARATION
OF THE
FAITH, CHURCH ORDER, AND DISCIPLINE
OF THE
CONGREGATIONAL, OR INDEPENDENT DISSENTERS,
ADOPTED AT THE ANNUAL MEETING OF THE CONGREGATIONAL
UNION, MAY, 1833.

THE CONGREGATIONAL Churches in England and Wales, frequently called INDEPENDENT, hold the following doctrines, as of Divine authority, and as the foundation of Christian faith and practice. They are also formed and governed according to the principles hereinafter stated.

PRELIMINARY NOTES.

1. It is not designed, in the following summary, to do more than to state the leading doctrines of faith and order maintained by Congregational Churches in general.

2. It is not proposed to offer any proofs, reasons, or arguments, in support of the doctrines herein stated, but simply to declare what the Denomination believes to be taught by the pen of inspiration.

3. It is not intended to present a scholastic or critical confession of faith, but merely such a statement as any intelligent member of the body might offer, as containing its leading principles.

4. It is not intended that the following statement should be put forth with any authority, or as a standard to which assent should be required.

5. Disallowing the utility of creeds and articles of religion as a bond of union, and protesting against subscription to any human formularies as a term of communion, Congregationalists are yet willing to declare, for general information, what is commonly believed among them, reserving to every one the most perfect liberty of conscience.

6. Upon some minor points of doctrine and practice, they, differing among themselves, allow to each other the right to form an unbiassed judgment of the Word of God.

7. They wish it to be observed, that, notwithstanding their jealousy of subscription to creeds and articles, and their disapproval of the imposition of any human standard, whether of faith or discipline, they are far more agreed in their doctrines and practices than any Church which enjoins subscription and enforces a human standard of orthodoxy; and they believe that there is no minister and no church among them that would deny the substance of any one of the following doctrines of religion, though each might prefer to state his sentiments in his own way.

PRINCIPLES OF RELIGION.

I. The Scriptures of the Old Testament, as received by the Jews, and the books of the New Testament, as received by the Primitive Christians from the Evangelists and Apostles, Congregational Churches believe to be Divinely inspired, and of supreme authority. These writings, in the languages in which they were originally composed, are to be consulted, with the aids of sound criticism, as a final appeal to all controversies, but the common version they consider to be adequate to the ordinary purposes of Christian instruction and edification.

II. They believe in one God, essentially wise, holy, just, and good; eternal, infinite, and immutable in all natural and moral perfections; the Creator, Supporter, and Governor of all beings, and of all things.

III. They believe that God is revealed in the Scriptures, as the Father, the Son, and the Holy Spirit, and that to each are attributable the same Divine properties and perfections. The doctrine of the Divine existence, as above stated, they cordially believe, without attempting fully to explain.

IV. They believe that man was created after the Divine image, sinless, and in his kind, perfect.

V. They believe that the first man disobeyed the Divine command, fell from his state of innocence and purity, and involved all his posterity in the consequences of that fall.

VI. They believe that, therefore, all mankind are born in sin, and that a fatal inclination to moral evil, utterly incurable by human means, is inherent in every descendant of Adam.

VII. They believe that God having, before the foundation of the world, designed to redeem fallen man, made disclosures of His mercy, which were the grounds of faith and hope from the earliest ages.

VIII. They believe that God revealed more fully to Abraham the covenant of His grace, and, having promised that from his descendants should arise the Deliverer and Redeemer of mankind, set that patriarch and his posterity apart, as a race specially favoured and separate to His service; a peculiar church, formed and carefully preserved, under the Divine sanction and government until the birth of the promised Messiah.

IX. They believe that, in the fulness of the time, the Son of God was manifested in the flesh, being born of the Virgin Mary, but conceived by the power of the Holy Spirit; and that our Lord Jesus Christ was both the Son of man and the Son of God; partaking fully and truly of human nature though without sin – equal with the Father and 'the express image of His person'.

X. They believe that Jesus Christ, the Son of God, revealed, either personally in His own ministry, or by the Holy Spirit in the ministry of His apostles, the whole mind of God, for our salvation; and that, by His obedience to the Divine law while He lived, and by His sufferings unto death, He meritoriously 'obtained eternal redemption for us'; having thereby vindicated and illustrated Divine justice, 'magnified the law', and 'brought in everlasting righteousness'.

XI. They believe that, after His death and resurrection, He ascended up into heaven, where, as the Mediator, he 'ever liveth' to rule over all, and to 'make intercession for them that come unto God by Him'.

XII. They believe that the Holy Spirit is given, in consequence of Christ's mediation, to quicken and renew the hearts of men; and that His influence is indispensably necessary to bring a sinner to true repentance, to produce saving faith, to regenerate the heart, and to perfect our sanctification.

XIII. They believe that we are justified through faith in Christ, as 'the Lord our righteousness', and not 'by the works of the law'.

XIV. They believe that all who will be saved were the objects of God's eternal and electing love, and were given by an act of Divine sovereignty to the Son of God; which in no way interferes with the system of means, nor with the grounds of human responsibility; being wholly unrevealed as to its objects, and not a rule of human duty.

XV. They believe that the Scriptures teach the final perseverance of all true believers to a state of eternal blessedness, which they are appointed to obtain through constant faith in Christ, and uniform obedience to His commands.

XVI. They believe that a holy life will be the necessary effect of a true faith and that good works are the certain fruits of a vital union to Christ.

XVII. They believe that the sanctification of true Christians, or their growth in the graces of the Spirit, and meetness for heaven, is gradually carried on through the whole period during which it pleases God to continue them in the present life, and that, at death, their souls, perfectly freed from all remains of evil, are immediately received into the presence of Christ.

XVIII. They believe in the perpetual obligation of Baptism and the Lord's Supper; the former to be administered to all converts to Christianity and their children, by the application of water to the subject, 'in the name of the Father, and of the Son, and of the Holy Ghost'; and the latter to be celebrated by Christian churches as a token of faith in the Saviour, and of brotherly love.

XIX. They believe that Christ will finally come to judge the whole human race according to their works; that the bodies of the dead will be raised again; and that, as the Supreme Judge, He will divide the righteous from the wicked, will receive the righteous into 'life everlasting', but send away the wicked into 'everlasting punishment'.

XX. They believe that Jesus Christ directed His followers to live together in Christian fellowship, and to maintain the communion of saints; and that, for this purpose, they are jointly to observe all Divine ordinances, and maintain that church order and discipline which is either expressly enjoined by inspired institution, or sanctioned by the undoubted example of the apostles and of apostolic churches.

Principles of Church Order and Discipline.

I. The Congregational Churches hold it to be the will of Christ that true believers should voluntarily assemble together to observe religious ordinances to promote mutual edification and holiness, to perpetuate and propagate the Gospel in the world, and to advance the glory and worship of God, through Jesus Christ; and that each society of believers, having these objects in view in its formation, is properly a Christian church.

II. They believe that the New Testament contains, either in the form of express statute, or in the example and practice of apostles and apostolic churches, all the articles of faith necessary to be believed, and all the principles of order and discipline requisite for constituting and governing Christian societies; and that human traditions, fathers and councils, canons and creeds, possess no authority over the faith and practice of Christians.

III. They acknowledge Christ as the only Head of the Church, and the officers of each church under Him, as ordained to administer His laws impartially to all; and their only appeal, in all questions touching their religious faith and practice, is to the sacred Scriptures.

IV. They believe that the New Testament authorises every Christian church to elect its own officers, to manage all its own affairs, and to stand independent of, and irresponsible to, all authority, saving that only of the Supreme and Divine Head of the Church, the Lord Jesus Christ.

V. They believe that the only officers placed by the apostles over individual churches are the bishops or pastors and the deacons; the number of these being dependent upon the number of the church; and that to these, as the officers of the church, is committed respectively the administration of its spiritual and temporal concerns – subject, however, to the approbation of the church.

VI. They believe that no persons should be received as members of Christian churches, but such as make a credible profession of Christianity, are living according to its precepts, and attest a willingness to be subject to its discipline, and that none should be excluded from the fellowship of the church, but such as deny the faith of Christ, violate His laws, or refuse to submit themselves to the discipline which the Word of God enforces.

VII. The power of admission into any Christian church, and rejection from it, they believe to be vested in the church itself, and to be exercised only through the medium of its own officers.

VIII. They believe that Christian churches should statedly meet for the celebration of public worship, for the observance of the Lord's Supper, and for the sanctification of the first day of the week.

IX. They believe that the power of a Christian church is purely spiritual and should in no way be corrupted by union with temporal or civil power.

X. They believe that it is the duty of Christian churches to hold communion with each other, to entertain an enlarged affection for each other, as members of the same body, and to co-operate for the promotion of the Christian cause; but that no church, or union of churches, has any right or power to interfere with the faith or discipline of any other church further than to separate from such as, in faith or practice, depart from the Gospel of Christ.

XI. They believe that it is the privilege and duty of every church to call forth such of its members as may appear to be qualified by the Holy Spirit to sustain the office of the ministry; and that Christian churches unitedly ought to consider the maintenance of the Christian ministry in an adequate degree of learning as one of the especial cares, that the cause of the Gospel may be both honourably sustained and constantly promoted.

XII. They believe that church officers, whether bishops or deacons, should be chosen by the free voice of the church; but that their dedication to the duties of their office should take place with special prayer, and by solemn designation, to which most of the churches add the imposition of hands by those already in office.

XIII. They believe that the fellowship of every Christian church should be so liberal as to admit to communion in the Lord's Supper all whose faith and godliness are, on the whole, undoubted, though conscientiously differing in points of minor importance; and that this outward sign of fraternity in Christ should be co-extensive with the fraternity itself, though without involving any compliances which conscience would deem to be sinful.

Document II.5

Quaker Testimony to the Authority of Christ in his Church, 1840

Following the Beacon controversy of the 1830s (see II.25), the Quakers issued an official statement that reaffirmed traditional belief. The document, however, attempts to meet the concerns of those members of the Society of Friends who, under the influence of Evangelicalism, were tempted to repudiate their inheritance. Thus the testimony acknowledges the value of the Bible and the need for redemption, but stresses, in accordance with Quaker principles, the work of the Holy Spirit. The ordinances observed by the rest of Christendom are rejected, and it is insisted that the ministry, which should be open to women, must involve no preparation, no pay and no training. On the context, see E. Isichei, *Victorian Quakers*, Oxford, 1970.

The source is *A Testimony to the Authority of Christ in his Church*, London, 1840, pp. 1–3. The document goes on to reaffirm Quaker resistance to such ecclesiastical impositions as tithes.

A TESTIMONY
TO THE AUTHORITY OF CHRIST IN HIS CHURCH,
AND
TO THE SPIRITUALITY OF THE GOSPEL DISPENSATION;
ALSO
AGAINST SOME OF THE CORRUPTIONS OF PROFESSING CHRISTENDOM.

Given forth by the Yearly Meeting of the religious Society of Friends, held in London by adjournments, from the 20th to the 29th inclusive of the fifth month, 1840

We feel engaged at the present time to remind our members, and also to submit to the serious reflection of others, those views of the spiritual reign of our holy Redeemer, which have, from its origin, distinguished our religious Society.

Accepting with thankfulness the Holy Scriptures, as a revelation from God to the children of men, we have ever received these writings as an invaluable blessing, and believed that they are profitable for doctrine, for reproof, for correction,

Theology

for instruction in righteousness. It is therefore our earnest desire that, under the enlightening influence of the Holy Spirit by which they were given forth, they may be read and meditated upon, and followed by all men.

They do clearly record for our instruction the setting up, and the continuance through successive generations, under the immediate direction of the Most High, of an outward priesthood, of ceremonial laws and ordinances, of tithes, of feasts and sacrifices, of types and figures, which however were all to be fulfilled in Christ, and which were abolished by that one offering of Himself, by which He hath perfected for ever all them that are sanctified.

He is come in the flesh: He hath made reconciliation for iniquity, and hath appeared, to put away sin by the sacrifice of Himself: He is the propitiation for the sins of the whole world: He is our unchangeable and only High Priest, who ever liveth to make intercession for us, and through Him by one Spirit we have access unto the Father. The Mosaic institutions, and all the rituals of a ceremonial law are terminated. The Levitical priesthood has ceased, being superseded by Christ, who has ascended into heaven, and now sitteth at the right hand of the Father. No outward provisions similar in nature or character was established by Him. He conferred no power on man to provide a line of successors to his apostles. An outward priesthood has notwithstanding been set up, and a power has been assumed and exercised over the hearts and consciences of men, which He never bestowed. These evils and others in the church had their origin in the corrupt will and wisdom of man, they have long obstructed, and are still obstructing the reign of the Messiah, by interfering with that prerogative to reign in the church, and in the hearts of the children of men, which belongeth to Him alone.

Unto out Lord, risen from the dead and glorified with the Father, is given all power in heaven and on earth. He is appointed for a leader and commander to the people. His kingdom is an everlasting kingdom, and of the increase of his government and peace there shall be no end. It is one of the very striking features of his religion, that through Him we receive the Holy Spirit, to reprove the world of sin. The dark heart of man is thereby enlightened to see his undone condition by nature. By the effectual working of the grace of God the sinner is brought to tremble for his sins, to repent, and to forsake them, and to flee for refuge to the hope set before him in the Gospel, seeking redemption through the blood of Christ, even the forgiveness of sins.

The work of the Spirit is a deep and a heart-searching work. Its office is not only to cleanse the evil heart of man from the grosser enormities of sin, but to crucify the flesh, with the affections and lusts thereof, to subject the will and wisdom of the creature to its own divine power, to bring every thought into captivity to the obedience of Christ. We do therefore earnestly desire that all men may be brought to take more heed to this heavenly Teacher, who would, as believed in and obeyed, carry forward and complete a mighty change in the heart.

It is the prerogative of Christ to call and qualify by the Holy Spirit his servants to minister in word and doctrine, and to preach repentance towards God and faith towards our Lord Jesus Christ. In the earliest period of the Christian church his Spirit was, agreeably to ancient prophecy, poured upon servants and upon handmaidens, and we believe He continues to call, from the young and from the old, from the unlearned and from the poor, from the wise and from the rich, from women as well as from men, those whom He commissions to declare unto others the way of salvation. And seeing that this gift of the Holy Spirit cometh from God only, the ministry ought not, in our apprehension, to be performed at stated times of human appointment, neither ought there to be any previous preparation by the minister, of matter to be communicated by him to an audience, when met for the purpose of performing the solemn duty of worship unto God. But it should be exercised in that ability which He giveth on the occasion, and which He graciously renews from time to time, as it seemeth Him good.

The servants of Christ, who labour in the ministry, are to be highly esteemed for their work's sake, and when they leave their outward avocations, at his call, to preach the Gospel, their outward wants should be cheerfully supplied, if needful; yet we consider the gift of the ministry to be of so pure and sacred a nature, that no payment should be made for its exercise, and that it ought never to be undertaken, for pecuniary remuneration. As the gift is free, the exercise of it ought to be free also, in accordance with the precept of our Lord, 'freely ye have received, freely give.' We think that all payments to the ministers of the Gospel, for their services, are calculated, in their effects, to obstruct the faithful ministration of the word – to hinder the honest declaration of the whole counsel of God, in the authority of Him who is given to be Head over all things to his church.

In accordance with the views already stated, we consider that no provision of man's arrangement ought to be resorted to for qualifying those who feel themselves called to minister unto others. We believe it to be the duty of the ministers of the Gospel, to be diligent in the fear of God in reading the Holy Scriptures; neither do we undervalue human learning. But to subject any such to a course of teaching, as a necessary preparation for the ministry, is, in our apprehension, to interfere with that work of the Holy Spirit, which our Lord carries forward in the hearts of those whom He calls to preach his Gospel unto others, or to minister to the conditions of the people.

Our Lord leadeth not only his ministers in the path of duty, but He giveth to all his believing children, as they are individually concerned to look unto Him, rightly to occupy with those talents which He entrusts to them for the good of others. And we believe that He will, as the eye is single unto Him for spiritual light and guidance, open their understandings more clearly and experimentally to see, that as all the types and shadows and ordinances of the Law were fulfilled in Him, that as He established no outward priesthood, so He established no new ordinances to be administered or to be observed in his church. His baptism is that of the Holy Ghost and of fire. He himself is the bread of life. It is He who giveth the meat which endureth unto everlasting life. He maketh all his faithful followers members of that royal priesthood and holy nation of which the Apostle Peter writes; and as they are concerned to order their households in the fear of God, He enables them to instruct their families in the truths of his blessed Gospel, and to train them up in the way of holiness.

Theology

Document II.6

Unitarian Opinion, 1846

In the period up to 1850 there are few published descriptions of Unitarian beliefs that are not either sententious propaganda typical of the disputes amongst the Dissenting denominations, or contained in long and learned books on the Bible. John Relly Beard (1800–76) adopted a different approach and was one of the most active compilers of popular dictionaries of his time – see DNB. He attempted to explain Unitarianism in dictionary style in *Unitarianism Exhibited in its Actual Condition consisting of Essays by Several Unitarian Ministers and Others Illustrative of the Rise, Progress and Principles of Christian Anti-Trinitarianism in Different Parts of the World*, London, 1846. It remains a valuable source on global Unitarianism.

This extract is taken from the section entitled 'Anti-Trinitarianism in England', pp. 160–62, by William Turner, tertius (1788–1853; see DNB). Miracles, because they were clearly described in the Bible, were accepted as literally true by the older branch of Unitarian thinking, but Turner expresses the newer view of the content of the Bible that later became universal in the denomination.

With regard to our actual opinions – as we have no public creed, as we lay more stress on broad general principles than on particular doctrines, and as different views certainly prevail amongst us, it is, of course, difficult to describe them with the precision which would be possible, were there any book that could be appealed to, as authoritatively recording them. I may, however, affirm, in general, as a correct representation of our present belief – that we receive Christianity as a religion of divine origin, and regard Jesus Christ as the last and greatest of the prophets, completing and terminating the preparatory dispensation of Moses, and establishing in place of it, a religion for universal humanity. We further agree in considering God, the supreme Father, as the only proper object of religious worship, and as a being of essential love and mercy, who requires no other propitiation from frail and erring man than a penitent and humble spirit; and a will earnestly devoted to his service. In Christ we receive the highest form of spiritual excellence, in which are at one manifested to us the holiness and benignity of the Being, in whose name we believe he spoke, and a model of human virtue after which we should constantly aspire. Cleaving to his spirit and example, we take to be the sure road to everlasting life. But, although by the contemplation of Christ, we feel ourselves better able to conceive of God in his moral relation to mankind, and constantly offer up our prayers to God through him – yet we regard it as contradictory to the first principles of natural religion and the plainest commands of scripture, to address worship to Christ, who is himself a creature, and, as most of us regard him, in nature a man. The doctrinal points therefore on which we feel ourselves most at variance with other Christians are, first, the doctrine of the Trinity, according to which the Father, the Son, and the Holy Spirit are to be worshipped as equal and co-eternal God, making up the idea of Deity amongst them; secondly, the worship of Christ; and thirdly, the common doctrine of the Atonement, according to which, God is declared unable or unwilling to forgive the truly penitent without the satisfaction made by the sufferings of Christ to his offended justice. For none of those doctrines, as they are popularly understood, can we find any satisfactory warrant in the language of the New Testament; and besides this, the first of them seems to us to involve a self-contradiction, the second strikes at what we deem the fundamental doctrine of religion; and the third we cannot reconcile with our notions of the paternal benevolence of God. More difference of opinion exists among us, as to the degree of authority which is due to the literal meaning of the words of Scripture. Some are of opinion, that whatever can be clearly shewn to be taught by Christ and his Apostles, must be received with unquestioning deference as a divine command; another, and I am inclined to believe, an increasing party, think, that it is rather the *spirit* than the letter of Christ's religion – the great general principles of faith and conduct embodied in his teachings and life, which should be embraced as divine; that in the application to the events and persons of his own time, as described in the New Testament, these principles have been largely modified by the popular belief and opinions then prevalent among the Jews; and that, therefore, studying the Christian Scriptures with the same free and unprejudiced spirit as we should any other writing of an equal antiquity, it should be an object to separate in them the permanent from the transient; the eternal truth which is designed for all ages and countries, from the fleeting form of opinions which has only a relative value for the state of society in which it is sincerely entertained.

With respect to the miraculous, which enters so largely into the narratives of the New Testament, the great majority of Unitarians in this country take it in its literal sense, and regard it as a superhuman conformation of the truth and divinity of the doctrines therein contained; making it, in fact, the great and only certain distinction of a divine revelation from a merely human system. There are some, however, and I must confess myself to be among the number, who cannot go to this extent. We believe in direct revelations of spiritual truth from God, and in the divine origin of the Gospel. Convinced, from the calm, deliberate testimony of our own hearts and minds, of the intrinsic truth and excellence of Christianity; persuaded there must have been a divine power and presence in the workings and teaching of Jesus of Nazareth, and unable, by any process of interpretation or criticism that has yet been suggested, to remove the supernatural from the Christian narrations, without destroying their very texture, we take it, unexplained, for the sake of the precious truths and great example which are involved in it; but it is not to us the primary basis of our faith. We dare not make it a *sine qua non* to the acceptance of Christianity as a Divine system; and feeling, the more we comprehend the spirit of the ancient world, how widely different were its conceptions of moral and religious truth, and even of the fidelity of historical narration, from those which now prevail; and further observing, how obviously some of the miracles recorded in the New Testament possess rather a symbolical than an historical character, we judge it the wiser course, to rest the evidence of Christianity on deeper and firmer grounds, to suspend an absolute judgement on this difficult and mysterious question, and without discussing it, in the present state of knowledge, in our public assemblies

Theology

for worship and edification, to leave it open for calm and serious investigation among the learned and philosophical.

Document II.7

Evangelical Alliance Basis of Faith, 1846

Evangelicalism was the common creed of the vast majority of Nonconformists, and in the mid-nineteenth century it was shared with a substantial section of the Church of England, most Scottish Presbyterians and a vast diaspora of Christians in the English-speaking world and beyond. In 1846 an international body, the Evangelical Alliance, was created to represent the global interests of this diverse constituency. Its doctrinal basis, the first formal definition of the Evangelical faith ever attempted, represented the lowest common denominator of its members' beliefs. Nevertheless the ninth clause, as was pointed out at the time, excluded Quakers. The eighth clause was added, along with lesser modifications, between the drafting stage in 1845 and the adoption of the basis in the following year. See J. B. A. Kessler, *A Study of the Evangelical Alliance in Great Britain*, Goes, Netherlands, 1968, pp. 27–9, 39–42; and J. R. Wolffe, 'The Evangelical Alliance in the 1840s', in W. J. Sheils and D. Wood, eds, *Voluntary Religion*, Studies in Church History 23, Oxford, 1986.

The extract is taken from D. King, *Historical Sketch of the Evangelical Alliance*, Glasgow, 1851, pp. 34–5.

That the parties composing the Alliance shall be such persons only as hold and maintain what are usually understood to be Evangelical views, in regard to the matters of Doctrine understated, namely:–

1. The Divine Inspiration, Authority, and Sufficiency of the Holy Scriptures.
2. The Right and Duty of Private Judgment in the Interpretation of the Holy Scriptures.
3. The Unity of the Godhead, and the Trinity of the Persons therein.
4. The utter Depravity of Human Nature, in consequence of the Fall.
5. The Incarnation of the Son of God, His work of Atonement for sinners of mankind, and His Mediatorial Intercession and Reign.
6. The Justification of the sinner by Faith alone.
7. The work of the Holy Spirit in the Conversion and Sanctification of the sinner.
8. The Immortality of the Soul, the Resurrection of the Body, the Judgment of the World by our Lord Jesus Christ, with the Eternal Blessedness of the Righteous, and the Eternal Punishment of the Wicked.
9. The Divine institution of the Christian Ministry, and the obligation and perpetuity of the ordinances of Baptism and the Lord's Supper.

It is, however, distinctly declared: – First, that this brief Summary is not to be regarded, in any formal or Ecclesiastical sense, as a Creed or Confession, nor the adoption of it as involving an assumption of the right authoritatively to define the limits of Christian Brotherhood; but simply as an indication of the class of persons whom it is desirable to embrace within the Alliance: – Second, that the selection of certain tenets, with the omission of others, is not to be held as implying that the former constitute the whole body of important Truth, or that the latter are unimportant.

Document II.8

Salvation Army Religious Doctrines, 1878

General William Booth (see IX.18), always thorough in organisational matters, formally created the Salvation Army by a legally binding Foundation Deed that specified its doctrines. The document, which was enrolled in 1878, names the organisation the 'Christian Mission' because the title 'Salvation Army' had only just been introduced. The list of doctrines shows Booth's origins in Methodism by following Wesley's Arminianism in clauses 6 (universal redemption), 8 (the witness of the Spirit), 9 (the defectibility of faith) and 10 (entire sanctification). See R. Sandall, *The History of the Salvation Army*, vol. 1, London, 1947, p. 233.

The extract is taken from the same work at pp. 288–9.

That the religious doctrines professed believed and taught by the Members of the said Christian Mission are and shall for ever be as follows : –

1. We believe that the Scriptures of the Old and New Testaments were given by inspiration of God and that they only constitute the Divine rule of Christian faith and practice.
2. We believe there is only one God who is infinitely perfect the Creator Preserver and Governor of all things and who is the only proper object of religious worship.
3. We believe that there are three persons in the Godhead the Father the Son and the Holy Ghost undivided in essence and co-equal in power and glory.
4. We believe that in the person of Jesus Christ the Divine and human natures are united so that He is truly and properly God and truly and properly man.
5. We believe that our first parents were created in a state of innocency but by their disobedience they lost their purity and happiness and that in consequence of their fall all men have become sinners totally depraved and as such are justly exposed to the wrath of God.
6. We believe that the Lord Jesus Christ has by His suffering and death made an atonement for the whole world so that whosoever will may be saved.
7. We believe that repentance towards God faith in our Lord Jesus Christ and regeneration by the Holy Spirit are necessary to salvation.
8. We believe that we are justified by grace through faith in our Lord Jesus Christ and that he that believeth hath the witness in himself.

9 We believe that continuance in a state of salvation depends upon continued obedient faith in Christ.

10 We believe that it is the privilege of all believers to be 'wholly sanctified' and that 'their whole spirit and soul and body' may 'be preserved blameless unto the coming of our Lord Jesus Christ' (1 Thess. v. 23).

11 We believe in the immortality of the soul in the resurrection of the body in the general judgment at the end of the world in the eternal happiness of the righteous and in the endless punishment of the wicked.

Document II.9

Baptist Union Declaratory Statement, 1888

The Baptist Union of Great Britain and Ireland, by contrast with its Congregational equivalent (see II.3), formulated no statement of faith at its relaunching in 1832, merely confining itself to saying that its members agreed in 'the sentiments usually denominated evangelical'. When the Union was rocked by the Down Grade controversy (see II.37), however, its council prepared a Declaratory Statement that was adopted by its assembly on 23 April 1888. The circumstances explain why the statement shows signs of discomfort and haste – in omitting, for example, the doctrine of the Trinity. See E. A. Payne, *The Baptist Union*, London, 1959, pp. 60–61, 140–41 and (for the text of the document) 271.

Whilst expressly disavowing and disallowing any power to control belief or restrict inquiry, yet in view of the uneasiness produced in the churches by recent discussions, and to show our agreement with one another, and with our fellow Christians on the great truths of the Gospel, the Council deem it right to say that:

(*a*) Baptized in the name of the Father, and of the Son, and of the Holy Ghost, we have avowed repentance towards God and faith in the Lord Jesus Christ – the very elements of a new life; as in the Lord's Supper we avow our union with one another, while partaking of the symbol of the Body of our Lord, broken for us, and of the Blood shed for the remission of sins. The Union, therefore, is an association of churches and ministers, professing not only to believe the facts and doctrines of the Gospel, but to have undergone the spiritual change expressed or implied in them. This change is the fundamental principle of our church life.

(*b*) The following facts and doctrines are commonly believed by the Churches of the Union:

1. The Divine Inspiration and Authority of the Holy Scriptures as the supreme and sufficient rule of our faith and practice: and the right and duty of individual judgment in the interpretation of it.

2. The fallen and sinful state of man.

3. The Deity, the Incarnation, the Resurrection of the Lord Jesus Christ, and His Sacrificial and Mediatorial Work.

4. Justification by Faith – a faith that works by love and produces holiness.

5. The Work of the Holy Spirit in the conversion of sinners, and in the sanctification of all who believe.

6. The Resurrection; the Judgment at the Last Day, according to the words of our Lord in Matthew xxv, 46.[1]

Note

1. It should be stated, as an historical fact, that there have been brethren in the Union, working cordially with it, who, whilst reverently bowing to the authority of Holy Scripture, and rejecting dogmas of Purgatory and Universalism, have not held the common interpretation of these words of our Lord.

Document II.10

Evangelical Free Church Catechism, 1899

During the 1890s, the various Evangelical Free Churches, aware of a high degree of unity, combined in local and national councils (see X.4). In 1899 the National Council issued *An Evangelical Free Church Catechism for Use in Home and School* 'to express the Christian doctrines held in common'. Drafted by Dr Oswald Dykes, the Presbyterian principal of Westminster College, Cambridge, it was revised by a large committee dominated by Hugh Price Hughes (see I.9). It shows rising contemporary theological trends in describing God primarily as Love and as Father (clauses 2 and 3) and by its assertion of the visibility of the Holy Catholic Church (clauses 33 and 34), a principle beloved by Hughes. Although the catechism was sold for only one penny, it was not widely used. Nevertheless it is an important statement, substantially reflecting the common faith of the great bulk of Nonconformists at the end of the nineteenth century. See E. K. H. Jordan, *Free Church Unity: History of the Free Church Council Movement, 1896–1941*, London, 1956, pp. 61–3; and [D. P. Hughes], *The Life of Hugh Price Hughes*, London, 1905, pp. 460–69, 477–80.

The text is from pp. 7–23 of the *Catechism*, omitting only item 27, which lists the ten commandments.

1. *Question. What is the Christian religion?*
   Answer. It is the religion founded by our Lord and Saviour Jesus Christ, Who has brought to us the full knowledge of God and of Eternal Life.

2. *Q. How must we think of God?*
   A. God is the one Eternal Spirit, Creator and Sustainer of all things; He is Love, boundless in wisdom and power, perfect in holiness and justice, in mercy and truth.

3. *Q. By what name has Jesus taught us to call God?*
   A. Our Father in Heaven.

4. *Q. What do we learn from this name of Father?*
A. We learn that God made us in His own image, that He cares for us by His wise providence, and that He loves us far better than any earthly parent can.

5. *Q. What does Jesus say about Himself?*
A. That He is the Son of God, Whom the Father in His great love sent into the world to be our Saviour from sin.

6. *Q. What is sin?*
A. Sin is any thought or feeling, word or act, which either is contrary to God's holy law, or falls short of what it requires.

7. *Q. Say in brief what God's law requires.*
A. That we should love God with our whole heart, and our neighbour as ourselves.

8. *Q. Are we able of ourselves to do this?*
A. No: for, although man was made innocent at the first, yet he fell into disobedience, and since then no one has been able, in his own strength, to keep God's law.

9. *Q. What are the consequences of sin?*
A. Sin separates man from God, corrupts his nature, exposes him to manifold pains and griefs, and, unless he repents, must issue in death eternal.

10. *Q. Can we deliver ourselves from sin and its consequences?*
A. By no means, for we are unable either to cleanse our own hearts or to make amends for our offences.

11. *Q. How did the Son of God save His people from their sins?*
A. For our salvation, He came down from Heaven, and was incarnate by the Holy Ghost of the Virgin Mary, and was made man, and was crucified also for us under Pontius Pilate. He suffered and was buried, and the third day He rose again according to the Scriptures, and ascended into Heaven, and sitteth on the right hand of the Father.

12. *Q. What benefit have we from the Son of God becoming Man?*
A. We have a Mediator between God and men; one who as God reveals to us what God is; and, as perfect Man, represents our race before God.

13. *Q. What further benefits have we from our Lord's life on earth?*
A. We have in Him a brother man who is touched with the feeling of our infirmities, as well as a perfect example of what we ought to be.

14. *Q. What did He accomplish for us by His death on the Cross?*
A. By offering Himself a sacrifice without blemish unto God, He fulfilled the requirements of Divine Holiness, atoned for all our sins, and broke the power of Sin.

15. *Q. What does the resurrection of Jesus teach us?*
    A. It assures us that He has finished the work of our redemption; that the dominion of death is ended; and that, because He lives, we shall live also.

16. *Q. What do we learn from His ascension into Heaven?*
    A. That we have in Him an Advocate with the Father, Who ever liveth to make intercession for us.

17. *Q. What do we learn from His session at the right hand of God?*
    A. The He is exalted as our Head and King, to Whom has been given all authority in heaven and on earth.

18. *Q. How does Jesus Christ still carry on His work of salvation?*
    A. By the third person in the blessed Trinity, the Holy Spirit, Who was sent forth at Pentecost.

19. *Q. What is the mystery of the blessed Trinity?*
    A. That the Father, the Son, and the Holy Spirit, into Whose Name we are baptized, are one God.

20. *Q. What must we do in order to be saved?*
    A. We must repent of our sin and believe on the Lord Jesus Christ.

21. *Q. What is it to repent?*
    A. He who truly repents of his sin not only confesses it with shame and sorrow, but above all he turns from it to God with sincere desire to be forgiven and steadfast purpose to sin no more.

22. *Q. What is it to believe on the Lord Jesus Christ?*
    A. It means that we rely on Him as our Teacher, Saviour and Lord, putting our whole trust in the grace of God through Him.

23. *Q. How are we enabled to repent and believe?*
    A. By the secret power of the Holy Spirit working graciously in our hearts, and using for this end providential discipline and the message of the Gospel.

24. *Q. What benefits do we receive when we repent and believe?*
    A. Being united to Christ by faith, our sins are freely forgiven for His sake; our hearts are renewed; and we become children of God and joint-heirs with Christ.

25. *Q. In what way are we to shew ourselves thankful for such great benefits?*
    A. By striving to follow the example of Jesus in doing and bearing the will of our Heavenly Father.

26. *Q. Where do we find God's will briefly expressed?*
    A. In the Decalogue or Law of the Ten Commandments, as explained by Jesus Christ. ...

28. *Q. How has our Lord taught us to understand this Law?*
    A. He taught that the Law reaches to the desires, motives and intentions of

the heart, so that we cannot keep it unless we love God with our whole heart and our neighbour as ourselves.

(i.) Q. *What does the First Commandment teach us?*
A. To take the one living and true God for our own God, and render unto Him the honour which is due to Him alone.

(ii.) Q. *What does the Second Commandment teach us?*
A. To worship God in spirit and in truth, not by the use of images or other devices of men but in such ways as He has Himself appointed.

(iii.) Q. *What does the Third Commandment teach us?*
A. Never to blaspheme and never to utter profane words, but always to regard and use with deep reverence the Holy Name of God.

(iv.) Q. *What does the Fourth Commandment teach us?*
A. That we ought to be diligent in our calling during six days of the week, but keep one day hallowed for rest and worship; and because Jesus rose from the dead on the first day of the week, Christians observe that day, calling it the Lord's Day.

(v.) Q. *What does the Fifth Commandment teach us?*
A. That God regards with special favour those who reverence and obey their parents.

(vi.) Q. *What does the Sixth Commandment teach us?*
A. To hold human life sacred, and, instead of hating or hurting our fellow-men, even our enemies, to do all we can to preserve them in health and well-being.

(vii.) Q. *What does the Seventh Commandment teach us?*
A. To honour God's ordinance of marriage, to preserve modesty, and to keep ourselves chaste in thought, speech and behaviour.

(viii.) Q. *What does the Eighth Commandment teach us?*
A. To be honest and fair in all our dealings, and in no wise to take unbrotherly advantage of another by fraud or force.

(ix.) Q. *What does the Ninth Commandment teach us?*
A. To avoid false testimony, and never to deceive anyone or spread reports to our neighbour's hurt.

(x.) Q. *What does the Tenth Commandment teach us?*
A. Not even in our heart to grudge our fellow-man his prosperity or desire to deprive him of that which is his, but always to cultivate a thankful and contented spirit.

29. Q. *What special means has God provided to assist us in leading a life of obedience?*
A. His Word, Prayer, the Sacraments, and the Fellowship of the Church.

30. Q. *Where do we find God's Word written?*
A. In the Holy Bible, which is the inspired record of God's revelation given to be our rule of faith and duty.

31. Q. *What is Prayer?*
A. In prayer we commune with our Father in heaven, confess our sins, give Him thanks for all His benefits, and ask, in the name of Jesus, for such things as He has promised.

32. Q. *Repeat the Lord's Prayer.*
A. 'Our Father, Which art in heaven, hallowed by Thy Name. Thy Kingdom come. Thy will be done in earth, as it is in heaven. Give us this day our daily bread. And forgive us our trespasses, as we forgive them that trespass against us. And lead us not into temptation; but deliver us from evil; for Thine is the kingdom, the power, and the glory, for ever and ever. Amen.'

   (i.) Q. *What is meant by the words – 'Hallowed be Thy Name'?*
   A. That our Heavenly Father would lead all men to acknowledge and reverence Him as Jesus has made Him known, so that everywhere His glorious praise may be proclaimed.

   (ii.) Q. *What do we pray for in the words – 'Thy Kingdom come'?*
   A. We pray that the Gospel may spread and prevail in all the world, till the power of evil is overthrown and Jesus reigns in every heart and governs every relation of human life.

   (iii.) Q. *What is meant by the words – 'Thy will be done in earth as it is in heaven'?*
   A. That all men may be led to accept God's holy will, and cheerfully to do whatever He requires, so that His gracious purpose may be fulfilled.

   (iv.) Q. *What shall we desire when we say – 'Give us this day our daily bread'?*
   A. That God would prosper our daily labour and provide what is needful for the body, ridding us of anxiety and disposing us to contentment.

   (v.) Q. *Explain this petition – 'Forgive us our trespasses, as we forgive them that trespass against us'.*
   A. Here Christ teaches us that we may confidently ask God to forgive us our sins, but that He will not do so unless we ourselves from the heart forgive those who have wronged us.

   (vi.) Q. *What do we ask for in the last petition – 'Lead us not into temptation, but deliver us from evil'?*
   A. We entreat that we may not need, for our humbling, to be exposed to severe temptations, and that we may be kept from the power of every spiritual enemy.

33. Q. *What is the Holy Catholic Church?*
A. It is that Holy Society of believers in Christ Jesus which He founded, of which He is the only Head, and in which He dwells by His Spirit; so that, though made up of many communions, organised in various modes, and scattered throughout the world, it is yet One in Him.

34. *Q. For what ends did our Lord found His Church?*
A. He united His people into this visible brotherhood for the worship of God and the ministry of the Word and the Sacraments; for mutual edification, the administration of discipline, and the advancement of His Kingdom.

35. *Q. What is the essential mark of a true branch of the Catholic Church?*
A. The essential mark of a true branch of the Catholic Church is the presence of Christ, through His indwelling Spirit, manifested in holy life and fellowship.

36. *Q. What is a Free Church?*
A. A Church which acknowledges none but Jesus Christ as Head, and, therefore, exercises its right to interpret and administer His laws without restraint or control by the State.

37. *Q. What is the duty of the Church to the State?*
A. To observe all the laws of the State unless contrary to the teaching of Christ; to make intercession for the people, and particularly for those in authority; to teach both rulers and subjects the eternal principles of righteousness, and to imbue the nation with the spirit of Christ.

38. *Q. What is the duty of the State to the Church?*
A. To protect all branches of the Church and their individual members in the enjoyment of liberty to worship God, and in efforts to promote the Religion of Christ, which do not interfere with the civil rights of others.

39. *Q. What is a Christian minister?*
A. A Christian minister is one who is called of God and the Church to be a teacher of the Word and a pastor of the Flock of Christ.

40. *Q. How may the validity of such a Ministry be proved?*
A. The decisive proof of a valid Ministry is the sanction of the Divine Head of the Church, manifested in the conversion of sinners and the edification of the Body of Christ.

41. *Q. What are the Sacraments of the Church?*
A. Sacred rites instituted by our Lord Jesus to make more plain by visible signs the inward benefits of the Gospel, to assure us of His promised grace, and, when rightly used, to become a means to convey it to our hearts.

42. *Q. How many Sacraments are there?*
A. Two only : Baptism and the Lord's Supper.

43. *Q. What is the visible sign in the sacrament of baptism?*
A. Water: wherein the person is baptized into the name of the Father and of the Son and of the Holy Spirit.

44. *Q. What inward benefits does this signify?*
A. The washing away of sin and the new birth wrought by the Holy Spirit in all who repent and believe.

45. *Q. What are the outward signs in the Lord's Supper?*
A. Bread and wine: which the Lord has commanded to be given and received for a perpetual memorial of His death.

46. *Q. What is signified by the Bread and Wine?*
A. By the Bread is signified the Body of our Lord Jesus Christ in which He lived and died; by the Wine is signified His Blood, shed once for all upon the Cross for the remission of sins.

47. *Q. What do they receive who in penitence and faith partake of this sacrament?*
A. They feed spiritually upon Christ as the nourishment of the soul, by which they are strengthened and refreshed for the duties and trials of life.

48. *Q. Why do Christians partake in common of the Lord's Supper?*
A. To shew their oneness in Christ, to confess openly their faith in Him, and to give one another a pledge of brotherly love.

49. *Q. What is a Christian's chief comfort in this life?*
A. That in Christ he belongs to God, Who makes all things work together for good to them that love Him.

50. *Q. What hope have we in the prospect of death?*
A. We are well assured that all who fall asleep in Christ are with Him in rest and peace; and that even as He rose from the dead, so shall we also rise and be clothed with glorified bodies.

51. *Q. What has Jesus told us of His Second Advent?*
A. That, at a time known only to God, He shall appear again with power, to be glorified in His saints and to be the Judge of all mankind; and that for His Appearing we should be always ready.

52. *Q. What is the Christian's hope concerning the future state?*
A. We look for the life everlasting, wherein all who are saved through Christ shall see God and inherit the kingdom prepared for them from the foundation of the world.

Theologians

Document II.11

Andrew Fuller on Duty Faith, 1801

Andrew Fuller (1754–1815), minister of the Particular Baptist Church in Kettering, and a tireless worker for the cause of the Baptist mission to India, was also the leading Baptist theologian of his day. He wrote *The Gospel Worthy of All Acceptation* (1781), in order to answer those Calvinists who were questioning whether it was right for preachers to invite their hearers to accept the gospel. William Gadsby (see I.3) and John Stevens together with their high Calvinist Strict Baptist followers, strongly opposed Fuller's teaching, but its effect was to encourage the growth of missionary activity at home and abroad. See J. W. Morris, *Memoirs of the Life and Writings of the Rev. Andrew Fuller*, London, 1826; E. F. Clipsham, 'Andrew Fuller and Fullerism: A Study in Evangelical Calvinism', *Baptist Quarterly*, 20 (1963–64), pp. 99–114, 146–54, 214–25, 268–76; P. J. Morden, *Offering Christ to the World: Andrew Fuller (1754–1815) and the Revival of Eighteenth Century Particular Life*, Milton Keynes, 2003; and DNB.

This extract is taken from the 1801 edition of *The Gospel Worthy of All Acceptation*, reprinted in *The Complete Works of the Rev. Andrew Fuller*, ed. A. G. Fuller, London, 1831, vol. 2, pp. 65–6, in which Fuller answers objections made by some of his critics.

If the atonement of Christ were considered as the literal payment of a debt – if the measure of his sufferings were according to the number of those for whom he died, and to the degree of their guilt, in such a manner as that if more had been saved, or if those who are saved had been more guilty, his sorrows must have been proportionably increased – it might, for aught I know, be inconsistent with indefinite invitations. But it would be equally inconsistent with the free *forgiveness* of sin, and with sinners being directed to apply for mercy as *supplicants*, rather than as claimants. I conclude, therefore, that an hypothesis which in so many important points is manifestly inconsistent with the Scriptures cannot be true.

On the other hand, if the atonement of Christ proceed not on the principle of commercial, but of moral justice, or justice as it relates to *crime* – if its grand object were to express the divine displeasure against sin (Rom. viii. 3) and so to render the exercise of mercy, in all the ways wherein sovereign wisdom should determine to apply it, consistent with righteousness (Rom. iii. 25) – if it be in itself equal to the salvation of the whole world, were the whole world to embrace it – and if the peculiarity which attends it consist not in its insufficiency to save more than are saved, but in the sovereignty of its application – no such inconsistency can justly be ascribed to it.

If the atonement of Christ excludes a part of mankind *in the same sense* as it excludes fallen angels, why is the gospel addressed to the one any more than to the other? The message of wisdom is addressed to *men* and not to devils. The former are invited to the gospel-supper, but the latter are not. These facts afford proof that Christ, by his death, opened a door of hope to sinners of the human race as *sinners: affording a ground for their being invited, without distinction, to believe and be saved.*

But as God might send his Son into the world to save men, rather than angels, so he may *apply* his sacrifice to the salvation of some men, and not of others. It is certain that a great part of the world have never heard the gospel; that the greater part of those who have heard it disregard it; and that those who believe are taught to ascribe not only their salvation, but faith itself, through which is obtained, to the *free gift of God*. And, as the application of redemption is solely directed by sovereign wisdom, so, like every other event, it is the result of *previous design*. That which is actually done was *intended* to be done. Hence the salvation of those that are saved is described as the *end* which the Saviour had in view: 'He gave himself for us, that he might redeem us from all iniquity, and purify unto himself a peculiar people, zealous of good works.' Herein, it is apprehended, consists the peculiarity of redemption.

There is no contradiction between this peculiarity of *design* in the death of Christ, and a universal obligation on those who hear the gospel to believe in him, or a universal invitation being addressed to them. If God, through the death of his Son, have promised salvation to all who comply with the gospel; and if there be no *natural* impossibility as to a compliance, nor any obstruction but that which arises from aversion of heart; exhortations and invitations to believe and be saved are consistent: and our duty, as preachers of the gospel, is to administer them, without any more regard to particular redemption than to election; both being secret things, which belong to the Lord our God, and which, however they be a rule to him, are none to us.

Document II.12

Edward Williams on Moderate Calvinism, 1809

Edward Williams (1750–1813) was the leading Independent theologian at the opening of the nineteenth century. While maintaining pastoral ministries, he acted as principal of the academies at Oswestry and, from 1795, Rotherham. *An Essay on the Equity of the Divine Government and the Sovereignty of Divine Grace* (London, 1809), his chief work, was a defence of Calvinism against the Arminianism of John Fletcher of Madeley ('the system I am opposing' in the extract). Like Andrew Fuller among the Baptists (see II.11), he propounded a nonfatalistic version of Calvinism, rejecting the doctrine of absolute necessity upheld by rational Dissenters led by Joseph Priestley as well as by high Calvinists. See W. T. Owen, *Edward Williams, D.D.*, Cardiff, 1963; and DNB.

Theology

The extracts are taken from the *Essay*, pp. 337–8 and 341–2.

Not content with barely shewing the inconsistency and absurd consequences of the system I am opposing, it is my wish, if possible, to give my readers fully to understand the system I am now establishing, under the name of *true Calvinism*, in opposition to Mr. F's. *frightful picture* of what he is pleased to call, on every occasion, 'Calvinian Necessity.' What is now pleaded for is utterly repugnant to the hypotheses that make *all actions*, the good and bad alike, to proceed from the *divine decrees*. For,

1. *Bad* actions, as before observed, arise from *ourselves*, as *essentially* not *decretively* defectible; and not from a *positively good* self-determining *principle*, the absurd and impossible source to which Arminians refer them. It will not avail to say, that the *abuse* of free-will, and not free-will itself is the cause of sin; for such *abuse*, if any thing *bad*, is itself the first-born of sins. Is it not astonishing that inquisitive Free-willers, in the Arminian sense of the word, do not see the necessary consequence of their doctrine, that it makes GOD himself the positive cause and ordainer of sin?

2. Instead of representing the blessed GOD as a fountain sending forth 'sweet water and bitter,' the present system represents the adorable Creator as the source of *good only*, and of *all good*, universally and continually. We say, that evil, or *moral defect*, originates in *ourselves*, that is, our essential defectibility, in such a manner, that *God alone* can prevent its existence; and that, not in virtue of Equity but of sovereign *favour*. The denial of this, is in fact the same thing as to say, that GOD might, if he pleased, make a creature which needed no support, and with whom his providence had no concern. ...

These views, if I am not mistaken, most exactly and unexceptionably correspond with the whole tenor and every part of Scripture. I know of neither precept nor promise, invitation nor threatening, which is not in perfect harmony with the above representations. On the contrary, the Arminian hypothesis, I think it is fairly shewn, tends to rob GOD of his rights of sovereignty, and fathers all the sins in the universe, tho' not designedly, yet eventually, on the *author* of free-will. While the *absolute* necessitarians, as most of the modern pretended *rational*, exclusively rational *divines* are, together with infidel speculatists, from whose pernicious opinions some Calvinists, thro' better motives and for different ends, have not kept quite clear – while *such necessitarians*, I say, who make *moral evil* of positive and voluntary appointment, as one *link* of a *decretive chain*, must either father sin upon the *decreer*, or deny the existence of sin, as distinct from *natural* evil, and consequently of a *moral* system.

To this we may add, the system now advanced attributes what is *good* in all actions to GOD; not only the *power* but the *natural act*; even the *natural* act of actions *morally* bad; which causation is *positive*, and every way worthy of an infinitely good and perfect being. But all moral defect, or sin, is the *obliquity* of an act naturally good; which obliquity, in every shape and respect, has only a *deficient cause*, and therefore infinitely remote from all divine causation.

Document II.13

Richard Watson on Arminianism, 1829

Richard Watson (1781–1833) was the first Methodist systematic theologian. As secretary of the Wesleyan Methodist Missionary Society and president of Conference in 1826, he played a full part in the life of his denomination. His *Theological Institutes* (1829), significantly named so as to form a counterblast to Calvin's *Institutes*, insisted on the Arminian teaching of his connexion that Christ died for all and not just for the elect. See T. Jackson, *Memories of the Life and Writings of the Rev. Richard Watson*, London, 1834; E. J. Brailsford, *Richard Watson, Theologian and Missionary Advocate*, London, 1906; and DNB.

The extracts are taken from Watson's *Theological Institutes*, 14th edn, London, 1865, vol. 3, pp. 408–9 and 413.

With respect to this controversy, we may also observe, that it forms a clear case of appeal to the Scriptures; for to whom the benefits of Christ's death are extended, whether to the whole of our race, or to a part, can be matter of revelation only; and the sole province of reason is, therefore, that of interpreting with fairness, and consistently with the acknowledged principles of that revelation, those parts of it in which the subject is directly or incidentally introduced.

The question before us, put into its most simple form, is, whether our Lord Jesus Christ did so die for all men, as to make salvation attainable by all men. The affirmative of this question is, I think, the doctrine of Scripture.

It is plainly EXPRESSED,

1. In all those passages which declare that Christ died 'for all men,' and speak of his death as an atonement for the sins 'of the whole world.'

We have already seen, in treating of our Lord's atonement, in what sense the phrase, 'to die for us,' must be understood; that it signifies to die in the place and stead of man, as a sacrificial oblation, by which satisfaction is made for the sins of the individual, so that they become remissible upon the terms of the evangelical covenant. When, therefore, it is said, that Christ 'by the grace of God tasted death for every man;' and that 'he is the propitiation for our sins, and not for ours only, but also for the sins of the whole world;' it can only be fairly concluded from such declarations, and from many other familiar texts, in which the same phraseology is employed, that, by the death of Christ, the sins of every man are rendered remissible, and that salvation is consequently attainable by every man. ...

2. The same doctrine is also stated in those passages which attribute an equal extent to the effects of the death of Christ as to the effects of the fall of our first parents: 'For if through the offence of one many be dead, much more the grace of God, and the gift by grace, which is by one man Jesus Christ, hath abounded unto many.'

... It will now be necessary for us to consider what those who have adopted a different opinion have to urge against these plain and forcible declarations of Scripture. It is their burden, that they are compelled to explain these passages in a more limited and qualified sense than their literal and obvious meaning suggests; and that they must rely upon inference merely; for it is not even pretended that there is any text whatever to be adduced, which declares, as literally, that Christ did not die for the salvation of all, as those which declare that he did so die. We have no passages, therefore, to examine, which, in their clear literal meaning, stand opposed to those which we have quoted, so as to present apparent contradictions which require to be reconciled by concession on one side or the other. This is, at least, *prima facie*, strongly in favour of those who hold that, in the same sense, and with the same design, 'Jesus Christ tasted death for every man.'

Document II.14

William Arthur on Entire Sanctification, 1856

William Arthur (1819–1901) was a missionary in India and France, a secretary of the Wesleyan Methodist Missionary Society, first principal of the Methodist College, Belfast, and president of Conference in 1866. His most influential writing was *The Tongue of Fire*, London, 1856, a restatement in assured and polished prose of John Wesley's doctrine of entire sanctification. Arthur contended that the great need of the church was the experience of perfect love, which he envisaged as the power of the Holy Spirit that the disciples of Jesus received at Pentecost, ten days after his ascension. For an instance of entire sanctification, see V.11; and on its history, D. W. Bebbington, 'Holiness in Nineteenth-Century Methodism', in W. M. Jacob and N. Yates, eds, *Crown and Mitre: Religion and Society in Northern Europe since the Reformation*, Woodbridge, Suffolk, 1993. On Arthur, see N. W. Taggart, *William Arthur*, London, 1993; and DNB.

The extract is taken from *The Tongue of Fire*, 10th edn, London, 1857, pp. 309–11.

As to the way in which this power may be obtained, here we have only to recall the lesson of the Ten Days, – 'They continued with one accord in prayer and supplication.' Prayer earnest, prayer united, and prayer persevering, these are the conditions; and, these being fulfilled, we shall assuredly be 'endured with power from on high.' We should never expect that the power will fall upon us just because we happen once to awake and ask for it. Nor have any community of Christians a right to look for a great manifestation of the Spirit, if they are not all ready to join in supplication, and, 'with one accord,' to wait and pray as if it were the concern of each one. The murmurer who always accounts for barrenness in the Church by the faults of others, may be assured that his readiest way to spiritual power, if that be his real object, lies in uniting all, as one heart, to pray without ceasing.

Above all, we are not to expect it without persevering prayer. Prayer which takes the fact that past prayers have not yet been answered, as a reason for languor, has already ceased to be the prayer of faith. To the latter, the fact that prayers remain unanswered, is only evidence that the moment of the answer is so much nearer. From first to last, the lessons and example of our Lord all tell us that prayer which cannot persevere, and urge its plea importunately, and renew, and renew itself again, and gather strength from every past petition, is not the prayer that will prevail.

When John in the Apocalypse saw the Lamb on the throne, *before that throne* were the seven lamps of fire burning, 'which are the seven Spirits of God sent forth into all the earth;' and it is only by waiting before that throne of grace that we become imbued with the holy fire; but he who waits there long and believingly, will imbibe that fire, and come forth, from his communion with God, bearing tokens of where he has been. For the individual believer, and, above all, for every labourer in the Lord's vineyard, the only way to gain spiritual power is by secret waiting at the throne of God, for the baptism of the Holy Spirit. Every moment spent in real prayer is a moment spent in refreshing the fire of God within the soul. We said before, that this fire cannot be simulated; nothing else will produce its effects. No more can the means of obtaining it be feigned. Nothing but the Lord's own appointed means, nothing but 'waiting at the throne,' nothing but keeping the heart under 'the eyes of the Lamb,' to be again, and again, and again penetrated by His Spirit, can put the soul into that condition, in which it is a meet instrument to impart the light and power of God to other men.

Document II.15

James Martineau on the Incarnation, 1861 and 1864

James Martineau (1805–1900) was one of the leading Dissenting theologians and philosophers of the nineteenth century, becoming nationally prominent in the last twenty-five years of his life. A Unitarian minister from the 1820s until his death and a college principal, he never took a narrow sectarian view. He was widely admired by Anglicans, for example W. E. Gladstone, whose view of the church and theology was very different. This extract from his massive output (he was still writing when over 90) gives his very distinct view of the incarnation, the first sentence being widely quoted by the Liberal Christian wing of Dissent late in the century. See J. Drummond and C. B. Upton, *The Life and Letters of James Martineau*, 2 vols, London, 1902; and R. Waller, 'James Martineau: the Development of his Thought', in B. Smith, ed., *Truth, Liberty, Religion*, Oxford, 1986, pp. 225–64.

The extracts are taken from Martineau's *Essays, Reviews, Addresses*, London, 1891, vol. 2, sections XI ('Tracts for Priests and People', extracted from *National Review*, 1861), p. 443; and XII ('The Crisis of Faith', extracted from *National Review*, 1864), pp. 488–9.

(a)
The Incarnation is true, not of Christ exclusively, but of Man universally, and God everlastingly. He bends into the human to dwell there; and humanity is the susceptible organ of the divine. ...

(b)
When the incrustations on the original picture are cleared from the canvas, the dress of mythological pretensions, the attitude of self-glorification, which are nowhere less at home than in the divinest nature, will disappear: and the figure will come out, grand in its simplicity, of the true Son of Man, standing in the light of a new consciousness that just for that very reason he is also Son of God, and must draw others to be so too. The Incarnation, taken in the Church sense, as predicable exclusively of his personality, is not only unsustained by proof, supernatural or natural, but an absolute reversal of the animating principle of his life and faith. The Church makes it the most stupendous of miracles that he individually was at once human and divine: to him it was an everyday fact that all men are mingled of human and divine. The Church sets the two natures in such contrariety that the rules of the universe must be set aside to blend them in a single instance; to him it was revealed – and the revelation bathed the world in a sanctity constant as the daylight – that they were in the closest kindred, living together, whether the consciousness was mutual or not, in every soul, and incapable, without sorrowful breach and unfulfilled perfection, of parting from one another. To set him up on a pedestal alone – the unique form in which God's essence has entered the limits of our humanity – is to frustrate the very aim and prayer of his life, by appropriating to him the consecration for which he cared only so far as it was universal. Not till we say of all men what the creed says of him exclusively, that two natures go to make one person, both that which is born after its kind, and that which is 'of one substance with the Father' – the blended conditions of the *creature* and the *Son* of God – do we make any confession which he would own: and the truth of the Incarnation first comes out, when, in virtue of it, he represents us all, and by exhibiting it on the level of our life, makes us aware that our humanity is human only, but, beyond the sphere of self, has fellowship and rest in God.

Document II.16

R. W. Dale on the Atonement, 1878

Robert William Dale (1829–95) was the greatest intellect of Victorian Congregationalism. His ministry at Carr's Lane Church in central Birmingham led to his early chairmanship of the Congregational Union in 1869 and was crowned by his presidency of the first International Congregational Council in 1891. He was prominent in Birmingham Liberalism and published on political matters (see IX.27, 28). But his most influential work was his book on *The Atonement*, London, 1875. See the excellent biography by his son, A. W. W. Dale, *The Life of R. W. Dale of Birmingham*, London, 1898; C. Binfield, ed., *The Cross and the City: Essays in Commemoration of Robert William Dale, 1829–1895*, Supplement to the *Journal of the United Reformed Church History Society*, vol. 6, supplement no. 2, 1999; M. Hopkins, *Nonconformity's Romantic Generation: Evangelical and Liberal Theologies in Victorian England*, Carlisle, 2004, chap. 3; and DNB.

The document is taken from *The Atonement*, 22nd edn, London, 1902, pp. lvii–lxi. The influence of F. D. Maurice is evident in the claim that 'the life which dwelt in Christ is the true life of man'; but Dale wrestles to square this new intellectual current with received Evangelical orthodoxy. The resulting obscurity in the first edition was clarified in the preface to the seventh edition (1878), from which the extract comes.

Our whole conception of the redemptive work of the Lord Jesus Christ rests upon our faith in His Divine dignity. He was the Son of God. But He was also the Son of man. That it should have been possible for a Divine person to reveal Himself under the conditions of human nature, and in a human history, is very wonderful, and throws an intense light on the vast possibilities of perfection which belong to our race. These possibilities are still more gloriously illustrated when we discover – what, indeed, seems to me to be implied in the Incarnation, but is also distinctly affirmed in the New Testament – that the life which dwelt in Christ is the true life of man, that we were created in order that this life might be ours. Hence, while the Lord Jesus Christ is the brightness of God's glory, and the express image of His Person, He is also the visible manifestation of the glory of human nature, the 'idea' and prophecy of its moral and spiritual excellence, and of its true relation to God. ...

When I, a sinful man, come to God through Christ, I acknowledge that I am not what I ought to be, nor what I desire to be. ...

I confess that I do not submit, as I should, to the perfect justice of the Divine anger against my sin, or to the perfect justice of the tremendous penalty which is threatened against sin. At times I may acknowledge from my very heart that I deserve to perish in the fires of the Divine wrath, but at other times I resent the stern severity of the eternal Law of Righteousness, and think that if I perished God would deal hardly with me. But Christ, with all His love for the human race and with all His eagerness for their salvation, never shrank from acknowledging the justice of the Divine condemnation. He spoke of the chaff being burned up by the unquenchable fire, and of the dead soul being utterly consumed by the undying worm. Coming to God through Him, I place myself by His side and consent to all that He says about my ill desert: my consent may be imperfect, but I am sure that Christ is right and that I am wrong. I wish to have the same mind that was in Him, and meanwhile I ask God to receive Christ's acknowledgment as my own.

But Christ not only felt and confessed the justice of God's punishment for sin, He actually submitted to Death, and, what was more terrible than physical Death, the loss of the consciousness of God's presence, and this spiritual agony appears to have been the immediate cause of His death. Having become man, He submitted, though sinless Himself, to these dreadful consequences of sin. In His last hours there was more than the acknowledgment that we deserved to suffer, there was the voluntary endurance of suffering which we had deserved; there was an *act* of moral homage to the righteousness of the Divine penalty with which sin is menaced. Coming to God through Him, I say that I desire to make this act of His my own, and I ask God to accept it as expressing my own submission and homage to the righteousness of the penalty which I have deserved by my sin.

Document II.17

W. B. Pope on Theology as a Science, 1880

William Burt Pope (1822–1903) was tutor in systematic theology at the Wesleyan Theological Institution at Didsbury and editor of the connexional learned journal, *The London Quarterly Review*. In 1877 he was president of Conference. The published version of his doctrinal lectures, *A Compendium of Christian Theology*, in the expanded second edition of 1880, formed the standard exposition of the Methodist standpoint in the late nineteenth century. See R. W. Moss, *The Rev. W. B. Pope, D.D.*, London, [1909]; and DNB.

The extract, which clearly reveals the contemporary prestige of science, is taken from *A Compendium of Christian Theology*, 2nd edn, London, 1880, vol. 1, pp. 25–6.

The methods of theology are scientific. It observes, tests, and arranges facts and makes generalisations; it uses both the inductive and deductive processes of argument; it depends upon the same primary laws of thought upon which those processes rest; and it sets out, as all legitimate human inquiry must set out, with a firm faith in certain truths which lie behind experience, being inwrought into the fabric of our minds: such as the primary law of causation and all that it involves, and the validity of those laws of belief which are innate. But the facts of our science are gathered from regions some of which are thought to be interdicted to scientific observation. There is the sacred deposit of original truths in the constitution of man's nature. There are the economies of Creation and Providence. There is the boundless storehouse of the Word of God; and there are the innumerable testimonies of common experience, of which Scripture is the test, while they confirm the Scripture. Strictly speaking, all these regions of observation are one, inasmuch as every element of religious consciousness, and every lesson of the external universe, is wrought up into the fabric of Divine revelation. We cannot take a step further without the assurance that these are legitimate fields of observation, the facts or phenomena of which are as real as the facts with which physical science has to do. Theological science is dissipated at once if this is denied. Supposing it granted, then there remains only the careful, honest, and religious observance of the accepted laws of reasoning. The result, whether by analysis or synthesis, is the scientific presentation of each doctrine and class of doctrine and the entire compass of theology. In this way, that is by the rigorous processes of induction and deduction, systematic theology arrives at a clear and distinct apprehension of every article of the Faith. For instance, its doctrine of sin is the result of a wide and exhaustive examination of a large number of testimonies in Scripture and in experience which force conviction on the mind that one, and one only, theory can account for all the facts. The same may be said of its doctrine of the Person of Christ, which is inductively established by a comparison of many passages, none of which individually contains a formal statement. Of this we shall have manifold other illustrations as we proceed.

Document II.18

A. M. Fairbairn on the Kingdom of God, 1893

Andrew Martin Fairbairn (1838–1912) was a Scot who first served in the ministry of the Evangelical Union, a revivalist and anti-Calvinist denomination. Experience of theological study in Berlin qualified him for the principalship of Airedale Congregational College, Bradford. In 1883 he was elected chairman of the Congregational Union and in 1886 he became the founding principal of Mansfield College, Oxford (see III.6). See W. B. Selbie, *The Life of Andrew Martin Fairbairn*, London, 1914; R. S. Franks, 'The Theology of Andrew Martin Fairbairn', *Transactions of the Congregational History Society*, 13 (1939), pp. 140–50; and DNB.

The extract is taken from Fairbairn's most influential work, *The Place of Christ in Modern Theology*, London, 1893, pp. 515–17. It illustrates the general shift in contemporary theology away from identifying the kingdom of God with the church and, typically for its period, polemicises heavily against the Anglo-Catholics.

Now, our first question is, How did Christ conceive and describe His society? And here we note as most characteristic that His familiar phrase was not 'the Church,' but 'the kingdom of heaven' or 'of God,' or simply 'My kingdom.' The mere figures are significant: the term 'kingdom' is used in the Gospels to denote His society 112 times, and almost always by Himself; but 'Church' only twice. Now, the names are either synonymous or they are not. If they are synonymous, it must be possible to translate the Church into the terms of the kingdom, and the kingdom into the terms of the Church. If they are not, then the kingdom, as Christ's most used, most emphasized, and most descriptive name for His society, must contain His determinative idea – *i.e.*, the Church must be construed through the kingdom, not the kingdom through the Church. If the first position be chosen, then the neo-Catholics who seem almost with one consent to have forgotten the kingdom, have failed to interpret the Church; if the second, then there is behind and beneath the Church another notion, as it were, the aboriginal ideal of the Christian society, to which they have given no adequate recognition, and for which they have found no fit place. In the one case, their idea of the Church is not adequate; in the other, their Church is not the ultimate normal polity or social ideal of Jesus.

The idea of the kingdom, then, is primary ... .

Now, it is remarkable that in the language of Christ as to the kingdom the emphasis falls, not upon the officials, if officials there be, or on Sacramental acts, if such acts there be, but upon the people, upon persons, their personal qualities, conduct, character, their state and living before God, their behaviour and ministry among men. He, indeed, calls disciples and commissions apostles, but He deals with them as men who must be of a given spirit if they would enter the kingdom; their eminence in it depends, not on office, but on spiritual qualities; and their rewards, not on dignities possessed, but on range and kind of service – none being sacerdotal, all spiritual and human.

Document II.19

P. T. Forsyth on God the Holy Father, 1896

Peter Taylor Forsyth (1848–1921) was a graduate of the University of Aberdeen who then studied under Ritschl in Germany. During successive Congregational ministries at Shipley, Hackney, Manchester, Leicester and Cambridge he shed his early theological liberalism and became a passionate exponent of an approach in which the cross was the criterion of truth. In 1901 he became principal of Hackney Congregational College and in 1905 chairman of the Congregational Union. His greatest works were composed in the twentieth century and include *Positive Preaching and the Modern Mind* (1907) and *The Person and Place of Jesus Christ* (1909). See W. L. Bradley, *Peter Taylor Forsyth*, London, 1952; T. Hart, ed., *Justice the True and Only Mercy*, Edinburgh, 1995; and L. McCurdy, *Attributes and Atonement: The Holy Love of God in the Theology of P. T. Forsyth*, Carlisle, 1999.

The extract is taken from a sermon on John 17: 11 preached before the Congregational Union autumn assembly in 1895, and reprinted in P. T. Forsyth, *God the Holy Father*, London, 1957, pp. 4–5. The sermon's title, 'God the Holy Father', is a manifesto for his mature theology in which holiness tempers love to generate the grace of the atonement.

The ethical standard is becoming supreme with us to-day, not only in conduct, but also in theology. We may welcome the change. It carries us farther – to a standard truly spiritual. It plants us on God's holiness as His perfect nature, His eternal spirit, His ruling self and moving centre. We have been overengrossed with a mere distributive equity, which has made God the Lord Chief Justice of the world. Or we have recoiled from that to a love slack and over-sweet. But this lifts us up to a more spiritual and personal standard, to the Fatherly holiness whose satisfaction in a Holy Son is the great work and true soul of Godhead. The divine Father is the holy. And the Holy Father's first care is holiness. The first charge on a Redeemer is satisfaction to that holiness. The Holy Father is one who does and must atone. Atonement wears a new glory when read in Christ's own light. We see it flowing in grief *from that very holiness* of the Father to which it returns in praise. As Holy Father He is the eternal Father and maker of sacrifice no less than of man. He offers a sacrifice rent from His own heart. It is made to Him by no third party ('for who hath first given unto Him'), but by Himself in His Son; and it is made to no foreign power, but to His own holy nature and law. Fatherhood is not bought from holiness by any cross; it is holiness itself that pays. It is love that expiates. 'Do not say, "God is love. Why atone?" The New Testament says, "God has atoned. What love!"' The ruling passion of the Saviour's holy God is this passion to atone and to redeem.

All this and more is in that *'Holy Father'*, which is the last word in the naming of God. The Church of to-day has gained greatly in its sense of the *love* of God. There are still greater things waiting when she has moved on as far again, to that *holiness* whose outward movement is love, which love is but the passion to impart. You can go behind love to holiness, but behind holiness you cannot go. It is the true consuming fire. Any real belief in the Incarnation is a belief in the ultimacy, centrality, and supremacy of holiness for God and man. We may come to holiness by way of love, but we only come to love by reason of holiness. We may be all aglow for the coming of the kingdom, but there is a prior petition. It is the kingdom's once condition, 'Hallowed be Thy Name'. That hallowing was done in Christ's death which founded the kingdom. We are in some danger of inverting the order of these prayers to-day. 'Thy kingdom come' is not the first petition. The kingdom comes from the satisfaction of holiness. It does not make it. 'God is Love' is not the whole gospel. Love is not evangelical till it has dealt with holy law. In the midst of the rainbow is a throne. There is a kind of consecration which would live close to the Father, but it does not always take seriously enough the holiness which *makes* the fatherhood of the cross – awful, inexhaustible, and eternal, as full of judgment as of salvation.

Document II.20

J. S. Lidgett on the Fatherhood of God, 1897

John Scott Lidgett (1854–1953) was a Wesleyan minister who, in 1891, became the first warden of the Bermondsey Settlement. In the twentieth century he was to be the editor of *The Methodist Times*, the leader of the Progressives on the London County Council and the chief Free Church influence on the 1944 Education Act. In 1906 he was president of the National Free Church Council, in 1908 president of the Wesleyan Conference and in 1932 first president of the reunited Methodist Church. See J. S. Lidgett, *My Guided Life*, London, 1936; R. E. Davies, ed., *John Scott Lidgett: A Symposium*, London, 1957; A. F. Turberfield, *John Scott Lidgett: Archbishop of British Methodism?*, London, 2003; and DNB.

The extracts are taken from the published version of Lidgett's Fernley Lecture before the Wesleyan Conference in 1897, *The Spiritual Principle of the Atonement*, 2nd edn, London, 1898, pp. 226, 229 and 233–4. The book consists of the author's reinterpretation of traditional Evangelical views on the atonement in the light of the theology of F. D. Maurice; the passage presented here expounds the characteristic stress of the period on the Fatherhood of God.

Coming to the first question, What is the relationship of God to mankind, in virtue of which He demands and provides Atonement? – our unhesitating answer is, His Fatherhood ...

The divine Fatherhood is supreme, all-embracing and all-controlling. It is clear, at first sight, that Fatherhood is a higher, more vital, intimate, and gracious relationship than any other which can be named; than, for example, that of creator, king, or judge. It is equally true, though not so immediately apparent, that Fatherhood includes all these other relationships in a higher and larger whole. ...

... not the least weighty reason why it is necessary to treat the Fatherhood of God as the relation which determines the Atonement lies in the revelation of the Holy Trinity and of the constitution of mankind in the Son of God. From these we learn that God becomes the Father of man in time on account of what He eternally is. The Godhead exists in the eternal unity of the Father, the Son, and the Holy Spirit. It is in and through those relationships that God is what He is; the primacy, in a sense, being with the Father. It is in and through the Son that creation has been brought into being, is constituted, and has vital union with God. Thus the world stands in the closest connexion with the immanent life of the Godhead. The creative process has its source in the Father, its mediator in the Son. The creative product is conditioned by the Son, and has the Son as its head, through whom it has access to God. The external acts of God, in creation and redemption, have their ground in, correspond to, and reflect the immanent relations of the Godhead. Fatherhood as the source of the divine life, Sonship as the eternal expression of it, the Holy Spirit as completing the fellowship of love, in and through these the Godhead subsists. And the manifestation of God is the unfolding of what He is. The primacy of Fatherhood in the interior life of the Godhead means the supremacy of fatherly purpose in the exterior action of the Godhead. The headship of the Son over creation involves that His nature and His relationships in the Godhead give the law to those who hold their being of and in Him. However loudly we may profess our belief in the *doctrine* of the Holy Trinity, we are indeed trifling with it, and jeopardying faith in it, unless we receive it with the seriousness which makes *the fact* of the Holy Trinity the key of nature and of the history of the world. The primacy of the Father in the Holy Trinity makes the creation and redemption of man fatherly; the eternal headship of the Son over man necessitates that the true nature of man should be filial.

Controversies and Issues

Document II.21

William Huntington on the Divine Law, 1804

William Huntington (1745–1813) had little formal education, and worked for a time as a coal-heaver. Following a dramatic conversion experience in a Surrey garden, he began to preach and in 1782 moved to London where, until his death, he preached to congregations numbering about 2,000. He was a high Calvinist and was strongly isolationist, believing there were probably not more than three faithful ministers in the whole country. He opposed the seventeenth-century confessions of faith by denying the moral law to be a rule of life for the believer, fiercely denouncing all who opposed him. This antinomianism became a cause of division in a number of Particular Baptist churches. See [J. Lincoln], *The Voice of Years*, London, 1814; T. Wright, *The Life of William Huntington*, London, 1909; and DNB.

This extract comes from 'Every Divine Law in the Heart of Christ and his Spiritual Seed; But the Unbelieving Disobedient to the Faith and Without Law', 1804, in *The Select Works of the late Rev. William Huntington, S.S.*, vol. 3, Collingridge edition, London, 1856, pp. 414–17.

Now my reasons for not setting the law as a rule of life before the children of God are,

1. Because I do not find this rule in any one commission given forth of God to any of his evangelical servants; no, not in the commission of Christ himself. 'The spirit of the Lord is upon me, because he has anointed me to preach the gospel to the poor: he hath sent me to heal the broken-hearted; to preach deliverance to the captives, and recovering of sight to the blind; to set at liberty them that are bruised. To preach the acceptable year of the Lord,' Luke, iv. 18, 19. And although it is true that he preached the law in all its spiritual meaning as no other ever did, yet he never sent sensible and seeking sinners to it, but always directed them to the good-will of the Father in himself. 'He that doeth the will of my Father which is in heaven shall enter into the kingdom,' Matt. vii. 21. 'It is not the will of your Father which is in heaven that one of these little ones should perish,' Matt. xviii. 14. 'And this is the will of him that sent me, that every one which seeth the Son, and believeth on him, may have everlasting life, and I will raise him up at the last day,' John vi. 40. Our Lord here sets the Father's will before the children, which is his good-will of purpose and of promise in Christ. But God is a master as well as a Father. 'If I be a Father, where is my honour, and if I be a master, where is my fear?' Malachi, i. 6. Believers are not servants but sons; and before these sons he sets the heavenly Father's will; but the self-sufficient servant he always sends to the law, which is the commanding will of the master, and the servant's only rule.

'What is written in the law; how readest thou? This do and thou shalt live,' Luke, x. 26, 28. But our Lord never once called the law the believer's rule of life: nor does he call it the believer's law, but applies it to his enemies. 'But this cometh to pass, that the word might be fulfilled that is written in their law,' John, xv. 25. ...

12. I believe in my heart that I am redeemed, and delivered from the curse of the law, by the application of the atoning blood of Christ, sprinkled on my conscience by the Holy Spirit of God; and that, by the imputation of Christ's obedience to the law for me as my surety, and being placed to my account, I am delivered from the galling yoke of precept, 'Do, and live.' This is what I firmly believe; this I have long experienced, felt, and enjoyed; and, was I to deviate from this, I should preach lies, and preach what I do not believe; 'and whatsoever is not of faith is sin,' Rom. xiv. 23.

13. I believe that none of those who have written against me, calling me antinomian, ever performed one good work themselves in all their lives, being wholly destitute of a good root: and their performances destitute of the real properties of a good work. Good fruits must be fruits of the Spirit, and spring from union with the living vine: they must be done in the exercise of faith, and under the constraints of experienced love. But men destitute of the Spirit must be in the flesh; and 'they that are in the flesh cannot please God,' Rom. viii. 8.

Document II.22

William Steadman on Believer's Baptism, 1812

William Steadman (1764–1837) combined his duties as president of the newly formed Horton Academy (later Rawdon) with the pastoral oversight of Bradford (Westgate) Particular Baptist Church and an extensive village preaching itinerary. He was highly respected in Bradford, and enjoyed cordial relationships with ministers who did not share his baptist beliefs. Although he was a strict communionist, he was willing to conduct the communion service in open-communion churches (on which see II.23). See T. Steadman, *Memoir of the Rev. William Steadman*, London, 1838; and S. James, 'Revival and Renewal in Baptist Life: The Contribution of William Steadman (1764–1837)', *Baptist Quarterly*, 37 (1998), pp. 263–82.

This defence of his denomination's distinctive baptismal practice is from *Persons who have put on Christ the Only Proper Subjects of Christian Baptism, A Sermon*, Leeds, 1812, pp. 17–19, the text being Galations 3: 27.

To you however my hearers, I address myself with the greatest freedom; and in the first place, Let me entreat you to consider whether the prevailing practise [*sic*] of administering baptism to infants, can at all be made to accord with the view here given us of the sacred ordinance. Can it be said on this principle, That as many of you as have been baptized into Christ have put on Christ? – Whether, the party baptized, be the infant of an ungodly or a godly parent, he is quite unconscious of what is done to him, he can have formed no previous acquaintance with

Christ, can have had no sense of his need of Christ, or the worth of his righteousness, or his grace, nor have exercised any reliance on either, nor can he in any respect whatever profess his reliance on Christ in his baptism, it being a work in which he is wholly incapable of any personal concern or choice. Nor do we see that it at all alters the case to admit, that an infant may be regenerated by the Spirit of Christ, and so have a principle of faith wrought in him. Of the possibility of this, we have no hesitation, and have, from the hints afforded us in Scripture, the pleasing hope, that such as die in infancy are the happy subjects of such a work, and are therefore saved. But when we recollect, that this happy change is not effected in all infants, nay not even in all the infants of believing parents, and that it is therefore impossible to distinguish at that early period in whom it is wrought; and farther, when we remember that it is not by the principle of faith, but by the exercise of that principle that persons put on Christ, and that this exercise supposes knowledge and choice; when, I say, we consider these things, we can by no means admit that the possibility, or the existence of such a principle in a few, or even in the majority, would afford any ground at all for asserting of infants who are baptized, that as many of them as have been baptized into Christ, have put on Christ. Much less are we able to admit the justness of its application, on account of the introduction of sponsers [sic] to engage in the child's behalf, whether those sponsers are indifferent persons or its parents; for not to mention that such sponsers universally enter into engagements they are wholly unable to perform, it is sufficient to observe, that the profession of faith by proxy is a measure wholly unknown in the New Testament; and that in my text in particular, the inspired Apostle most plainly represents the putting on of Christ connected with baptism, as each one's personal act. But perhaps it may be said, That though the apostle affirms, that those who have been baptized into Christ have put on Christ, he must not be necessarily understood to assert, that they have put on Christ previous to their baptism, or even at it; but, on the contrary, it may be sufficient to justify his assertion if such persons in their future lives should most certainly put on Christ.

But to this we reply, That the Apostle's language is decisive, and refers not to what may in the future come to pass, but to what had in fact already taken place. He does not say, as many of you as have been baptized into Christ, may in some future period of your lives put on Christ, but, *you have put on Christ*. He manifestly affirms this of them, immediately upon their being baptized. But were we for a moment to admit, that his words may be so construed as to allow of this meaning, yet we are free to affirm, that even such a sentiment does by no means correspond with matters of fact.

Document II.23

Robert Hall on Terms of Communion, 1815

In 1816 Robert Hall (see I.1) entered the long-running debate among Particular Baptists on the terms of admission to church membership and to the Lord's Supper by

Theology

advocating that membership and participation at the Lord's Table should be open to both Baptists and non-Baptists. He was opposed by Joseph Kinghorn of Norwich. Apart from the high Calvinist Baptists, Hall's views on an open Lord's Table were increasingly adopted, but during the nineteenth century there was little acceptance of open membership. See M. Walker, *Baptists at the Table*, Didcot, Oxfordshire, 1992.

The following extract is taken from *The Works of Robert Hall, A.M.*, ed. O. Gregory, London, 1839, vol. 3, p. 77.

Having shown, we trust to the satisfaction of the reader, that paedobaptism is not an error of such magnitude, as to prevent the society which maintains it from being deemed a true church, I proceed to observe that to repel the members of such a society from communion is the very essence of schism. Schism is a causeless and unnecessary separation from the church of Christ, or from any part of it; and that secession cannot urge the plea of necessity, where no concurrence in what is deemed evil, no approbation of error or superstition, is involved in communion. In the case before us, by admitting a paedobaptist to the Lord's supper, no sanction whatever is given to infant-sprinkling, no act of concurrence is involved or implied, nothing is done, or left undone, which would not have been equally so, if his attendance were withdrawn. Under such circumstances, the necessity of preserving purity of worship, or of avoiding an active cooperation in what we deem sinful or erroneous (the only justifiable ground of separation), has no place. The objection to his admission is founded solely on a disapprobation of a particular practice, considered, not as it affects us, since no part of our religious practice is influenced by it, but in relation to its intrinsic demerits.

Division amongst christians, especially when it proceeds to a breach of communion, is so fraught with scandal, and so utterly repugnant to the genius of the gospel, that the suffrages of the whole christian world have concurred in regarding it as an evil, on no occasion to be incurred, but for the avoidance of a greater – the violation of conscience.

Document II.24

Suffolk and Norfolk Baptist Association Circular Letter, 1829

In 1829 representatives from six of the twenty-four churches in the Suffolk and Norfolk Association (formed 1769) met at Grundisburgh to form a new association. The reasons given for this separation, together with rules for the new association, were given in a letter addressed to all Suffolk and Norfolk Particular Baptist churches. Extracts from this letter, together with the three leading rules of the new association, affirming an adherence to high Calvinism and restricted communion, are given below. Duty faith (see II.11) is explicitly repudiated. After the division the two associations continued as separate bodies on friendly terms. When the old association came to an end in 1849 some churches joined the new association, and others the newly formed Suffolk Union. For an account of the Suffolk and Norfolk Associations, and of the 1829 division, see, A. J. Klaiber, *The Story of the Suffolk Baptists*, London, 1931.

After many years' union and co-operation with the Suffolk and Norfolk Association of Baptist Churches, we have this day mutually agreed, in the fear of the Lord, and with a single eye to the Redeemer's glory, and the spiritual interest of his holy kingdom upon earth, to withdraw, and form ourselves into a separate Association, upon the principles, and for the objects, expressed in the annexed articles.

In taking this step, we trust we have not been actuated by feelings of personal disaffection towards our brethren, from whom we separate. Gladly would we have continued with them, and most cordially would we have aided them in promoting the benevolent design of the Association, if we could have done so, consistently with a steady conscientious zeal, for the spread and defence of the pure and precious truths of the everlasting gospel. But when our union can be maintained only by an implied compromise of what we esteem sound doctrine, a sense of duty compels us to dissolve it. ...

We beg to have it clearly understood, that our separation from the Suffolk and Norfolk Association has not been occasioned by a departure from the original *Articles*, but from the original PRINCIPLES, of the Association. The articles were not 'the basis of our union,' but the rules of our proceedings. The basis of our union is to be found in the doctrines of grace and salvation, avowedly maintained by the Churches. These have ever been held, to the exclusion of the *sentiment*, that it is the duty of all men to believe with the faith of God's elect; and in opposition to the *practice* of general and indiscriminate offers and exhortations in the ministry. We identify the doctrines thus held with the faith once delivered to the saints, and regard them as the *original principles* of the Association. Under this view, we need not inform you there has been a departure from them. A defection has taken place in several Churches, and as some of our brethren appear more disposed to countenance than oppose that defection, we know of no means of securing our own comfort, and uniting our efforts, to advance the true glory of our Lord's kingdom, other than that of adopting the measures we have taken. ...

Doctrines and Articles. ...
1. That this Association be formed of Churches of the Particular Baptist denomination maintaining the important doctrines of three equal Persons in the Godhead; eternal and personal election; original sin; particular redemption; free justification by the imputed righteousness of Christ alone; efficacious grace in regeneration; the final perseverance of real believers; the resurrection of the dead; the future judgment; the eternal happiness of the righteous; and everlasting misery of such as die impenitent; together with the necessity of Baptism upon a profession of faith, as a pre-requisite to the Lord's Supper; the obligation of believers to practical obedience to the declared will of Christ as King in Zion; and the Congregational order of the Churches inviolable.
2. That the doctrines expressed in the preceding article are held by this Association to be wholly incompatible with the doctrine which asserts that *saving faith is the duty of all men*, and are therefore maintained by the respective Churches to the exclusion of that doctrine.

Theology

3. That the leading objects of our union are to promote and defend the above stated doctrines of Grace, with a view to the peace and prosperity of the Churches, and the glory of God; – to cultivate a spirit of love and sympathy with each other, and spiritual communion with our ascended Lord; – to render mutual assistance by counsel, by prayer, and other means; and to further the kingdom of Christ, as opportunity and ability shall be given.

Document II.25

Isaac Crewdson's Resignation from the Quakers, 1836

The Beacon controversy of the 1830s was a symptom of the impact of Evangelicalism on the Society of Friends. Isaac Crewdson (1780–1844), a Manchester textile manufacturer and a Quaker minister, embraced an Evangelical faith after a severe illness. In 1835 he issued *A Beacon to the Society of Friends*, in which he contended that the Quakers were maintaining unscriptural teachings. In the following year he resigned from the Society to form a breakaway body of Evangelical Friends, but the group barely survived his death. See M. Grubb, 'The Beacon Separation', *Journal of the Friends Historical Society*, 60 (1977), pp. 190–98; and DNB.

The extract is the substance of Crewdson's letter of resignation to his local Monthly Meeting dated 9/11/1836 (the Quakers repudiated conventional names of months) and taken from the anonymous work, *The Crisis of the Quaker Contest in Manchester*, Manchester, 1837, appendix, pp. 1–4. It repudiates the teaching of Robert Barclay, the seventeenth-century apologist for the Quakers, and of their founder George Fox. It asserts that the Society's basic principle of the 'inward light' led to the rationalism professed in America by the Quakers who followed Elias Hicks.

To the Monthly Meeting of Hardshaw East.

Dear Friends,

I believe the time has arrived, when the connexion which has subsisted for more than fifty-six years, between myself and the Society of Friends, and in which I have been a Minister upwards of twenty years, must be dissolved.

To my dear Friends of every class, from whom I have received *much kindness*, and to whom I have been bound by many and strong ties, – towards whom my heart has often been enlarged in the love of the Gospel, and for whom my prayers have been put up to the Throne of Grace; – that love I hope will never be extinguished.

In taking leave of you, I trust you will bear with me, while I make a few remarks, and allow them to have your candid attention.

The first apprehensions in my mind, with regard to the doctrines held by the Society, were produced by reading Barclay's Apology – I was forcibly struck with what then appeared to me the unscriptural way in which he treats on the light, seed, grace, and Word of God, particularly in the 13th Section of his V. and VI. Propositions. ...

This occurred probably ten or twelve years ago. My views, as to the errors of the Society, I confess have opened very slowly, (even since that period; –) I was warmly attached to the Society, – it was painful to me to think, that the body to which I was united, was in error, and I have been ready to close my mind against conviction. Steadily, yea tenaciously have I clung to the hope, that whatever errors of doctrine or practice we may have been in – that, on those errors being exhibited, and Scriptural Truth held up, we might, and should reform. I was aware, when in the beginning of 1835, I published the Beacon, that Hicksism did exist to some extent among Friends in this country; and I believed that under different modifications, many held the unscriptural and dangerous doctrine of the 'Inward Light' – *the very root of the heresy* promulgated by Hicks; and my design in publishing that work was, that Friends should be warned of the danger; and I did hope, that in having before them the deadly errors of Hicksism, in contrast with the *Truth of God*, as revealed in Holy Scripture, if in any respect they should see their own faces as in a glass, their hearts might be inclined to receive the warning, and to take the Scripture ground. I had little idea that a Scriptural book (and such it is proved to be on a stern and rigid examination,) would so generally, throughout the Society, have been met with decided hostility. Even so lately as when I wrote the first part of my Reply to the Statement of the Committee, I confess I had a very inadequate idea of the radical unsoundness of the system, and I fondly hoped that the Scriptures might yet be admitted, (practically I mean,) as the paramount standard; and that unitedly fleeing to the refuge set before us in the Gospel, we might have striven together, for the faith once delivered to the saints; and it is but very lately that the deep and painful conviction has been forced upon me, with *irresistible evidence*, that Quakerism, as set forth in some of the writings of George Fox, and other early Friends, is not Christianity, and that some of his delusive assumptions were of a truly awful, and even blasphemous character.

Document II.26

Epistle from the Meeting for Sufferings, 1836

The official Quaker response to the Beaconite agitation (see II.25) came in an epistle dated 5/12/1836 issued by the Meeting for Sufferings, the highest executive body of the Society of Friends. It called for unity, but restated the doctrine of the special illumination of the Holy Spirit as the bedrock of Quaker testimony. For a fuller and more measured response, see II.5.

The extract is taken from the separately printed *An Epistle from the Meeting for Sufferings* ..., London, 1836, p. 1.

To Friends in the Quarterly and other Meetings within the limits of this Yearly Meeting.

Dear Friends,

We have observed with much pain the printing and industrious circulation of various papers and pamphlets, put forth apparently for the purpose of weakening the attachment of the members of our religious society to those views of Christian truth and practice which have ever been entertained by Friends. ...

Whilst, as a Christian church, we have ever believed and received with thankfulness all the glorious truths of the Gospel, we have been more particularly distinguished by a union of sentiment on the convictions, guidance, and teachings of the Holy Spirit:– free and immediate in their communication to the soul of man; and, when it pleaseth God, independent of all external instrumentality. And were we in any way to let down this high spiritual view, which is however, no other than what is taught in Holy Scripture, we believe that we should frustrate the purposes of the Lord in gathering us to be a distinct people; endanger our existence in that character; and bring condemnation upon ourselves, by having proved unfaithful in that which the Lord hath committed to us.

Document II.27

Samuel Davidson on Biblical Criticism, 1839

The issue of the higher criticism of the Bible first aroused a major public controversy in England when, in 1856–57, Samuel Davidson (1806–98) was arraigned for erroneous religious teaching while he was on the staff of the Lancashire Independent College. Davidson, an Ulster Presbyterian, was recruited to join the college at its foundation in 1843. In 1856 there were orthodox complaints that the views he expressed in his new edition of the standard work, T. H. Horne's *Introduction to the Critical Study and Knowledge of the Holy Scriptures*, were unacceptable. In 1857, after much debate, he resigned. See R. Tudur Jones, *Congregationalism in England, 1662–1962*, London, 1962, pp. 254–6.

The extract is from an earlier work, S. Davidson, *Lectures on Biblical Criticism*, Belfast, 1839, pp. 2–3. It shows that already, before his appointment to the Lancashire College, Davidson had embraced the principles of higher textual criticism practised on the continent but neglected in Britain – except among Unitarians.

Now if it be a laudable thing to attempt to restore the unvitiated text of a heathen author, surely it ought to be much more so in regard to that of the Bible. The great Author from whom it proceeds, the consequent importance of its contents, and the design of its bestowment on man, conspire to place it infinitely above the emanations of the highest and brightest intellects. All our attention should therefore be directed, in the first place, to the ascertainment of the true and proper reading of the original. When this is accomplished, we may proceed with confidence to interpret and to explain it. We must first judge whether an alteration has been made in a passage, so that the condition in which it originally came from the hands of its author does not appear. The incorruptness of the text must be considered; the changes which it may have undergone are to be discovered; and those readings must be restored into whose place others have intruded. This is followed by interpretation. The science embracing these two departments of knowledge has not been cultivated in these countries with the zeal and ardour which it has awakened in modern times on the continent of Europe. The learning it demands has been abortive. But we begin to see the tokens of better things, and we rejoice that the day is appearing in which we shall not be behind our continental brethren.

Document II.28

J. Angell James on the Postmillennial Hope, 1848

John Angell James (1785–1859) was commonly regarded as the model of an Evangelical minister. From 1805 to his death he served Carr's Lane Independent Church, Birmingham, and in 1838 was chairman of the Congregational Union. He was a prolific author (see also V.7 and VII.8). See R. W. Dale, *The Life and Letters of John Angell James*, London, 1861; and DNB.

The extract is taken from James's *The Church in Earnest* [1848], London, 1861 edn, pp. 356–8. It expresses the expectation, widespread in Nonconformity, of a millennium of peace and plenty to be brought about within history, and so before the second advent, by the triumph of the gospel. This postmillennial hope contrasts with the premillennialism of II.29.

The church on earth ... is assured of increase, triumph, and universal dominion. She is not always to be shut up within her present narrow limits, a little band scorned by pride, oppressed by power; the circumference of the globe is to be the circle of her domain, and all nations are to be her subjects. The Lord shall arise upon thee, 'O thou afflicted, tossed with tempest, and not comforted.' 'The Gentiles shall see thy righteousness, and all kings thy glory. Lift up thine eyes round about, and see: all they gather themselves together, they come to thee: thy sons shall come from afar, and thy daughters shall be nursed by thy side. Then thou shalt see and flow together, and thy heart shall fear and be enlarged, because the abundance of the sea shall be converted unto thee, the forces of the Gentiles shall come unto thee.' A thousand such promises as these, though partially fulfilled by the incarnation of the Son of God, and the setting up of his kingdom in the world, await their consummation in the latter day glory. ...

The sabbath of our world shall have arrived. The worship of Jehovah shall be universal. The Name which is above every name shall be heard on every plain, and echoed from every mountain. The Bible shall be in every hand, a house of prayer in every village, and an altar for God in every habitation. The groans of creation shall be lost amidst the songs of salvation, and this vale of tears, even to its darkest nook and deepest recess, be irradiated with the sunshine of joy and praise. The throne of tyranny, cemented by blood, and occupied by oppression, shall be overturned, and the vine and fir tree, overshadowing its seat, and yielding the fruit of liberty, shall be planted in its place. Slavery, that veriest type of selfishness, cruelty, and lawless power, shall be abolished as one of the greatest crimes and direst curses of humanity. The Prince of Peace, whose throne is for ever and ever, 'shall judge among the nations, and shall rebuke many people; and they shall beat their swords into plough shares, and their spears into pruning hooks: nation shall not lift up sword against nation, neither shall they learn the art of war any more.' Commerce shall be purified from its cupidity, legislation from its injustice, literature from its pride, and philosophy from its scepticism. The principles of Christianity shall permeate every thing, and leaven the whole mass of society with the spirit of that kingdom, 'which is righteousness, peace, and joy, in the Holy Ghost.' Then will be realised all the glowing descriptions contained in the chapters of Revelation, to which I have already alluded, and men, and angels, and God himself, rejoice over 'the new heavens and new earth, wherein dwelleth righteousness.'

Document II.29

B. W. Newton on Premillennialism, 1850

After gaining academic distinction at Exeter College, Oxford, Benjamin Wills Newton (1807–99) returned to this native Plymouth, where he became one of the leaders of a group known as the 'Plymouth Brethren', who were calling for separation from all organised religion (the 'apostasy'), and for a return to primitive first-century Christianity. Great stress was laid on a right understanding of prophecy; on the rise of Antichrist, and a period of tribulation prior to the return of Christ for a millennial reign in Jerusalem. John Nelson Darby (see IX.24) joined the Plymouth meeting but came into serious disagreement with Newton over whether or not the church would pass through this period of tribulation, resulting in two distinct Brethren traditions. See H. H. Rowdon, *The Origins of the Brethren*, London, 1967.

Newton wrote profusely on prophetic issues. In this extract he recounts the recent rise of premillennial teaching, that is, the conviction that the second coming of Christ would precede the millennium. For the contrasting postmillennial position, see II.28. The extract comes from *Aids to Prophetic Enquiry, First Series*, London, 1850, pp. 5–6.

The Advent of the Lord Jesus in glory, was now recognised as the alone means appointed of God, for the introduction of the Millennium; and it was clearly seen, that not only the conversion of Israel, but the binding of Satan and the release of creation from its groan, were made dependent upon agency entirely different from any which God had connected with the suffering period of His Church's testimony. Indeed, no moral instrumentality such as the preaching of the Gospel, *could* either bind Satan, or raise the bodies of the saints who sleep. Both these things must be the result of *manifested* almighty power, and both, according to the arrangements of God, are made precursors to the Millennial reign.

The *eleventh* and *fourteenth* chapters of Zechariah – the third of Joel, and the last of Isaiah, were among the passages appealed to, as clearly revealing, that the manifestation of Christ in glory, was to precede the conversion of Jerusalem, and the subsequent blessing of the Earth.

Document II.30

John Harris on the Inspiration of the Scriptures, 1851

John Harris (1802–56) was a tutor at Cheshunt College, primarily serving the Countess of Huntingdon's Connexion, and from 1851 the first principal of New College, London, the result of a merger of the Congregational colleges of the capital. He was chairman of the Congregational Union in 1852. See DNB.

The extract is taken from *New College, London: The Introductory Lectures at the Opening of the College, October 1851*, London, 1851, pp. 31–5. It reveals that Harris, a representative figure in his denomination, did not believe in verbal inspiration, let alone the idea that the Bible was dictated to its human authors. Like most Evangelical Nonconformists of his time, he was no Fundamentalist. See D. W. Bebbington, *Evangelicalism in Modern Britain: A History from the 1730s to the 1980s*, London, 1989, pp. 86–91.

Do the Scriptures themselves affirm that inspiration uniformly relates, not merely to the thought, but that it extends to the language in which the thought is expressed, in this sense, that all the previous knowledge which the writers possessed of their own language was entirely superseded, and that the very words and phrases which would otherwise have spontaneously embodied the same thoughts, were supplied to them immediately by the Holy Spirit?

Now, we not only freely but gratefully acknowledge, and earnestly contend, that, in certain instances, distinctly specified in the Bible, verbal inspiration is represented as taking place. ...

But the sacred writers nowhere claim for themselves immediate and universal verbal inspiration, in the sense we have described. ...

Miracle was not lavished. The supernatural never interposed and displaced the natural, except as a means to an end; and the end was attained, in this particular, without verbal infusion. The Divine did not supersede the human, but appropriated and guided it. The individuality of the man – as expressed in his vocabulary, mental associations, range of knowledge, and general dispositions – remained, and moved with conscious freedom, under the eye of the Divine Agent. That eye was never withdrawn. Its watchfulness is evident in the presence of what may be called a *scriptural* style – a character resulting from the *selection* and the *proportion* of subjects, and from the absence of everything inappropriate in the treatment of them – pervading the canonical books in general, so as to distinguish them from all other books. But this superintendence left the sacred writers the free use of their human faculties and characteristics.

Document II.31

T. T. Lynch on the *Rivulet* Controversy of 1855–57

Thomas Toke Lynch (1818–71), a London Congregational minister, published in 1855 *Hymns for Heart and Voice: The Rivulet*. The collection was attacked for containing signs of German pantheism; prominent ministers defended it; *The British Banner* sustained the assault; and it was only after a special January meeting of the Congregational Union assembly that the controversy was settled in 1857. See A. Peel, *These Hundred Years: A History of the Congregational Union of England and Wales, 1831–1931*, London, 1931, pp. 221–34; and DNB.

Lynch's personal hurt at the original censure in *The Morning Advertiser* is evident in the extract; so is the advancing spirit of freedom of enquiry and hostility to creeds that he believed he championed. It is taken from W. White, ed., *Memoir of Thomas T. Lynch*, London, 1874, pp. 132–3, 187–9.

I went into the office of the *Advertiser* and bought a copy of 'yesterday's paper.' On getting home, as a sort of dessert at dinner-time, we read domestically the following information about the 'good man of the house:' – That he had published a book in which, 'from beginning to end, there was not one particle of vital religion or evangelical piety;' that 'nearly the whole of his hymns might have been written by a Deist, and a very large portion might be sung by a congregation of Freethinkers;' that it was a 'painful fact he should preach twice every Sunday' as an avowed 'minister of the gospel,' being the Author of this 'spiritually dead and dreary book;' and that he had 'palmed off' his hymns as 'Christian,' when they were merely 'endeavours to look through nature up to Nature's God,' such endeavours being, even if the hymns were no more, at least *possibly; very* Christian. Here was an attack upon book and minister not gratifying. ...

When people call you Christless, they often mean no more than that you are creedless, and creedless only in the sense of not accepting all their phrases about truths as full and final, though perhaps you understand and revere and obey these truths far more than your accusers. Christ is the Truth, and he that loves the Truth loves truths. There is no fear that we shall be indifferent to truths, if we be thoughtful lovers of Christ Jesus. But the love of creeds is not the love of truths; it is the proud antagonist of that higher love. What think ye of Christ? Sirs, ye will not let us think of Christ; as soon as we tell you a little of our thought ye strike us on the mouth. Reader, we must guard the liberty of the learner, and that we shall the most certainly do if we ourselves have learned Christ in the exercise of our own liberty. I do not myself ask tolerance from the orthodox, as if I were only in an early stage of thinking, not knowing as yet unto what principal convictions my thoughts would grow. I know in whom I have believed, and my belief, thank God, is grounded and rooted, and thereupon are both buds and fruits. But I affirm it to be my right and duty to shield the liberty of inquirers, and to encourage its exertion.

Document II.32

J. Howard Hinton's Critique of J. Baldwin Brown's *The Divine Life in Man*, 1860

James Baldwin Brown (1820–84) was an early graduate of London University and from 1843 minister of Claylands Independent Chapel, London, which moved to the suburbs in 1870 as Brixton Independent Church. Deeply influenced by romantic – in the broadest sense – currents of thought, he became the leading liberal theologian in Congregationalism. John Howard Hinton (1791–1873), a patriarchal Baptist leader who was minister of the Devonshire Square Church and secretary of the Baptist Union, criticised Baldwin Brown's *The Divine Life in Man* (1859) as a break with Evangelical Calvinism. The episode represents the beginning of the theological divergence between the Congregationalists, who tended to take a more liberal path, and the Baptists, who remained more doctrinally conservative. For Baldwin Brown, see Elizabeth Baldwin Brown, ed., *In Memoriam: James Baldwin Brown*, London, 1884; M. Hopkins, *Nonconformity's Romantic Generation: Evangelical and Liberal Theologies in Victorian England*, Carlisle, 2004, chap. 2; and DNB. For Howard Hinton, see *The Theological Works of the Rev. John Howard Hinton, M.A.*, 7 vols, London, 1864–67; I. Sellers, 'John Howard Hinton, Theologian', *Baptist Quarterly*, 33 (1989), pp. 119–32; and DNB.

The extract is taken from J. H. Hinton, 'Strictures on Some Passages in the Rev. J. B. Brown's "Divine Life in Man"', *The Baptist Magazine*, March 1860, pp. 134–7. Hinton first quotes a passage that he saw as raising the fundamental question at issue: Baldwin Brown was dropping the insistence on the role of God as governor that Hinton had learned from Andrew Fuller. For Hinton, the fatherhood of God had eclipsed his sovereignty.

'The attempt to establish a fundamental distinction between a father's government and a ruler's,' says Mr. Brown, 'has done much mischief, and for a century and a half has exercised a most debasing influence on theology. The idea that, as a father, God sustains one set of relations to men, and as the ruler of the universe another – that the key to certain manifestations is to be found in his love, while others can only be explained by his justice – could only satisfy an age in which the real foundations both of divine and human order were obscured.' – P. 26. ...

An habitual regard to this distinction would not only be useful in the understanding of Scripture; it would also be an important aid in theological controversy. In opposition to what I believe to be the scriptural doctrine of atonement for sin, no argument is more promptly or more confidently adduced than the incongruity of such a fact with God's parental relation to mankind. Now, for my own part, I entirely admit this alleged incongruity, and, if I believed that God held to mankind no other than a paternal relation, I would at once abandon my present views of the atonement; I have, however, no such belief. I affirm, on the contrary, that, besides being a father, God is also a moral governor; and on this relation I base the doctrine of the atonement. To me, consequently, it is no argument at all to say that such a doctrine is incongruous with the fatherhood; the real question to be discussed with me is, whether God is, or is not, a moral governor – a question, let me be permitted to say, which would be more convincingly treated by a little sound reasoning, than by a curt denunciation.

Document II.33

James Wells and William Bidder on the Eternal Sonship of Christ, 1860

In 1859 J. C. Philpot (see IV.23) wrote three articles in *The Gospel Standard* maintaining the eternal Sonship of Christ or eternal generation. An acrimonious controversy ensued, chiefly surrounding the term 'eternal generation'. James Wells, the provocative high Calvinist Baptist minister of the Surrey Tabernacle, Southwark, entered the field against Philpot in October 1860 with the first of four letters in *The Earthen Vessel* written under the pseudonym 'A Little One'. The editor, C. W. Banks (see IV.9), believed the truth to lie with Philpot rather than with his friend Wells, but allowed further articles to appear, believing debate would do good. He also requested William Bidder, another London minister, to respond to Wells. The controversy quickly died down, but was to have serious repercussions among Strict Baptists when it was revived in the twentieth century. See K. Dix, *Strict and Particular: English Strict and Particular Baptists in the Nineteenth Century*, Didcot, Oxfordshire, 2001, pp. 93–6.

The first extract (a) is from Wells's opening letter in *The Earthen Vessel*, October 1860, p. 258; the second extract (b) is from Bidder's answer in *The Earthen Vessel*, December 1860, pp. 301–2.

(a)
There is, among even good men, *serious and real* difference of sentiment relative to this vital subject [the Sonship of the Saviour]. The difference is *not* a difference of mere words; there is a *real difference* between the meaning of those who place the Sonship of the Saviour in his divinity, independent altogether of his humanity, and those who place his Sonship in his complexity. They both hold it is true, that Christ is properly, underivedly and essentially God. Yet, while both hold fast this great truth, there is, nevertheless, a most *serious* difference in the two opposite sentiments; but as both avow the co-equal Godhead of Christ, with the Father and the Holy Spirit, the one ought not to charge the other with any *intentional* derogation from the dignity of his Person, but that there is a real and serious difference between the two is clear, the one holding that Christ is by nature, as God considered the Son of God; that the three divine Persons are properly, essentially, and of necessity Father, Son, and Holy Spirit; the other sentiment teaching, that God is a Father not by nature or necessity, but by choice, and by creative act; that Christ is a Son, not by nature as God, or of necessity, but by choosing to take human nature, and so becoming a complete Person; and that the Holy Spirit is called the Holy Spirit, not so much to denote what he is by nature, as to denote what he is in his life-giving and sanctifying work in the souls of men. ...

... there is, as I have said, a real difference between these two opposite doctrines – concerning the Sonship of the Saviour; just look at it; the one doctrine teaches that the Father is a father by nature, and of course, co-eval with his existence; the other doctrine teaches, that when taken in a gospel sense, that he chose to be by covenant relationship that which he was not by nature, or of necessity. Again one doctrine teaches that Christ, independent of his human nature, is as God, also the Son of God, begotten by the Father from all eternity, yet self-existent; the other doctrine teaches that he is no more the Son of God apart from his complexity, than the Father is the Son of God.

(b)
Now he [Wells] must know, or he ought to know, that such advocates believe no such thing as that the Divine essence is, or was, begotten; nor do they dare think so – much less say so. They believe that God the Son, as a Person, subsisting in that essence, was eternally begotten of the Father; not made or created, but begotten, and in the same nature in which he is God. And there being nothing in the Divine nature, but what is eternal – then this generation must be eternal generation; a phrase which is no more a contradiction than a Trinity in Unity ... One would suppose that common sense might dictate to the people that an everlasting Father supposes and proclaims an everlasting Son; and that the one could not possibly be without the other: and that they both co-eternally exist together without being or ending; for what is eternal is devoid of commencing or cessation.

Document II.34

Leicester Conference on the Terms of Religious Communion, 1877

On 16 October 1877 at Wycliffe Congregational Church, Leicester, there was held a conference designed for those who held that theological opinion was no bar to religious communion. The occasion was a celebration of anti-credalism. It was the week of the Congregational Union's autumn assembly in the town, and so the event created alarm – represented by some of the cries of dissent in the following extract – lest Congregationalism should be seen to identify itself with the toleration of non-Evangelical faith. The spring assembly in the following year overwhelmingly reaffirmed the adhesion of the Union to Evangelical doctrines. See M. D. Johnson, 'Thomas Gasquoine and the Origins of the Leicester Conference', *Journal of the United Reformed Church History Society*, 2 (1982), pp. 345–53 and M. Hopkins, *Nonconformity's Romantic Generation: Evangelical and Liberal Theologies in Victorian England*, Carlisle, 2004, chap. 4.

The extract is taken from the *Report of the Conference on the Terms of Religious Communion*, London, 1878, pp. 15–16. The speech is by Joseph Wood, a Leicester Congregational minister and secretary of the organising committee, in response to a question from Henry Allon (see IV.24): could they all worship Jesus Christ? The reply makes plain that Wood respected eminent Unitarians such as the men he named and wanted to end barriers to fellowship with them.

I take up this position. For my own part, I can hold communion with a man who does not worship Jesus Christ, if he has the life of goodness within him – ('oh, oh!') – which I conceive such a man has. Will you tell me that a man like Dr. Channing had not the life of goodness in him? ('Hear, hear,' and applause.) If you do, of course it is not possible for me to believe you. If you tell me that many other men – like Dr. Martineau, the Rev. J. J. Tayler, and other men I might mention – have not the life of goodness in them, and real spiritual goodness and Christlikeness, such as can be found in the members of our evangelical Churches – if you tell me so, it appears to me that you are blind to the fact. (A voice: 'We do not.') I say I can hold religious communion with these men, for they manifest a Christlike life and spirit – a life of spiritual goodness. I can sit down with them to the Lord's table; I can go into their pulpits and preach, and they can come into my pulpit and preach; I can join them in any common work which has for its end the advancement of the cause of righteousness and the kingdom of God. I feel personally no difficulty in that, and one reason why we are met together is to give that idea a public platform, to see how far there is any feeling in favour of it. It appears to some of us that there is a feeling in that direction, that it is possible to hold communion with persons who differ as widely as Unitarians differ from Evangelicals. ('No, no.') If not, then there is an end of it as far as you are concerned. We who say yes intend to go on – (applause) – and to show to the best of our ability that it is practicable. I will try and give the best answer I can to Dr. Allon's question. This is the position that we take up, that neither circumcision nor uncircumcision, neither belief in the Trinity, nor the acceptance of the physical resurrection of Christ, nor the opinion that these things are essential to religious life, is essential to spiritual communion as far as we are concerned. You may deem them essential to your life; but cannot we who differ yet meet, because we both have the same life, because we both rejoice in a common spirit? We think it is an admirable thing that men should meet who thus widely differ from each other.

Document II.35

Samuel Cox on the Larger Hope, 1877

Samuel Cox (1826–93) was a scholarly Baptist minister who served at Southsea, Ryde (Isle of Wight) and Mansfield Road, Nottingham. From 1875 he was editor of *The Expositor*, but in 1884 resigned rather than undertake to exclude allusions to the larger hope – that is, universalism. He had expounded his case for this position in *Salvator Mundi* (1877), arguing from scripture and the assumption that punishment should be reformatory. See memoir by his widow in S. Cox, *The Hebrew Twins*, London, 1894; G. Rowell, *Hell and the Victorians*, Oxford, 1974, pp. 131–3; and DNB.

The extract is taken from S. Cox, *Salvator Mundi*, 2nd edn, London, 1878, pp. 191–3.

Now is it not well nigh impossible to gather these passages together from the Old Testament and the New, to listen to this 'pure concent' of the Hebrew Prophets and the Christian Apostles with the direct words of Jehovah and of Christ, without being convinced that the doctrine of an universal redemption and restitution, however long we may have overlooked it, is interwoven with the very texture of Holy Writ and pervades it from end to end? And how is the eternal purpose of the unchangeable God to be accomplished if there be no possibilities of salvation beyond the grave, when it is only too certain that many pass out of this life loving darkness rather than light, many more to whom the good news of Redemption have never been either adequately or attractively presented, and most of all who have never so much as heard the joyful sound?

I am not mindful of the fact that he who so searches the Scriptures as to find this happy prospect of eternal life for all men in them, will also find many passages which denounce the wrath of God against all unrighteousness of men, which threaten the wicked with the terrors of judgment, with death, and with being destroyed from the presence of the Lord and the glory of his power. We have examined many of these passages, and have ascertained what they mean. It is no part of our argument that wrath and judgment and punishment are not to be elements of the life to come. Rather we affirm, and rejoice to affirm, that in every age and in every world unrighteousness must be hateful to God; and that so long as men cleave to it, and refuse to submit themselves to the righteousness of God, they must be searched through and through with unspeakable miseries. We admit that if men pass out of this age unrighteous and impenitent, they must be banished from the presence and glory of God in the age to come, must pass through the pangs of death before they can be born again into life. But we ask why death, judgment, punishment should change their nature and function the very moment we pass from this æon, or life, into the next? They are remedial and corrective here; why should they be uncorrective and merely punitive hereafter? On the authority of the New Testament itself we maintain that God is the Father of the spirits of all flesh, and that He can never chasten us save for our profit. Nay, more, on the authority both of the Hebrew Prophets and of the Christian Apostles we maintain that this law of the Divine punishments holds in the world to come no less than in the present world, since their visions of future judgment are almost invariably followed by visions of a redemption which is to extend to all nations and to cover the whole earth. And this conclusion is sustained by our Lord Himself in those memorable passages in which He speaks of the unrighteous as going away from his bar into 'an age-long pruning,' and affirms that 'every one shall be *salted* with fire,' *i.e.*, saved by it.

Document II.36

Charles Beard on the Person of Christ, 1881

Charles Beard (1827–88) was a graduate of London University who became minister of Hyde Chapel, Cheshire, and, from 1867, of Renshaw Street Chapel, Liverpool (see DNB). In 1881 he was one of a group of lecturers on the 'positive aspects of Unitarian thought and doctrine'; his topic was Christology. While repudiating Evangelicalism, he strives, as the capital letters at the end of the extract illustrate, for as high a doctrine as he can manage.

The extract is taken from Charles Beard, 'Jesus Christ', in *Unitarian Christianity*, 4th edn, London, n.d., pp. 138–41.

We shall again do something to define our characteristic attitude to Christ, if we ask and answer the question, Does the centre of gravity of the Christian system lie in his life or in his death? in the charm of his character and the wisdom of his teachings, or in the interpretation put by Apostles and Evangelists on his cross and his resurrection? For it remains a fact that it is very difficult to find any trace of what are called the peculiar doctrines of the gospel in Christ's own words; and that if Paul's Epistles had never been written, and the world had been left to the sole instruction of the Evangelists, what is called Evangelical Christianity would never have existed. The doctrine of the Atonement and that of the Deity of Christ are more closely associated than may always have been seen at first sight: it was not without a meaning that Anselm laid down those lines of the vicarious sacrifice, which so many centuries accepted, in a treatise on the Incarnation – *Cur Deus Homo* – Why was God made man? Both conceptions belong to the same order of ideas: the logical necessities of the Atonement demand the God-man. From this point of view, then, Christ's appearance upon earth is a divine transaction, the fulfilment of a plan conceived in the secrecy of the Eternal Councils before time was. ... Whereas, on the other hand, if you leave on one side the anger of God, the wiles of the devil, the flames of the pit, the universal depravity of man, as figments of the theological imagination, you may conceive of Christ's life as simply, naturally, beautifully human. ... I claim this life in all its strength, its beauty, its symmetry, for humanity: without it, my conception of what humanity is and may be would be maimed and incomplete. I cannot consent to make it a mere factor in a divine transaction; I want to feel its inspiring, soothing, liberating influence on my soul. And that cannot be if I am to conceive of Christ as a mysterious being, altogether without parallel in the world's history: in whom was a side of strength to which nothing that is in me presents any analogy: who, while mortal, was immortal; while ignorant, was omniscient; while confined within the bounds of a human personality, was the Omnipresent, the Omnipotent, the Infinite, the Absolute. My sorest need is for the strong, bright, beautiful Son of Man.

Document II.37

C. H. Spurgeon on the Down Grade, 1887

Spurgeon (see I.4) enjoyed by far the greatest prestige of any Baptist minister and so there was a crisis when, in 1887, he criticised the Baptist Union for tolerating heresy in its ranks. One of the former students of his college had written two anonymous articles in his church magazine, *The Sword and the Trowel*, alleging that the theological decline of Dissent during the eighteenth century was being replicated in the nineteenth. Spurgeon took up the same issue, charging that there was a contemporary 'Down Grade'. Spurgeon left the Union, but, having drawn up a declaration of faith in 1888 (see II.9), it retained the loyalty of most of its adherents. See E. A. Payne, *The Baptist Union*, London, 1959, pp. 127–43; *idem*, 'The Down Grade Controversy: A Postscript', *Baptist Quarterly*, 28 (1979), pp. 146–58; M. T. E. Hopkins, 'Spurgeon's Opponents in the Down Grade Controversy', *Baptist Quarterly*, 33 (1988), pp. 274–94; *idem*, 'The Down Grade Controversy: New Evidence', *Baptist Quarterly*, 35 (1994), pp. 262–78 and *idem*, *Nonconformity's Romantic Generation: Evangelical Theologies in Victorian England*, Carlisle, 2004, chap. 7.

The extract is taken from C. H. Spurgeon, 'Another Word concerning the Down Grade', *The Sword and the Trowel*, August 1887, pp. 397–8. It is clear that Spurgeon was concerned by the general state of Nonconformity as evidenced by its worldliness as well as by its doctrinal declension.

No lover of the gospel can conceal from himself the fact that the days are evil. We are willing to make a large discount from our apprehensions on the score of natural timidity, the caution of age, and the weakness produced by pain; but yet our solemn conviction is that things are much worse in many churches than they seem to be, and are rapidly tending downward. Read those newspapers which represent the Broad School of Dissent, and ask yourself, How much farther could they go? What doctrine remains to be abandoned? What other truth to be the object of contempt? A new religion has been initiated, which is no more Christianity than chalk is cheese; and this religion, being destitute of moral honesty, palms itself off as the old faith with slight improvements, and on this plea usurps pulpits which were erected for gospel preaching. The Atonement is scouted, the inspiration of Scripture is derided, the Holy Spirit is degraded into an influence, the punishment of sin is turned into fiction, and the resurrection into a myth, and yet these enemies of our faith expect us to call them brethren, and maintain a confederacy with them!

At the back of doctrinal falsehood comes a natural decline of spiritual life, evidenced by a taste for questionable amusements, and a weariness of devotional meetings. At a certain meeting of ministers and church-officers, one after another doubted the value of prayer-meetings; all confessed that they had a very small attendance, and several acknowledged without the slightest compunction that they had quite given them up. ...

As for questionable amusements – time was when a Nonconformist minister who was known to attend the play-house would soon have found himself without a church. And justly so; for no man can long possess the confidence, even of the most worldly, who is known to be a haunter of theatres. Yet at the present time it is matter of notoriety that preachers of no mean repute defend the play-house, and do so because they have been seen there. Is it any wonder that church members forget their vows of consecration, and run with the unholy in the ways of frivolity, when they hear that persons are tolerated in the pastorate who do the same?

Document II.38

R. F. Horton on Inspiration, 1888

In 1888 R. F. Horton (see I.10) published a book entitled *Inspiration and the Bible*. Designed to communicate recent biblical scholarship, it provoked great antagonism for apparently denigrating the scriptures. Even an aunt of Horton's ceased to attend his ministry. The episode was an instance of the friction surrounding the acceptance of the higher criticism in the churches. See W. B. Glover, *Evangelical Nonconformists and Higher Criticism in the Nineteenth Century*, London, 1954, pp. 176–84.

The extract is taken from R. F. Horton, *Inspiration and the Bible*, London, 1888, pp. 235–40.

Two or three conclusions may be stated with some distinctness. First of all, we may say that *the writers of the Bible are all subject to certain limitations of culture and knowledge imposed by the age in which they lived*; thus frequently the widening view of the later writer may correct the narrower view of the earlier, and even the views of the latest writers remain subject to the revision of subsequent experience; of this last observation the readiest example is the general expectation of the Apostolic age, expressed so vividly in the Revelation, that the second coming of Christ was quite near at hand. It follows, of course, that a principle of conduct, though it be prefaced by an imposing 'Thus saith the Lord,' is not to be taken at once as applicable to our life, authoritative as an absolute ethical law everywhere and at all times; but it must be examined in the light of after revelations and after experience; and generally, only that which is in accordance with the spirit of our Lord Jesus Christ can be ultimately accepted as valid. This is all contained germinally in our Lord's own simple statements when He drew into parallel lines of contrast what was 'said to them of old time' and what He Himself says unto us.

Then, again, we may say that *historical writings in the Bible are by no means guaranteed against error*; in fact the Bible itself, by furnishing us in almost all cases with more than one account of the same transactions, implicitly warns us against the idea that they are. In this point of course our desire for certainty inclines us to demand that there should be infallibility, and our eager dogmatism therefore hastens to maintain that there is; but it is beyond question that infallibility there is not. ...

Perhaps one other conclusion may be stated: *that the traditional authorship of the several Books of the Bible is by no means to be relied upon*, because frequently writings would cluster round the nucleus formed by a great name, and would ultimately all be treated as if they came from the one pen ...

At the outset we attempted to frame a provisional definition of what we must mean by inspiration. At the close it may be worth while to reconsider this definition. *We call our Bible inspired, because by reading it and studying it we can find our way to God, we can find what is His will for us and how we are to carry out His will.*

Document II.39

John Clifford on the Social Gospel, 1888

John Clifford (1836–1923) was the outstanding General Baptist minister of the later nineteenth century. Serving at Praed Street, Paddington, he moved the congregation to larger premises in Westbourne Park in 1877. He was president of the Baptist Union twice, in 1888 and 1899, and first president of the Baptist World Alliance, 1905–11. Clifford led the Nonconformist passive resistance to the Education Act of 1902. With Hugh Price Hughes (see I.9), he was the chief English exponent of the social gospel. His address as president to the Baptist Union assembly in 1888, entitled 'The New City of God; or the Primitive Christian Faith as a Social Gospel', shows that his Evangelicalism was entirely compatible with a passion for social betterment. See J. Marchant, *John Clifford, C.H.*, London, 1924; D. M. Thompson, 'John Clifford's Social Gospel', *Baptist Quarterly*, 31 (1986), pp. 199–217; and DNB.

The extract is taken from *The Baptist Handbook*, 1889, pp. 68–9.

All social problems are spiritual at heart, pierce to the throbbing nerve of souls, concern shattered ambitions and broken hearts, defeated energies and maimed lives, wasted efforts and blighted hopes, starving children and crushed old age, agonised women learning at death's door how they should have lived; men educated in theft as if it were an accomplishment, and trained in vice as the readiest means of living; bitter despairs breeding weakness and wickedness and keen miseries that make darkness more welcome than light, and the grave the only gospel of rest. Are not these the things of the spirit? Do not the sorrows and sins, anxieties and agonies born of the monopoly of land, the exactions of landlords, the huddling of large families in town and city, the fierce race for riches – do they not carry us, if the heart of the Saviour and fried of the poor be not dead within us, to the very sanctuary of souls, to the throne of the Holy Ghost, and to the unspeakably sweet and welcome consolations of the Spirit of Jesus? For us there are no exclusively material problems. Man *is* spirit and has the world, as he has his body, as his dwelling place and school house, tool box and temple; and in the degree in which our aims are completely human, and directed to the absolute and universal best, we shall find our divinest duties in unravelling the tangled skein of life, helping to a juster distribution of the natural and appointed rewards of industry, abolishing the depraving and destructive fierceness of competition, lessening poverty so that it may only exist as the just punishment of indolence and guilty incapacity, drying up the sources of social vice, substituting wise and sustained personal sympathy for spasms of 'charity,' creating decent, chaste and comfort-bringing homes in the place of huts that generate impurity, and make the healing courtesies of life impossible; and thereby we shall authorise again the forcible reply to those who question the validity of our mission, 'Go your way, and tell John the things which ye do hear and see: the blind receive their sight, and the lame walk, the lepers are cleansed, and the deaf hear, and the dead are raised up, and the poor have good tidings preached to them. And blessed is he who shall find none occasion of stumbling in Me.' There is no true service of God that is not a service of man. The New City of God is, and must be, the city of the new man.

Document II.40

D. W. Simon on Congregational Thought, 1891

David Worthington Simon (1830–1909) was unusual among English Nonconformists in having a thorough acquaintance with the theology of Germany as a result of spending many years there. He acted as principal successively of the Spring Hill (from 1869), Edinburgh (from 1884) and Bradford (from 1893) Congregational Colleges. He encouraged serious theological study and produced ministers of independent mind. His chief work, *Reconciliation by Incarnation* (1898), is an instance of the general late nineteenth-century intellectual trend to focus more on the incarnation than on the atonement. See F. J. Powicke, *David Worthington Simon*, London, 1912.

In 1891 Simon delivered an acute analysis of recent developments in denominational thought at the first International Congregational Council meetings in London. The extract is taken from *The International Congregational Council, London, 1891*, London, 1891, pp. 77–8. Pye Smith (see III.9), Payne (see III.1) and their contemporaries upheld the position represented in this volume by Edward Williams (see II.12).

The first thing that calls for notice is the pronounced and widespread distaste, not to say aversion or hostility to the theological or scientific treatment of Christian truth. ... The theological tone of our colleges is, I believe, higher than it ever was, but the anti-theological and falsely practical current outside is to strong that even the best students have difficulty in stemming it – the majority prefer to float with it.

It is scarcely necessary for me to adduce specific facts in support of the statements I have made; but I will mention three: First, that during the last thirty-five years only one 'Systematic Theology' has been published by British Congregationalists; that out of some 600 registered Congregational publications during, say, twenty-five years, scarcely 50 are scientifically theological; and that out of upwards of 450 discourses by Congregational ministers printed during the last five years or thereabouts in *The Christian World Pulpit*, scarcely thirty were properly doctrinal. ...

But it is time I turned to what is decidedly the more important part of my theme – namely, the attitude of Congregationalists towards the subject-matter of theology. Thirty-five years ago the field was held by Moderate Calvinism of the type expounded by Pye-Smith, Payne, Wardlaw, and last, not least, Lindsay Alexander – a system, so far as it deserves the name, which had slowly supplanted what it was not unusual, forty years ago, to speak of as 'the mighty inheritance received from Howe and Charnock' – the so-called 'Puritan theology.' Since then our theological thought has been passing through a process of disintegration, in the course of which some doctrines have been dropped, others modified, others transmuted. The impulse under which we have acted, however, has been only to a slight extent spontaneous; it originated in and has been guided partly by ideas flowing directly from Germany, partly by the writings of Coleridge, McLeod Campbell, Maurice, Bushnell, Carlyle, Tennyson, and Robertson, and partly by a changing evangelical consciousness. Allowing for the relative instinctiveness of our theological thinking – for, like our nation generally, we are only too indifferent to philosophical or even logical consistency – I might generalise on the movement as follows. Something like the third of a century ago theocentric Calvinism practically had passed over into soteriological moderate Calvinism with its two co-ordinate foci, the Divinity and the atonement of Christ; since then we have been and still are working our way towards a Christocentric system, or perhaps, to speak more exactly, towards one with the two foci of the Fatherhood of God and the Living Personality of Christ.

PART III

WRITINGS

Introduction

The nineteenth century witnessed an explosion of religious publishing. Much of it is illustrated in other parts of this volume – a popular work encouraging conversion at V.7, a missionary report at VIII.11 and so on – but some particular genres not covered elsewhere are included here. Philosophy was a field in which Nonconformists were much less innovative than in the previous century, but it remained important to them, especially in their training for the ministry. Evangelicals in general adopted the common sense school of philosophy pioneered by Thomas Reid and popularised by Dugald Stewart. It meshed readily with their theology, as is illustrated in III.1, where it is deployed to vindicate revelation. The place of the Bible in the scheme of things is commended in an altogether more light-hearted way in III.3. There is scholastic reasoning of a kind that harks back to Aquinas in III.2; and Kant is invoked as an exponent of the moral argument for the existence of God in the popular apologetic of III.5. Much writing was concerned with the borderland between theology and natural philosophy – what today would be called science – and can properly be labelled natural theology. It is exemplified in III.8 and III.9. The apparent threat to Christian belief from evolutionary theory was met with remarkable confidence within the framework of natural theology (III.10, 11). Social Darwinism also seemed acceptable, at least to some (III.7). The self-assured intellectual posture of Nonconformity is apparent in the attitude to the philosophers of the age (III.4) and the arrival of its representatives in the University of Oxford (III.6).

The miscellaneous writings covered here include a defence of Dissenting principles (III.12; see also X.18), a claim that those principles, when thoroughly followed out, led to a Unitarian position (III.14) and a critique of Evangelical phraseology by an insider (III.13). The outpouring of periodical literature (see also III.4, 13, IV.9; IV.13, 23) is illustrated from the Unitarians (III.15), Evangelical Nonconformity in general (III.16) and progressive Methodists (III.17). There are fictional portrayals of Nonconformity written by outsiders (III.18, 19), insiders (III.20, 22) and an insider who became an outsider (III.21).

There is discussion of Nonconformist philosophical opinion in A. P. F. Sell, *Philosophy, Dissent and Nonconformity*, Cambridge, 2004. Natural theology is ably covered in J. H. Brooke, *Science and Religion: Some Historical Perspectives*, Cambridge, 1991. The fictional treatment of Nonconformity is equally ably analysed in V. Cunningham, *Everywhere Spoken Against: Dissent in the Victorian Novel*, Oxford, 1975.

Philosophy and Apologetic

Document III.1

George Payne on Reason in Religion, 1828

George Payne (1781–1848) was a graduate of the University of Glasgow who showed metaphysical ability in the Scottish school of common sense philosophy. Having served as minister in Edinburgh and as co-secretary of the Congregational Union of Scotland at its inception in 1812, he went on to be president of Blackburn Academy (from 1823) and of the Western Academy (from 1829). See DNB.

The extract is taken from Payne's chief work, *Elements of Mental and Moral Science*, London, 1828, pp. 523–7. His debt to the Scottish Enlightenment is evident in his defence of the role of reason in expounding natural theology and in establishing the credentials of scripture. His thought was parallel to that of Thomas Chalmers, the Evangelical leader in the Church of Scotland, from whom he quotes.

We know nothing of God but what he has revealed to us; that Revelation, then, must be the standard of Rectitude, by exhibiting to us his perfect and glorious nature. The inquiry which presents itself, then, is, 'Where is this revelation to be found?' To this question, I answer,

First, in the material creation. 'The heavens declare the glory of God.' ... We sometimes hear it asserted, that the works of nature do not teach any thing of God – and that reason has nothing to do in matters of religion. It may be possible, perhaps, to attach a meaning to the latter assertion, against which no great exception can be taken; yet it is often ignorantly made, and is adapted to lead into very great and deplorable mistakes. The words, understood in their obvious sense, are so far from being true, that it is by the aid of reason we arrive at the knowledge of the fundamental truth of all religion, *viz.* the Divine Existence. We see marks of contrivance in the universe; we immediately conclude that there must have been a contriver. But this is a deduction of reason. Discard the use of reason, and we shall be constrained to surrender our confidence in the being of a God. Should it be said, in reply, that the existence of God is affirmed in his word; I would ask, how we know that this word merits our confidence – that it is the word of God – that the Scriptures were, indeed, given by inspiration of God? Is it not by the aid of reason? Should it be further said, that the character of Jehovah, as drawn by the inspired penmen, approves itself to us, as being a true description of Him in whom we live and move; and thus establishes the Divinity of the Bible; I admit the truth of the remark, while I ask, if it be not to our reason, that this character approves itself. Let us, then, be careful not to misunderstand the statement, that reason has nothing to do in matters of religion. If we are determined to extinguish the light of nature – or rather to affirm that there is no such thing – to place no confidence in the decisions of reason,

Writings

we must surrender our faith in divine revelation, admit that we are left without any moral guide whatever, and abandon ourselves to an universal scepticism. ...

Secondly, ... we must seek for a revelation of God in the Scriptures of truth. ... Having examined the claims of the Bible to be a revelation from God; having subjected the evidence by which this important fact is sought to be established, to the test of those rules by which the value and credibility of evidence is, in all cases, tried, and found it to be sufficient and convincing; I agree with Dr. Chalmers in thinking, that the question then is, 'not, What thinkest thou? but, How readest thou?' I am disposed to concede that the apparent reasonableness, or unreasonabless, of any doctrine which is manifestly revealed, does not supply a legitimate ground either of reception or rejection. I would grant to the Roman Catholic that we are not justified in rejecting the doctrine of transubstantiation itself, on the ground of its apparent absurdity. The exclusive inquiry concerning this, and every other sentiment, ought to be the following – Is it the doctrine of Scripture? If that be the case, it must be true. I would not, however, be understood as affirming that reason is to be totally excluded here; since it is only by the upright use of this faculty that we can ascertain the meaning of Scripture. All that is intended is, that the divine authority of the Bible being established, the sole office of reason is to ascertain the meaning of its communications; and not to sit in judgment upon the reasonableness of those doctrines which are clearly shewn to constitute integral parts of that communication.

Document III.2

Adam Clarke on the Being of God, 1829

For Adam Clarke, see I.2. The extract (remarkably) is taken from a sermon on Hebrews 11: 6 called 'Some Observations on the Being and Providence of a God', printed in Clarke's *Discourses on Various Subjects*, vol. 2, London, 1829, pp. 374–5. The giving of weight to abstract reasoning (*a priori*) for the existence of God in scholastic manner is unusual for the period, though, after six more reasons of this kind, Clarke goes on to offer evidence from creation (*a posteriori*).

Metaphysicians and philosophers, in order to prove the existence of God, have used two modes of argumentation:–

A priori, proofs drawn from the necessity that such a Being as God is, must exist: arguments of this kind do not produce any thing in evidence which is *derived* from His works.

A posteriori, proofs of the being and perfections of God drawn from His own works.

Propositions à Priori.

Prop. I. – If there be no one being in the universe but such as might possibly *not have existed*, it would follow, that there might possibly have been *no existence* at all: and if that could be so, it would be also possible that the present existence might have arisen from total *non-existence*, which is absurd. Therefore, it is not possible that there might have been no existence at all. Consequently, an impossibility of not existing must be found somewhere; there must have been a Being whose non-existence is impossible.

II. – The *whole nature* of an unoriginated Being, or *aggregate* of His attributes, must be *unoriginated*, and necessarily what it is. A being cannot produce its own attributes; for this would suppose it acted before it existed. There is nothing in the nature of this Being that is *contingent*, or could have been *otherwise* than it is; for whatever is *contingent* must have a cause to determine its mode of existence.

III. – The attributes of an unoriginated Being must be possessed by it *unlimitedly*; for, to possess an attribute *imperfectly*, or only in a *certain degree*, must suppose some cause to have *modified* this Being so as to make Him incapable of having that attribute in any other than an *imperfect degree*. But no cause can be admitted in this case, because this is the First of all beings, and the cause of all things. Farther, an imperfect attribute, or any one that is not in its *highest degree*, must be capable of improvement by exercise and experience; which would imply that the unoriginated Being must be originally imperfect; and that He was deriving farther degrees of perfection from the exercise of His own powers, and acquaintance with His own works.

Document III.3

Henry Rogers from *The Eclipse of Faith*, 1852

Henry Rogers (1806–77) was a Congregational minister whose delicate throat prevented him from preaching so that he was able to devote himself to writing and (oddly) lecturing. He served at Highbury College from 1832, and, in parallel, was professor of English literature and language at University College, London, from 1836. From 1839 he was at Spring Hill College, Birmingham, and from 1858 president of Lancashire Independent College. See R. W. Dale, 'Biographical Sketch of Henry Rogers', in H. Rogers, *The Superhuman Origin of the Bible*, 8th edn, London, 1893; DNB; and A. P. F. Sell, 'Henry Rogers and the Eclipse of Faith', *Dissenting Thought and the Life of the Churches*, San Francisco, 1990.

The extract is taken from Rogers's most popular work, first published in 1852, *The Eclipse of Faith*, 5th edn, London, 1854, pp. 206–13. The book is a reply to the scepticism about historic Christianity in F. W. Newman's *Phases of Faith* (1850). In this passage, using the literary device of a dream, Rogers imagines that all copies of the Bible, together with every quotation from it in other works, had disappeared overnight. Deploying irony and wit in an oblique form of apologetic, he suggests the importance of divine revelation.

Never before had I had any adequate idea of the extent to which the Bible had moulded the intellectual and moral life of the last eighteen centuries, nor how intimately it had interfused itself with habits of thought and modes of expression;

nor how naturally and extensively its comprehensive imagery and language had been introduced into human writings, and most of all, where there had been most of genius. A vast portion of literature became instantly worthless, and was transformed into so much waste paper. It was almost impossible to look into any book of merit, and read ten pages together, without coming to some provoking erasures and mutilations, some 'hiatus valde deflendi,' which made whole passages perfectly unintelligible. Many of the sweetest passages of Shakespeare were converted into unmeaning nonsense, from the absence of those words which his own all but divine genius had appropriated from a still diviner source. As to Milton, he was nearly ruined, as might naturally be supposed. Walter Scott's novels were filled with perpetual *lacunæ*, I hoped it might be otherwise with the philosophers and so it was; but even here it was curious to see what strange ravages the visitation had wrought. Some of the most beautiful and comprehensive of Bacon's Aphorisms were reduced to enigmatical nonsense.

Those who held large stocks of books knew not what to do. Ruin stared them in the face; their value fell seventy or eighty per cent. All branches of theology, in particular, were a drug. One fellow said, that he should not so much have minded if the miracle had spunged out what was *human* as well as what was divine, for in that case he would at least have had so many thousand volumes of fair blank paper, which was as much as many of them were worth before. ...[m]any of our modern infidels gave an entirely new turn to the whole affair, by saying that the visitation was evidently not in judgment, but in mercy; that God in compassion, and not in indignation, had taken away a book which men had regarded with an extravagant admiration and idolatry, and which they had exalted to the place of that clear internal oracle which he had planted in the human breast; in a word, that if it was a rebuke at all, it was a rebuke to a rampant 'Bibliolatry.' As I heard all these different versions of so simple a matter, and found that not a few were inclined to each, I could not help exclaiming, 'In truth the devil is a very clever fellow, and man even a greater blockhead that I had taken him for.' But in spite of the surprise with which I had listened to these various explanations of an event which seemed to me clear as if written with a sunbeam, this *last* reason, which assigned as the cause of God's resumption of his own gift, an extravagant admiration and veneration of it on the part of mankind – it being so notorious that those who professed belief in its divine origin and authority had (even the best of them) so grievously neglected both the study and the practice of it – struck me as so exquisitely ludicrous that I broke into a fit of laughter, which awoke me. I found that it was broad daylight, and the morning sun was streaming in at the window, and shining in quiet radiance upon the open Bible which lay on my table. So strongly had my dream impressed me, that I almost felt as though, on inspection, I should find the sacred leaves a blank, and it was therefore with joy that my eyes rested on those words, which I read through grateful tears: 'The gifts of God are *without repentance.*'

Document III.4

The British Quarterly Review on J. S. Mill, 1860

The British Quarterly Review was launched in 1845 by Robert Vaughan (see VI.2) as a cultured vehicle of orthodox Dissenting opinion. Vaughan was succeeded as editor in 1866 by H. R. Reynolds (see DNB) and Henry Allon (see IV.24), who, after Reynolds retired in 1874, remained in charge until the periodical folded in 1886. *The British Quarterly* was the Evangelical Nonconformist equivalent of the great Victorian organs, *The Edinburgh Review*, *The Quarterly Review* and *The Westminster Review*. A. Peel, *Letters to a Victorian Editor*, London, 1929, contains Allon's editorial correspondence.

The extract is from the review of John Stuart Mill's classic *On Liberty* (1859) in *The British Quarterly Review*, January 1860, pp. 174–6. Although the anonymous reviewer does not penetrate to the premises of Mill's thought, he treats the philosopher as an equal.

[W]e shall, in this article, confine our criticisms for the most part to the chapter on 'Free Thought and Discussion.'

Mr. Mill seems to think that there is still a great deal to be done before we can be said fully to enjoy this inestimable right. We cannot agree with him. As far as legal penalties go, we are as free as any people can well be. For any remaining inconveniences which may attend the patron or champion of unpalatable or obnoxious opinions (not from the *hands*, for they are tied; but) from the looks or even tongues of his fellow-men, or from any other methods of showing aversion that cannot be recognised or repressed by law without greater social 'tyranny' than the law can ever cure, we do not flatter ourselves that Mr. Mill, or any one else, can devise a remedy; further, we doubt whether it would be good for the progress of truth (partly on Mr. Mill's own showing), if exemption from all such opposition could be secured for its champions. ... [I]t is quite true (and, we think, every day sufficiently confirms it) that there is practically, in this country the most unfettered freedom of discussion. We heartily wish indeed that every remnant of obsolete law which savours of forcible repression, may be abolished, if only for consistency's sake; but we cannot say that, practically, any serious let or hindrance is given to the most free (if only tolerably decent) discussion of any opinions, however paradoxical or obnoxious.

Document III.5

Thomas Cooper on the Moral Argument for God, 1875

Thomas Cooper (1805–92), after a time as a journalist and Wesleyan lay preacher, achieved fame as a Chartist and spent two years in prison for sedition. He subsequently became a freethought lecturer, but in 1856 dramatically announced his conversion to theism. Three years later he joined the New Connexion General Baptists and acted as an itinerant Christian apologist. See *The Life of Thomas Cooper written by Himself*, London, 1873; T. Larsen, *Contested Christianity: The Political and Social Contexts of Victorian Theology*, Waco, Texas, 2004, chap. 8; and DNB.

The extract is taken from T. Cooper, *God, the Soul and a Future State*, London, 1875 edn, pp. 97–9. In this popular critique of the socialist thinker Robert Owen, the placing of words in the mouth of the audience is a striking feature of the orator's style.

'But all this is very contrary to the teaching we used to hear some years ago, when Robert Owen was in the height of his fame,' some of you who hear me may be saying; – 'and it seemed very clear to us, then, that he was right. We thought he had proved it – that Man is the mere creature of circumstance – that his character is formed for him and not by him – and that there ought to be no praise and no blame.'

Ay, ay, I remember it all. But you felt you *must* praise and blame, and you felt you could not help praising and blaming. And the funniest thing was that Robert Owen himself was perpetually praising and blaming! ... You cannot get quit of your sense of duty, with all your prate about being 'creatures of circumstance.' No more could Robert Owen. He was perpetually talking about men fulfilling their duties, and perpetually praising and blaming men according as they neglected or fulfilled their duties.

Now, how is it that you cannot get quit of this sense of duty? How is it that you feel remorse when you have violated your sense of duty? One of you to whom I am speaking is the father of a family. I say to him – One day, you lose your temper, and you ill-treat your wife, or your children. I don't care whether you call yourself Freethinker, Sceptic, Socialist, or Secularist: you feel you have violated your sense of duty. While your ill-temper remains, you strive to maintain that what you have done is right. But, when it subsides, and reflection returns, you say to yourself – 'I was very wrong in treating my poor wife so unfairly and cruelly. How often I charge myself with this bad conduct, and say, I will never be guilty of it again. Yet I *am* guilty of it again. How I hate myself for it!' – or, if it were your child that you ill-used, you say to yourself, 'What a wretch I was to ill-use my poor child so cruelly! I was *not* correcting it for its faults, though I pretended I was: I was only indulging my vile bad temper.'

You know that I am telling you the home-truth. How is it that, involuntarily, you experience this self-recrimination when you have done wrong? Because you have this Moral Nature which we are talking of. How come you to have it? There is but one possible answer:– Because it has been given you by the Moral Governor to Whom you are responsible. Your very possession of the Moral Nature proves His existence. And it was the conviction of the great thinker, Immanuel Kant, that it is the strongest and most undeniable of all the proofs of God's existence.

Document III.6

A. M. Fairbairn on Mansfield College, Oxford, 1889

In 1889 Mansfield College opened as the first institutional presence of Nonconformity in the University of Oxford. Eighteen years before, the tests that excluded Nonconformists from attending the university had been relaxed (see IX.10), and now the college was established to allow candidates for the ministry to take advantage of the facilities of Oxford. See E. Kaye, *Mansfield College, Oxford: Its Origin, History and Significance*, Oxford, 1996. A. M. Fairbairn (see II.18), the principal of the new institution, delivered his inaugural lecture at the opening, triumphantly declaring that the college would exclude nobody by fresh tests.

The extract is taken from *Mansfield College, Oxford: Its Origin and Opening*, London, 1890, pp. 97–8.

An occasion like this suggests certain very obvious questions:– What do we mean by these buildings? What is their idea, purpose, end? What is the work we intend to attempt or hope to achieve? Why have we entered this classic home of stately and historical colleges, where learning is cultivated amid traditions that endear the past and are like plastic hands that hold and shape the present? And why have we built here a home for a people and a cause which Oxford is thought never to have loved, while they are believed never to have loved Oxford? But the obvious are not always the radical and relevant questions. It were fitter indeed to ask, not why have we come to Oxford now, but why only now? why not earlier? For our coming at all ought not to need to be vindicated; rather our coming so late has need to be explained. Oxford is England's, and to be of the English people is to be a joint heir to what is, in its own order, their noblest inheritance. Not willingly did we lose our part and lot in the inheritance, but the loss made us neither forget our love nor surrender our claim; and even now we believe we do honour to our fathers by seeking to live in the heart and under the influence of the mother they loved.

Perhaps it may be as well at the outset to state anew the idea and design of the College. It is essentially a special school: its exclusive concern is theology. Its course is post-graduate, its students men already possessed of degrees. It does not aim at drawing its men from schools, but from colleges and universities. They are meant to be men who have received a liberal education, and been searched and tried by the fires of their various schools, and yet have chosen theology as their special study, and some form of the Christian ministry as their peculiar work. The ministry primarily intended is the ministry of the Congregational churches, but while the men who told tutorships or scholarships on the foundation must belong to these churches, the classes and the services of all our teachers are absolutely free to students of theology, whatever their Church – Baptist, Methodist, Presbyterian, or Anglican. In these respects no distinction has been or will be drawn; the College, as a place of instruction in a special subject, is to the competent and the qualified as open and free as the day. We may define it, then, as a society or body of men, all possessed of given academic qualifications, associated with a view to the study of theology.

Document III.7

Hugh Price Hughes on Social Evolution, 1894

In the editorials of *The Methodist Times* (see III.17), Hugh Price Hughes (see I.9) ranged over a wide range of contemporary social, political and intellectual issues. His confident, swashbuckling style is well illustrated by an editorial that praises without a trace of criticism a newly published work, Benjamin Kidd's *Social Evolution*. The book was one of many that tried to apply Darwin's idea of evolution to social affairs. Kidd decided that in the competition between the races the Anglo-Saxons were destined to emerge triumphant.

The extract is taken from *The Methodist Times*, 12 April 1894, p. 1.

Until now, unless we are much mistaken, Mr Kidd has been unknown to literary or philosophic fame. But when we laid down this volume we thought of the remark with which, thirty years ago, an *Edinburgh* Reviewer opened his article on Mr. Lecky's 'History of the Rise and Progress of Rationalism in Europe.' He said that until he began to read the work he had never met its author's name, but when he laid the volume down he felt that Mr. Lecky was one of the greatest literary men of the age. A similarly profound impression must be produced upon every capable and educated reader of Mr. Kidd's extraordinary book. We have never read any study of human society which has impressed us so much since we were enchained by Mr. Lecky's great work thirty years ago. Singularly enough, this book is the long-delayed, probably unconscious, but completely crushing reply to Mr. Lecky's brilliant eulogy of modern Rationalism. Mr. Kidd proves, with overwhelming and almost mathematical demonstration, that modern progress is due, not to loudly-trumpeted and much-idolised Rationalism, but to the ethical and altruistic influence of Christianity. He condemns in severe terms the prejudice, bigotry, and intolerance which have blinded so many exponents of modern science to the fact that Christianity has been the main factor of European progress. He proves beyond the possibility of effective contradiction that the essential condition of progressive evolution is not cleverness, but goodness. ... The astonishing peculiarity of Mr. Kidd's achievement is that he has vanquished modern materialistic infidelity with its own chosen weapon. David cut off Goliath's head with Goliath's own sword, and Mr. Kidd has given fatal blows both to modern Atheism and to materialistic Socialism with a sword manufactured and sharpened in the workshop of Darwinism. From the standpoint of thorough-going Evolution, Mr. Kidd has exhibited the unspeakable folly both of Atheism and of Atheistic Socialism. Facts and arguments which have constantly been flaunted by sincere but half-educated men on the anti-Christian side, must henceforth be counted among the most powerful evidences of the truth and value of the Christian religion.

Science

Document III.8

The Methodist Magazine on Natural Theology, 1825

Like John Wesley before it, *The Methodist Magazine* that circulated widely in its denomination culled useful and edifying material from wherever it could be found. In 1825 it included a passage from *The Christian Philosopher* (1823) by Thomas Dick, a Scottish Presbyterian Seceder who was an enormously influential exponent of popular science. In a manner typical of early nineteenth-century Evangelicals, Dick – and his Methodist readers – put science in the context of natural theology. By contrast with earlier exponents of the tradition such as William Paley who dwelt exclusively on the theme of creation revealing the greatness, wisdom and goodness of God, Evangelicals normally argued that the dysfunctional dimensions of nature illustrated the degradation of the world as a result of the fall of humanity into sin. See D. W. Bebbington, 'Science and Evangelical Theology in Britain from Wesley to Orr', in D. N. Livingstone *et al.*, eds, *Evangelicals and Science in Historical Perspective*, New York, 1999.

The extract is taken from *The Methodist Magazine*, April 1825, pp. 243–4.

Is it not reasonable, then, to conclude, that such awful phenomena as storms, volcanoes, and earthquakes, are so many occasional indications of the frown of an offended Creator, upon a race of transgressors, in order to arouse them to a sense of their apostacy from the GOD of heaven? We cannot conceive that such physical operations, accompanied by so many terrific and destructive effects, are at all compatible with the idea that man is at present in a *paradisiacal* state, and possessed of that *moral* purity in which he was created. Such appalling displays of ALMIGHTY power are in complete unison with the idea, that man is a transgressor, and that the present dispensations of GOD are a mixture of mercy and of judgment; but if he belong to an innocent race of moral intelligences they appear quite anomalous, and are altogether inexplicable, on the supposition, that a Being of infinite benevolence and rectitude directs the operations of the physical and moral world; more especially when we consider the admirable care which is displayed in the construction of animal bodies, in order to prevent pain, and to produce pleasurable sensations. When man was first brought into existence, his thoughts and affections, we must suppose, were in unison with the will of his Creator, his mind was serene and unruffled; and, consequently, no foreboding apprehensions of danger would, in such a state, take possession of his breast. But after he had swerved from the path of primeval rectitude, and especially after the Deluge had swept away the inhabitants of the Antediluvian world, the constitution of the earth and the atmosphere seems to have undergone a might change, corresponding to the degraded state into which he had fallen, so that those very elements which may have formerly ministered to his enjoyment, by being formed into different combination, now conspire to produce terror and destruction.

Document III.9

John Pye Smith on Science and Religion, 1839

John Pye Smith (1774–1851), though almost entirely self-taught, became probably the most distinguished thinker among the Independents in the early nineteenth century. A tutor at Homerton College from 1800, he was its principal from 1806 almost until his death. His book *On the Relation between Holy Scripture and Some Parts of Geological Science* (London, 1839) was the chief Evangelical Nonconformist contribution to the rising debate on religion and science. See J. Medway, *Memoir of the Life and Writings of John Pye Smith*, London, 1853; R. Helmstadter, 'Condescending Harmony: John Pye Smith's Mosaic Geology', in P. Wood, ed., *Science and Dissent in England, 1688–1945*, Aldershot, Hampshire, 2004; DNB.

The extract, taken from pp. 17–19 of the book on geology mentioned above, insists that there is a complete harmony between revelation and science, between the word and the works of God. The author goes on to reject the idea that creation took place only some 6,000 years before, along with many other beliefs that had gained currency without, Pye Smith insists, adequate biblical evidence. He refers at the beginning of the passage to astronomy and geology.

Are then the discoveries and deductions of those sciences consistent, or are they not, with the declarations of primeval divine revelation?

We cannot but expect such consistency. Our Creator has given us faculties suited to the perception and the right appreciation of it. Cases indeed are conceivable, and they do occur, in which difficulties appear, because we see only detached portions of the truth, and the intervening parts of our field of view are covered with an obscurity which we cannot dispel. Yet such cases are not those of contradictory propositions, in which the affirming of one destroys that of the other. But this is the predicament of the subject which we have to consider. If from the discoveries of Astronomy and Geology we infer that the created universe, including our own globe, has existed through an unknown but unspeakably long period of time past; and IF, from the records of revelation *we draw the conclusion* that the work of creation, or at least so far as respects our planet, took place not quite six thousand years ago; it is evident that the two positions cannot both stand: one destroys the other. One of them must be an error; both may be wrong; only one can be right.

Our first care must be to ascertain the true state of the facts, on each side. Are the propositions respectively drawn from their premises, by sound reasoning? Have we guarded sufficiently against all causes of error? Are the facts in nature satisfactorily proved? And is our interpretation of the Scriptures legitimate?

TRUTH, therefore, is our object: Truth, in religion, in morals, and in natural science. The more completely we attain it, if we faithfully apply it to its proper purposes, the more we shall bring happiness to ourselves and our fellow creatures, and reverential honour to our God.

Document III.10

John Clifford on Darwinian Evolution, 1882

For John Clifford, see II.39. In 1882, within a fortnight of the death of Charles Darwin, Clifford preached a sermon to his congregation as a tribute to the memory of a great man. Darwin and the Bible agreed, he argued, on the lowly origins of humanity and the creative work of God. As the extract shows, he did not totally endorse evolution; but he had no fears about its implications for Christian belief. In holding this position, Clifford was like most other Evangelical Nonconformists who wrote about the subject. On the compatibility of Darwinism and orthodoxy, see J. R. Moore, *The Post-Darwinian Controversies: A Study of the Protestant Struggle to come to Terms with Darwin in Great Britain and America, 1870–1900*, Cambridge, 1979; and D. N. Livingstone, *Darwin's Forgotten Defenders: The Encounter between Evangelical Theology and Evolutionary Thought*, Grand Rapids, Michigan, 1987.

The extract is taken from J. Clifford, 'Charles Darwin; or Evolution and Christianity', *Typical Christian Leaders*, London, 1898, pp. 232–4.

These points of agreement between Evolution and Revelation being allowed, where then is the difference? First, it is here, and it is simple. The Bible says God 'made man,' and made him from 'dust,' and Darwin says 'Yes'; but (and here comes the critical addition) man was evolved from the 'dust' *through innumerable gradations of being*. Of those gradations Genesis has no hint. It is silent: and it *seems* to speak as if God made man, the whole man, instantly, and placed him on the earth there and then, and at one particular moment of time. 'He spake and it was done.' The creative act was special, immediate and instantaneous. Such, at least, has been the interpretation usually given on the Scriptural statements.

But we must not forget–

(*a*) That no one contends that the evolutionary *theory* is positively *proved*. It is only a high probability, and it is accepted simply in that character. But I am anxious to say, –

(*b*) That even if it were proved, it does not seem to me that it would conflict with a fair and just interpretation of Scripture, or in any way lessen the force of the witness for design borne by the physical nature of man. For the words 'He spake and it was done' are not intended to declare the immediateness of God's creative deeds, so much as the ineffable ease and invincible certainty with which the Almighty works; and it is a childish illusion which sees in the startling visit of a comet a greater proof of power than in the steadfast brilliance of the daily sun; and cites the instant flash of lightning as a mightier marvel than the slow evolution, from the tiny dweller within the acorn-cup, of the gigantic and far-spreading oak. Hence I have felt from the beginning of this controversy that even supposing the evolutionary theory of our origin indisputably proved, the Biblical record remains intact; for in saying that the 'Lord made man' and made him 'from the dust,' it declares nothing concerning any gradations of being, any processes of formation; and where God's Word is silent, surely we do no wrong in getting to know all we can from God's works.

Document III.11

W. H. Dallinger on the Creator, 1887

William Henry Dallinger (1842–1909) was a Wesleyan minister who was also a practising scientist. He acted as president of Wesley College, Sheffield (1880–88), and as president of the Royal Microscopical Society (1884–87). He was also president of the Wesley Scientific Society that in the 1880s tried 'to associate Wesleyan Methodism with the advances of modern science'. Dallinger had no difficulty in reconciling Darwinian evolution with the idea of design by the Creator. See DNB; and on the Wesley Scientific Society, S. Andrews, 'The Wesley Naturalist', *History Today*, November 1971, pp. 812–16.

The extract is taken from W. H. Dallinger, *The Creator*, London, 1887, pp. 60–62. The book contains the Fernley Lecture delivered at the Wesleyan Conference in that year.

Science finds that phenomena are self-acting, and self-adjusting. The energy is competent; the method is perfect for bringing about the result investigated. Science can find no more; it asks no more; and materialism says, there is no more. There is no design in it; it is, because to be at all, it must be that. There is no design in the form of the river-bed which the mighty waters have engraved for themselves in their irresistible movement down the mountain slope and along the windings of the valley to the sea. It is the result of the force of gravity. Such is the argument.

But while science as such, in strict obedience to its canons, must stop at the self-adjustment of immediate phenomena, and materialism will stop there, the reasoning faculties of the race, as we have seen, will not stop there. They must come at last, by the laws of reason, upon the power and the intelligence by which the methods of nature were made self-acting. Gravitation and the properties of water will account for the perfect adaptation of the river to its bed, and the bed to the purpose of a river. But how came gravity? How came the properties of water? There may be, there is, no direct design in the path of the Amazon or the Danube; but surely there is magnificence in the design that caused the great, the cosmic *methods* of nature so to co-operate as to cause those rivers inevitably to carve their perfect paths? The dynamics of nature are self-acting up to the very limit of our power of research; but after that, and beyond it, what? Why is the *direction* of nature's dynamical methods always and everywhere, through all time and space, beneficent and beautiful?

It is only the design, the teleology, of the old school, touched by the Ithuriel spear of modern knowledge, and changing into a conception of universal design, that can only have originated in an infinite mind.

The 'law of evolution' and that of 'variation and the survival of the fittest' may, if you will, be held to account for all that narrower knowledge had attributed to direct design. But evolution, like gravitation, is only a method; and the self-adjustments demonstrated in the 'origin of species' only make it, to reason, the clearer, that variation and survival is a method that took its origin in mind. It is true that the egg of a moth, and the eye of a dogfish, and the forearm of a tiger *must* be what they are to accomplish the end of their being. But that only shows, as we shade our mental eyes, and gaze back to the beginning, the magnificence of the design that was *in*volved in nature's beginning, so as to be *e*volved, by the designed rhythm of nature's methods.

Whatever matter may be; whatever force is; or whether or not both are the one inseverable product of omnipotent volition; the first affection of matter by force carried with it, potentially, the finished purpose of the All-wise, whatever that may be. Every instance of what such writers as Darwin are obliged to write of as 'contrivance' or 'adaptation' throughout this universe as it now is, or that shall yet arise in it through all duration, are, and will be, but factors of related harmony in a stupendously vast interlocked 'mosaic' of design, which in its entirety has a 'final purpose' too great for man to see.

It is admitted by the fullest and farthest thinkers, that the teleological, and the mechanical views, of phenomena and their origin, are not antagonistic. Instead of mutually excluding each other in thought, they are the complement of each other.

Other Non-Fiction

Document III.12

David Bogue and James Bennett, *History of Dissenters*, 1808

David Bogue (1750–1825) and James Bennett (1774–1862), Bogue's former pupil (see DNB for both), were leading Independent ministers, and their pioneering four-volume *History of Dissenters from the Revolution in 1688 to the Year 1808*, London, 1809, remains a classic to which all scholars of the period need to refer. At the start of their work (vol. 1, pp. 292–3), they set out the principles on which they believe a Dissenter rests his faith.

The fundamental principle on which I build the whole of my system is 'That Jesus Christ is the sole head of the church.' A legislative authority in it belongs to him alone. This authority he has exercised by framing a divine constitution in every respect perfect and complete. To this, in all its parts, I feel myself indispensibly bound to adhere. Whatever he has revealed, that I am called on to receive. Whatever he commands, that I am obliged to obey. Whatever he forbids, it is my duty to avoid. Whatever he has left indifferent, that no man, or body of men, has a right to enjoin, or to forbid: for who should make either a duty or a sin of what Christ has made neither the one nor the other? If any man, or body of men, make additions to Christ's constitution, fidelity to him constrains me to reject them, as a criminal encroachment on the sovereign [*sic*] authority of the great Head of the church. Or if they take away, or leave out a part of Christ's constitution, and do not enjoin the whole, from the same principle I am under the necessity of refusing to embrace their system; because they impeach the wisdom of the divine Legislator, as if in his constitution there was something superfluous; and assume an authority in his kingdom to which they have not the shadow of a claim.

Document III.13

John Foster on the Aversion of Men of Taste to Evangelical Religion, 1819

John Foster (1770–1843) was a Baptist minister whose erudition made his pulpit addresses inaccessible to his congregations, at a succession of which he stayed for only a short period. But his wide reading made him an ideal contributor to *The Eclectic Review*, which, from its foundation in 1805, set out to represent Evangelical Nonconformity in the cultured world. Foster's essays, often republished, blend refinement with doctrinal allegiance and independence of mind. See J. E. Ryland, ed., *Life and Correspondence of John Foster*, London, 1846; and DNB.

The document is an extract from what is probably Foster's most celebrated essay, 'On Some of the Causes by which Evangelical Religion has been rendered less acceptable to Persons of Refined Taste', *Essays*, London, n.d., pp. 216–27. He criticises the jargon that many other writers were also to censure.

[T]he mode of expression of the greater number of evangelical divines, and of those taught by them, is widely different from the standard of general language, not only by the necessary adoption of some peculiar terms, but by a continued and systematic cast of phraseology; insomuch that in reading or hearing five or six sentences of an evangelical discourse, you ascertain the school by the mere turn of expression, independently of any attention to the quality of the ideas. If, in order to try what those ideas would appear in an altered form of words, you attempted to reduce a paragraph to the language employed by intellectual men in speaking or writing well on general subjects, you would find it must be absolutely a version. You know how easily a vast mass of exemplification might be quoted; and the specimens would give the idea of an attempt to create, out of the general mass of the language, a dialect which should be intrinsically spiritual; and so exclusively appropriated to Christian doctrine as to be totally unserviceable for any other subject, and to become ludicrous when applied to it. And this being extracted, like the Sabbath from the common course of time, the general range of diction is abandoned, with all its powers, diversities, and elegance, to secular subjects and the use of the profane. It is a kind of popery of language, vilifying everything not marked with the signs of the holy church, and forbidding any one to minister to religion except in consecrated speech. ...

These pages have attempted to show in what particulars the language adopted by a great proportion of Christian divines might be modified, and yet remain faithful to the principles of Christian doctrine. Such common words as have acquired an affected cast in theological use, might give place to the other common words which express the ideas in a plain and unaffected manner, and the phrases formed of common words uncouthly combined, may be swept away. Many peculiar and antique words might be exchanged for other single words, of equivalent signification, and in general use. And the small number of peculiar terms acknowledged and established as of permanent use and necessity, might, even separately from the consideration of modifying the diction, be often, with advantage to the explicit declaration and clear comprehension of Christian truth, made to give place to a fuller expression, in a number of common words, of those ideas of which these peculiar terms are the single signs.

Now such an alteration would bring the language of divines nearly to the classical standard. If evangelical sentiments could be faithfully presented, in an order of words of which so small a part should be of specific cast, they could be presented in what should be substantially the diction of Addison or Pope.

Document III.14

John Kenrick on Christian Liberty, 1836

John Kenrick (1788–1877) was a respected biblical and classical scholar, of wide repute (see DNB). As a Unitarian he took an 'advanced' view of biblical interpretation, arguing for example in mid-century that Mark's gospel was the first to be written. He was also a noted preacher and advocate of education.

The following extract comes from a sermon which argued strongly for religious liberty from a Unitarian viewpoint: *The Respect Due to Christian Liberty in Religious Education*, London, 1836, pp. 14–15. The allusion to the rejection of a human creed refers to the Salters' Hall meeting of 1719 (M. R. Watts, *The Dissenters*, Oxford, 1978, vol. I, pp. 375–7).

[T]he Protestant religion had scarcely secured for itself the free exercise of its worship and profession of its faith, when it began to make that faith and worship a national standard, and employ such means as it could persuade the civil power to lend it, in order to coerce into uniformity all who had judged differently of Scripture from the predominant party in the state. Hence a fresh excitement of the evil spirit of religious faction, new persecutions, and alternate triumphs and proscriptions, till those who proved finally the stronger drove the weaker from their communion, to seek, as Dissenters, the freedom which they could no longer enjoy as members of the National Church. Even these had not fully learnt, so deeply rooted is the love of spiritual domination, what it was to stand fast in the liberty with which Christ had made them free; and they too began their petty warfare of persecution and exclusion against all who departed from nonconformist orthodoxy. Again, it was necessary that those who valued the birthright of religious freedom should be sifted from the multitude with whom liberty of conscience meant liberty for themselves, constraint and silence for all who differed from them. When the Presbyterian Dissenters of England, above a century ago, refused to bear a part in the imposition of a creed framed in human language, declaring thereby that the recognition of the divine authority of Scripture ought to be the sole bond of communion, then first, as it appears to me, was the true principle of Christian liberty professed among us. Stop short of this, and you will find yourself involved in some inconsistency: you must recognise somewhere or other an authority, which in these things limits, if it do not supersede, the authority of God and Christ. Go beyond this, and the name of Christian ceases to have a meaning. I may without presumption assume this latitude of religious liberty as the characteristic of our part of the Nonconformist body, since it is the very ground on which we are reproached by the rest. As Presbyterian Dissenters, then, we may reasonably boast, that 'we are children not of the bondwoman, but of the free.'

Document III.15

The Inquirer, 1842

The Inquirer was the first weekly newspaper to be published with Unitarians and other similar Dissenters in mind, and it was considered a speculative venture at the start in 1842. Edward Hill, the founder (who gave up after a few weeks), engaged a staff which included as editor William Hincks (1794–1871; see DNB), a sub-editor, a writer on the monkey market and a drama critic. It was an unusual assemblage for a religious journal and many thought it would soon fold. However, it has never failed to appear over almost 160 years and is the oldest Dissenting newspaper in existence, though the journal *The Gospel Standard* is older, having been founded in 1835. Hincks was the driving force behind *The Inquirer* in its early years, and his first editorial was rather different from the offerings from editors in the opening number of other religious newspapers. See K. Gilley and A. Ruston, *The Inquirer: a History and Other Reflections*, London, 1992.

THE INQUIRER
TRUTH – FREEDOM – CHARITY
London July 9 1842

... Whilst we collect with diligence the information which may seem likely peculiarly to interest those who we look to already as our friends, we hope to make our paper entertaining and useful to the general reader and to give it a character which shall deserve the patronage of all who have cultivated minds, enlarged views and liberal feelings.

It will be a leading object with us to advocate the rights of conscience and the most extended views of religious freedom and charity.

We rest our hopes for the spread of pure and rational religion in the world on improved education and diffused knowledge. The effects we anticipate from the progress of truth are improved moral condition, and, consequently, increased happiness.

Where we can we will communicate knowledge and submit prevailing sentiment to searching but candid inquiry. Where we can we will defend and apply great principles, and exhibit popular errors in their true characters. But we will endeavour also to contribute our share to innocent and rational enjoyment, and to give the information which is useful to various classes of readers with that kind of selection which suits our pretensions to supply a *family* newspaper.

Document III.16

Mary Ann Hearn (Marianne Farningham) on *The Christian World*, 1857

The Christian World was one of the leading weekly religious journals of the second half of the nineteenth century and set out to be unsectarian in approach, but soon came to serve Nonconformists almost exclusively. Founded by Jonathan Whittemore in 1857, it had as one of its most regular contributors Mary Ann Hearn (1934–1909), who wrote under the pseudonym Marianne Farningham (see DNB). She joined the staff at its inception and continued writing for it until her death; many of her contributions were published in separate volumes which had a wide readership. In her autobiography, *A Working Woman's Life*, London, 1907, pp. 76–7, she recalls the first issue of 9 April 1857.

The first number of *The Christian World* had a very modest appearance. It thus introduced itself to the public in –

A WORD TO OUR READERS

The proprietors of this journal believe that the progress of popular education cannot be more effectively advanced than by a cheap and thoroughly healthy literature, such as that which it is their purpose to supply. They rejoice to know that of late years numerous efforts, more or less successful, have been made by Christian philanthropists to create reading for the people of so attractive a nature, and at so low a price, as to drive out of the market much debasing rubbish produced by a ribald press. But, notwithstanding all that has yet been done, there is still unhappily abundance of room, and great necessity for augmented exertions in the same good cause; and we appeal, therefore, to all true friends of the people – especially to those who are ever foremost in labours of this sort, ministers of the Gospel, Sunday school teachers, and Church members generally – to aid us in establishing a cheap family newspaper conducted on pure principles, and pervaded by a Catholic spirit.

Intimation was given of the future standpoint and policy of the journal. In politics it would advocate Reform, Retrenchment, and Peace. It would be the friend of Progress, but the foe of Revolution. In Religion it would be decidedly evangelical, but wholly unsectarian.

Its appearance was timely. A general election was just over, and the leading article had for its subject Lord Palmerston's Cabinet. It contained two sermons, and instalments of two serial stories. The sermons were by the late Rev. W. Jay, of Bath, and the coming man, Charles Haddon Spurgeon. The 'Chronicle of the Churches' was a feature in this first number, as it has always been; and there was an article which contained a warning for young men who smoke!

Document III.17

The Methodist Times, 1885

For Hugh Price Hughes, the editor, see I.9. Hughes came to London in 1884 with the aim of creating a forward movement within Methodism, and one of his first acts was the foundation of *The Methodist Times* as 'a Journal of Religious and Social Movement'. It proved to be one of the key Nonconformist journals of the late nineteenth and early twentieth centuries.

This extract is taken from Hughes's editorial in the first issue of 1 January 1885, which set out what he intended to do.

The younger generation of Methodists have hitherto had no literary organ through which they could freely interchange thoughts, convictions, and aspirations. Thackeray said that a great need of English society was a journal written by gentlemen for gentlemen. The great need of that vast movement called Methodism is a journal written by young Methodists for young Methodists. During the last quarter of a century a silent educational revolution has been gradually effecting an immense change. We do not believe that the younger generation has abandoned any one of the essential doctrines of John Wesley. We at any rate are prepared to argue in detail that the broad, catholic, tender-hearted theology of early Methodism is the goal towards which the best modern thought, the discoveries of science, and the generous humanitarianism of our day are perpetually tending. Nevertheless, the intellectual environment of the younger generation is widely different from that in which their fathers lived. The standpoint is greatly changed. The horizon is indefinitely widened. New worlds of thought and fact have come into full view. The modern revolution we describe began with the creation of the University of London. The crowning phase has followed the opening of Oxford and Cambridge to Nonconformists. An ever-increasing stream of young Methodists is now perpetually flowing towards both of the residential Universities. These great centres of intellectual and moral activity already exert an immense influence over us. They affect our modes of thought, our methods of speech, the whole attitude of our minds, in a way of which many of the older generation appear to be quite unconscious. It is high time that the younger generation had some literary organ in which they could fully express and discuss their thoughts, their duties, and their hopes. The first list of literary contributors, published in another volume, will show that we are already in a position to speak with some authority on their behalf. All young Methodists, of both sexes, may always look to us for sympathy and appreciation. One main object of our existence is to discover and to discuss what the younger Methodists think and want.

Fiction

Document III.18

George Eliot, *Adam Bede*, 1859

The novelist George Eliot (Mary Ann Evans) was for a time at a school run by two of the daughters of Francis Franklin, minister of Cow Lane Baptist Church, Coventry. Her aunt Elizabeth Evans, a Wesleyan preacher, was the model for Dinah Morris in *Adam Bede*. Eliot's other sources included biographies of Wesley and of Mary Fletcher (née Bosanquet). For these female preachers, see D. A. Johnson, *Women in English Religion, 1700–1925*, New York, 1983, and P. W. Chilcote, *She Offered them Christ*, Nashville, 1993.

This extract is from Chapter 2, 'The Preaching', when Dinah Morris makes her first appearance to deliver an evening sermon in the village of Hayslope. The prayer vividly portrays the zeal of these female evangelists.

'Dear friends', she said, in a clear but not loud voice, 'let us pray for a blessing.'

She closed her eyes, and hanging her head down a little, continued in the same moderate tone, as if speaking to some one quite near by:

'Saviour of sinners! when a poor woman, laden with sins, went out to the well to draw water, she found Thee sitting at the well. She knew Thee not; she had not sought Thee; her mind was dark; her life unholy. But thou didst speak to her, Thou didst teach her, Thou didst show her that her life lay open before Thee, and yet Thou wast ready to give her that blessing which she had never sought. Jesus! Thou art in the midst of us, and Thou knowest all men: if there is any here like that poor woman – if their minds are dark, their lives unholy – if they have come out not seeking Thee, nor desiring to be taught; deal with them according to the free mercy which Thou didst show to her. Speak to them, Lord, open their ears to my message; bring their sins to their minds, and make them thirst for that salvation which Thou art ready to give.

'Lord! Thou are with Thy people still: they see Thee in the night watches, and their hearts burn within them as Thou talkest with them by the way. And Thou are near to those who have not known Thee: open their eyes that they may see Thee – see Thee weeping over them, and saying, "Ye will not come unto me that ye might have life" – see Thee hanging on the cross and saying, "Father, forgive them, for they know not what they do" – see Thee as Thou wilt come again in Thy glory to judge them at the last. Amen.'

Document III.19

Margaret Oliphant, *Salem Chapel*, 1863

Margaret Oliphant (1828–97) had no direct experience of English Dissent. 'I knew nothing about chapels, but took the sentiment and a few details from our old church in Liverpool, which was Free Church of Scotland, and where there were a few grocers and other such good folk whose ways with the ministers were wonderful to behold.' However, she demonstrated a sure grasp of the atmosphere of Dissent and the often uneasy relationship between fiercely independent congregations and the minister they employed to preach to them. Arthur Vincent is the new young minister of Salem Chapel, fresh from college, and Lady Western with whom he had mixed socially was a grand aristocratic supporter of the Church of England. Tozer is a deacon, Pigeon a disgruntled church member. See *Autobiography and Letters of Mrs M. Oliphant*, ed. H. Coghill, Leicester, 1974, and V. Cunningham, *Everywhere Spoken Against*, Oxford, 1975, chap. 9.

The extracts are taken from Margaret Oliphant, *Chronicles of Carlingford – Salem Chapel*, London, 1863, republished 1986, pp. 174–5 and 362.

Meantime Vincent went angry and impetuous downstairs. 'I will not submit to any inquisition,' cried the young man. 'I have done nothing wrong that I am ashamed of. If I dine with a friend, I will suffer no questioning on the subject. ... What right has any man in any connection to interfere with my actions? Why, you would not venture to attack your servant so! Am I the servant of this congregation? Am I their slave? ...

'If a minister ain't a servant, we pays him his salary at the least, and expects him to please us,' said Tozer, sulkily. 'If it weren't for that, I don't give a Sixpence for the Dissenting connection. Them as likes to please themselves would be far better in a State Church, where it wouldn't disappoint nobody; not meaning to be hard on you as has given great satisfaction, them's my views; but if the Chapel folks is a little particular, it's no more nor a pastor's duty to bear with them, and return a soft answer. I don't say as I'm dead again' you, like the women,' added the butterman, softening; 'they're jealous, that's what they are; but I couldn't find it in my heart, not for my own part, to be hard on a man as was led away after a beautiful creature like that. But there can't no good come of it, Mr Vincent; take my advice, sir, as have seen a deal of the world. ... A man as goes dining with Lady Western, and thinking as she means to make a friend of him, ain't the man for Salem. We're different sort of folks, and we can't go on together.'

...

'Why, what have I ever done to Pigeon? if he has anything to find fault with, he had much better come to me, and have it out.'

'Mr Vincent, sir,' said Tozer solemnly, '... them ain't the sentiments for a pastor in our connection. That's a style of thing as may do among fine folks, or in the Church where there's no freedom; but them as chooses their own pastor, and pays their own pastor, and don't spare no pains to make him comfortable, has a right to expect different. Them ain't the sentiments, sir, for Salem folks. I don't say if they're wrong or right – I don't make myself a judge of no man; but I've seen a deal of our connection and human nature in general, and this I know, that a minister as has to please his flock, has got to please his flock whatever happens, and neither me nor no other man can make it different ... It's flock as has to be considered – and it ain't preaching alone as will do that.'

Document III.20

M. G. Pearse, *Daniel Quorm and his Religious Notions*, 1875

Mark Guy Pearse (1842–1928) was a Wesleyan minister who, despite preaching for C. H. Spurgeon, developed unusually liberal theological views for his denomination. His fictional output began with *Daniel Quorm and his Religious Notions*, London, 1875, which is often classed as the first Methodist novel but which has a tract-like religious message. Daniel is a wise Cornish class leader who has to deal with difficult characters like Widow Pascoe. See Mrs. G. Unwin and J. Telford, *Mark Guy Pearse*, London, 1930.
  The extract is taken from pp. 144–7 of the novel.

On Winning Souls.

Strangely enough, it was Widow Pascoe who most commonly suggested this topic. Partly by the selfishness of her sentiments, partly by her dismal looks and tones, but still more by the impression that all about her made on one's mind. Though she never said it in so many words, there were a hundred things about her that kept saying it over and over again – 'The Lord's people are a *peculiar* people, a *little* flock. You only know that the way leads to Heaven if a very few there be that find it. Therefore receive all new comers with cold suspicion. Most likely they are hypocrites, and if not, they will probably be back in the world again in a month. Keep the way as much as you possibly can to yourself.' ...
  Dan'el listened with a sigh, and spoke slowly and sadly, – 'Well, if we don't take care, I'm 'fraid some of us'll never get to Heaven.'
  This was threatening: it even disturbed Widow Pascoe's composure for a moment.
  Dan'el continued, as if explaining what had gone before, – 'Or if we get there it won't be like the Lord Jesus went. You remember that Jesus wouldn't go to Heaven alone, even He took a soul with Him, and said: *"To-day shalt thou be with me in Paradise."* An' the only safe way for us is to go like the Blessed Master went.' ...
  'You know, my dear sister, you'll never get anybody to go along such a dismal old road as you make of it, never. An' what'll you do if you get up to the golden gate all by yourself? You know the Lord wouldn't let the beasts go into the ark one by one – not even the unclean beasts; not a cat or a dog could go in by itself. An' if 'tis anything like that, what will folks do who've never got a soul to go to Heaven with 'em. Besides, it would be a'most impudence to knock to the door an' ask the glorious great Archangel to open it just to let in one.'

Document III.21

W. H. White, *Autobiography of Mark Rutherford*, 1888

William Hale White (1831–1913) trained for the Independent ministry and served as a minister at Bedford. Theological and other problems led to his resignation and he became minister of the Old Meeting House, Ditchling, Sussex, in 1850. It was General Baptist in origin (built 1740) but the congregation had become part of the Unitarian denomination. In the following extract White describes his candidature for the pulpit, and the low ebb to which some rural Unitarian foundations had fallen at this time. He left the ministry in 1851 never to return. For background on his life, see C. M. Maclean, *Mark Rutherford*, London, 1955; and DNB.

White composed a series of novels on Dissenting life. This extract is taken from the semi-fictional *Autobiography of Mark Rutherford, Edited by his friend Reuben Shapcott*, 2nd edn, London, 1888, pp. 92–5.

The old Presbyterian chapels throughout the country have many of them become Unitarian, and occasionally, even in an agricultural village, a respectable red brick building may be seen, dating from the time of Queen Anne, in which a few descendants of the eighteenth century heretics still testify against three Gods in one and the deity of Jesus Christ. Generally speaking, the attendance in these chapels is very meagre, but they are often endowed, and so they are kept open. There was one in the large straggling half-village, half-town of D——, within about ten miles of me, and the pulpit was then vacant. The income was about £100 a year. The principal man there was a small general dealer ... and I had come to know him slightly, because I had undertaken to give his boy a few lessons ... The money in my pocket was coming to an end, and as I did not suppose that any dishonesty would be imposed upon me, and although the prospect was not cheering, I expressed my willingness to be considered as a candidate ... I was therefore invited to preach. I was so reduced that I was obliged to walk the whole distance on the Sunday morning, and as I was asked to no house, I went straight to the chapel, and loitered about in the graveyard till a woman came and opened the door at the back. I explained who I was, and sat down in a Windsor chair against a small kitchen table in the vestry. It was cold, but there was no fire, nor were any preparations made for one. ... I waited in silence for about twenty minutes, and my friend the dealer came in, and having shaken hands and remarked it was chilly, asked me for the hymns. These I gave him and went into the pulpit. I found myself in a plain-looking building designed to hold about two hundred people. ... I counted my hearers, and discovered that there were exactly seventeen, including two very old labourers, who sat on a form near the door. The gallery was quite empty, except a little organ or seraphine, I think it was called, which was played by a young woman. The dealer gave out the hymns, and accompanied the seraphine in a bass voice, singing the air. A weak whisper might be perceived from the rest of the congregation but nothing more. ... I talked for about half-an-hour about what I considered to be the real meaning of the death of Christ, thinking that this was a subject which might prove as attractive as any other. After the service the assembly of seventeen departed, save for one thin elderly gentleman, who ... said, 'Mr Rutherford, will you come with me, if you please?' I accordingly followed him almost in silence ... till we reached his house. ... We had dinner in a large room with an old fashioned grate in it, in which was stuck a basket stove. ... Very little was spoken during dinner-time by anybody. ... At twenty minutes to two we sallied out for the afternoon service, and found the seventeen again in their places, excepting the two labourers. ... The service was a repetition of that in the morning, and when I came down my host again came forward and presented me with nineteen shillings. The fee was a guinea, but from that two shillings were abated for my entertainment.

Document III.22

W. H. Mills, *Grey Pastures*, on a Bazaar of c. 1890

William Haslam Mills (1874–1930) was the chief reporter for *The Manchester Guardian* during the First World War. His fictional account of the Congregational chapel where he grew up, Albion Chapel, Ashton-under-Lyne ('Wyclif'), is a vivid evocation of Northern Nonconformist life in the closing years of the century. It was first published in *The Manchester Guardian* and then reissued as *Grey Pastures* in 1924. On Albion, see C. Binfield, 'The Dynamic of Grandeur: Albion Church, Ashton-under-Lyne', *Transactions of the Lancashire and Cheshire Antiquarian Society*, 85 (1988), pp. 173–92.

The extract is from *Grey Pastures*, London, 1924, pp. 8–11. This section describes 'The Big Bazaar', an event characteristic of the period combining a sale of prepared articles with amateur entertainments in order to raise money, commonly, as here, to remove a chapel debt. Bazaars were unusual among chapel events in being run by women. See F. K. Prochaska, *Women and Philanthropy in Nineteenth-Century England*, Oxford, 1980, chap. 2.

Like other big things in our history, it was traceable ultimately to the accident that 'a few of us got talking.' On this occasion they got talking in the chapel yard after a deacons' meeting – that chapel yard in which a good deal of half-obliterated reading-matter on the flags attests the presence below of a considerable company of the long-since departed. The subject of the talk was the chapel debt. Though considerable in amount and not slightly over-due, the debt was wholly free from that moral taint which attaches to the unpaid bills of individuals. Perhaps the difference was faintly indicated in the words in which they referred to its extinction – it was not so much to be 'paid' as to be 'wiped out.' Moreover, it had been in some rather special and exotic sense of the word 'incurred,' and, as they talked beneath the gas-jet which fought precariously for its life in the draught round the corner of the chapel yard, it was figured as 'hanging over' the congregation as though its imminence over the head of the congregation was something for which the congregation was in no sense to blame. In the street outside the chapel yard was the carriage of Mr. Henry Stonor, at once a deacon of Wycliffe and Member for the borough. It was a definite enrichment of life to everybody in the talk to be familiar with Mr. Stonor, who in turn was distinctly though distantly known to Mr. Gladstone. The talk, at any rate, came to a head at the door of Mr. Stonor's carriage. The moment was favourable for getting something done because the general meeting of the deacons had dissolved half an hour before, and had precipitated into its essential constituents of power and purpose. We were governed by committees, but committees never make history. It is only made by strong men. The door of Mr. Stonor's carriage closed with a snap. His bay horses struck a hoof-full of sparks from the stone sets. The other square-hatted figures separated into the night, and when Mr. Ogden Green half an hour later sat down with the wife of his bosom and the daughters of his house to the coffee and pastry which he had not found in a pretty long life to do him any harm, he announced that 'there would probably be a Bazaar.'

It tells us something of what that Bazaar had been that for years we were not tired of talking about it. Long after the reminiscence was exhausted in what we may call its scope and rotundity, it could still be discussed with pleasure in detail. Its leaf, as the Psalmist says – its leaf as distinguished from its fruit – never withered. It registered, for example, the high-water mark of 'giving,' and that, not only in money but in hams and tongues and jellies and cheese-cakes. I believe it to be moreover an historical fact – though I cannot prove it – that it marked the climax and culmination of English needlework. It stood out from others, again, in the size of the sum at which it aimed, but this was only a difference in degree not distinguishing it essentially from the mere 'sale of work' which anyone could see it was not. Very exquisite things had been and were indeed done any year for sales of work – things which 'it was a sin to let go at a guinea.' The real distinction of the big Bazaar lay in the bold and innovating spirit which disclosed itself in the entertainments. In nothing was it shown more signally than in the Tableaux Vivants. The inclusion of the Tableaux Vivants among the entertainments was a striking movement, an approach to the questionable arts of the drama and the stage which probably had its critics, though opposition was not organized, partly because the project introduced itself and made some progress towards preparation under the slightly frigid name of 'living statuary'. It was in the formulation of ideas for living statuary that Miss Cheeseman, who was known chiefly as an authority on the vicissitudes of the Children of Israel, disclosed an unexpected acquaintance with the more prominent personages of pagan mythology ...

PART IV

WORSHIP

Introduction

Nonconformist worship showed immense variety during the nineteenth century. The general trend over time was from simplicity to elaboration, from free worship towards greater liturgical structure, but there were many counter-currents and eddies. Thus the exuberance of early Primitive Methodism (IV.1, 22) gradually subsided (IV.7), but instances of religious excitement could be found late in the century, particularly in Wales (IV.11) and the Salvation Army (IV.26). Throughout the century the Society of Friends maintained its tradition of quietness (IV.12), and the Brethren were recruits to the same cause (IV.5). A desire to reach the unchurched masses induced proposals for greater, rather than less, simplicity (IV.4), but respectability encouraged a more devotional temper in ordinary services (IV.10) and imitation of the Church of England led to the wider use of liturgical elements (IV.6, 14).

Preaching was the central act of services of worship in most Nonconformist denominations. Instances of sermons are given in Part I, but here there are descriptions of two of the pulpit giants of the early years of the century (IV.2, 3) together with guidance on sermon preparation from one of the later masters of the craft (IV.8). There is an instructive insight into the actuality of preaching in the results of a survey of sermon texts from 1896 (IV.13). Occasionally there would be objections that preaching was rated so highly as to eclipse other elements in worship (IV.9), but Nonconformists generally did not neglect the sacraments. Baptists ensured that the questions of the proper mode and subjects of baptism were kept on the agenda (see II.22 as well as IV.17), but others were happy to reply (IV.19) and Baptists became less disposed to insist on their views (see II.23). There was a tendency to react against the Oxford movement by minimising the mysterious in the communion service, and there was a wish to recover the practice of the earliest Christians (IV.16). Yet there were traces of a higher eucharistic doctrine, especially in Wesleyanism (IV.15), but also in unlikely places such as the Primitive Methodist Conference (IV.16) and the thought of C. H. Spurgeon (IV.20). The most elaborate of all eucharistic liturgies, far more ritualist than what was observed by most Anglican ritualists, was to be found in the astonishing order used by the Catholic Apostolic Church (IV.18).

Inherited patterns of worship entailed having a precentor lead the singing. That approach was defended by traditionalists (IV.23), but there were successive innovations – organs (IV.25), choirs (IV.24) and even brass bands (IV.26). The century was notable for a flowering of Anglican hymnody, but Dissenting hymn-writers were less outstanding than the great figures of the previous century: Watts and Wesley continued to form the staple of the Nonconformist repertoire. Yet there were new compositions aplenty, including rousing revivalist choruses (IV.22), solid doctrinal compositions (IV.21) and broad-minded affirmations of human potential (IV.27). Praise rang out in buildings that were at first, especially in the villages, little different from barns, but gradually architect-designed structures became normal. A great debate raged over whether Nonconformists should follow the Church of England in adopting the Gothic revival style (IV.28, 29). By the end of the century Gothic had triumphed (IV.30) and the big question was whether the caretaker was fulfilling his onerous duties (IV.31).

The subject of worship is covered in H. Davies, *Worship and Theology in England*, vols 3 and 4, Princeton, New Jersey, 1961–62, and, for Methodism, in N. P. Goldhawk, 'The Methodist People in the Early Victorian Age: Spirituality and Worship', in R. Davies *et al.*, ed., *A History of the Methodist Church in Great Britain*, vol. 2, London, 1978. Congregational and Presbyterian worship and architecture on both sides of the Atlantic are covered in C. D. Cashdollar, *A Spiritual Home: Life in British and American Reformed Congregations, 1830–1915*, University Park, Pennsylvania, 2000, chaps 3, 5 and 11. Trends affecting the communion service among Methodists are analysed in J. C. Bowmer, *The Lord's Supper in Methodism, 1791–1960*, London, 1961, amongst Congregationalists in B. D. Spinks, *Freedom or Order? The Eucharistic Liturgy in English Congregationalism, 1645–1980*, Allison Park, Pennsylvania, 1984, and among Baptists in M. Walker, *Baptists at the Table: The Theology of the Lord's Supper amongst English Baptists in the Nineteenth Century*, Didcot, Oxfordshire, 1992. There is some material on Dissenting hymnody in J. R. Watson, *The English Hymn*, Oxford, 1997. There are introductions to chapel architecture in K. Lindley, *Chapels and Meeting Houses*, London, 1969, and A. Jones, *Welsh Chapels*, Cardiff, 1984. A superb case study of a Dissenting architect is provided in C. Binfield, *The Contexting of a Chapel Architect: James Cubitt, 1836–1912*, London, 2001. There are pioneering studies of the relationship between the chapels and the visual arts in John Harvey, *The Art of Piety: The Visual Culture of Welsh Nonconformity*, Cardiff, 1995; and in *idem*, *Image of the Invisible: The Visualization of Religion in the Welsh Nonconformist Tradition*, Cardiff, 1999.

General

Document IV.1

Hugh Bourne on the Camp Meeting Preacher, c. 1820

Hugh Bourne (1772–1852) was a Wesleyan revivalist in north Staffordshire who decided to import the American technique of camp meetings, that is long, open-air preaching sessions (see VIII.2). When he held one at Mow Cop in 1807, he was expelled from the Wesleyans and then gradually built up his own connexion, the Primitive Methodists, the least inhibited of the main Nonconformist denominations. Remaining unmarried, he devoted his life to organising Primitive Methodism. See J. Walford, *Memoirs of the Life and Labours of the Late Venerable Hugh Bourne*, 2 vols, London, 1855–56; J. T. Wilkinson, *Hugh Bourne, 1772–1852*, London, 1952; and DNB.

The extract is a set of guidelines for camp meeting preachers drawn up by Bourne and printed in Walford's *Memoirs* (above), vol. 2, pp. 76–7.

A camp meeting or open-air preacher should go straightforward, and should strike home at every blow. Set sermons, prepared for chapel pulpits, are of little use. The open-air preacher should have his mind upon Luke xxiv. 46, 47, 'Thus it is written, and thus it behoved Christ to suffer, and to rise from the dead the third day; and that repentance and remission of sins should be preached in his name among all nations.' He preaches man's fall and lost state; he preaches the atonement; he preaches repentance; he preaches the forgiveness of sins, justification by faith, the new birth, the being born again, created anew in Christ Jesus unto good works. He endures the travail in birth, presses through temptation, gets into the full exercise of faith, the unction of the Holy One descends, liberty opens, and, as much as in him lies, he preaches the gospel with the Holy Ghost sent down from heaven. He often produces a greater effect in a quarter of an hour, than many a pulpit preacher does in a full hour. Some preachers in chapel pulpits spend portions of time in proving what they advance; but the straightforward open-air preacher does no such thing. He preaches the lost state of man, the death and resurrection of Christ, repentance, faith, and holiness. He warns, by setting forth the terrors of hell, and encourages by preaching the glories of heaven; but he leaves his preaching to prove itself. He looks to God, and to the prayers and faith of himself and people, and watches for effects – watches for the conviction and conversion of sinners, and the quickening of believers. A sound camp meeting preacher avoids apologies and frivolous remarks. He preaches a free, full, and present salvation. He redeems his time, and completes his work. He does not squander away his own, and the people's time, by attempting to tell what others have preached, or will preach; but he attends to his own work, occupies his own portion of time, and makes an end without attempting to occupy the time that belongs to others. He is prompt and attentive, and closes at the signal given, if not before.

Document IV.2

Robert Hall as a Preacher, 1821

For Robert Hall, see I.1. The powerful impression he made as a preacher was described by the editor of the *London Magazine* (February 1821), and was reprinted in *The Works of Robert Hall, A.M.*, ed. O. Gregory, London, 1839, vol. 1, pp. 187–9.

Mr. Hall, though perhaps the most distinguished ornament of the Calvinistic dissenters, does not afford the best opportunity for criticism. His excellence does not consist in the predominance of one of his powers, but in the exquisite proportion and harmony of all. The richness, variety, and extent of his knowledge, are not so remarkable as his absolute mastery over it. He moves about in the loftiest sphere of contemplation, as though he were 'native and endued to its element.' He uses the finest classical allusions, the noblest images, and the most exquisite words, as though they were those which came first to his mind, and which formed his natural dialect. There is not the least appearance of straining after greatness in his most magnificent excursions; but he rises to the loftiest heights with a childlike ease. His style is one of the clearest and simplest – the least encumbered with its own beauty – of which ever has been written. It is bright and lucid as a mirror, and its most highly-wrought and sparkling embellishments are like ornaments of crystal, which, even in their brilliant inequalities of surface, give back to the eye little pieces of the true imagery set before them. ...

There is nothing very remarkable in Mr. Hall's manner of delivering his sermons. His simplicity, yet solemnity of deportment, engage the attention, but do not promise any of his most rapturous effusions. His voice is feeble, but distinct; and as he proceeds, trembles beneath his images, and conveys the idea that the spring of sublimity and beauty in his mind is exhaustless, and would pour forth a more copious stream if it had a wider channel than can be supplied by the bodily organs. The plainest and least inspired of his discourses are not without delicate gleams of imagery, and felicitous turns of expression. He expatiates on the prophecies with a kindred spirit, and affords awful glimpses into the valley of vision. He often seems to conduct his hearers to the top of the 'Delectable Mountains,' whence they can see from afar the glorious gates of the eternal city. He seems at home among the marvellous revelations of St. John; and while he expatiates on them, leads his hearers breathless through ever-varying scenes of mystery, far more glorious and surprising than the wildest of oriental fables. He stops when they most desire that he should proceed, when he has just disclosed the dawnings of the inmost glory to their enraptured minds – and leaves them full of imaginations of 'things not made with hands' – of joys too ravishing for smiles – and of impulses which wing their hearts 'along the line of limitless desires.'

Document IV.3

Adam Clarke as a Preacher, 1833

For Adam Clarke, see I.2. This account of his pulpit style is taken from An Account of the Infancy, Religious and Literary life of Adam Clarke, LL.D., F.A.S., &c., *London, 1833, vol. 3, pp. 473–5. It comes from an appendix written by his Anglican clergyman son, J. B. B. Clarke.*

The appearance of my Father, and his effect, while in the pulpit, upon a stranger, would probably be something like this:– he would see a person of no particular mark, except that time had turned his hair to silver, and the calmness of fixed devotion gave solemnity to his appearance: he spreads his Bible before him, and opening his hymn-book reads forth, in a clear, distinct, full voice, a few verses, after the singing of which, he offers up a short prayer, which is immediately felt to be addressed to the Majesty of Heaven: the text is proclaimed and the Discourse is begun:– in simple yet forcible language he gives some general information connected with his subject, or lays down some general positions drawn from either the text or its dependencies; on these he speaks for a short time, fixing the attention by gaining the interest; the understanding feels that it is concerned; a clear and comprehensive exposition gives the hearer to perceive that his attention will be rewarded by an encrease of knowledge, by new views of old truths, or previously unknown uses of ascertained points: – he views with some astonishment the perfect collectedness with which knowledge is brought from far, and the natural yet extensive excursions which the Preacher makes to present his object in all its bearings; laying heaven and earth, nature and art, science and reason, under contribution, to sustain his cause:– now, his interest becomes deeper, for he sees that the Minister is beginning to condense his strength, that he is calling in every detached sentence, and that every apparently miscellaneous remark was far from casual, but had its position to maintain, and its work to perform; and he continues to hear with that rooted attention which is created by the importance and clearness of the truths delivered, by the encreasing energy of the speaker, and by the assurance in the hearer's own mind that what is spoken is believed to the utmost and felt in its power:– the Discourse proceeds with a deeper current of fervour, the action becomes more animated, the certainty of the Preacher's own mind and the convinced feelings of his own heart are shewn by the firm confidence of the tone and a certain fulness of voice and emphasis of manner; the whole of the œconomy of God seems laid open before him; the infinite nature of Jehovah, – His unchangeable being as a God of mercy and truth are made manifest; the counsels of the Most High for the salvation of the human soul are displayed; – all the attributes and perfections of the Deity are exhibited, as engaged to accomplish the designs of His love to man; the heights of heaven are ascended, and the Propitiation for sin is seen before the throne; the recesses of the heart are pierced, its state, its wants, its helplessness are made known; the God of Love, Jesus the Saviour, the Spirit of Power and of Holiness, are displayed as the Source, the Hope, the Fulfilment, of all that Truth has promised, of all that Love can do:– the soul thus informed, or established, or alarmed, feels as in the immediate presence of its God, and beholds the Lord as a God of knowledge, or as the Confidence of the ends of the earth, or as that Being toward whom all its changed affections turn with the cry, 'the Lord He is the God, the Lord He is the God.' – Such was the general nature and tendency of my Father's preaching.

Document IV.4

Edward Miall on the Reform of Worship, 1849

For Edward Miall, see IX.7. In 1849 he wrote a critique of the churches' strategy of mission entitled *The British Churches in Relation to the British People*, proposing a variety of measures to overcome the alienation of many of the working classes. One was the abolition of pew rents, the system by which seats in chapel were let to particular worshippers (which made non-subscribers feel unwelcome), together with the transformation of religious services into something more akin to political meetings. See D. Smith, 'Church and Society in Britain: A Mid-Nineteenth-Century Analysis', *The Evangelical Quarterly*, 61 (1989), pp. 141–58.

The extract is taken from Miall's book mentioned above, 2nd edn, London, 1850, pp. 283–5.

The advantages ... which would probably be concurrent with, or follow close upon, our rising superior to those feelings which originate in attaching an idea of sanctity to brick walls, would suggest some improvements in the structure of our places of worship, and remove some of the inconveniences which tend to produce an unhappy moral impression. We might get rid of pews – we might get rid of pulpits – we might throw open our chapels to all comers, as unreservedly as we do a public hall, leaving every one, without distinction, to take any place which at the time of his entrance might remain unappropriated – we might eschew, and the sooner the better, the entire system of pew-rents, and meet such expenses as we might incur by voluntary subscription – and we might turn to useful account, during the week, the edifice in which we assemble for devotion and instruction on the Lord's day. ...

It appears to me that their place of assembly might be thrown open by most Christian organizations once a week – not for a religious service, in the common acceptance of that phrase, but for 'disputing and persuading the things concerning the kingdom of God.' At such meeting, under no further restriction than is obviously necessary to prevent confusion, intelligent members of the Church should be encouraged to enforce the message of mercy upon those assembled, with the same freedom as they would, on other occasions, commend a political truth, or urge on a social reform. I would put no interdiction upon the manifestation of feeling, whether assenting or dissenting, by the audience. I would give all present full liberty to ask questions, to start objections, or to speak in opposition. In fact, I would have the gospel propounded, illustrated, discussed, commended, on these occasions, as any other great truth, or system of truth, is dealt with, when the intention is to make it known far and wide, and induce men to receive it.

Document IV.5

William Trotter on Brethren Worship, c. 1850

William Trotter was a minister of the Methodist New Connexion who seceded in 1841 because of dissatisfaction with Conference policies. He joined the so-called Plymouth Brethren, the body of Evangelicals who from the 1830s formed assemblies that eschewed the institutionalisation of the existing denominations. Their weekly observance of the Lord's Supper was characterised by silence and spontaneous contributions of the kind described by Trotter. For Trotter, see H. Pickering, *Chief Men among the Brethren*, 2nd edn, London, n.d., pp. 31–2; and H. H. Rowdon, *The Origins of the Brethren, 1825–1850*, London, 1967, p. 175. For Brethren worship, see N. Dickson, '"Shut in with Thee": The Morning Meeting among Scottish Open Brethren', in R. N. Swanson, ed., *Continuity and Change in Christian Worship*, Studies in Church History 35, Woodbridge, Suffolk, 1999.

The extract is taken from W. Trotter, *Five Letters on Worship and Ministry in the Spirit*, London, n.d., pp. 4–5.

Have there not been times when His presence has been realised as a fact? and how blessed were such seasons! There might be, and there were, intervals of silence; but how were they occupied? In solemn waiting upon God. Not in restless anxiety as to who was next to speak or pray; not in turning over the leaves of Bibles or hymn books to find something that we thought suitable. No; nor in anxious thoughts about those who were lookers-on, wondering what they would think of the silence that existed. God was there. Each heart was engaged with Him; and for any to have broken silence, for the sake of doing so, would have been felt to be an interruption indeed.

When silence was broken, it was with a prayer that embodied the desires, and expressed the breathings of all present; or a hymn in which all could with fulness of heart unite; or a word which came home to our hearts with power. And though several might be used in such hymns, and prayers, and ministrations, it was as evidently one Spirit who guided and arranged the whole, as though a plan of it had been made before-hand, and each one had had his part assigned. No human wisdom could have made such a plan. The harmony was divine. It was the Holy Ghost acting by the several members, in their several places, to express the worship or to meet the need of all present.

Document IV.6

James Martineau's Call to Worship, 1862

For James Martineau, see II.15. His 'liturgical genius' (Horton Davies) was expressed in *Common Prayer for Christian Worship* (1862), which blended dignity in the divine presence with a typically Unitarian sense of the mildness of the divine attributes. The book was to be a model for the growing number of Free Churches that adopted liturgical worship over the next eighty years. See H. Davies, *Worship and Theology in England*, vol. 4, Princeton, New Jersey, 1962, pp. 271–81.

The extract is taken from the Ninth Service in the revised form of *Common Prayer* which was published as *Ten Services of Public Prayer*, London, 1879.

Call to Worship.

Dearly beloved brethren, the heavenly Father in whose presence we now stand is always more ready to hear than we to pray: nor does anything hide him from us but the veil of our impure and earthly mind. And since the preparations of even the willing heart are not without him, let us inwardly pray for the grace of a humble and holy spirit: that for a little while we may be alone with him; and, as his beloved Son went up into the mountain to pray, so we may rise above the haste and press of life, and commune with him in spirit and in truth.

Let us pray.
¶ *All kneeling.*

O God, who art, and wast, and art to come, before whose face the generations rise and pass away: age after age the living seek thee, and find that of thy faithfulness there is no end. Our fathers in their pilgrimage walked by thy guidance, and rested on thy compassion: still to their children be thou the cloud by day, the fire by night. Where but in thee have we a covert from the storm or shadow from the heat of life? In our manifold temptations, thou alone knowest and art ever nigh: in sorrow, thy pity revives the fainting soul: in our prosperity and ease, it is thy Spirit only that can wean us from our pride, and keep us low. O thou sole source of peace and righteousness; take now the veil from every heart, and join us in one communion with thy prophets and saints who have trusted in thee, and were not ashamed. Not of our worthiness, but of thy tender mercy, hear our prayer. *Amen.*

Document IV.7

Saul Street Primitive Methodist Chapel, Preston, 1869

The fervour of Primitive Methodism decayed only slowly as it settled into the groove of urban respectability. At Saul Street, the chief chapel of the denomination in Preston, Lancashire, the interior might not be prepossessing and the ministers might not be distinguished, but the worship, as observed by a visiting journalist in 1869, was still lively – though not as lively as it once had been.

The extract is taken from A. Hewitson, *Our Churches and Chapels*, Preston, 1869, pp. 72–4.

The chapel has a somewhat spacious interior; and has a large gallery fixed on six rather slender iron pillars. The pews have at some time had one or more coats of light delicate green paint – the worst colour which could be chosen for endurance – put upon them, and many are now curiously black at the rear, through people leaning back against them. A glance round shows the various sombre places, and their relative darkness gives a fair clue as to the extent of their use. At one end there is a small gallery for the choir and the organ, and in front of it the pulpit, a plain moderately-substantial affair, is located. The organ is a very poor one. It has a tolerably good appearance; but it is a serious sinner with reference to its internal arrangements. We quietly examined it very recently, and should have gone away with a determination not to be comforted if an intimation had not been made to the effect that 'the organist was organising a plan for a new organ,' and that there was some probability of a better instrument being fit up before very long. The members of the choir are of a brisk, warbling turn of mind, and can push through their work blithely. The singing is thoroughly congregational – permeates the whole place, is shot out in a quick, cheerful strain, is always strong and merry, is periodically excellent, is often jolly and funny, has sometimes a sort of chorus to it, and altogether is a strong, virtuously-jocund, free and easy piece of ecstacy which the people enjoy much. It would stagger a man fond of 'linked sweetness long drawn out,' it might superinduce a mortal ague in one too enamoured of Handel and Mozart; but to those who regularly attend the place, who have got fairly upon the lines of Primitive action, it is a simple process of pious refreshment and exhilaration. The chapel will hold between 700 and 800 persons; if hydraulicised 1000 might be got into it; but such a number is rarely seen in the place; and the average attendance may be set down at about 500. ... The congregation of Saul-street chapel is almost entirely of a working-class character. In the front and on each side of the body of the building there are a few free seats, which are mainly used by very poor humble-looking people. The ministers are the Rev. J. Judson, who is the superintendent, and the Rev. W. Graham. ... Reverting to Mr. Judson, it may be said that he is a quiet, earnest, elderly, close-shaven, clerical looking gentleman – has a well-defined, keen solemnity on his countenance, looks rather like a Catholic priest in facial and habilimental cut, is one of the old school of Primitive preachers, is devout but not luminous, good but not erudite, is slow and long-drawn in his utterances, but he can effervesce on a high key at intervals, and can occasionally 'draw out' the brethren to a hot pitch of exuberance. His general style is sincere; he means well; but his words, like cold-drawn castor oil, don't go down with over much gusto. The junior preacher – Mr. Graham – is more modernised in manner and matter. He is an earnest, thoughtful, plodding man, can preach a fair sermon, [sheds] tears a little sometimes, and can 'bring down the house' in tolerably good style. ... Not much time is lost by the

Saul-street Primitives: every Monday evening they have preaching at the place; on Tuesday evening three or four class meetings, in which singing, praying, and talking are carried on; on Wednesday ditto; on Thursday evening the singers work up their exercises; on Friday evening there is a meeting of leaders, or committee men; on Saturday evening a band of hope meeting; and on Sundays they are throng from morning till night. Their prayer meetings are pious and gleeful affairs. Throughout the whole of such gatherings, and in fact generally when prayer is being gone on with, the steam is kept well up, and the safety valve often lifts to let off the extra pressure. Sharp shouts, breezy 'Amens,' tenderly-attenuated groans, deep sighs, sudden 'Hallelujahs,' and vivacious cries of 'Just now,]' 'Aye,' 'Glory,' 'Yes,' 'Praise the Lord,' &c. – all well meant – characterise them. But prayer meetings are not half so stormy as they used to be; twenty or thirty years since they were tremendously boisterous; now, whilst a fair amount of ejaculatory talk is done at them, they are becoming comparatively quiet, and on Sundays only a few of the old-fashioned and more passionately devoted members make noises.

Document IV.8

R. W. Dale on Preaching, 1877

For R. W. Dale, see II.16. In 1877 Dale delivered the Lyman Beecher lectures at Yale on preaching. He was himself a majestic preacher, though fearing that he was too cerebral in approach; but the weakness of young preachers that he describes must have been all too common – and not just among the young.

The extract is taken from R. W. Dale, *Nine Lectures on Preaching*, London, 1877, pp. 131–4.

What is the sermon to do? The answer to this question determines the whole method of preparation.

Is it your principal intention to prove some Christian doctrine, to support the teaching of a particular text by appealing to the concurrent authority of other parts of Holy Scripture? – then your line of preparation is clear. If you do not happen to have in hand, as the result of your previous studies, an organised statement of the Scripture evidence – direct and indirect – of the truth on which you are about to preach, you must rely on your general knowledge of the contents of the Bible, and you must hunt up the proofs you want, and carefully verify them.

Is it your intention to state and explain some truth which you have reason to suppose is not generally understood? Then you may be greatly helped by thinking of two or three members of your congregation who are least likely to understand it, and you should consider by what lines of thought and by what class of illustrations you would be able to make the truth clear to them if you were talking to them in private. …

Perhaps your principal object is practical; you want to get the people to discharge some duty which they neglect, or to break with some sin. If you have reason to believe that they have no clear understanding of the nature of the duty, or that they do not believe that the sin is forbidden by the law of Christ, your first endeavour must be to instruct their consciences; and until the necessary instruction has been given, your appeals and warnings, no matter how solemn, vehement, and passionate, will have no effect. You will then consider what motives will most powerfully influence the particular class of persons who are neglecting the duty on which you are insisting, or who are committing the positive sin from which you are trying, with God's good help, to rescue them. ...

I believe that many young preachers, when they sit down to prepare a sermon, start like Abraham, who 'went out, not knowing whither he went.' Or perhaps it would be truer to say that for half an hour or an hour they do not start at all, but look idly round their subject, and wonder whether they will be able to make anything of it. At last, by some accident, they find what looks like a path, and after trying it they find that it leads nowhere, and so they come back to the place where they began. The preacher who has a definite end to reach, rarely loses any of the time which he gives to preparation; he sees in the distance the point to which he has to travel, and he either finds or makes a road to it.

Document 4.9

A Strict Baptist View of Worship, 1879

Charles Waters Banks (1806–86), a London pastor and printer, commenced a monthly Strict Baptist periodical known as *The Earthen Vessel* in 1845. See K. Dix, *Strict and Particular: English Strict and Particular Baptists in the Nineteenth Century*, Didcot, Oxfordshire, 2001, pp. 184–8; and DEB. In the January 1879 issue of *The Earthen Vessel* (pp. 21–3) B. G. Walker of Willenhall, Staffordshire, contributed an article asking the question, 'Do we worship God in spirit and in truth?' He wrote after having witnessed the profound emotion of a woman as she bowed in worship and prayer before a statue in a Roman Catholic cathedral. The 'rage for sermons' that he mentions was widespread in Nonconformity.

We often feel sorrowful when we witness the placid coldness and the lukewarm spirit in which the worship of God is carried on in many places, and especially in Churches which profess to hold the doctrines of grace. ...

I have been pained, when at chapels, to hear the minister say something like this: 'Our time this morning (or evening) is rather short, so we will curtail the preliminaries in order to have more time for the sermon.' This is surely not worshipping God in spirit. To impress the people with the idea that you are anxious to get through the hymns, reading, and prayer as soon as possible, and the sooner the better, is scarcely to be called spiritual worship, and, to my mind, is calculated to be very injurious. If there is any preference in our accustomed order of worship, the sermon appears to be last in the scale. Singing ought to be the grateful breathing of our our hearts in praise to the Lord for His continual blessings. The reading of the Word is a very solemn part of our worship, for it is the voice of God speaking to us, and should be received as a blessing direct from God. But the sermon is not addressed to God; it is an opening up, explaining, and illustrating passages of Scripture, and drawing from thence comfort for poor souls who are traversing this wilderness world, and a warning to the sinner to flee from the wrath to come.

I would not for one moment under-rate the sermon, for sermons have been greatly blessed in being instrumental in awakening sinners and in confirming feeble knees; but this I would urge, that seeing what a great God it is with whom we have to do, let our worship be as much as possible freed from hindrances which would cause it to be void of spirit. The rage for sermons has reached such an extent that it matters not how apt a man might be in visiting the poor and afflicted, however consistent in walk and conversation, however firm in the faith, however solemn and impressive in conducting the worship of God, yet if he is not just what his hearers would have him to be in preaching, he is accounted of little worth.

Document IV.10

Gideon Congregational Church, Newfoundland Street, Bristol, 1880

Gideon Congregational Church stood in a densely populated part of Bristol. Its morning service at 11 and evening service at 6.30 (typical times) were visited in 1880 by a sympathetic lay observer who was actually invited to offer prayer. He comments on the 'devout manner' of what was evidently a decorous though socially mixed congregation. The sermon lengths, at around forty minutes, were also typical.

The extract is taken from R. D. Robjent, *The Bristol Nonconformist Sunday Services*, Bristol, n.d., pp. 9–11.

Inside it is a large place of worship, painted and neatly decorated; there are galleries, the choir and organ gallery being at the rear of the pulpit, which stands on a platform. The organ is ornamented, and the numbers of the hymns and tunes are placed in a frame near thereto, a very convenient plan when the organist's curtain does not prevent the congregation in any part of the building seeing the numbers. The boarding under the seats hinders kneeling. The service on Sunday morning, November, 1880, was conducted by the Minister, who commenced with a short prayer. Previously to his reading the second portion of Scripture, he said he observed two friends present, and wished them to pray, after he had concluded the reading. I considered it to be a privilege to be one of the friends; the other was a stranger to me. After our prayers, the Minister prayed – hymns were sung, and the devout manner of the choir and congregation was such that I not only knew I was in the House of God, but I felt it also! The sermon occupied thirty-seven minutes, the text being a part of the 11th verse in the 43rd chapter in Genesis,

'And carry down the man a present.' The Minister, who made several references to the Bible, was earnest and thoughtful, the sermon was extemporary. There were several vacant seats, especially in the galleries. After the conclusion of the service, a working man in the congregation, who had passed the middle age of life, went to the Minister, who was in the Church, having left the pulpit, and informed him that he had found 'peace in the Saviour!' Having an opportunity of speaking to him, I asked him, at what portion of the service; his reply was, partly through the whole service, but particularly when the hymn 'Rock of ages' was being sung. 'Something then came over me,' he said, 'and I felt bound to go and tell the Minister!' Such a circumstance as this is exceptional in these days, and there is nothing I record with so great a pleasure. The Minister, as well he may be, was also heartily glad!

The Minister conducted the service in the evening of the same Sunday, November, 1880, commencing with a hymn which was sung. He prayed devoutly, and read portions of Scripture. The extemporary sermon was solemn and able, and occupied forty minutes. The text was a portion of the 6th verse in the 64th chapter in Isaiah, 'And we all do fade as a leaf.' His earnestness as to the salvation of souls made me come to the conclusion that he may rightly be called one of the successors of John Wesley! There was a larger congregation than in the morning, and several persons were in the galleries. The time will come when Churches and other places of worship will be filled, where there are sincere and godly preachers. Notice was given both morning and evening, of the week-evening prayer meeting. After the service, a prayer meeting was held in the school room adjoining the Church, at which a large number of persons assembled. It was a worshipping company, and a happy meeting.

Document IV.11

The Welsh *Hwyl*, c. 1880

David Davies (1834–1908) was an unpretentious Baptist farmer-minister at Maesyrhelem Baptist Chapel, Radnorshire, who claimed not to be able to grasp Maclaren's sermons (see I.8). His son describes Davies producing the *hwyl*, a phenomenon exclusive to Wales that involved both preacher and congregation in an intense form of suppressed excitement and could give rise to an involuntary sound like a shrill humming.

The extract is taken from R. Davies, 'An Estimate and an Appreciation', in E. Davies, *The Life of the Late Rev. David Davies*, Maesyrhelem, Brecon, 1914, pp. 68–9.

His style of pulpit oratory was typically Welsh, and was distinctly of the pulpit and not of the platform order. He was a past-master in that mellifluous, song-like speech of inspired preaching which has been so characteristic of the Principality. It is not every aspirant to this kind of preaching that can perform the feat successfully, and with agreeable results to his congregation, as many who have endured such attempts can feelingly testify. Painful recollections remain with some congregations as the result of the ambitions of certain individuals to acquire this style of eloquence. An English lady once asked a Welsh preacher if he used the 'Welsh howl' in his pulpit ministrations. Of course, it was the 'Welsh hwyl' she meant, and it was the limitation of the Saxon tongue that accounted for the mispronunciation and its unintended and unconscious insinuation. But in some cases, perhaps, 'howl' would be no misnomer. Unless one has a natural aptitude for that particular kind of oratory, there will certainly be more 'howl' than 'hwyl' about it. But Mr. Davies could do the 'hwyl' with consummate skill. He possessed the necessary gifts in a perfect form, so that as a piece of vocal execution, even, his preaching was sometimes astonishing, and exerted a kind of wizardry over the congregation that held them spell-bound, or roused them into uncontrollable manifestations of feeling. He could mesmerize the multitudes with the magic of his tones and overwhelm them by the sheer effect of his 'hywl.' It was, indeed, a marvellous performance, and few who heard it will ever forget its thrill.

Document IV.12

Caroline Stephen on Quaker Silent Waiting, 1891

Caroline Amelia Stephen (1834–1909), a sister of Sir Leslie Stephen, the first editor of *The Dictionary of National Biography*, was a Quaker by convincement, that is a convert to the Society of Friends. Doubts about the affirmations of the Anglican liturgy led her to accept an invitation to a Friends' meeting where the atmosphere induced her to throw in her lot with the Society in 1879. This passage is an account of her experience on that occasion. See DNB.

The extract is taken from C. Stephen, *Quaker Strongholds*, 3rd edn, London, 1891, pp. 12–13.

When lo, on one never-to-be-forgotten Sunday morning, I found myself one of a small company of silent worshippers, who were content to sit down together without words, that each one might feel after and draw near to the Divine Presence, unhindered at least, if not helped, by any human utterance. Utterance I knew was free, should the words be given; and before the meeting was over, a sentence or two were uttered in great simplicity by an old and apparently untaught man, rising in his place amongst the rest of us. I did not pay much attention to the words he spoke, and I have no recollection of their purport. My whole soul was filled with the unutterable peace of the undisturbed opportunity for communion with God – with the sense that at last I had found a place where I might, without the faintest suspicion of insincerity, join with others in simply seeking His presence. To sit down in silence could at the least pledge me to nothing; it might open to me (as it did that morning) the very gate of heaven. And since that day, now more than seventeen years ago, Friends' meetings have indeed been to me the greatest of outward helps to a fuller and fuller entrance into the spirit from which they have sprung; the place of the most soul-subduing, faith-restoring, strengthening and peaceful communion, in feeding upon the bread of life, that I have ever known.

Document IV.13

The British Weekly on Sermon Texts, 1896

The British Weekly was edited from its foundation in 1886 by William Robertson Nicoll (1851–1923), a minister of the Free Church of Scotland who had to retire from the pulpit because of a delicate throat. The journal targeted Nonconformists as well as Scottish Presbyterians with news of public affairs together with theological and literary material of a high order. Its innovations included occasional surveys of its readership, one of which, in 1896, asked for the texts of sermons on a single Sunday. The results showed that the sermons tended to concentrate on the more familiar parts of the Bible. The length of sermons, reported on 19 March 1896, p. 356, varied from 1 hour 28 minutes, by Mr E. W. Bishop at Clay Cross Methodist New Connexion Chapel, Derbyshire, to 5.75 minutes, by the Rev. G. Bicheno at the Primitive Methodist Chapel in Clitheroe, Lancashire. For Nicoll, see T. H. Darlow, *William Robertson Nicoll*, London, 1925; and DNB.

The extract is taken from *The British Weekly*, 26 March 1896, p. 379.

From the large collection of coupons and postcards sent in response to our request a fortnight ago, we have been able to make some comparisons as to the books of the Bible from which texts were principally chosen on Sunday, March 8th. Three-fourths of the entire number were from the New Testament, and in the New Testament the favourite book was the Gospel of St. John. Texts from St. John's Gospel introduced about one-sixth of all the sermons on the New Testament.

Next to this Gospel, and very near it, comes the first Epistle of St. John, which supplies texts for one-sixth of the remaining discourses. St. Luke, St. Matthew and St. Mark follow next in order; then the Epistle to the Hebrews, the Acts, the first Epistle to the Corinthians, and the Romans. The other books are in the following order: Ephesians, Philippians, Revelation (the last two equal), Galatians, 1st Peter, Colossians, 1st Timothy, 2nd Timothy, Titus, Epistle of St. James, 1st Thessalonians, Jude. No texts were sent us from Philemon, or 2nd and 3rd John.

A fifth of the Old Testament texts were from the Psalms. Next comes the book of Genesis, which supplies texts for one-seventh of the whole. Isaiah follows, and curiously enough the book of Nehemiah is the next on the list. It is an interesting fact that one out of every eleven Old Testament texts sent in to us is from Nehemiah. Exodus follows, but at a considerable distance. Deuteronomy, Joshua, 2nd Kings, and Jeremiah (the last three equal), 1st Kings and Proverbs (equal), Numbers, 2nd Samuel, Job, Daniel (equal), 1st Samuel, Ezekiel, Hosea, Zechariah, all provided a fair number of texts. Very few sermons were preached from Haggai, Jonah, Amos, Leviticus, Joel, and Malachi; none on Lamentations, Obadiah, Micah, Nahum, Habakkuk, and Zephaniah.

Many texts were chosen several times by preachers in different parts of the country. Among the favourite texts were the following:

Gen. v. 24, 'And Enoch walked with God.'
Gen. xxii. 1, 'God did tempt Abraham.'
Gen. xl. 23, 'Yet did not the chief butler remember Joseph, but forgat him.'
Josh. v. 13, 14. The meeting between Joshua and the captain of the Lord's host.
Psalm xiv. 1, 'The fool hath said in his heart, There is no God.'
Psalm lxxii. 17, 'His name shall endure for ever: his name shall be continued as long as the sun,' etc.
Isa. lv. 1, 2, 'Ho, every one that thirsteth,' etc.
Isa. lvii. 15, 'For thus saith the high and lofty One that inhabiteth eternity,' etc.
Hosea vii. 8, 'Ephraim is a cake not turned.'
Matt. iv. I, The story of the Temptation.
Matt. v. 13, 'Ye are the salt of the earth.'

The passages which provided most sermons were the trial of Abraham (Genesis xxii.) and the Temptation in the Wilderness (St. Matthew iv.). The single verse on which most sermons were preached was Galatians ii. 20, 'I am crucified with Christ,' etc.

Other favourite passages were St. Matthew xi. 28–30, ii. 28, xvi. 24, xxii. 42; St. Luke ix. 56, xi. 22; Philippians iii. 8; St. John viii. 12, xx. 26–29, xiii. 34, xiv. 1, xvii. 3; St. Mark viii. 34.

Document IV.14

C. Silvester Horne and T. H. Darlow: Orders for Morning and Evening Service, 1897

At the end of the nineteenth century liturgical worship was making headway in the Nonconformist churches (see IV.6). The Congregational pioneer was John Hunter, who published *Devotional Services for Use in Nonconformist Chapels* in 1882. He was imitated by, amongst others, Charles Silvester Horne (1865–1914) and Thomas Herbert Darlow (1858–1927). Horne, one of Fairbairn's first students at Mansfield College, Oxford (see III.6), was serving as minister of the fashionable Allen Street Congregational Church, Kensington; he later became superintendent of Whitefield's Central Mission, Tottenham Court Road, chairman of the Congregational Union in 1910 and MP for Ipswich in the same year. See W. B. Selbie, *The Life of Charles Silvester Horne, M.A., M.P.*, London, 1920; and C. Binfield, *So Down to Prayers: Studies in English Nonconformity, 1780–1920*, London, 1977, chap. 9. Darlow, a Cambridge graduate, was minister at Crosby, warden of Browning Hall, Walworth, and minister of New College Chapel, Hampstead, before becoming, in 1898, literary superintendent of the British and Foreign Bible Society. See *Who Was Who, 1916–1928*.

The extract is taken from C. S. Horne and T. H. Darlow, *'Let Us Pray': A Handbook of Selected Collects and Forms of Prayer for the Use of Free Churches*, London, 1897, pp. 14–15.

Worship

An Order of Morning Service.

ANTHEM.
Prayer. – Opening Sentences
  A Confession
HYMN.
LESSON.
CHANT.
COMMANDMENTS OF CHRIST WITH RESPONSES.

Prayer. – A Collect.
  The Lord's Prayer.
ANTHEM.
Prayer. – By the Minister.
CHILDREN'S HYMN.
WORDS TO CHILDREN.
NOTICES [*if any*].
HYMN.
SERMON.
OFFERTORY [*if any*].
HYMN.
Prayer. – Collects
  Benediction.

An Order of Evening Service.

HYMN.
Prayer. – Opening Sentences
  A Collect
  The Lord's Prayer.
CHANT.
LESSON.
ANTHEM.
Prayer. – A Thanksgiving
  or An Intercession
  or A Short Litany
HYMN.
Prayer. – By the Minister.
HYMN.
NOTICES [*if any*].
SERMON.
OFFERTORY [*if any*].
HYMN.
Prayer. – Collects
  Benediction.

Sacraments

Document IV.15

Adam Clarke on Holy Communion, 1830

> For Clarke, see 1.2. Here he expounds a Wesleyan view of holy communion, which, while primarily treating the rite as a memorial, approaches as close as he dare to discerning a sacrificial element as well. The extract is taken from a sermon on Luke 22: 19 called 'The Nature and Design of the Holy Eucharist' published in A. Clarke, *Discourses on Various Subjects*, vol. 3, London, 1830, pp. 221–2.

It may be just necessary to state a few reasons for frequenting the table of the Lord, and profiting by this ordinance ...

1. Jesus Christ has commanded His disciples to do this in remembrance of Him: and, were there no other reason, this certainly must be deemed sufficient by all those who respect His authority as their Teacher and Judge. *He who breaks one of the least of His commandments*, (and certainly this is not one of the least of them,) *and teaches others*, either by precept or example, *so to do, shall be called least in the kingdom of heaven*. What an awful reproof must this be to those who either systematically reject, or habitually neglect, this holy ordinance.

2. As the oft-repeated sacrifices in the Jewish church, and particularly the *Passover*, were intended to point out the Son of God till He came; so, it appears, our blessed Lord designed that the Eucharist should be a principal mean of keeping in remembrance his passion and death; and thus shew forth Him who *has* died for our offences; as the others did Him who, in the fulness of time, *should* die.

I believe it will be generally found, that those who habitually neglect this ordinance, seldom attach much consequence to the doctrine of the atonement, and those kindred doctrines essentially connected with it.

Though I am far from supposing that the Holy Eucharist is itself a *sacrifice*, which is a most gross error in the Romish church; yet I am as fully convinced that it can never be scripturally and effectually celebrated by any but those who consider it as *representing* a *sacrifice*, even that of the life of our blessed Lord, the only available sacrifice for sin; and that the Eucharist is the only ordinance, instituted by divine appointment among men, in which any thing of the ancient sacrificial forms yet remains; and that this, in its *form*, and in the *manner* of its administration, partakes so much of the ancient expiatory offerings, *literally* considered, and so much of the *spirit* and *design* of those offerings, as ever to render it the most lively exhibition both of the *sign* and the *thing signified*; and, consequently, a rite the most wisely calculated to shew forth the death of the Son of God, till He shall come to judge the quick and dead.

Document IV.16

Primitive Methodist Communion at Conference, 1841

In the following account of the communion service held at the Primitive Methodist Conference at Reading on 11 June 1841 there is evident a 'primitivist' desire to imitate exactly the practices of the apostolic church, characteristic of the more popular types of Nonconformity. Yet there are other features which are specifically Methodist, reflecting the Wesleyan background of the Primitives' leaders, if not a still older tradition: the elevation of the bread, kneeling to receive the elements, the ordained receiving before the laity and the sending back of 'consecrated' bread to the circuits. For Hugh Bourne, see IV.1; James was his brother and Clowes the co-founder of the denomination.

The extract is taken from *The Primitive Methodist Magazine*, 1841, pp. 305, 353–6.

The Holy Sacrament of the Supper of the Lord...This proved to be one of the crowning ordinances...administered by Bros Hugh Bourne, James Bourne and William Clowes...After singing and prayer one of the brethren stood up and spoke of the first institution of the feast of the Passover in Egypt...He next spoke of our Lord continuing it in the christian church...He then took up a plate from the table which had on it a number of unleavened cakes and held it up in the presence of the people, using the words of the apostle 1 Cor.xi.24...He then took up a bottle (there were four bottles on the table) and he poured out into a cup and spoke of the blood of Christ which was shed for us...A quantity of bread was immediately broken into small pieces on one of the plates; and the three appointed to minister took the sacrament. A number then came forward and kneeled at the forms, placed there for that purpose...and when they had partaken...a verse was given out; and while it was singing they rose from their knees and retired; and a number more took their places...at the close many of the delegates wished for and obtained each a piece of the bread that remained to take with them to their respective circuits.

[Further note by Hugh Bourne on the bread] We got information from several quarters relating to the Jewish Passover cakes...Now if any respect should be paid to the primitive institution, in the celebration of this divine ordinance, then unleavened, unyeasted bread should be used.

[Further note by Hugh Bourne on the wine] Our sister Ride purchased six pounds of good raisins, which cost two shillings and nine pence. She had them cut and put into an earthen vessel; poured on them as much boiling water as she thought proper; covered the vessel over, and set it warm, stirring it occasionally. And the next day the wine was ready for bottling.

Document IV.17

Baptist Noel on Believer's Baptism, 1849

Baptist Wriothesley Noel (1795–1873) came from a prominent aristocratic Evangelical Anglican family, served in London as minister of the Anglican proprietary chapel at St John's, Bedford Row, and was a prolific author. In 1848 he created a stir by seceding from the Church of England on the ground that its establishment was unscriptural. On 9 August 1849 he was baptised as a believer in John Street Chapel, where he subsequently ministered to a Baptist congregation. See D. W. Bebbington, 'The Life of Baptist Noel', *Baptist Quarterly*, 24 (1972), pp. 389–411; and DNB.

The extract is taken from a tract, *Address of the Hon. and Rev. B. W. Noel on the Occasion of his Baptism*, [London, 1849], pp. 1–2.

I have not come to the resolution to obey what I believe to be Christ's command, without having fully weighed the grounds upon which that step is to be taken. Without having read anything whatever in favour of the exclusive right of believers to Christian baptism, I have read all the strongest arguments that I could meet with upon the other side. I believe I have weighed well every considerable argument that has ever been adduced in the maintenance of infant baptism, as an addition to, and which evidently becomes a substitution for, the baptism of believers in Christian Churches; and I have come distinctly to these two conclusions, which appear to me, at least, to be certain. I will not speak of the convictions of others, but I speak of the conviction of my own mind, after very much examination. It appears to me to be distinctly proved, first, that baptism, as ordained by Christ, is an immersion in water, a being buried in the water; and, secondly, that immersion is meant to be a profession of faith in Christ. If these two conclusions are correct (and I believe they will completely prevail with the Christian world eventually), then it follows that a person who, like myself, has only been sprinkled in infancy, is unbaptised; because such a person has neither been immersed, nor has he made a baptismal profession of faith; and these two things constitute Christian baptism. So that, if these conclusions are correct, then I, and others, who have been only sprinkled in infancy, are in neither sense baptised.

Document IV.18

Catholic Apostolic Church Eucharist, 1850

The Catholic Apostolic Church arose from the work of Edward Irving (1792–1834), a minister of the Church of Scotland in London who, after astonishing the world by announcing the imminent second coming and approving speaking in tongues, was deposed from the ministry in 1832 for Christological heresy. His congregation came to believe that apostles had been restored to the church and, after Irving's death, twelve of them organised its global mission. Primarily the achievement of John Bate Cardale (1802–77), the 'Pillar of the Apostles' (see DNB), the elaborate liturgy of the church derived from Eastern Orthodox as well as Roman Catholic and Anglican models. See P. E. Shaw, *The Catholic Apostolic Church sometimes called Irvingite*, Morningside Heights, New York, 1946; C. G. Flegg, *'Gathered under Apostles': A Study of the Catholic Apostolic Church*, Oxford, 1992.

The extract is from *The Order for the Celebration of the Holy Eucharist*, n.p., 1850 edn, pp.10–11, 17. The prayer of consecration uses the epiclesis or invocation of the Holy Spirit that is characteristic of Eastern rites; the prayer before communion embodies the continuing advent hope.

THE CONSECRATION.

Look upon us, O God, and bless and sanctify this bread.

In the Name of the Father, and of the Son, and of the Holy Ghost, we bless ✠ this bread; and we beseech Thee, heavenly Father, to send down Thy Holy Spirit, and make it unto us the Body of Thy Son Jesus Christ: Who, the same night in which He was betrayed, took bread;[1] and after He had given thanks, He brake it,[2] and said, Take, eat, THIS IS MY BODY, which is broken for you: this do ye in remembrance of Me.

R.   Amen.

Look upon us, O God, and bless and sanctify this cup.

In the Name of the Father, and of the Son, and of the Holy Ghost, we bless ✠ this cup; and we beseech Thee, heavenly Father, to send down Thy Holy Spirit, and make it unto us the Blood of Thy Son Jesus Christ: Who in like manner also took the cup[3] after He had supped, saying, THIS CUP IS THE NEW TESTAMENT IN MY BLOOD: this do ye, as often as ye drink it, in remembrance of Me.

R.   Amen.

...

THE CONCLUDING PRAYER BEFORE COMMUNION.

Hasten, O God, the time when Thou shalt send from Thy right hand Him whom Thou wilt send; at whose appearing the saints departed shall be raised, and we which are alive shall be caught up to meet Him, and so shall ever be with Him. Under the veil of earthly things we have now communion with Him; but with unveiled face we shall then behold Him, rejoicing in His glory, made like unto Him in His glory; and by Him we, with all Thy Church, holy and unspotted, shall be presented with exceeding joy before the presence of Thy glory. Hear us, O heavenly Father, for His sake, to whom, with Thee and the Holy Ghost, One living and true God, be glory for ever and ever.

R.   Amen.

Notes

1. Here the Celebrant shall take the bread into his hands.
2. Here he shall break the bread.
3. Here he shall take the cup into his hands.

Document IV.19

A Primitive Methodist Defence of Pouring in Baptism, 1862

Public controversies about the principles separating the denominations were a feature of the earlier and middle years of the century. One recurring issue was the proper mode of baptism because the Baptists, apart from holding that the ordinance should be restricted to believers, maintained that it should be administered by total immersion. One such debate took place at Coalville in Leicestershire in 1862. The local Baptist minister named Porter put forward the case for immersion; the Primitive Methodist minister called Cresswell, stationed at nearby Church Gresley, answered him – successfully, if the account published by his side is to be credited.

The extract is taken from *The Coalville Discussion*, 2nd edn, Loughborough, [1862], pp. 6–7.

Mr. Cresswell then rose, and said: – The first thing which my opponent advanced in favour of immersion was John baptizing in Jordan. He appeared to me to want to make the impression that in Jordan signified under Jordan. We will allow this, examine it. In John 10th chapter 40th verse, we find an account of the Jews seeking to apprehend Christ; but he 'escaped out of their hands, and went again beyond Jordan into the place where John at first baptized, and there abode.' So that if John's baptizing in Jordan signifies under Jordan, it will make it appear that our Lord went and dwelt under the river. Again it is said that John baptized in the wilderness, and preached the baptism of repentance. I think we may fairly suppose that the wilderness was nearly as full of sand as the river Jordan was of water, so that this will make it appear that John dipped his candidates under the sand. Again we read that John was baptizing in Enon. Now Enon was not a river, but a place, and this will make it appear the he dipped them under Enon. Is my opponent prepared to admit the construction which he places on the words in Jordan? Now I do not believe that John dipped his candidates under the sand, or that our Saviour dwelt under the river, or that John dipped his candidates under Enon. I understand it to mean this, that John baptized at those places.

Document IV.20

C. H. Spurgeon on the Real Presence, c. 1880

Spurgeon (see I.4) believed in a weekly observance of the Lord's Supper. Some of the addresses given by him on these occasions, either in the Metropolitan Tabernacle or in his sitting-room when he was staying at Mentone in the south of France, were publishing in *'Till He Come'* (1894). This affirmation of the real presence of Christ comes from an address entitled 'Over the Mountains', based on the Song of Solomon 2: 16–17 (p. 69). See M. Walker, *Baptists at the Table*, Didcot, Oxfordshire, 1992, chap. 5.

In the sacred emblems now upon this supper table, Jesus is already among us. Faith cries, 'He has come!' Like John the Baptist, she gazes intently on Him, and cries, 'Behold the Lamb of God!' At this table Jesus feeds us with His body and His blood. His corporeal presence we have not, but His real spiritual presence we perceive. We are like the disciples when none of them durst ask Him, 'Who art Thou?' knowing that it was the Lord. He is come. He looketh forth at these windows, – I mean this bread and wine; showing Himself through the lattices of this instructive and endearing ordinance. He speaks. He saith, 'The winter is past, the rain is over and gone.' And so it is; we feel it to be so: a heavenly springtide warms our frozen hearts. Like the spouse, we wonderingly cry, 'Or ever I was aware, my soul made me like the chariots of Ammi-nadib.' Now in happy fellowship we see the Beloved, and hear His voice; our heart burns; our affections glow; we are happy, restful, brimming over with delight. The King has brought us into his banqueting-house, and His banner over us is love. It is good to be here!

Music and Hymnody

Document IV.21

William Gadsby's Hymn of Praise to Christ, 1814

In 1814 Gadsby (see I.3) published *A Selection of Hymns for Public Worship* to counteract what he believed to be Arminian and legalistic tendencies in Isaac Watts's *Psalms and Hymns* and John Rippon's *Selection*, the hymn books then in use in his Manchester congregation. Gadsby's original selection contained 513 hymns by various authors in Part I, and in Part II a further 157 by Gadsby himself. 'Immortal honours' is numbered 667, and entitled, 'Safety in Christ – Heb. xiii. 6; Phil. iv. 19.' In this hymn Gadsby sees Christ as the sufficient source of all his spiritual support. His response, in the first line of verse 4, reflects William Cowper's, 'O for grace to love thee more!'

Further parts have been added to the hymn book, and the latest edition of 1977 contains 1,156 hymns. It is still used by those Strict Baptists subscribing to *The Gospel Standard*.

Immortal honours rest on Jesus' head;
My God, my Portion, and my Living Bread;
In Him I live, upon him cast my care;
He saves from death, destruction and despair.

He is my Refuge in each deep distress;
The Lord my strength and glorious righteousness;
Through floods and flames He leads me safely on,
And daily makes his sovereign goodness known.

My every need he richly will supply;
Nor will his mercy ever let me die;
In him there dwells a treasure all divine,
And matchless grace has made that treasure mine.

O that my soul could love and praise him more,
His beauties trace, his majesty adore;
Live near his heart, upon his bosom lean;
Obey His voice, and all his will esteem.

Document IV.22

Hymn on Revival from the Primitive Methodist Short Hymn Book, 1829

Hugh Bourne (see IV.1) issued *A Collection of Hymns for Camp Meetings, Revivals, &c.* to supplement the main Primitive Methodist hymn book first published in 1824. *The Short Hymn Book*, as the newer collection was called, contained some of the most upbeat compositions for the occasions when the 'Ranters' were at their least inhibited. The anonymous hymn 13, not by Bourne himself, urges its hearers to 'Catch the fire' and culminates in an attractive rustic metaphor of bees swarming. See I. Sellers, *The Hymnody of Primitive Methodism*, n.p., 1993.

The hymn is taken from H. Bourne, *A Collection of Hymns for Camp Meetings, Revivals, &c.*, Bemersley, near Tunstall, 1829.

Revival

1 Haste again ye days of grace,
 When assembled in one place,
 Signs and wonders mark'd the hour!
 All were fill'd, and spoke with power;
 Hands uplifted, eyes o'erflow'd,
 Hearts enlarged, self destroy'd!
 All things common, now we'll prove,
 All our common stock be love.
   CHO. – Jesus now his work revives,
      Now his quick'ning spirit strives,
      Oh! let preachers, people – all,
      Listen to the glorious call!
      Join the simple lively throng,
      Catch the fire, and swell the song,
      Heart in heart, and hand in hand,
      Spread the life through all the land.
2 Oh! that each may now prevail!
 Act the faith that cannot fail!
 Rise and pull the blessing down!
 Seize the kingdom for their own!
 Fire our hearts with holy zeal,
 Glowing still for Zion's weal;
 Heaven open! blessings pour!
 Spirit work this present hour! – Jesus now, &c.
3 Lo! the knife we boldly take,
 Bind our Isaacs to the stake;
 Freely part with all for thee,
 Welcome King of liberty!

Now we die to self and sin,
Nothing feel but love within,
May this faith in works abound,
Shine and burn to all around.
> Cho. – Pilgrims! soon the journey's done!
> Warriors! soon the battle's won;
> Where your doubts, your cares, your fears!
> See! the glitt'ring crown appears!
> Hark! the angels shouting cry,
> 'Welcome! Welcome! to the sky!'
> Jesus calls, and calls for thee;
> 'Faithful servant come to me.'

4 Satan fill'd with hellish spite,
Veil'd in robes of borrow'd light
Strove to scatter ruin wide,
Disunite and then divide!
Still his utmost skill shall fail,
Patient love shall still prevail;
Clust'ring closer, now we'll cling,
Swarm and hive around our King. – Pilgrims, &c.

Document IV.23

J. C. Philpot on Singing in Worship, 1859

J. C. Philpot's reviews in *The Gospel Standard*, one of the Strict Baptist periodicals, were frequently essays on a subject, rather than appraisals of the book named at the heading of the review. In commenting on two collections of hymns (*Sacred Hymns from the German*, translated by Frances Elizabeth Cox, and *Hosannah to the Son of David*, by William Williams) in the June issue of 1859 (pp. 193–4), he offered some practical advice on congregational singing. (For Philpot, see X.19). The discussion of the precentor's role is a reminder that many strict communion Baptists, and some others, including Spurgeon, would not countenance musical instruments in worship.

And now, as the opportunity offers itself, will our readers permit us to drop a few thoughts upon singing as a part of the service of the sanctuary. We have already said that it is the sweetest, but we must add that it is the most difficult to carry on as a spiritual and acceptable service, and for the following reasons:

Of all our public services it is *the most mixed*. In the reading, expounding, praying, and preaching, the minister exercises a virtual and practical monopoly. It may be good or it may be bad; but it is a monarchy; not an aristocracy as in the prayer-meeting, nor a republic as in the singing, where rebellious voices – rebellious, we mean, against all the laws of melody and harmony, time and tune, are generally the loudest. Unhappily, a discordant voice is the sure fruit of an unmusical ear; and as this unmusical ear cannot detect its own discords, it is unashamed and unabashed at its own tones – tones which jar upon the musical ear worse than the knife-grinder's wheel or the ungreased hay-cart. Could we, then, have our own way, these jarring notes should either be silenced or softened, wholly mute, or lost in the crowd.

Another difficulty is, that the Lord's people who *should* sing, often from want of ear and voice, *cannot* sing, whilst those who for want of grace should not sing both can and do. ...

Congregational singing, not choral, is the only fit service of the sanctuary. A well tuned choir, with their fugues and their anthems, their singing in parts and their selections from Handel and Haydn, may please the ear, but they certainly grieve the heart which has in it any living faith and godly fear. Choral and congregational singing are not necessarily incompatible, but they almost invariably become so through the musical pride of the choir. The choir do not like their airs and graces, their new tunes and difficult pieces to be drowned, and, as they consider it, totally spoiled by the congregation. They, therefore, often purposely choose tunes which the congregation cannot sing, that their monopoly may be preserved intact, and that the singing may be not to the praise of God but themselves. And the congregation, continually beaten and baffled by the new and difficult tunes, at last cease to interfere with the singing gallery, which thus at last becomes, like the musical service at the London Magdalen or Foundling Hospital, a mere orchestra of performers.

The best plan, we think, is the London way, which is for a precentor (or clerk) to lead the air and the congregation to follow. When the precentor has a good ear so as not to drop or lower the key, and has a strong, clear tenor voice, which can lead the air without faltering, the congregation will be sure to follow, and to follow well too. The false notes of the bad singers are lost in the body of voice which sustains the air, and the general result is not only pleasing to the ear, but is what singing should be – congregational worship.

Document IV.24

Henry Allon on Church Choirs, 1870

Henry Allon (1818–92) was minister of the magnificent Union Chapel, Islington, and chairman of the Congregational Union in 1864 and 1881. A highly refined man, he encouraged music in worship, editing several collections of hymns. Yet in 1870 he was still insisting that choirs must lead worship rather than perform anthems independently. See W. H. Harwood, *Henry Allon*, London, 1894; and DNB.

The extract is taken from H. Allon, 'The Worship of the Church', in H. R. Reynolds, ed., *Ecclesia*, London, 1870, pp. 424–6.

This conception of Church services involves the further question whether it is essential to the worship of the congregation, that all its members should vocally contribute to it. That this should be the rule of worship-song admits of no question. Congregational praise should manifestly be expressed in forms in which all ordinary worshippers may easily join, so that the sacrifice of praise may go up to God, a great offering of united vocal song. ... The scientific musician or the fastidious amateur may not silence the great bulk of a congregation, because it has not attained to his culture. The same principle applies to the place and functions of Church choirs. The only legitimate conception of them is, that they lead the song of the congregation. God cannot be worshipped vicariously, and few perversions are more incongruous than for a congregation to be listening while a choir is performing. ... The consentaneous vocal song of a whole congregation is a higher degree of worship than the vicarious song of some twelve or twenty members of it. Hardly, we fear, would experience testify to any very great degree of devotional feeling produced by mere choir singing; not even in the judgment of the broadest charity, would either the deportment or the song of cathedral choirs produce generally the impression that they are pre-eminent ministers to the devout feeling of the congregation. ... Those who wish for the laudable enjoyment of sacred music, can hear it in almost any music-hall, and at almost any time, especially in towns large enough to have cathedral services.

Document IV.25

Presbyterian Views on Organs, 1856–70

The Presbyterian Church in England observed the same prohibition of organs as its sister churches in Scotland because it was thought that there was no scripture warrant for such instruments. The growing popularity of organs, however, led to their introduction in fashionable churches in Liverpool and Warrington, and, despite objections, they were allowed to remain. By 1870 the church dropped all pretence of resisting the innovation, as had the Church of Scotland in 1865. See D. Murray, 'Disruption to Union', in D. Forrester and D. Murray, eds, *Studies in the History of Worship in Scotland*, Edinburgh, 1984, p.90.

The extract is taken from L. Levi, ed., *Digest of the Actings and Proceedings of the Presbyterian Church in England, 1836–1876*, London, 1877, pp. 74–6. The passage also illustrates the legal form of procedure in Presbyterian church government.

INSTRUMENTAL MUSIC.

At Liverpool, 1856, the Synod took up an Overture from Dr. Hamilton and other members of the Court on the subject of Instrumental Music, which having been read and discussed, it was agreed by a majority of 58 to 32 as follows: – The Synod of the Presbyterian Church in England declare that the introduction of instrumental music in public worship is not approved by this Church, and enjoin all Presbyteries to take order that no such innovation be introduced in any of the congregations within their bounds, but to take steps, so far as practicable, to encourage and cultivate the harmonious exercise of vocal praise. A dissent was thereupon entered by Mr. W. Chalmers and others. ...

At Newcastle-on-Tyne, 1857, there was a reference from the Presbytery of Lancashire as to proceedings with regard to the continued use of an organ at St. George's Presbyterian Church, Liverpool, and at St. John's, Warrington; and after discussion, on the motion of Mr. Chalmers, seconded by Mr. Anderson (Morpeth), it was agreed by 53 to 49 as follows: – Dismiss the reference, find that the use of instrumental music in public worship, though not without precedent, is not in accordance with the ordinary practice of this Church, and ought not to be introduced in any case without the permission craved and obtained of the Supreme Court, and enjoin Presbyteries to take order accordingly. But with regard to the cases of St. John's, Warrington, and St. George's, Liverpool, inasmuch as instrumental music had been introduced into them by the sanction, express or implied, of the Presbytery of Lancashire, and is agreeable to the feelings and wishes of said congregations, while its prohibition would disturb their peace, destroy their prosperity, and endanger their very existence, the Synod instruct the Presbytery of Lancashire to take no further action in regard to them; and renews its injunctions to all Presbyteries to take steps, so far as practicable, to encourage and cultivate the harmonious exercise of vocal praise. ...

At London, 1870, the Synod took up the Overtures from the Presbyteries of London, Lancashire, and Berwick anent the use of instrumental music in public worship, and after discussion, by a majority of 121 to 49, the Synod, on the motion of Mr. Charles E. Lewis, and seconded by Rev. R. H. Lundie, resolved as follows: – The Synod, having taken into consideration the Overtures of the Presbyteries of Berwick, Lancashire, and London on the subject of the use of instrumental music in public worship, and having regard to the unsatisfactory position in which the question has been left by the previous deliverances of Synods, and being of opinion that the Church ought not, by any general resolution, to fetter the action of Sessions and congregations in this matter, hereby records the several resolutions of Synod passed on the subject in the years 1856, 1857, 1858, 1861, 1862, but urges congregations to continue their efforts for the better cultivation of vocal praise, and enjoins Presbyteries to take order that the substantial prosperity and harmony of congregations be regarded. From this deliverance the Rev. George Wallace, in his own name, and in the name of all who would adhere to him, entered his dissent, intimating his intention of assigning reasons in due time.

Document IV.26

Salvation Army Regulations on Brass Bands, 1881

Originally designed to drown interruptions at Salisbury in 1878, the brass band soon became a standard feature of the larger corps of the Salvation Army. It was simultaneously part of its military ethos and a stimulus to the hearty singing that was one of its hallmarks. See R. Sandall, *The History of the Salvation Army*, vol. 2, London, 1950, chap. 20.

The extract is taken from Sandall's *History*, vol. 2, pp. 323–4. In a typical blunt directive, measures are taken to ensure the loyalty of the bands to the Army. The signatory, William Bramwell Booth, was the oldest son of the General.

In order to prevent misunderstanding, and to ensure the harmonious working of the brass bands with the various corps to which they are attached, the following regulations are to be strictly observed.

1. None will be admitted or retained a member of any band who is not a member of the Army.
2. All the instruments in every band are to be the property of the Army, no matter by whom they may be purchased, or through whom they may be presented. The words 'Salvation Army brass band,' followed by the number of the corps, must be marked on every instrument. In no case are instruments to be used to play anything but salvation music, or on any but Salvation Army service.
3. In the event of any member of the band resigning his position as such, he will leave his instrument behind him.
4. In no case will any committee be allowed in connection with any band.
5. In every case the captain of the corps to which the band is attached shall direct the movements of the band, and shall appoint the bandmaster.
6. In no case will any band, or member of any band, be allowed to go into debt, either for instruments, or anything else, connected with the band.
7. In no case is the practice of the band, or any member of the band to interfere with the meetings of the corps.
8. It is strongly recommended that in cases where a treasurer or secretary is required by a band, the treasurer or secretary of the corps to which it is attached shall act in that capacity.
9. Any band that may have been, or may have formed, which does not carry out this order will not be recognized as a Salvation Army band, and must not in future be allowed to take part in the operations of the Army.
10. Any band failing to carry out this order will at once be disbanded.

By order of the General,
W. Bramwell Booth, Chief of the Staff

24 February 1881

Document IV.27

W. G. Tarrant's Easter Hymn, c. 1890

This hymn by William George Tarrant (1853–1928) was composed about 1890 and has been taken from *The Essex Hall Hymnal*, London, 1902. He was the leading Unitarian hymn writer of his day, whose work appeared in hymn books of various Dissenting denominations. It is a good example of the optimism for the future of humankind which was common amongst Liberal Christians within Dissent in the late nineteenth century.

The Light along the ages
Shines brighter as it goes
From age to age more glorious
Its radiant splendour grows.
Man's life, begun so lowly,
Now soars to heaven above,
To share, in life eternal,
The joys of endless love!

We thank thee, O our Father!
For every gift of thine;
All speak alike the bounty
Of tenderness divine;
But, every gift surpassing,
This wondrous thought we own, –
The Son of man is risen
To dwell before thy throne!

Wherever goodness reigneth
The soul of Christ lives on,
And every Christ-like spirit
Shall rise where he hath gone:
Earth's dust hath served its mission;
Henceforth the soul is free,
And through the heights of being
Ascends, O God, to thee!

Architectural Setting

Document IV.28

John Blackburn on the Gothic Style, 1847

John Blackburn (1891–55) served in Ireland and at Finchingfield, Essex, before becoming, in 1822, Independent minister at Claremont Chapel, Pentonville. He was secretary of the Congregational Union (1834–47), first editor of *The Congregational Magazine* (1818–45) and editor of the first two issues of *The Congregational Year Book* (1846–47). See DEB.

The extract is taken from Blackburn's 'Remarks on Ecclesiastical Architecture as applied to Nonconformist Chapels' in *The Congregational Year Book*, London, 1847, p. 161. Despite his reservations about the Roman Catholic associations of the Gothic (or 'English') style, he comes down decisively in its favour on aesthetic as well as utilitarian grounds. See C. Binfield, *So Down to Prayers: Studies in English Nonconformity, 1780–1920*, London, 1977, chap. 7.

The English or pointed style was a few years ago not likely to obtain favour with the nonconformist public. If we remember rightly, when Mill Hill grammar school was about to be erected, a beautiful plan and elevation in the English style was rejected, upon the ground of its ecclesiastical associations, and a more costly plan of a Grecian edifice was adopted instead, which, though it gave to the structure a noble portico, left the building as a whole, very destitute of appropriate decorations.

The new Lancashire Independent college, with its cloisters and dormitories, its gothic tower and oriel windows, demonstrates that a taste for the English style is now cultivated by nonconformists themselves. This has extended to our chapels also. Highbury chapel, Bristol, and the Congregational church, Holloway, are the most complete edifices we have seen in this style, and we must confess, in spite of all our prejudices, that the beauty and flexibility, the copious resources and power of adaptation, and, above all, the moderate cost of what is popularly denominated the Gothic style, compel us to give it our suffrages.

But we need not regard its symbolic mysteries, or adopt those ornaments which we know have been prostrated to purposes of superstition. We have our Protestant character to maintain in its integrity; and in these times of fearful apostacy to the church of Rome, it would afflict many honest Christians in other denominations, as well as in our own, if they should see our taste leading us to questionable conformities. But let us avail ourselves of those attractive forms, which are most agreeable to the eye, and are so flexible as to permit the erection of organ lofts, schools, lecture rooms or vestries, in harmony with the general edifice. This the Grecian style will not often allow, and then only at great expense ...

Worship

Document IV.29

Philip Sambell on the Gothic Style, 1867

Philip Sambell was an architect, practising largely in Cornwall, who had been responsible for a designing a large number of chapels. He had also been a Baptist church member at Falmouth for forty-six years when, in 1867, he wrote an impassioned plea for Nonconformists to avoid the Gothic style, which he preferred to call 'pointed'. Still, twenty years after Blackburn's championship of Gothic (IV.28), the style seemed tainted by its Catholic affinities.

The extract is taken from a letter dated 5 February 1867 written by Sambell to the editor of *The Baptist Magazine*, March 1867, pp. 171–2.

Pointed architecture is, *par excellence*, from its origin, the Romish-Priest architecture, and was designed to thoroughly subserve their superstition. That style flourished in the greatest perfection, and was elaborated and attained the richest decoration in Britain. The power of its association grew strong, and penetrated deep into the popular mind, so that Pointed architecture and Romanism became synonyms, and could with difficulty be dissociated, so as to permit the mind to appreciate the real beauty of that architecture by itself.

I submit that the Pointed style is misapplied when used by Protestant Dissenters for their chapels – nay, it is dangerous, because insidious in its approaches to induce a yearning after Ritualism. It cuts up and wastes valuable accommodation-space and costs far more than a chaste and simple classical edifice; and I would earnestly protest against any more imitations of the Pointed style.

We have no need for steeples, towers, &c., except as expensive ventilators or ornaments; yet we even build two spires, in the vain attempt at ambitious display. The stone and wood tracery, arches, painted glass, steep roofs, multiplicity of detail, – requiring lead, elaborate interior roof-timbering, and other matters essential in the Pointed style – all absorb so large a share of laboriously-collected money which would be better bestowed on comfort and greater accommodation.

As the classic style will meet all the reasonable requirements of Protestant Dissenters, in the manner I have indicated, let us not copy any part of a style that ministers to superstition – not even the cross, on that account.

Document IV.30

Penmaenmawr Wesleyan Chapel, 1890

Penmaenmawr is a small watering place on the north Welsh coast, a few miles west of Llandudno. On 10 December 1890 the memorial stones of a new chapel were laid there. The initiative had been taken by the superintendent of the Bangor circuit and money had been given by two rich Wesleyans from Whitchurch and Liverpool who no doubt spent holidays in Penmaenmawr.

The extract is taken from the *Wesleyan Chapel Committee Report*, 1890, p. 171. The building, designed by John Wills (see IV.31), was Gothic but severely practical, allowing for future expansion and also for the drastically different sizes of congregation in winter and summer.

The Chapel is in the Early Gothic style, and is planned with a view to make it a model sea-side place of worship.

Its plan is cruciform, with a nave and transepts, and chancel.

At present the nave and one transept only will be built, and this will be done in a manner to provide for a winter congregation of 100 in the transept, or, as the season advances, of 200 in the nave, or, in the height of the season, when transept and nave are thrown into one, for a congregation of 300.

The future transept and chancel will provide for 110 additional sittings, making an ultimate provision for 410 worshippers, who may all see and hear the preacher.

The adaptability of the Chapel to congregations of varying sizes, as at present, will be preserved, without in any way disturbing the present fabric.

Besides the Chapel there is a vestry, and on the basement floor an assembly room, large class-room, tea-room, etc., etc. None of the basement rooms are underground, but are entered from the level of the side road, while the Chapel is entered from the level of the front road.

The walls are of local Penmaenmawr stone, with limestone quoins and Tallacre stone dressings.

The windows are all glazed with cathedral glass in geometrical pattern; that to the chancel end being circular, with geometrical tracery. All the floors are wood block on concrete. The fittings throughout are in pitch-pine.

The roof is partially open and is a handsome piece of Early English work with octagon and moulded tie beams, and the spandrils filled in with cusped arches and panels. The heating is by hot water, by Mr. Smith, of Whitchurch.

The entire cost of the buildings is £2,030.

The Architect is Mr. John Wills, F.S.Sc., of Derby, and the Builders are Mr. Evan Evans of Penmaenmawr, and Mr. John Williams, of Bangor.

Document IV.31

John Wills on Duties of Caretakers, 1893

John Wills was a local preacher and class leader at Green Hill Wesleyan Church in Derby, where he practised as an architect. Between 1875 and 1900 he was responsible for more than seventy-five chapels for the Wesleyans alone, though he built many others for various Nonconformist denominations. He was twice a lay representative to Conference, president of the Derby and Derbyshire Band of Hope Union and a town councillor. See D. A. Barton, 'John Wills (1845–1906)', unpublished typescript, 1997.

Worship

The extract is taken from John Wills, *Hints to Trustees of Church Property*, 5th edn, Wisbech, 1893, pp. 19–20. It illustrates the brisk manner of a successful professional and the high expectations of chapel caretakers.

CONDENSED MANUAL
OF
CARE TAKER'S DUTIES.

Where practicable, the Care Taker should live on the premises, so as to attend more regularly and thoroughly to his duties; and should be chosen with great care. He should be cleanly, methodical, and civil. A surly, rough, cantankerous Care Taker has spoilt many Sunday Schools, and impaired the prosperity of churches. It is advisable, also, that his faculties should be unimpaired. A deaf, or near-sighted Care Taker, is most undesirable. There are occasions when a look or a whisper conveys a wish from an official; and alertness is required. Infirmities should not cause us to despise their possessor, neither should they be a passport or recommendation (as before now they have been) to a post involving great responsibilities. The wages of the Care Taker should not be too niggardly. If he does his duty well, he will deserve at least wages equal to a respectable mechanic.

The following summary of duties is suggested:–

1st. – As to Damp. – To keep outside of building clear of refuse; prune trees or bushes whose foliage makes walls wet. Report to officials first appearance of damp, and ascertain the cause. Examine and clean all eaves gutters at least three times in the year – April, October, and December. Where windows have tubes in theirs sills to let water off, examine them frequently and keep them clear of dust and dirt. Where windows have not these tubes, wipe up the 'sweat' after each service with a cloth duster.

2nd. – As to Cleaning. – Whole interior of buildings to be swept and dusted; hassocks, cushions and carpets of pews to be cleaned once a week. Classrooms or other parts of building used during the week to be swept and dusted after each meeting in addition to the weekly cleaning. Once a month clean all glass, and carefully dust all carved work, mouldings, ceilings, cornices; sweep walls, &c., &c. Matting to be taken up every three months and cleaned. Floors to be washed and scrubbed every six months. Door mats to be kept clean, and yards well swept. W.Cs. or other closets and urinals to be attended to as described in this book.

3rd. – As to Ventilation. – Open all ventilators on dry sunny days, and also on other days if weather allows; those that are not affected by weather to be kept *always open during the week.* Ventilate *during services* and *meetings* when possible and without inconvenience. See that air bricks to foundation are not broken or stopped, and that all ventilators are in proper repair and working order.

4th. – As to Warming. – Keep stoves or apparatus clear of wood or clothes. Keep fuel in place where it cannot by accident catch fire. Light fires in good time in winter. Keep heat to 60 degrees during service. When thermometer is four degrees below freezing point, keep low continual fire if the apparatus is steam or hot water. If there is frost in the pipes, wait for *natural thaw* before firing, and heat meanwhile with gas. If stoves are used, keep a vessel with water near the stove that the water may gradually steam off.

5th. – As to Lighting. – Complete lighting 15 minutes before doors are opened; keep ventilators open the while so that all smell may escape. When gas is turned low or turned on during service, do it very gradually. Regulate stop cock at meter with judgment, turn on only force actually required, and turn off at night.

Care Takers adopting the above summary of duties, should make themselves fully acquainted with the preceding contents of this book, where more complete information will be found under the various heads.

Note. – That Cards with the CONDENSED MANUAL printed on them, to hang on Vestry walls, may be had of the Author, Victoria Chambers, Derby, post free 6d. each, three for 1/-, eight for 2/-.

PART V

SPIRITUALITY

Introduction

The spirituality of the nineteenth century is only just becoming a subject of thorough investigation. It has often been taken for granted, but souls as well as minds and bodies have a history. Here the subject has been approached broadly so as to include not only the opening of the spiritual life in conversion, its close in death and its growth and vicissitudes in between but also its expression in activities inside and outside the home. Although several of the extracts refer to female experience, more material on these themes will be found in Part VII on women.

Conversion was not normally expected by Unitarians, but nearly all other denominations in Nonconformity, including a growing section of the Society of Friends (V.6), looked for the experience. It was essentially the arrival of faith in Christ (V.7). It could be gradual as well as sudden, but most of the instances given here are of datable occurrences. The most common age at conversion was the teenage phase (V.4), but the event could take place when a person was younger (V.8) or older (V.5). Theologically it was originally conceived as containing a divine element alongside a human response (V.1). The perceptibly supernatural could be involved (V.2); in the Calvinist tradition it was expected that there would be a time of waiting in conviction of sin before the divine disclosure (V.3); and in Methodism there was also normally a period of earnest seeking before the gift of assurance was vouchsafed (V.4, 8). The trend over time was for the human element to eclipse the divine. By the end of the century, when details of conversion experiences are much harder to come by, conversions could be planned for in large-scale organised missions (V.9). There was now no need to wait: true faith was there for the taking at any time.

The most traditional Calvinists retained the anxious piety of the seventeenth century that saw doubt of salvation as a virtue that threw the soul into repeated self-examination (V.12). All Calvinists were suspicious of claims that there was some second decisive experience to be sought beyond conversion (V.10). Methodists, however, followed John Wesley in hoping for entire sanctification in this life (V.11). Although that tradition fell into decay, it enjoyed a revival with a fresh terminology in the last years of the century (V.15). Physical healings of a type more common in African Christianity were known among the Peculiar People of Essex (V.14). But the normal patterns of spirituality concentrated on private prayer (V.23), family prayer (V.18) and the reading of the Bible together with other books (V.13). The home, especially in smaller groups such as the Brethren, could have its own taboos (V.21); or else it could be unfriendly to Dissenting religion (V.16). Outside the home, devotion could bring worldly success (V.17, 19), but it was generally insisted that religion should be the priority – even to the extent of discouraging emigration (V.20). One ideal was to bring spiritual methods to bear on the practical problems of the day such as homelessness among children (V.22).

Death was a time to testify to the authenticity of faith. Confidence and calm in the face of pain and imminent departure from this life were faithfully recorded (V.25, 26, 29). Sometimes deaths could accurately be described as triumphant (V.28). Spiritual struggle, however, could also be part of the experience of dying (V.24). After death there were relatives to be comforted (V.27) and, in a few cases of the distinguished, memorials to be erected (V.30).

Spirituality is covered, for the Methodists, in G. S. Wakefield, *Methodist Spirituality*, Peterborough, 1999; and, for two great Dissenting figures, Dale and Spurgeon, in J. M. Gordon, *Evangelical Spirituality*, London, 1991, chap. 6. Male religious experience is compared with its female equivalent in L. Wilson, *Constrained by Zeal: Female Spirituality amongst Nonconformists, 1825–1875*, Carlisle, 2000. Patterns of conversion are considered in M. R. Watts, *The Dissenters*, vol. 2, Oxford, 1995, pp. 49–80, and in D. W. Bebbington, 'Evangelical Conversion, c. 1740–1850', *Scottish Bulletin of Evangelical Theology*, 18 (2000), pp. 102–27. The deathbed scene is discussed in H. D. Rack, 'Evangelical Endings', *Bulletin of the John Rylands University Library of Manchester*, 74 (1992).

Conversion

Document V.1

John Rippon on the Theology of Conversion, 1801

John Rippon (1751–1836) was the minister of Carter Lane, Southwark, the largest Baptist church of his day. From 1790 to 1802 he edited *The Baptist Annual Register*, the first Particular Baptist periodical, which, alongside news and biography, considered moot points in theology. The distinction between conversion and regeneration was among them. After the passage given below, Rippon elaborates the distinction by a series of epigrams from the Puritan Stephen Charnock. The upshot is that, while regeneration is a divine act, conversion is both divine and human. On Rippon, see K. R. Manley, *'Redeeming Love Proclaim': John Rippon and the Baptists*, Carlisle, 2004; and DNB.

The extract is taken from *The Baptist Annual Register*, 1801–02, p. 664.

CONVERSION. – Consists both of God's act upon men in turning them, and of acts done by men under the influence of converting grace: they turn, being turned.

REGENERATION – Is the MOTION OF GOD in the heart of a sinner: – Conversion is the MOTION OF THE HEART of a sinner towards God.

In Regeneration, men are wholly passive – in Conversion, they become active.

Expressed passively – *Ye are returned*, 1 Pet. ii. 25. :

Expressed actively – *A great number turned*, Acts xi. 21.

Effectual Vocation is the call of men out of darkness to light; and Conversion answers to that call, and is the *actual turning* of men from the one to the other: – is the turn of the *heart* to God; – a turn of the *thoughts* of the heart; – a turn of the *desires* of the heart; – a turn of all the *affections* of the heart; – a turn of the mind from carnal to spiritual things; – a turn of the *will* to be flexible; – a turn from *darkness* to light; – a turn from the *devil* to God; – a turn from heart-*idols*, and cursed favourites, to the living God; – a turn from our own *righteousness* to the righteousness of Christ; – an active turn from *self-will* and wisdom, to the whole scheme of salvation in Christ.

Document V.2

An Independent Conversion, 1804

John Armitage, who later became an Independent minister, recounted long afterwards a strange episode that decisively influenced his conversion. At about the age of sixteen he was serving as an apprentice in Liverpool, where he regularly attended a Baptist chapel.

The extract is taken from a memoir of Armitage in *The Evangelical Magazine*, November 1850, pp. 567–8. The editor leaves the reader 'to put upon it what construction he may please'.

About this period, when labouring under conviction of my sins, I was most remarkably arrested, or rather visited, by a messenger from the world of spirits. ... Its appearance was in the year 1804. I went to bed at my usual time, and after reading my usual portion of Scripture, and soliciting the protection of Heaven, I retired to rest; and when in profound sleep I was awakened by a voice calling me – 'John! John! John!' three times, but I could perceive no one. As there was another person sleeping in the same room, I called to him to know if he wanted anything, or if he had called; to which he replied he had not spoken. After this, I composed myself again to sleep. The night following, I was awakened in a similar manner. I replied by asking what was wanted, and immediately I saw a most beautiful figure, who thus, with pleasing accent, addressed me:– 'Knowest thou there is a God?' I answered, though much agitated, 'Yes.' 'Seek Him while He may be found; call upon Him while He is near.' After thus addressing me, the figure instantaneously disappeared.

Document V.3

A Particular Baptist Conversion, 1809

John Kershaw (1792–1870) was a close associate of William Gadsby (see I.3), and for over fifty years pastor of Hope Chapel, Rochdale (see DEB). In his autobiographical *Memorials of the Mercies of a Covenant God* (1870), he recounts his experiences when as a young man he came under an acute conviction of sin. Through the preaching of John Hirst of Bacup, he realised that Christ was able to save him, but questioned whether he was willing to do so. After a struggle Kershaw was persuaded of the doctrine of election, but could find no internal evidence that he was one of God's chosen people. He regularly attended Sunday worship, and walked miles to be at prayer meetings, but continued to doubt whether he was a child of God. Deliverance came through the experience related in his autobiography (pp. 58–61), and typifies a traditional form of introspective Calvinistic piety.

I hope never to forget the night the Lord brought my soul out of bondage into the glorious liberty of the gospel. It was on a Lord's day evening. I went in the morning to the house of God in a very distressed state of mind, and remained so all day. The preaching only tended to increase my misery, the enemy telling me that, like Simon Magus, I had neither part nor lot in the matter. Having attended three services, I was returning home (it was a fine summer evening), in my feelings worse than when I set out in the morning. So sinful, miserable, and wretched did I feel myself that I was ready to give all up for lost, the accuser of the brethren harassing me with his temptations, saying it was of no use going any more either to chapel or prayer meetings. It was folly and presumption to read and pray, for the more I attended to these things the more wretched I grew. My soul gave way under these temptations, and I said within myself, 'I will give all my religion up, for its is nothing but a stench in my own nostrils. What must it be then to the Lord of Hosts?' So engaged was my mind that I stood still in the road, when this question arose within me: 'What am I to do? Go back into the world I cannot. I have tried again and again to do this, and found their society more and more distasteful.' I then concluded that I would have nothing to do either with the world or the people of God. ...

Whilst pondering on these things, the following words came with such power upon my mind, as though I had heard them spoken by an audible voice: 'O wretched man that I am, who shall deliver me from this body of sin and death?' I was so struck with their import that I stood amazed, saying to myself, 'These are the words of St. Paul in the seventh chapter to the Romans. He was a good and gracious man, a minister of Jesus Christ, and the great apostle of the Gentiles. If he had thus to complain of sin and wretchedness, who can tell but I may be a child of God after all my fears and temptations?' ... My soul was greatly encouraged. I found I was a brother and companion with Paul in this path of internal tribulation and Christian experience. I hastened home to get my Bible, in order to examine the chapter through. I read it with such light, power, and comfort as I had never felt before; so pleased and blest in my soul that I began to read the next chapter, commencing thus: 'There is, therefore, now no condemnation to them which are in Christ Jesus, who walk not after the flesh but after the Spirit.' As I read these precious words, their blessed contents were brought into my soul with power and glory. I saw and felt that I was in Christ Jesus, saved with an everlasting salvation. The burden of sin was removed, my conscience cleansed by an application of the precious blood of Jesus Christ. I felt the sealing testimony of the Holy Spirit of God that I stood complete and accepted in the Beloved. I read the chapter through with a joy I cannot describe. I now knew my election of God, and that no charge could ever be brought against me, because Christ had died for my sins, and was raised again from the dead for my justification; that he ever lived to make intercession for me, and would receive me into his kingdom of glory. The love of Christ was shed abroad in my heart; I saw and felt that nothing could separate me from the love of God, which is in Christ Jesus our Lord. How precious and glorious were the truths contained in this chapter to my soul on that memorable evening; and often, in reading and preaching, when I have cited portions of it, I have felt a little of the same sweetness and savour.

Document V.4

A Wesleyan Conversion, 1812

Elizabeth Wood was a chapel-going girl in Bradford who was converted at the age of sixteen in 1812, the year after she had lost her mother. The following narrative, written by her sister, illustrates the potential of the Methodist love feast (see VI.17) as a converting agency and the aptness of hymnody for expressing the experience. It also offers a typical account of the subject's pre-conversion frivolity and her subsequent transformation. It is taken from *The Wesleyan Methodist Magazine*, February 1825, pp. 78–9.

The family were accustomed regularly to attend the Methodist Chapel; but no particular impression had been made on the mind of Elizabeth; she indulged herself in card-playing, and other vain amusements. The Methodist Preachers, who occasionally visited the family, sometimes favoured the children with notes of admittance to the Love-feasts. But on the 29th of December, 1811, it was with some difficulty that the subject of this Memoir, and a younger sister, obtained admission into a meeting of that description. Her feelings on this occasion she thus describes:– 'As soon as the service commenced, my heart began to melt: I cannot express what I felt; I wept bitterly. One person who spoke, concluded with these words; "I hope to be such a one as the Lord will accept when he makes up his jewels." I thought, Well, if I am not such a one, too, I shall be lost. I thought I was lost, and that there was no hope for me.' From that time her convictions of sin increased, and she sought the Lord, with many tears, till the 18th of February, 1812, and then the burden of her guilt was removed, and she was enabled to say, –

'My God is reconcil'd,
His pardoning voice I hear;
He owns me for his child,
I can no longer fear.'

This entire change of principle was accompanied by a corresponding change of conduct. She laid aside every forbidden thing, and was so fearful of doing wrong, that she often gave up her own judgment rather than act contrary to the opinion of those whom she thought more pious than herself. Those who feared God were her companions; and the duties which tended to the glory of God, and to the furtherance of her salvation, she performed with diligence and regularity. She was an active Teacher in the Sunday-School, and devoted much of her time to visiting the sick and poor at their own habitations. She became a collector for the Missions, and frequently assisted in the Prayer-meetings, and continued thus actively and usefully engaged for several years.

Document V.5

A General Baptist Conversion, 1820

Christopher Hunter was an extremely elderly man living in the hamlet of Redburn, near Kirton in Lincolnshire. Conversation with a passing New Connexion General Baptist led to his conversion and his baptism at the age of ninety.

Spirituality

The extract is taken from *The General Baptist Repository*, December 1822, pp. 455–6.

Till his ninetieth year, he lived a stranger to vital godliness. About that time, Mr. R. Stocks, of Kirton, having occasion weekly to pass through Redburn, became acquainted with the old man; and improved the opportunities that frequently recurred of addressing him and several other aged people on the great importance of religion, their exposedness to eternal misery and the gospel way of salvation; and to read to them suitable portions of scripture. By the blessing of God on these means, Mr. H. was led to enquire, What shall I do to be saved? After some time, he was brought to enjoy peace in believing, offered himself as a candidate for church fellowship, and was baptized by Mr. Stocks, on Easter Tuesday, 1820, when he had almost completed his ninety-first year. After his baptism, his conversation gave satisfactory proof of the sincerity of his profession. He hungered and thirsted after righteousness; and was humble and teachable. He retained all his natural faculties in full vigour; and seemed to devote them all to the great things of God.

Document V.6

A Quaker Conversion, c. 1830

Quakers were deeply touched by Evangelical spirituality in the nineteenth century and so accounts of their conversions are often similar to those found in other bodies. Yet the stress on love and the place of illumination in the following recollection have a distinctive Quaker feel to them. Elizabeth N. Capper (1818–1907) had just heard an address on 'Thine is the Kingdom, the Power, and the Glory'.

The extract is taken from *The Annual Monitor for 1908*, London, 1907, pp. 46–7.

The words several times repeated, seemed to grasp my whole being. It was indeed a new creation. Nothing will describe it. The nearest thing I can say is, that I sat as one might do who had been born, and had lived in the far recesses of a coal mine, never seeing more than a faint glimmer of light conveyed by a narrow shaft, – such an one suddenly lifted into the full blaze of a grand summer day. I gazed on a vision of beauty so sunlit, that I did not see my own sin and misery, only the glory of the King. I only felt the warmth of His love. My ears heard no voice saying, 'Thy sins, which are many, are all forgiven,' but I was fully assured of it, and for months joy and peace abounded, and I was little troubled by temptation. I knew that I had entered into Life. Then I began to know and to believe the love that God hath toward us.

After such an experience of the Lord's goodness, what more can I say? No language can tell the sweetness of so beholding the beauty of the Lord. A change from distrust and grudged allegiance to as much love as my poor heart could hold. 'We love Him, because He first loved us,' but we must believe in that Love before we can begin to respond to it, and perhaps our love grows more by praise and thanksgiving then by anything else which we can render.

Document V.7

J. Angell James on Faith, 1834

For Angell James, see II.28. His book *The Anxious Inquirer after Salvation Directed and Encouraged* (1834) was one of the most popular works of the century. Issued by the Religious Tract Society, founded in 1799 to provide cheap evangelistic literature, the book fulfilled the purpose of a tract but at greater length. In this extract, taken from an undated edition at pp. 76–7, saving faith is described as personal trust (*fiducia*) to distinguish it from verbal assent (*assensus*).

I will now show you HOW you are to believe. But is this necessary? There is no mystery in faith when we speak of believing a fellow creature. When the rebel is required to believe in the proclamation of mercy sent out by his sovereign, and to come and sue for pardon, or when the beggar is required to believe in the promise of a benefactor who has promised him relief, does it enter into his mind to ask how he is to believe? What, in each of these cases, does faith mean? A belief that the promise has been made, and a confidence in the person who made it that he will fulfil his word. Behold, then, the whole mystery there is in faith! It is a belief that Christ really died for sinners; that all who depend upon him alone shall be saved; and a trust in him for salvation. Yes, it is, if we may substitute another word as explanatory of faith, TRUST in Christ. Faith, and confidence in Christ, are the same thing. 'I know whom I have believed,' says the apostle, 'and am persuaded he is able to keep that which I have committed to him,' 2 Tim. i. 12. Believing, being persuaded, and the act of committing, are the same act; they all mean faith. It is to rest upon the word and work of Christ for salvation; to depend upon his atonement and righteousness, and upon nothing else, for acceptance with God; and really to expect salvation, because he has promised it.

Document V.8

A Primitive Methodist Conversion, c. 1838

Annie Tolson, born near Leeds in 1830, became a Primitive Methodist evangelist and later, as a freelance, the pastor of a church as well as a travelling preacher. Her conversion experience, though it took place when she was only eight, was typical of earlier Methodism in being the culmination of a sustained quest. Immediately afterwards she began to evangelise other children through a prayer meeting held in a pig-cote.

Spirituality

The extract is taken from A. Auty, *The Life and Labours of Mrs Auty*, Leeds, 1887, pp. 6–7. Tolson was her first married name; her second marriage was to a man named Auty.

When I reached my ninth year I became concerned about my soul's welfare, though I cannot remember ever telling an untruth, or swearing, or doing anything disobediently to my parents; yet, I felt that I was the greatest sinner in the world. I wept, and prayed, and cried for mercy, for months; but found no relief. I never opened my mind to anyone on the subject until I became quite worn down with grief and sorrow for my sins. I felt I could not live unless deliverance came. After going home from my work one night, I went under a certain hedge, there being a deep ditch that was dry. I thought no one would see me; there I knelt, and prayed, and resolved to die, if I did not find peace. This was the language of my heart –

Saviour of sinners, lend thine ear,
    Accept the mourner's plea,
And listening to my feeble prayer,
    Descend and pardon me.

I'm sunk in sin, beset with grief,
    Condemned by Thy decree;
Thou, only Thou, canst give relief,
    O Jesus, pardon me!

Thy bloody cross, and garments stained,
    Augment my misery;
I cry distressed, by love constrained;
    O Jesus, pardon me!

Beneath Thy cross I'll urge my cry,
    Until my soul is free;
Both night and day I'll groan and sigh,
    O Jesus, pardon me!

'Tis done! 'tis done! I do believe!
    I feel my soul is free;
Thy great salvation I receive,
    Yes! Thou hast pardoned me.

At that moment I ran home jumping, clapping my hands, and praising the Lord. When I reached home I told mother that I had found Jesus, and that He had pardoned all my sins. We then praised the Lord together.

Document V.9

A Methodist Conversion, c. 1900

Thomas Waugh, born in 1853 and a Wesleyan connexional evangelist from 1883, used to tell stories of conversions as part of his gospel preaching. One was of a cousin of his, another Tom Waugh, who lived in a village six miles outside Chester. Tom went to hear the evangelist preach at Brunswick Chapel, Liverpool. There he was converted through the mass meeting and personal counselling – methods reflecting the techniques of the American evangelists Moody and Sankey and very effective in the last years of the century.

The extract is taken from T. Waugh, *Twenty-Three Years a Missioner*, London, n.d., pp. 127–8.

Though the chapel was packed to the rostrum, the man who took my cousin up into the chapel saw room for one at the end of a seat in the gallery. That steward did not know it, but the Lord had specially reserved that seat for his charge. The man did not know it then, but he set Tom next to a man who had known him, and whom he had known since they went to school and played together when lads at home. That man had been saved two years before in one of my meetings in Brunswick, and was just eager to win others to Christ.

When, from the rostrum, I saw where the Lord had seated my cousin, I felt sure he would be one of the first to decide for Christ that night, and my faith was not disappointed. The moment I gave the invitation in the after-meeting, Tom was the first of over thirty to come out publicly seeking Jesus. His old playmate came with him and showed him the way, and soon they rejoiced together. After my word of congratulation and advice, Tom had supper with his friend and then walked the twelve miles home. He arrived at two o'clock and found the wife waiting up for him. When she heard the glad news of his conversion she wisely saw that they must be as one in this thing. They began a prayer-meeting together, and she found the Lord at her own fireside.

Experience

Document V.10

A Baptist View of the Baptism of the Holy Ghost, 1810

Whereas in the twentieth century the baptism of the Holy Spirit as a distinct experience was to become widespread under Pentecostal influence, it was entirely otherwise in the nineteenth. The term was applied by Methodists to entire sanctification; by others, as this passage illustrates, the baptism of the Holy Spirit was identified with regeneration or sanctification, or else, as the author urges, it was restricted to apostolic times.

The extract is from 'On the Baptism of the Holy Ghost', *The Baptist Magazine*, June 1810, pp. 330–2.

From the manner in which it is frequently mentioned, it seems that by far the greater part of the christian world, suppose it to refer, either to the application of the word to the understanding in regeneration, or else to those gracious, and sanctifying influences of the Holy Spirit, of which every christian is undoubtedly a partaker. Nor is it surprising that this opinion, though entirely without foundation, should be very generally received, if it be considered, that preachers frequently speak of the baptism of the Holy Ghost, as if it were perfectly understood, that every christian partakes of it, though they might as well teach their people to expect to attain to sinless perfection. In the same incautious manner, authors, of different denominations, have written of themselves and others, as being baptized with the Holy Ghost. And so prevalent is this opinion, that the few who have examined the subject, have been frequently charged with denying the influences of the Holy Spirit, because they have asserted, that the baptism of the Holy Ghost was entirely confined to the apostolic age. ...

[In Acts 2] we see that the baptism of the Holy Ghost, was the extraordinary and miraculous power by which the apostles, and first christians, were enabled by the performance of miracles, to demonstrate the truth which they taught, namely, that Jesus was the Christ, the Son of God, and the Saviour of Sinners; and that God had raised him from the dead. While then it is readily granted, that every believer is regenerated by the power of the Holy Ghost, through the word of truth; and that every christian is a partaker of his gracious and sanctifying influences, it is denied, that the baptism of the Holy Ghost, which was always attended with miraculous Power, is *now* enjoyed by any one.

Document V.11

A Wesleyan Full Consecration to God, c. 1810

It was the teaching of John Wesley that the converted Christian should go on to seek entire sanctification, or full consecration, which was conceived as a decisive second stage of experience. According to Wesley, those who were fully consecrated committed no known sin and so their state was one of Christian perfection. This account of struggle leading to assurance is expressed in the words of Mary Porteus, who started as a Wesleyan but who later, in 1825, was to become a Primitive Methodist itinerant preacher.

The extract is taken from J. Lightfoot, *The Power of Faith: Life and Labours of Mrs Porteus*, Leeds, 1862, pp. 41–2.

One night ... I resolved to continue on my knees till I obtained the blessing I sought. My pain of mind was great. I struggled till near midnight. I cried, 'Lord, I cannot let thee go; I will not rise. Oh, for thy dear Son's sake, answer prayer.' At length that promise was applied with power to my soul – 'I will sprinkle clean water upon thee, and thou shalt be clean.' I laid hold of this by faith; and while contemplating the Great Being who had recorded this promise, was led to pray thus: 'O thou Eternal Jehovah, thy voice at first spake the world out of nothing, thy hands stretched the heavens, and planted the stars. Thy power upholds all things: then nothing is too hard for thee. Thy powerful word *can* speak my nature clean. And art thou not as willing as thou art able? Ah, yes. It was thy own love that moved thee to make this promise. None compelled thee to make it. Art thou not then willing to fulfil it to my soul? O yes, I do believe. If there be one thing in which thou canst take more pleasure than another, it must be this, to stamp thine image on the soul. Oh, then, do this for thy gasping dust. I long for the sprinkling of thy Spirit. Make my infected nature pure. I do believe thou wilt be as good as thy word. Thou hast promised, and thou also wilt do it. Now let it come. This moment is only mine. Thou hast given me no warrant to hope for to-morrow. Thy word has said, 'Now is the accepted time.' I take thee at thy word; let me have it now. Thou has said, 'I will;' yes, and my soul replies, 'I will, I do believe. Thou canst not falsify thy word. It is done.'

When I thus ventured to lay hold of the promise, the witness was given; my soul sank in solemn awe. I had no high-flowing rapture, but such a weight of glory as I cannot express. My soul, the room, and all around, seemed full of God. How long I continued gazing, praying, adoring, and wondering, I cannot tell.

Document V.12

A Religion of Experience, 1834

William Huntington (see II.21), William Gadsby (see I.3) and their followers believed that deep conviction of sin was essential for the possession of real religion. Only those knowing the plagues of the heart and who at times sensed the presence of Christ in the soul could have any hope of being numbered among God's elect. An example of this subjectivism, with its consequent lack of any real assurance, is taken from a letter of 1834 printed in the first issue of *The Gospel Standard*, August 1835, pp. 9–10.

Once we were blind, but now we see; we were dead in trespasses and sins, but now we are made alive by the mighty power of God. When I am brought to meditate on these things, I feel astonished that the Lord should ever have brought such a wretch as myself out of nature's darkness, and passed by others, leaving them to perish in their sins; for I feel that there is nothing in me to recommend me to his favour. O, no; it is all of free, sovereign, unmerited, discriminating grace. I feel that I am a vile, polluted, hell-deserving sinner, and when the blessed Spirit is pleased to lead me out of self, give me a faith's view of Christ, in all his glorious characters, and enable me to see myself chosen in him before the foundation of the world, it is then I can rejoice in the Lord as my salvation: it is then I am laid low in self-abasement, and can say, 'How is it, Lord, that thou manifesteth thyself unto me, and not unto the world?' it is then I can exclaim, 'Not unto me, not unto me, but unto they name, O Lord, be all the glory;' it is then Christ appears to me the chiefest among ten thousand, and the altogether lovely; it is then I feel a little of the sweetness of being on the Mount with Jesus; and O, what sweet and blessed moments these are to my poor tried, tempted, harassed, and perplexed soul! But, alas! how very short they are, yet, and very seldom too! Then again I return to my old place, and a sad place it is; for there I find nothing but sin and wickedness, evil thoughts, yea, and evil desires too. My Jesus seems to be gone; my confidence and interest in the Lord seem to be the same. Then I sigh, and cry, and pray for him to return, but seem to pray in vain. Sometimes I am so vain as to try to mend myself, and I think I will drive the world, evil imaginations, and evil desires out of my heart. But, alas! the more I strive, the more powerfully they work in me. I then endeavour to fix my thoughts and affections on things above, but cannot, for I find my evil propensities will still rise up. I then try to forget self altogether, and to read my interest in Christ, but all in vain. Then I run to my Bible, but that appears to condemn me. So that do what I will, I seem to be shut up, and unable to come forth. Then the devil comes with his suggestions, and says, Look at yourself; you are nothing but a mass of sin, and yet you profess to be a child of God. You have never had any true conviction, nor any real manifestation; it's altogether delusion. Thus I am filled with doubts and fears, and am ofttimes ready to conclude that I shall prove to be an hypocrite after all. But now and then the

Lord is pleased to apply his promises to my soul, which revive and refresh me; therefore, I am not wholly destitute of hope.

Document V.13

A Congregationalist's Spiritual Encouragement, 1838

Ann Gilbert, *née* Taylor, (1782–1866) was the wife of Joseph Gilbert, a Congregational minister in Nottingham, and herself the author of some attractive children's verse (see DNB). She suffered from endemic lack of assurance of salvation, but records in this passage an occasion when the depression lifted – as a result of reading John Newton and Thomas Scott, two Evangelical Anglican divines, of hearing a Methodist local preacher and of receiving communion. Reading, sermons and the Lord's Supper were the three basic means of grace.

The extract is taken from J. Gilbert, ed., *Autobiography and Other Memorials of Mrs Gilbert*, 3rd edn, London, 1878, pp. 109–10.

[I]n the summer of 1838 I was called to make a long sojourn at the sea, on a solitary coast. Our first Sabbath on the way thither was spent in a family where I should not have looked for religious improvement; but I was there singularly affected. It was an ordinance Sabbath, and in my usual state of feeling, a doleful sense of need and misery, I joined the communion, of the small church there. During the administration, the yearning of may heart for salvation expressed itself in a whispered, 'Oh that I could!' no sooner uttered than a response seemed to say, 'And what hinders? If you are willing, is God unwilling?' I was dumb. I could give no reply; and went from the chapel with a new feeling of hope. At the house I met with a book I should not have expected to find there – Newton's 'Cardiphonia.' I read it eagerly, and felt its suitableness to my condition.

Few spots in England could have appeared less favourable for spiritual improvement than the little sea-bathing place we were going to. At the parish church there was service only once on the Sunday, and I think only once a fortnight, and the sermon was an essay without an evangelical word. On the Sunday evenings, in the kitchen of a small shopkeeper, the humble teaching of a local brother among the Methodists was the only other opportunity; but it was gospel, and I enjoyed it. I had brought with me from home a volume of Scott's 'Essays,' and these formed my Sunday readings, and well I remember the delight, admiration, and gratitude with which, upon one occasion, while reading the essay on Justification, I perceived, as by a new revelation, the glorious wisdom, freeness, and sufficiency of the plan by which a helpless sinner may be saved! I rose from my seat, being alone, read the words aloud, and thanked God for them. From that time, and till long after, I felt a degree of peace and happiness which was new to me.

Spirituality

Document V.14

A Peculiar People Healing, c. 1875

The Peculiar People were a revivalist sect founded in Essex by James Banyard, a former Wesleyan local preacher. They were organised under bishops and adopted the title 'Peculiar People' in 1852. They believed in divine healing, and Banyard himself was disowned in 1855 for seeking medical aid for a sick child. They still exist in Essex, as the Union of Evangelical Churches.

The description of a divine healing at the Herongate chapel is taken from M. Sorrell, *The Peculiar People*, Exeter, 1979, pp. 79–80.

It is with great pleasure we make known a great and speedy deliverance, wrought on a poor woman by the power of God. This dear woman had been very ill during the week, but she feared and loved God and many times God had heard and answered her prayers and she felt that God could and would if she could get to the chapel on Sunday. She was conveyed in a cart to the Peculiar People's chapel at Herongate. While there she was taken much worse and said she must die. During the afternoon the preacher spoke about the woman who touched the hem of Jesus' garment; this increased her faith, she believed God would heal her and make her well and strong. Her faith was rewarded; while the preacher was telling forth the mighty power of God to heal, the power of God entered her body, she leaped from her seat and ran about the chapel, healed perfectly, praising God with all her heart, soul and strength. The cure was a permanent one, from that day until her death, which was many years later, she was able to get about, and did a lot of hard work, living until she was seventy-eight years of age.

Document V.15

Thomas Waugh on the Power of Pentecost, c. 1895

For Waugh, see V.9. The more enthusiastic Methodists of the last decade of the century such as Waugh began to speak often of the work of the Holy Spirit and to refer to the need for a fresh Pentecost. These developments foreshadowed the rise of Pentecostalism in the following decade.

The extract is taken from T. Waugh, *The Power of Pentecost*, Rochdale, n.d., pp. 95–8.

The great reason why so much earnest Christian work, prayer, and sacrifice to-day yield such meagre results is this – *a large proportion of our Lord's disciples are living on the wrong side of Pentecost. Chronologically* of course they are on the right side, but *experimentally* they have not reached it yet. Like the first disciples previous to that wonderful day, they know Jesus, they love Him, and they follow Him, some near and some afar off, but *they have never claimed their own personal Pentecost*. They have not received this the first great qualification, without which all other gifts and qualifications are practically powerless in the work of saving men.

Many of our people seem to have got very little further than those Ephesian converts who said, 'We have not so much as heard whether there be any Holy Ghost.' We seldom hear a prayer for the Holy Ghost which is based upon the assurance that His fulness is a personal present blessing that God urges upon us now. We are often grieved and amazed at the way in which some Christians refer to Him, and at their ignorance of His relations to Christian life and work. Yet we only have Christ with us as we have His Spirit in us, for in His glorified body Christ is with the Father. When He went there He sent the Holy Spirit to be His own continued life on earth. ...

We are often asked, 'Have not all Christians the Spirit?' Certainly. 'If any man have not the Spirit of Christ He is none of His.' But all are not 'filled with the Spirit;' and *having* the Spirit, and being *filled* with the Spirit, are different things in degree. The disciples *had* the Spirit before Pentecost, but on that day they were *filled*, and we have seen with what wonderful results.

Activities

Document V.16

Opposition to a Baptist, c. 1805

Dissent still carried a stigma, especially in the earlier part of the century and especially in the countryside. Elizabeth May (1785–1849) was brought up at Appledore in Devon, where her father was a gentleman's steward and a strict Anglican. The daughter, however, was converted through the Independent chapel, and soon opposition from her parents began.

The extract is taken from an obituary by her husband, J. H. May, the Baptist minister at Culmstock in Devon, published in *The Baptist Magazine*, February 1850, p. 99.

Not long after her conversion to God her attention was directed to the subject of baptism. The only baptist in the town was Miss Hernaman. She applied to her for some ideas on the subject. She replied, 'I shall say nothing to you on the subject, only "Search the scriptures."' She immediately formed the determination to do so, and her now bereaved husband well remembers, how in his evening visits to her, she would direct his mind to the same subject, and how they used to search the word together, until both were convinced that the immersion of believers was the only baptism of the New Testament. The change that had passed in her mind, would not pass unnoticed by her parents, and fears were entertained by them to what this might grow. On the visit of the bishop she was obliged to go to confirmation. This, however, did not cure her heresy, and her father determined to send her out of the way of danger. He sent her to the care of an uncle in the town of Brixham. The late Rev. Thomas Roberts of Bristol was then pastor of the baptist church at Brixham; she applied to him for baptism, and was baptized by him before her return to her own home. After her return, she had to endure the bitterness of opposition. Even a place of retirement was denied her, her own bedroom was not to be available for the purpose, and often has she been obliged to resort to places of secrecy where few would think of going. Being rendered so very unhappy at home, she resolved to leave, and seek a situation. She soon found one in a pious family in the town of Ilfracombe, where she engaged as an assistant in a draper's and grocer's shop. There she was very happy with the family, which was then almost the only evangelical family in the town.

Document V.17

Samuel Budgett's Business Policy, c. 1820

Samuel Budgett (1794–1851) was, with his brother, a wholesale grocer in Bristol (see DNB). He was a loyal Wesleyan Methodist and was presented in a classic 'how-to-succeed' biography of the 1850s as a model Christian businessman. For its author, William Arthur, see II.14.

    The extract is taken from W. Arthur, *The Successful Merchant*, London, 1852, pp. 161–2.

One thing which materially aided the Messrs. Budgett in their upward struggle, was their system of selling for cash. That system was begun at the outset, and maintained throughout. Customers in the neighbourhood paid for all purchases immediately. This could not be carried out in the same form with customers at a distance. When they ordered goods they could not, of course, pay for them till they had been received; and that in many cases would be days after the order was given, when no representative of the firm was on the spot. But a plan was adopted which came as near to prompt payment as possible. Each customer was waited upon by a traveller once in four weeks. Each customer knew what day and what hour to expect the visit. If Mr. S—— had called on a tradesman in Hereford on Monday at ten o'clock, that tradesman would expect Mr. S—— four weeks after on Monday at ten o'clock. If he had given Mr S—— an order on his former visit, the cash would be expected now; if he had ordered any goods in the meantime the cash for them also would be expected now; so that up to this moment, Monday at ten o'clock, the account would stand perfectly clear. If the tradesman was not at home or had not prepared himself with his cash, the traveller did not call again; and no order was taken from one who had not discharged his account. Mr. Budgett regarded the maintenance of these rules as of the first importance. He would at any time lose customers and sacrifice much prospective advantage rather than diverge from them. His case was not that of a house which waits till it has attained a commanding name for one particular article, and then imposes stricter terms of payment for that article. He began with his principle when he had everything to gain. He fought his way up with it, even though he found it continually blocking up his path, making him enemies, and abridging his sales. He was persuaded of its excellence, and by it he would stand.

Document V.18

Helen Herschell on Family Prayer, c. 1840

Family prayer, often around the huge family Bible, was the essence of Evangelical household religion. Normally taken by the head of household, it formed a midway point between public worship and personal devotion, from which, as this passage

Spirituality

points out, it differed significantly. The author was the wife of an undenominational minister in London who specialised in mission to his fellow Jews (see VIII.13).

The extract is taken from R. H. Herschell, ed., *Far Above Rubies*, London, 1854, pp. 180–81.

Family prayer is not, or, at least, never ought to be, the substitute for private devotion. It is to be presumed that the members of which the family is composed, have already offered up their individual petitions at the throne of grace. It is not, therefore, for this purpose that they unite in social prayer; but to return thanks for *family* mercies, to confess family sin, and ask for family blessings.

You are aware that the component parts of prayer are generally considered to be – praise, thanksgiving, confession, and petition. Now, although all these may properly enter into family prayer, it must be with much less detail and minuteness than is proper in private prayer. When we are pouring out our heart to God in private, we may tell him everything; entering, if we choose, into the most minute details, because *we know them to be true*; but when we profess to utter the feelings of a company, we must, to a certain extent, represent what may be considered as the *average* state of mind and feeling of that company. To hear a good man pouring forth the deepest feelings of self-abasement, or uttering that deep spiritual experience which only the advanced Christian can know, in a mixed company, where there are children and servants, in various stages of spiritual advancement, is very painful to the feelings of those who listen, and are conscious that, as the mouth-piece of the family, the statements he is making are positively false. He may confess the existence of sin in the family to a much greater extent than the generality of the family feel it; but he should avoid expressing it as the feeling of the family. He must, in short, ever keep in mind that he is not at that time giving forth his own feelings to God, as an individual, but as one representing the family who are associated with him in prayer.

Document V.19

Thomas Binney on the Best of Both Worlds, 1853

Thomas Binney (1798–1874) was the minister of the King's Weigh House Chapel, London, from 1829 to 1869. Twice chairman of the Congregational Union, he was probably the best known Congregational minister of his day. His enormously popular book, *Is it Possible to Make the Best of Both Worlds?* (1853), assured young men that it *was* possible, so contributing significantly to the self-help ethos of the period. See J. Stoughton, *Thomas Binney*, London, 1874; C. Binfield, *George Williams and the Y.M.C.A.*, London, 1973, pp. 24–34; and DNB.

The extract is taken from T. Binney, *Is it Possible...?*, 9th edn, London, 1855, pp. 62–6.

So in respect to *competency* and *success in life*. All the virtues inculcated by religion are favourable to a man's passing comfortably through the world, and even to his advancement in it, so far as that is regulated by ordinary laws, and looked for within reasonable limits. Sudden turns of fortune, singular talents, and remarkable opportunities, we put aside. At the same time, it should never be forgotten that the most astonishing aptitude for business will seldom secure solid and permanent success without virtue, while virtue, associated with average power, will often make a steadily advancing man. The habits of mind, speech, and behaviour which a sensible religious man will naturally cultivate, are all favourable to his retaining employment, securing confidence, improving his circumstances, and getting on, – at least, not going back. Whatever he is, whether master or servant, – and whatever he does, whether buying or selling, planning or accomplishing, working with the head or hand, – he will be conscientious, truthful, upright, just. He *ought* to be active and energetic – for the law under which he lives is, 'whatsoever thy hand findeth to do, do it will all thy might.' He will be punctual, exact, courteous, conciliatory. While under authority, he will be careful of the time and property of his employers; watchful of their interests; jealous of their reputation: – he will be ready to serve and please, will avoid giving offence, will neither be pert and assuming, nor sluggish and sulky; will be loyal himself, and promote loyalty and respect in others; will, without grumbling, make an effort to meet the demand of a pressing emergency, and feel as glad in securing a point for 'our house,' as if the concern and all that belonged to it were his own. Religious virtue is favourable to industry and economy, thriftiness, and forethought. ... Now, mind, I don't mean to say that goodness, religious virtue, is always, and as such, to expect secular success; other things besides virtue, – talents, opportunity, experience, tact, and so on, have to do with this, – but I do say, that without virtue, *the other things* won't of themselves avail, or avail permanently and securely; that virtue will always get a man respectably through life, and, in a general way, improve his condition; and that thus, for ordinary purposes, and up to a certain point, it is *sure* to have its reward.

Document V.20

A Strict Baptist View of Emigration, 1853

In 1844 a group of about sixty people from Ebenezer Strict Baptist Chapel, Brighton, emigrated to Australia (see J. Chandler, *Forty Years in the Wilderness*, Main Ridge, Victoria, Australia, reprint 1990). They were joined by a small number from Providence, Brighton, where the minister, John Grace (cf. *Recollections of John Grace*, London, 1893), a friend of J. C. Philpot (see X.19), was opposed to emigration. In answer to an 'Inquiry' Philpot took up the subject in *The Gospel Standard* (May 1853, pp. 148–56). Philpot acknowledged that emigration was a means of 'spreading the English language, civilisation, liberty and religion over the earth' (p. 148), but the motivation for the Brighton emigrants was purely a desire to find employment.

Spirituality

We are truly sorry to see the emigrating fever daily spreading, and already, we fear, infecting many members of Christian churches. However they may disclaim it even to themselves, we cannot help believing that the gold mines are secretly drawing their hearts over the sea. ...

But could [the intending emigrant] be certain of obtaining every worldly advantage, nothing can compensate for the loss of the gospel and the spiritual privileges which we here enjoy. To turn our back on the gospel is, we consider, a grievous departing from the right ways of the Lord, if not a first step towards apostacy: and no person could entertain such a project unless his heart had previously backslidden from God. Those whose minds are teeming with schemes of emigration are not those who are enjoying the Lord's blessing in the house of prayer, and count a day in his courts better than a thousand; but either worldly professors, who know nothing of the sweetness and preciousness of the word of God's grace, or the backsliders in heart, who are filled with their own ways. You had better suffer any degree of privation under the sound of the gospel and in the society of Christian friends here, than have your pockets filled with gold-dust and your soul empty and barren yonder; you had better be a door-keeper in the house of God in dear old England, than dwell in the tents of ungodliness in the wilds of Australia.

But we may further add, that there is now very little reason why persons should leave their own country. Business and trade are generally prosperous, employment abundant, wages good and increasing, and every prospect for honest industry. ... Our advice, therefore, to those who desire to fear God is, Do not emigrate, but continue where God has placed you. We admit there are exceptional cases; but we believe that the safer and better way is to go to the Lord instead of the ship-agent, and by honest industry dig into the mines of Providence here rather than toil and sweat in the mines over the water. Hitherto hath the Lord helped you. He has promised that your bread shall be given, and your water shall be sure. The gold and the silver are his, and the cattle on a thousand hills. Instead, therefore, of seeking misery beyond the waves, 'seek the kingdom of God and his righteousness, and all these (temporal) things shall be added unto you.'

Document V.21

Edmund Gosse, His Father and a Christmas Pudding, 1857

Philip Henry Gosse FRS (1810–88; see DNB) was one of leading marine zoologists of the 1840s and 1850s while at the same time he exercised a ministry amongst the so-called Plymouth Brethren (see IV.5). His only child, Edmund, following the death of his mother, had his father's close attention in all that he did. Later a leading literary figure, Sir Edmund Gosse (1849–1928; also see DNB) wrote on his early life in *Father and Son*, London, 1907. The extract given (1948 reprint, pp. 109–11) graphically shows the attitude of the more extreme Brethren towards Christmas. There is, however, reason to doubt the authenticity of the story (see A. Thwait,

Glimpses of the Wonderful: The Life of Philip Henry Gosse, 1810–1888, London, 2002, pp. 1–2).

On the subject of all feasts of the Church he held views of an almost grotesque peculiarity. He looked upon each of them as nugatory and worthless, but the keeping of Christmas appeared to him by far the most hateful, and nothing less than an act of idolatry. 'The very word is Popish,' he used to exclaim, 'Christ's Mass!' pursing up his lips with the gesture of one who tastes assafoetida by accident. Then he would adduce the antiquity of the so-called feast, adapted from horrible heathen rites, and itself a soiled relic of the abominable Yule-Tide. He would denounce the horrors of Christmas until it almost made me blush to look at a holly-berry.

On Christmas Day of this year 1857 our villa saw a very unusual sight. My Father had given strictest charge that no difference whatever was to be made in our meals on that day; the dinner was to be neither more copious than usual nor less so. He was obeyed, but the servants, secretly rebellious, made a small plum-pudding for themselves. ... Early in the afternoon, the maids, – of whom we were now advanced to keeping two, – kindly remarked that 'the poor dear child ought to have a bit, anyhow,' and wheedled me into the kitchen, where I ate a slice of plum-pudding. Shortly I began to feel that pain inside which in my frail state was inevitable, and my conscience smote me violently. At length I could bear my spiritual anguish no longer, and bursting into the study I called out: 'Oh! Papa, Papa, I have eaten of the flesh offered to idols!' It took some time, between my sobs, to explain what had happened. Then my Father sternly said: 'Where is the accursed thing?' I explained that as much as was left of it was still on the kitchen table. He took me by the hand, and ran with me into the midst of the startled servants, seized what remained of the pudding, and with the plate in one hand and me still tight in the other, ran until we reached the dust-heap, when he flung the idolatrous confectionery on to the middle of the ashes, and then raked it deep down into the mass. The suddenness, the violence, the velocity of this extraordinary act made an impression on my memory nothing will ever efface.

Document V.22

Caring for Orphans by Faith, 1867

Living by faith, that is without the support of subscribers, was a principle that steadily gained ground as a basis for Christian service. It entailed devoted prayer and subsequent dependence on divine provision. The principle was applied to overseas missionary work, producing the faith missions; and it was applied to looking after orphan children, most famously by George Müller of Bristol. Charlotte Sharman, born in 1832, was a member of York Street Congregational Church, Walworth, who began paying for the care of individual children in 1862, sending them on to Müller. She began her own orphanage in 1867.

The extract is taken from M. Williams, *Charlotte Sharman*, London, n.d., p. 62.

Spirituality

When, a few months later, the first small Home was actually opened, she wrote: 'How little the dear children are aware that I have not the means in hand for keeping them a month.' But through years of experimenting in faith, she was to find that the supply never failed. As the number of her children increased, and funds got very low while expenses mounted up, her heart was often heavy, but she never broke her rule and told of her pressing need. Later, with the memory of past experiences, she could write: 'It would be indeed faithless to enter on the new period with any trembling of heart, though the balance in hand is only a few shillings.' She proved the advantages of the life that is lived by faith.

> Instead of having, in time of trial, to look to any uncertain source of supply, to seek after patronage, or devise schemes for exciting public interest and raising money, we have only to look to Him Whose are the silver and the gold, in Whose hand are the hearts of all, and Who fainteth not neither is weary, and then stand still and see His salvation.

Again and again gifts reached her just in the nick of time, and she never ceased to feel the wonder of the love that so supplied every need that there was no lack. She never failed in her gratitude or in her acknowledgment.

Document V.23

Methodist Bible and Prayer Union Requests for Prayer and Praise, 1881

The Methodist Bible and Prayer Union began its regular monthly circular letters in 1878. Each letter contained daily Bible study notes and suggestions, supplied by members, for prayer and praise. The requests vividly conjure up the atmosphere of the revivalist dimension of Methodism at the period. The yoking of the gospel to total abstinence is a significant sign of the times.

The extract is taken from *The Methodist Bible and Prayer Union Monthly Letter*, January 1881, pp. 5–6.

SUNDAY, 9TH. – For the conversion of an entire family, long prayed for. That a large family may be greatly blessed. For the conversion of my six children. For a revival in the Pontypool services, and on a Revival Mission at Tondu to commence to-day. For the conversion of a brother and his wife. For a Revival at Harrogate. That great success may attend the Special Services to be held in Hereford Circuit during the third and fourth weeks in January. That a brother may give up intoxicating drink.

Praise. – For many mercies derived since becoming a member of the Union. For support in bereavement and the rich consolations of the Word. For God's great goodness and forbearance through the past year.

MONDAY, 10TH. – For a widow and child – that God will convert them, and provide a situation whereby they may be maintained. For a delicate youth – that a suitable situation be obtained. That God will keep three dear young people at Hale in the narrow way. Special, for a dear brother – that he may be saved from the power of strong drink. That a son may be guided. For a son long prayed for. For a daughter long an invalid. For the conversion of an aged father long prayed for.

Praise. – For a dear son's safe arrival at Mysore. For a wonderful and immediate answer to united prayer for the restoration of a dear mother, at the point of death, and for the conversion of a brother thereby. That the first request by the Union on September 22nd has been completely answered.

Death

Document V.24

A Wesleyan Death, 1803

> Methodist obituaries often linger over deathbed scenes. Rebecca Clemenson (born 1723) was a well-to-do widow and long-standing Wesleyan member who died in old age after being blind for twenty years. Her delight in hymns is typical of Methodist spirituality. So is the struggle to retain the assurance of salvation until the last.
>
> The extract is taken from *The Methodist Magazine*, March 1804, pp. 129–30.

During her illness the enemy of souls was often permitted to buffet her. At one time, under these conflicts, she asked a fried, – 'Do you think I shall land safe at last?' On her replying, 'We have no doubt of your being soon in glory,' her peace returned. Her last conflict was on the Lord's-day, a week before her death. When she was delivered, she said, with peculiar sweetness,

> 'O what are all my sufferings here,
>   If, Lord, thou count'st me meet,
> With that enraptur'd host to' appear,
>   And worship at thy feet!'

Sometimes, supposing herself to be alone when she was not, in consequence of being blind, she prayed aloud, and earnestly intreated the Lord, that those she loved might not pass thro' the sufferings she had endured. Like her blessed Master, being truly resigned to the Will of her heavenly Father, when, under the deepest affliction, she seemed most evidently to bear his image. After this conflict, not one doubt remained on her mind. Being asked by a Preacher, If she was under any fear of death? She answered, – 'None at all; only thoughts of the last struggle, in the separation of soul and body, sometimes exercise my mind; but I am enabled to leave all to God.' She continued happy, often conversing with God, and repeating hymns, to the astonishment of those around her. Her love to the poor followers of Jesus was great, and the company of his ministers was her delight. ...

On Saturday morning, when the clock struck one, she said, 'I should have liked to have gone with the rising morn.' She appeared quite recollected all the day. In the evening, when parting with her leader, she said, with a grateful smile, 'The Lord Jesus bless you: The God of Peace be with you.' Death drawing very near, and rendering her unable to respire, one asked, How she felt her mind? She replied; – 'Unto my sovereign Lord and King, My all I now commend.' She appeared to be quite serene and placid; and engaged in close communion with God. Her last words that could be distinctly heard were, 'Jesus! Master!' About one o'clock on Sunday morning, July 31, 1803, her happy spirit was taken to Paradise.

Document V.25

A Quaker Death, 1823

Quakers had always taken particular pains to record their members' spiritual experience down to death. Mary Dudley (1750–1823) was a Methodist turned Quaker who travelled as a minister. The account of her last days has particular pathos through having been written by one of her children. The distinctive dating terminology of the Society of Friends makes its appearance in 'First day' (Sunday) and '9 mo.' (September). For Dudley, see DEB.

The extract is taken from E. Dudley, ed., *The Life of Mary Dudley*, London, 1825, pp. 333–43.

On the 5th, conversing seriously respecting her situation, it was remarked that her seeming ignorant as to the issue still produced a degree of hope that the trial of separation was not yet at hand, to which she quickly replied; 'That this is my death illness I have not the least doubt, but the time may be wisely and mercifully concealed from me; the end may come in a moment, and if it be the Lord's will to save me from agonizing pain, and grant a quiet dismissal, what a favour it will be. Oh! to pass quietly away. I feel very poor, and have many infirmities, which I hoped might be less sensibly felt at this awful time; but I have this one testimony, I am nothing, Christ is all. My friends are dear to me, there is nothing in my heart but love to all. God is love; He has supported me through many trials, and now enables me to rely on His free, full and unmerited mercy. Glory, glory, glory be to His name now and for ever. *The earth shall be filled with the knowledge of the Lord, and from the rising of the sun to the going down of the same His name is to be praised.*'

First day, the 7th, she seemed like one on the verge of the eternal world, and evidently thought herself going. The difficulty of breath and occasional spasms on her chest being very distressing to herself, and to those around her. She several times said, 'Come Lord Jesus, come quickly. Into thy hand I commit my spirit.'

Observing that she felt too weak even to hear the scriptures read, she sweetly added, 'But I can think of their author.' When parting for the night she commended each of her children to Divine protection, imploring the heavenly blessing for them, under the influence of strong affection, and with the solemnity of christian concern.

Contrary to expectation she obtained some refreshing sleep, and became a little revived, saying next morning, 'I expected to be in another world by this time. Lord enable me to wait in the patience thy appointed time.' ...

Spirituality

The only evidence of approaching dissolution was a gentle sinking of the breath, which continued like that of a sleeping infant; until without any perceptible intermission or the slightest struggle, it ceased, and the immortal and redeemed spirit ascended with joy to the mansions of never ending rest and peace, about half-past eight o'clock on fourth day evening, the 24th of 9 mo. 1823.

Document V.26

A Congregationalist Death, 1824

Obituaries which appeared amongst the Independents tended to praise those who had seen the light some years ago, been a devoted servant of their chapel, and depended on the grace of God in their last hours, which were often described at length. Comments made by the deceased in a period of calm about reliance on, and endurance in, the faith without a doubt entering their minds were frequently quoted. This typical example is taken from *The Congregational Magazine*, February 1825, pp. 111–12.

On the 17th of November, 1824, died Mr. John Huntsman, of Boston, Lincolnshire, aged 44. ... Soon after the ministry of the Gospel was introduced into Boston, in connection with the Independent denomination, he became a hearer of the word; and at the formation of a Christian church, in 1819, he became a member of that community. ... For five years he was actively devoted to the cause of God, and laboured abundantly for the promotion of his glory. Nearly the whole of this time he sustained the office of Deacon, and performed the duties of that office with exemplary prudence and zeal. ...

Bright as was his character when in health, the grace of God, which was with him, appeared brighter still in his last affliction. For some time prior to his death, he had an impression that his end was approaching, and he contemplated it with peculiar composure, and spoke of it with unruffled serenity. When seized with his last illness he said, 'This sickness will be unto death.' Although, from the peculiar character of his disorder, his sufferings must have been severe in the extreme, not one murmuring word escaped his lips:– on the contrary, his state of mind was most delightful and heavenly. Absorbed in a contemplation of the goodness of God, his feelings were invariably joyful, and his language that of praise. He often observed that God had never permitted one doubt, or one fear, respecting his safety, to pass over his mind, and on one occasion he said, 'I cannot describe the communion which God holds with my soul. I know whom I have believed. Religion is no trick – the Bible is no fable. I am a dying man; and nothing but the truth of God could support me, but this does support me.' He enjoyed abundant peace of mind during ten days of excruciating pain, and on each successive day exhibited a growing meetness for a better world. During the last few days he seemed to live even above prayer – his whole soul was occupied in the *praises* of his God. He expressed himself as resigned to the will of the Most High, and often delighted in the thought that God's will must be done. It was, indeed, a privilege to hear the delightful assurances of God's love which he expressed, and to witness the growing fervour of his soul in the prospect of eternity. His end was peace; for without a struggle or a sigh, the spirit left its trembling tenement, and returned to God who gave it.

Document V.27

A Letter of Consolation, 1839

Letters expressing regret at the death of a loved one often relied on the formula that God knows best, and that was understandable in a time when death amongst the young was not infrequent. The suggestion that no further sin was possible now that death had taken place was common amongst the Congregationalists and Baptists. Martha Sherman (see VI.9) is writing to a member of her Bible class, and seizes the occasion as an evangelistic opportunity.

The extract is taken from J. Sherman, *The Pastor's Wife*, 2nd edn, London, 1849, pp. 51–3.

My Dear Young Friend,

The intelligence of your dear sister's removal did not reach me till half-an-hour before the post left Enfield, or I should have written a few lines to you immediately. ... I think I may truly say I sympathise with you, for when but a few years older than yourself, I was called to part with an only sister...I though it impossible to live without her. ... But this is the dark side of the painful dispensation. ... When my own Mary was taken from me, heaven, as the dwelling-place of God, had no attractions for me; my heart was unrenewed and unhumbled for sin; but when that heaven was the abode of her happy spirit, my thoughts were constantly there, and I longed to be with her – earth had lost its great attraction – nothing could fill the dreadful blank which her removal occasioned. It pleased God, at last, to convince me that it was sin which made me so desolate, and that place in my heart He could more than fill: this led me to seek that pardon, which alone could unite me to Jesus, and that 'holiness without which no man can see the Lord:' and my earnest prayer was, that I might prove my love to her, not by fruitless repining at my loss, but by following in her steps, by consecrating myself wholly to the service of Him whom she had loved and humbly sought to glorify.

... To our finite minds it may seem mysterious that one so beloved and useful should be taken from us in early youth; but remember how little we know what God designs by his providences. His thoughts are not our thoughts, nor his ways our ways, happily for us: if ever we reach yonder happy world, we shall understand why these painful dispensations were permitted; till then, ever bear in mind that 'God is love', not only when He grants us that which delights us, but when He sends deep affliction, bereavement and pain: and God designs your good, and seeks your happiness in this trial: do not lose the blessing. There is one tie less to earth; her happy spirit is now rejoicing in her Saviour's love: that Saviour's precious blood purchased heaven for her, and that blood and that heaven He offers to you. Remember, dear, this world is but the passage to that bright world; keep that in sight, and beware of any thing that may shade it from your view – sin only can do this – this separates the soul from God. Oh! Never rest until sin is pardoned through that precious 'blood which cleanseth from all sin,' and that righteousness which justifies the 'sinner that believes in Jesus'. Pant after holiness, that you may be fitted for that world where 'nothing can enter that defileth.' Take up your cross and follow Jesus: be satisfied with nothing short of the entire consecration of yourself to Him, who invited you 'to come unto Him that you may have life.' Think of the joy that will fill heaven, and the souls of your dear sainted mother and sister, to hear the tidings through some angelic messenger that A—— had 'chosen that good part that shall never be taken from her.' ... Be much in prayer, dear; you have need of much wisdom in your doubly responsible situation; seek it as a promised, as well as a desired blessing, and never lean to your own understanding.

Document V.28

A Huntingtonian Death, 1844

The subject of this obituary was a Mrs Cathery, who died aged 80 shortly after the death-bed scene described. Mrs Cathery attended the ministries of Jenkin Jenkins, at Jireh Chapel, Lewes, and William Brook of Brighton. Both were Independent ministers, and both were friends of William Huntington (see II.21). This extract, describing Mrs Cathery's affectionate final farewell to three friends, and to a lady who had been her companion for over fifty years, is taken from *The Gospel Standard*, July 1844, pp. 218–20. It appeared under the signature, J. L., Chichester.

... as soon as we entered the room, she said, 'O how glad I am to see you both again! how kind it is of you in visiting me so often! The Lord has done great things for me.' She then immediately entered upon spiritual things, and spoke most sweetly and blessedly of her experience, and of her then present enjoyments. She said, ... [when another visitor entered the room], 'What, are you come to see a poor dying saint, who is just going to leave this poor, miserable, dying, and perishing world? I am quite ready; I am only waiting to receive the summons, the messenger, death, to welcome me home. Why are his chariot wheels so long in coming? why drag they so heavily?' I then read the 71st Psalm, which she appeared to enjoy much, as she would frequently stop me whilst reading, to make several remarks, which were truly sweet and weighty. After I had engaged in prayer, she said, 'You are come just at a seasonable time; the Lord is with us again, as he hath been many times before. O how sweet and precious is the real communion and fellowship of saints, and to feel the oneness of soul which we shall all ere long enjoy in that upper and better world, where we shall sing the high praises of God and the Lamb, and that for ever and ever, in much stronger accents, and in a more noble strain of voice than we can possibly do whilst here!' She begged of us to present her Christian love to several of her dear friends, whom she named, and to assure them that she did not forget them in these her dying moments, after which she spoke of the happy prospect that was set before her of meeting many of her dear Christian friends now in glory, with whom when on earth, she had taken sweet counsel; but above all, she should see Jesus, whom her soul loved, and be for ever with Him who had done all things well. 'What pains did he take,' she said; 'what sorrows did he wade through, what griefs did he suffer, what wrath did he endure, and what a glorious righteousness and endless salvation has he wrought out and brought in for us poor ungodly sinners! O! I shall sing much louder by and by, when I get rid of this poor body of sin and death, and so will you too.' Being somewhat exhausted, and her tongue parched, she asked for a little jelly. As soon as she received it, she said, 'O what a mercy and favour granted to me, a poor worm of the earth! I have every thing of a temporal nature given me as soon as I ask for it; but, O! how was it with my dear Redeemer? They would not so much as give him a drop of cold water to cool his tongue, when he cried out, "I thirst," but gave him vinegar mingled with gall to drink, even in his greatest agonies and bitterest sufferings. Blessed be his precious name!'

Document V.29

A Baptist Death, 1852

Baptist obituaries at this period tended to dwell on consciousness of the saving nature of the blood of Christ, and the nearness of glory. They also included some of the most detailed descriptions of the last hours of the deceased to be found amongst Dissenters. The obituary of John Brown of Newbury, from *The Baptist Magazine*, March 1852, pp. 173–4, was written by J. Drew, who in his vivid prose gets carried away by Brown's felicity in death.

Mr Brown's last illness was brief, but extremely violent. He was with us at our annual tea meeting on the last day in the year, and in the evening addressed the church in terms of unusual endearment and wisdom. ... On Friday he attended the monthly church meeting, which was the last time that he was ever in the house of God. On Saturday he was taken very ill with violent spasms, which continued to return after short intervals till nature succumbed to their attacks. ... He prayed earnestly and long for clearer manifestations of the divine favour; his prayers were heard and were followed by even more than his ordinary rejoicing; nor was there ever again to be a cloud over his purified and gladdened spirit. He felt that his guilt was altogether removed, that the blood of Jesus Christ had cleansed him from all sin, that he had only to wait a short time for his release from suffering

Spirituality

and for an abundant entrance into the everlasting kingdom of his Redeemer. So far was he from murmuring under his almost frightful agonies, that he regarded them all as necessary, repeatedly thanked his heavenly Father for them, and told his friends that he had no doubt but that there was some evil still left in him which the Lord thus designed mercifully to remove before admitting him to his presence. Between these fatal paroxysms it was delightful to be with him, and to witness the triumphs of a divine faith over the pangs of dissolving nature, over the timidity natural to man in such a crisis, and over the shocks of approaching death. His mind was wholly at peace, his lips were full of the praises of the Redeemer; and he as calmly awaited the arrival of the final struggle as if it had been the commonest event of life. We heard but one complaint from his lips, and that was, that he had done so little for God, while his debt of gratitude was so deep and boundless. Seldom has the power of real religion to support its friends under the heaviest afflictions been more signally displayed than in the conflict through which our beloved brother passed to his unfading, everlasting crown. Death was here the conquered, not the conqueror. His sting was gone, and with it all his power to awe. He appeared as a bright and smiling angel drawing aside the curtain of heaven, rather than as a grim spectre presiding over the carnival of the grave. ... Mr Brown expired on Monday the 19th of January, 1852, in the sixty-eighth year of his age.

Document V.30

A Unitarian Memorial, 1862

Although wall monuments were more common in parish churches than in chapels, several were erected in some buildings, usually to the specially eminent. Thomas Paget was certainly in that category, for he was that uncommon phenomenon, a Nonconformist country gentleman. Nevertheless he was closely connected with the town of Leicester, where he was a banker and at one time mayor. His monument, embodying the values for which he stood, was erected in the Great Meeting, Leicester. See A. Temple Paterson, *Radical Leicester: A History of Leicester, 1780–1850*, Leicester, 1954.

The inscription is taken from *The Epitaphs in the Graveyard and Chapel of the Great Meeting, Leicester*, Leicester, 1912, p. 387.

In
Memory of
Thomas Paget,
only son of Thomas Paget Esquire of Ibstock,
and Mary Clara his wife.
Born at Ibstock Decr 30th 1778,
Died at his residence at Humberstone Novr 25th 1862,
He married the 18th of Feby 1807,

Anne, second daughter of John Pares Esqre
of the Newarke, Leicester and Hopwell Hall
in the County of Derby.

Being imbued from his earliest years with the great principles of Civil
and Religious Liberty, to which his family had long been attached he ever
remained their consistent and zealous advocate in days of doubt and danger.
Consistent as a Politician, Eminent as an Agriculturalist, beloved as a
Landlord, and possessing the devoted affection of his family and friends,
he was unanimously elected by the freeholders of his native county
to represent them as one of the Knights of this Shire in Parliament

on the 11th of May 1831.

Faithful to his trust he never wearied until he had assisted in
the achievement of the Second Charter of his Country's freedom,
when on the subsequent division of this County, he retired into
that private life which he ever preferred.
He lived to witness the fruits of that great Measure, and on the
passing of the Municipal Reform Act he was again called from retirement, and twice unanimously elected Mayor of this Borough in
testimony of the respect and gratitude of its burgesses, earned by a long and
active life spent in the immediate neighbourhood of their Town, in close and
intimate connection with its commercial and social interests which it was ever
his aim and happiness to promote.
By those whose day upon earth has by his death been turned into night, but who
still await in humble hope the dawn of that heaven, where sorrow and separation
shall be no more, this marble is erected to the memory of the best and kindest of
Fathers, the tenderest and most affectionate of Husbands, the generous friend of the
poor and oppressed, and the dauntless protector of the injured and the innocent.

Quis desiderio sit pudor aut modus
Tam cari capitis?   +   +   +
Cui pudor et justitiae soror
Incorrupta fides, nudaque veritas.
Quando ullum inveniet parem?

Shield, crest and motto: 'Espere et persevere.'
S. BARFIELD, Sculptor   *Welford Road, Leicester*

PART VI

CHAPEL

Introduction

The life of the chapel was often the focus for the whole surrounding community. The only alternative centre of social life, especially in the earlier years of the nineteenth century, would commonly be the public house, which those aspiring to respectability would shun. The chapel was the place for meeting one's friends and enjoying leisure pursuits as well as for nurturing the Christian life. In the years before Queen Victoria there was usually a concentration on the more strictly religious activities such as prayer meetings and listening to sermons – though many of them had a dimension of entertainment about them – whereas as the century wore on there was a tendency to provide a wider range of diversions such as bazaars (see III.22) and musical events. Although some such as Strict Baptists and Methodists adhering to the holiness tradition resisted the trend, there was definitely a tendency to broaden the corporate life of the chapels.

The leadership of the local Nonconformist communities was vested in the ministers. Although a few groups such as the Brethren and the Churches of Christ rejected a separated ministry, the great majority of the denominations regarded an ordained man as desirable or even essential for pastoral care and at least occasional (in the case of the Methodists) pulpit ministry. Ministers were often poor, which could necessitate the taking on of secular work (VI.1), and frequently moved from one place of service to another. Yet they could be greatly admired, especially as their educational standards improved (VI.2). Methodist ministers were stationed in a fresh circuit every two or three years, but, particularly among the Wesleyans, there was an effort to reinforce the authority of the minister by solemnly setting him apart (VI.3). The threat of Nonconformist ministers losing the common touch became real (VI.4). While ministers came and went, however, lay leadership provided continuity in each chapel. Methodists were served by an army of lay preachers, in 1883 among the Wesleyans seven times as numerous as ordained ministers (VI.5, 7). Methodist chapel life was organised by society stewards and a host of officials met at the regular leaders' meetings (see X.13). Congregationalists and Baptists were led by deacons (VI.6), occasionally together with elders (VI.10), and the chief office holders were the church secretary and church treasurer. Chapel supplied an opportunity for many people to discover skills that otherwise would have lain dormant.

The Congregationalists and Baptists insisted, as the basis of their ecclesiastical polity, that their churches should be gathered communities. The members, that is to say, had to be committed Christians (VI.13). Hence applicants for church membership were required to explain their experience of conversion either in writing (VI.9) or in person to the church meeting (VI.10). Those admitted to membership were subject to the discipline of the church, so that serious moral lapses were investigated and could lead to censure or exclusion (VI.11). Bodies in the Methodist tradition, on the other hand, originally accepted any who were in earnest about their souls, though insisting on a rigorous moral discipline (VI.8). Admission to Methodist membership was by a quarterly ticket issued by the minister, but later in the century more formal procedures for recognition of new members were devised (VI.12). The Salvation Army maintained the emphasis on discipline in the late Victorian period (VI.14) when other Nonconformists were gradually allowing it to fade away – usually by leaving it to the minister.

The activities of the chapel also differed by denomination. Methodists adopted a number of special practices including class meetings and love feasts (VI.15, 17). Congregationalists and Baptists had the church meeting, their supreme organ of government (VI.18). But many features of chapel life were common to most Nonconformists. A great deal of effort normally went into the Sunday school, which was approved even by some (but not all) Strict Baptists (VI.22). The regular weekly sessions could involve careful preparation (VI.25) and the Sunday school anniversary was the highlight of the chapel year (VI.16). The spiritual needs of the congregation were catered for by gatherings for prayer (VI.19) and Bible study (VI.24); its social side found expression in such events as the Christmas tea meeting (VI.26). The chapel bade farewell to its former members in distinctive funeral occasions (VI.24).

The corporate life of Nonconformists is celebrated in K. Young, *Chapel*, London, 1972, and illustrated in R. Moore, *Pit-Men, Preachers & Politics: The Effects of Methodism in a Durham Mining Community*, Cambridge, 1974, and in C. D. Cashdollar, *A Spiritual Home: Life in British and American Reformed Congregations, 1830–1915*, University Park, Pennsylvania, 2000. The ministry is discussed in K. D. Brown, *A Social History of the Nonconformist Ministry in England and Wales, 1800–1930*, Oxford, 1988, and in J. Munson, *The Nonconformists: In Search of a Lost Culture*, London, 1991, chap. 4. The fullest study of lay leaders is G. Milburn and M. Batty, eds, *Workaday Preachers: The Story of Methodist Lay Preaching*, London, 1995. J. W. Grant, *Free Churchmanship in England, 1870–1940*, London, n.d., covers church membership for Congregationalists and Baptists. Chapel histories are excellent sources for the range of activities undertaken, and the one that most fully captures the atmosphere of chapel life is C. Binfield, *Pastors and People: The Biography of a Baptist Church: Queen's Road, Coventry*, Coventry, 1984.

Ministry

Document VI.1

Ministers and Secular Business, 1812

> The question of whether ministers should have a second source of income was a concern to many Dissenters. It was not an issue for the Methodists, whose travelling preachers were separated to their work: nor was it for the Scotch Baptists and Churches of Christ, who insisted that each church should have a plurality of elders and so accepted that they would need secular employment, or for the Brethren, who rejected the whole idea of a distinct ministry. But among Independents and, especially, ordinary Baptists, who were usually poorer, low stipends from their flocks often forced reluctant pastors to find additional sources of income. This discussion of the subject incidentally defines the expected duties of a minister.
>
> The extract is taken from *The Baptist Magazine*, June 1812, pp. 231–3.

It must on all hands be allowed, that for ministers to engage in secular employments under certain circumstances cannot be criminal. The great Apostle of the Gentiles *laboured with his own hands* in order to supply his necessities and the necessities of those who were with him. And when ministers are connected with churches whose circumstances are such as cannot provide for their support, and have no sufficient resources from property already acquired, a necessity is evidently laid upon them to do something for their own subsistence. ...

But ... I am free to assert that where such necessity does not exist, a minister's engaging in secular business can by no means be justified. And I beg leave to submit to your consideration the following reasons in support of my opinion.

1. *It takes up a minister's time.* Every one who takes into serious consideration the nature of the ministerial office, must be sensible that it is very comprehensive. It includes in it not only the frequent public ministration of the word, and in order to that, the assiduous and careful study of it; but also the diligent inspection of his flock, the visiting of the sick, and the administering of such private admonitions, consolations, and reproofs, as the respective cases of the individuals may require. But if a minister be engaged in secular business, and spend a large portion of his time in the shop, the warehouse, or the field, how can ministerial duties be discharged? Will not many of them be partially, if not wholly, omitted; and others be very indifferently performed?

2. *It greatly unfits the mind for the duties of the sacred office.* Secular employ of any kind occupies a large portion of the thoughts and cares of every one who engages in it, to any considerable extent, and that to so great a degree as to make it matter of very serious caution in private christians to watch against its pernicious influence. How much more dangerous must that influence be to

ministers, whose office requires that they should be more habitually and more eminently spiritual than christians in common ...

3. *It brings ministers into a set of connections very unfavourable to their great employ.* As a tradesman, a minister must associate with tradesmen; and it is vain to expect that such should in general be those who are pious and likely to promote the piety of a minister, or to derive any religious advantage from him. Habitual converse with them will insensibly incline him to a temper and a strain of converse similar to them, and thereby greatly unfit him for intercourse with the poor, the timid, the humble, and those who are labouring under spiritual maladies. ...

4. *It is likely to engross a minister's chief attention, and the ministry is in danger of becoming only a secondary concern.* He is in great danger of becoming more the tradesman than the minister; and if the concerns of his trade come into competition with those of the ministry, as will be very frequently the case, he will feel strongly inclined to let the latter give way to the former.

Document VI.2

Robert Vaughan on the Ministry, 1843

Robert Vaughan (1795–68) was Independent minister at Worcester and Kensington before, in 1834, becoming professor of modern history at University College, London. In 1843 he moved to take up the presidency of the Lancashire Independent College and two years later he launched *The British Quarterly Review* (see III.4). In 1846 he was chairman of the Congregational Union. The author of several historical works, Vaughan tried to enhance the culture of the Congregational ministry. See DNB.

The extract is taken from Vaughan's inaugural lecture at the Lancashire College, *Protestant Nonconformity in its Relation to Learning and Piety*, London, 1843, pp. 44–50.

The design of this institute is, the education of students with a view to the Christian ministry. Its benefits are to be restricted to persons whose piety shall be beyond doubt. To such persons it will extend the advantages of mental discipline and learning, together with the cultivation of the kind of ability especially required in the discharge of the duties of the preacher and the pastor in churches of our order. ...

The service of God is the great service of humanity; and the men who conduct it should be, in a far greater degree than is common, the great men in the generations of the earth!

In no connexion are considerations of this nature more deserving of attention than among Protestant Dissenters. In the worship of the Church of England, scarcely anything is left to the discretion of the officiating clergyman, nearly everything being provided and determined by a higher authority. It is by this means that the services of the Established Church are made to partake of a measure of decorum and dignity which could not otherwise have been secured. The worshipper may not bring to those services a due feeling of spirituality, but in themselves they are not wanting in order, seriousness, and a fitness to produce impression. But among us, with whom so much is left to the ability, taste, or judgment of the minister, the same advantage is not to be expected, except as the result of attention and study, specially directed to that object. My solemn conviction is, that it is not so much the doctrines we preach, as the manner of our preaching, which renders our ministry so little acceptable to a large portion of the educated classes of society; and that it is not so much our mode of worship that is the ground of objection in such quarters, as our want of due consideration in regard to it, so as to give to it the dignity, the solemnity, the fitness to awaken devout emotion, of which it is susceptible. Society, generally, will more readily bear with the want of talent in a minister, than with deficiency in regard to certain general, though lesser proprieties, belonging especially to his office; and in the worship of God, there is a feeling in humanity, which will sympathize more readily in a service somewhat tinctured with the awe of superstition, than with a service which may seem to bespeak a mind devoid of a proper reverence toward sacred things. We are far from wishing to realize a precise order and decorum in worship at the cost of spirituality and power; but we could wish to see that patient and unprejudiced thought given to services of this nature, which might secure to us as much as possible of the advantages of our system on the one side, with as little as may be of its disadvantages on the other.

Document VI.3

The Wesleyan Ordination Service, 1848

As the travelling preachers of early Methodism gradually evolved into regularly ordained ministers, a high doctrine of the pastoral office emerged among the Wesleyans. Ministers were responsible for the souls of their flocks – and also for good order in the increasingly disciplined connexion – and so were accorded a respected status. The ordination service, first published in 1846 and modified two years later, provided that the president of Conference, asking the questions, should impress upon the minds of candidates the importance of firm discipline as well as sound doctrine, which was embodied in John Wesley's sermons and notes on the New Testament. See J. C. Bowmer, *Pastor and People: A Study of Church and Ministry in Wesleyan Methodism from the Death of John Wesley (1791) to the Death of Jabez Bunting (1858)*, London, 1975.

The extract is taken from the *Order of Administration of the Lord's Supper and Baptism together with the Ordination Service as used by the Wesleyan Methodists*, London, 1848, pp. 106–11.

Do you trust that you are inwardly moved by the Holy Ghost to take upon you this office and ministration, to serve God for the promoting of his glory, and the edifying of his people?
Answer. I trust so.

Are you persuaded that the holy Scriptures contain sufficiently all doctrine required of necessity for eternal salvation through faith of Jesus Christ? And are you determined, out of the said Scriptures, to instruct the people committed to your charge; and to teach nothing, as required of necessity to eternal salvation, but that which you shall be persuaded may be concluded and proved by the Scripture?
Answer. I am so persuaded, and have so determined, by God's grace.

As you are to exercise your ministry under the direction of the Wesleyan-Methodist Conference, I have further to inquire, whether you have read the first four volumes of Mr. Wesley's Sermons, and his Notes on the New Testament; and whether you believe that the system of doctrine therein contained is in accordance with the holy Scriptures?
Answer. I have read them, and do so believe.

I have also to ask you, whether you have read the Large Minutes of the Conference; and believe that the general system of discipline contained therein is agreeable to the holy Scriptures; and whether you will maintain and enforce it in the societies which shall be committed to your charge?
Answer. I have read them, and do so believe and resolve. ...

Will you reverently obey your chief Ministers, unto whom is committed the charge and government over you; following with a glad mind and will their godly admonitions, and submitting yourselves to their godly judgments?
Answer. I will do so, the Lord being my helper.

Document VI.4

C. H. Spurgeon on the Ministry, 1876

For Spurgeon, see I.4. One of his greatest qualities was the common touch. He despised the genteel wherever he encountered it, but most of all in the ministry. This was one of the supreme messages Spurgeon tried to convey to the young men training for the pastorate in the college attached to his Metropolitan Tabernacle. See D. W. Bebbington, 'Spurgeon and British Evangelical Theological Education', in D. G. Hart and R. A. Mohler, eds, *Theological Education in the Evangelical Tradition,* Grand Rapids, Michigan, 1996, pp. 217–34.

The extract is taken from the book embodying Spurgeon's Friday afternoon addresses to his trainees, *Lectures to my Students*, London, 1876, republished 1954, p. 166.

Our subject is to be the minister's common conversation when he mingles with men in general, and is supposed to be quite at his ease. How shall he order his speech among his fellow-men? First and foremost, let me say, *let him give himself no ministerial airs*, but avoid everything which is stilted, official, fussy, and pretentious. 'The Son of Man' is a noble title; it was given to Ezekiel, and to a greater than he: let not the ambassador of heaven be other than a son of man. In fact, let him remember that the more simple and unaffected he is, the more closely will he resemble that child-man, the holy child Jesus. There is such a thing as trying to be too much a minister, and becoming too little a man; though the more of a true man you are, the more truly will you be what a servant of the Lord should be. Schoolmasters and ministers have generally an appearance peculiarly their own; in the wrong sense, they 'are not as other men are.' They are too often speckled birds, looking as if they were not at home among the other inhabitants of the country, but awkward and peculiar. When I have seen a flamingo gravely stalking along, an owl blinking in the shade, or a stork demurely lost in thought, I have been irresistibly led to remember some of my dignified brethren of the teaching and preaching fraternity, who are so marvellously proper at all times that they are just a shade amusing. Their very respectable, stilted, dignified, important, self-restrained manner is easily acquired; but is it worth acquiring?

Lay Leadership

Document VI.5

A Primitive Methodist Preachers' Plan, 1854

Local preachers, unordained but trained, were the backbone of Methodism, always taking far more services than the small body of regular ministers. Their preaching engagements were organised on printed plans, of which this is a typical instance. It is headed '1854. Primitive Methodist Preachers' Plan of the Brandon Circuit'. Brandon was in Suffolk, close to the Norfolk border. See G. Milburn and M. Batty, eds, *Workaday Preachers: The Story of Methodist Local Preaching*, London, 1995.

Chapel

LORD'S DAY PLAN

	PLACES	TIME.	JULY.		AUGUST.				SEPTEMBER.				OCTOBER.		
			23	30	6	13	20	27	3	10	17	24	1	8	15
1	Brandon	10½	16	2	J	41	1c	40	38	35	1	23	5	21	42
		2½ 6	16	2	4L	41	1c	40	38	35	1s	17	5	21	42
2	Thompson	2 6	20	22	7	8	36	9c	10	26	31	22	18	32	34
3	Feltwell	2 6	25	1CA	11	27	15	CM	2c	39	21	16	35	5	3L
4	Wilton	2 6	35	21	15	25	16	17c	14	33	2	30	15	P	5
5	Methwold	2 6	11	16	35c	14	27	1L	15	21	5	2	3	35	11
6	Radmere	10½ 2	42c	P	25	33	3	2	21	14	15	25	1	3	33
7	Sedge Fen	10½ 2	3	25	33	16	42c	14	3	5	30	1 P	14	33	25
8	Eriswell	2 6	23	14	3	2c	P	25	42	16	33	3 1	25	42	14
9	Saham	10½	CM	10	F	1CA	7	22c	F	18	32	9	7	24	P
		2 6	19	18	13	1CA	20	22c	36	10	32	9L	7	24	31
10	Watton	2½ 6	18	20	32	10c	37	13	22	24	36	26	8	1s	9
11	L. Cressingham	6	7	32	19	13	26	10c	24	22	9	18	19	34	1s
12	Bodney	10½	31	36	26	22c	24	8	34		18	10	11	20	1s
		2½								9					
13	Igborough	10½	24	P	31	34	18	36c	26	8	P	11	24	9	10
		2													
14	Ovington	2 6	10	7	9	32c	34	26	19	1L	8	7	22	36	19
15	Foulden	2 6	13	*	14	35c	22	31	1c	11	16	8L	9	18	21
16	Northwold	2 6	*	43	1SA	31	11	CM	16c	14	27	35	2	31	44
17	Brandon T. S.	2 6	14	23c	4	17	30	P	J	15	29	33	4	30	35
21	Gooderstone	2 6	24	28	8c	9	*	P	27	34	10	14	28	16	*
22	Ashill	2 6	1CA	19	34c	7	8	18	31	36L	24	20	10	22	32

	Preachers' Names and Residences	
	CHURCH	1
1	Mallows	4
2	Woolnough	8
3	Webb	1
4	Addison J.	3
5	Scott	9
6	Rudderham	9
7	Webb	10
8	Boughen	10
9	Twaites	19
10	Elinor	16
11	Rome	16
12	Buckle	11
13	Hallox	3
14	Shackle	3
15	Hudson	3
16	Edwards	1
17	Garner	9
18	Crow	11
19	French	9
20	Addison H.	3
21	Moore M.	
22	Lingwood	1
23	Moore	
24	Goodman	6
25	Lake	2
26	Archer	16
27	Lambert	21
28	Farrow	1
29	Frewer	12
30	Howard	10
31	Dunnett	8
32	Reave	1
33	Williams	
34	Parrot	9
35	Vergerson and Walebelly	

REFERENCE

Q. Quarterly Collection.   L. Lovefeast.   S. Sacrament.   T. Tickets.
P. Prayer Meeting.   C. C. Chapel Fund Collection.   R. Revival Meeting.

Document VI.6

A Baptist Deacon from 1858

The lay leaders of Congregational and Baptist churches were the deacons. Their primary responsibility was chapel finances while the minister looked after the congregation's spiritual welfare. The deacon described here served for many years from 1858 at Maesyrhelem Baptist Chapel, Radnorshire, during the ministry of David Davies, the father of the writer (see IV.11).

The extract is taken from E. Davies, *The Life of the Late Rev. David Davies*, Maesyrhelem, Brecon, 1914, p.51.

Mr. [Evan] Kinsey ... was a lonely and solitary man – his wife died somewhat early in life – and consequently almost invariably he rode on horseback to the services in solitude and silence. It could hardly be said that he was of any build. More truly it might be said that the various members of his body were hung together, and none too compactly; and his clothes dangled from the rigid corners of his lean, lank, and bony frame. His face, which was almost colourless, was certainly very striking; a face which one was constrained to examine in sections rather than as a whole. It was one of the sternest and strongest faces I have ever looked into, the nose and chin being almost fearfully predominant. He was a man set in authority by nature herself; and he had no need to speak the word, for a look from him was sufficient to restore peace and quietness on our galleries. He was born to be a ruler and leader of men; and had he entered the army he might have easily won for himself the title of a distinguished soldier, 'the Iron Duke.' Had he not been a Christian he would have ruled his enemies with a rod of iron, and dashed them in pieces like a potter's vessel. Imbued as he was with the spirit of Jesus, he saw to it that the rules of the church were carefully observed, and that the discipline was rigidly administered. On one occasion, when extra money was being raised, my father deemed it his duty to interfere, but Mr. Kinsey interposed as gently as was possible for one so strong and stern, saying, 'You see to the preaching Mr. Davies and we will look after the money'; adding in explanatory terms and tones, that preaching was a sufficient task for any one man. I presume that many pastors would be glad if all officers took the same view of such matters.

Document VI.7

John Harvey on Local Preachers, 1864

John Harvey, a Primitive Methodist minister stationed at Keighley, delivered an address on local preachers to the ministers of the Leeds district, meeting at Barnsley, in 1864. He laid down that the first qualification of local preachers was 'a fluent utterance'.

The extract is taken from J. Harvey, *Local Preachers*, Leeds, 1864, pp. 6–7.

Those who hesitate or stammer very much in the delivery of their discourses, however wishful to do good, are either to be pitied or blamed; pitied, if the impediment cannot be overcome; blamed, if they have never attempted to conquer the difficulty. When the audience is kept in suspense or held in doubt that the speaker will 'stick fast,' what he says fails to produce the desired effect. Some pluralise the singular by sounding the S. at the end of almost every word, which grates upon the ear, such as 'God's', 'buts,' 'bloods,' &c., and others at every pause, both in prayer and in preaching, add a very emphatic '*Aha!*' The benefits would more than counterbalance the efforts requisite to suppress such acquired habits. All good and intelligent men are not adapted for public speaking. We must not be understood as arguing here for the graces of elocution, the precision of rhetoric, the art of logic, and the accuracy of grammar; however valuable to a public speaker these may be, they are not favourite topics with the majority of our local brethren. But we would urge the cultivation of a natural, easy, and fluent delivery, as being more profitable to the hearer and less injurious to the speaker. A proper command of the voice is also important. Some pitch their voices too high at the commencement, and especially when preaching in the open air; and anon are heard screaming vehemently at the top of them, while portions of the congregation are writhing under the tortures of a voice outside its natural and legitimate province.

When I was a boy, and heard a preacher of this description, and saw him galloping at full speed till he was black in the face and foamed at the mouth, I thought that the man was in a passion; of course I understand things now better than I did then.

But let none suppose from these observations that we are in favour of a stiff, dry, formal delivery; contrariwise, we plead for earnestness, but that does not consist in a vociferous declamation. 'I speak as unto wise men, judge ye what I say.'

Membership

Document VI.8

Calvinistic Methodist Rules of Discipline, 1801

The Welsh Calvinistic Methodists, while still a society more or less within the Church of England, adopted a code in 1801 specifying the requirements of applicants for membership that remained in force throughout the century. As rule II makes plain, members did not have to be Christians, only seekers. Yet the expectations of them were precise, copious and extended far into the economic and political realms. Another seventeen clauses follow these seventeen.

The extract is taken from *The History, Constitution, Rules of Discipline, and Confession of Faith of the Calvinistic Methodists or the Presbyterians of Wales*, Caernarvon, 1900, pp. 23–7.

None may be admitted into membership of whom we cannot entertain a reasonable hope that they possess these qualifications:–

I. That they be, in a measure, convinced of sin by the Holy Ghost, poor in spirit, sorrowing for sin after a godly sort, and seeking to be delivered from it ...

II. That they be, more or less, convinced of their need of Christ, his righteousness and grace, and their need of Him as a perfect Mediator and mighty Saviour ...

III. That they so hunger and thirst for Christ and his righteousness, as to show all diligence in the right use of the means of grace ...

IV. That they hold no opinions or views which are contrary to the fundamental doctrines of Christianity; for instance, that they do not deny the doctrine of the Trinity, &c., &c.

V. That they be not perverse disputers, 'doting about questions, and strifes of words' ...

VI. That they be bent upon forsaking all the paths of sin and shame, which are contrary to the word of God and mar the beauty of the Christian character; and that they have no fellowship with the vanities of the world, and the unfruitful works of darkness; such as gatherings for foolish pleasure, wakes, dances, plays, banquettings, revellings, carousals, and other things of like nature ...

VII. That they be not yoked together in marriage with unbelievers ...

VIII. That they be not covenant breakers, but conscientious in performing, as much as lies in them, all their lawful engagements. ...

IX. That they hold family worship at least twice a day, 'rule well their own house,' and 'bring up their children in the nurture and admonition of the Lord'. ...

X. That they, and all who are under their care, keep holy the Sabbath day, by abstaining on that day from worldly business, and those small matters which might have been attended to before, or left to another time, such as buying and selling, and speaking their own words, that is, speaking about the business of this life, the affairs of kingdoms, and the concerns of their neighbours; and not only so, but they are required, not to shorten the day by indulging in too much sleep, to spend it in holy deeds and words, in the worship of God, in hearing his word, in teaching the ignorant, and in such works as truly tend to God's glory and the good of immortal souls.

XI. That they be sober, temperate in meats and drinks, neither gluttons nor drunkards. ...

XII. They must avoid all those modes and fashions of dress which tend to foster pride, wantonness, or extravagance ...

XIII. They must be of pure lips; their words must be few and gracious; they must put away from them all oaths, curses, and corrupt communications, the taking God's name in vain, filthiness, foolish talking, and jesting ...

XIV. That they be men of few words in buying and selling, not contentious, not unduly praising what they sell, nor saying 'it is naught, it is naught' of what they buy, not taking advantage of others' ignorance to put two prices on the same thing; but, as far as they understand its value and the state of the market, asking and paying for all goods the due and proper price. ...

XV. That they do not make it their business to buy or sell running goods, nor dishonestly deal in anything that is subject to duty ...

XVI. They must not speak evil of dignities, or those that are in authority ...; but, on the contrary, they must prove themselves, by word and deed, sincere and faithful subjects of the government, honouring the king and all that are in authority under him, and acknowledging with thankfulness the great kindness shown us, and the temporal and spiritual liberty and privileges which we enjoy ... .

XVII. They must not be usurers,[1] oppressors,[2] or misers;[3] they must not play at lotteries or any other game of chance, but be merciful, compassionate and generous, giving according to their ability to every good cause, recompensing good for evil, blessing for cursing, kindness for unkindness ...

Notes

1. We are clearly of opinion that to exact fair and lawful interest is not usury in the worst sense of the word, nor forbidden in every case. For instance, when money is borrowed on interest for the purpose of trading and making a profit, is it not as just and proper for one man to gain by his money as it is for another to gain by his time or labour? The same thing may be said of other instances. But to exact *immoderate* interest is sinful, in the same way as it is sinful to demand so high a rent for land that the tenant cannot pay it. It is true the Israelites were forbidden to lend upon usury to their brethren (*Deut.* xxiii. 19, and in other places); but it is probable either that this formed part of the civil law of Israel, and was intended to remain in force so long only as the wall of partition between Jews and Gentiles stood, or else that it was forbidden to lend on usury, because the Israelites were never accustomed to borrow money for purposes of trade, but only for procuring the necessaries of life in time of trouble and poverty.

See *Exod.* xxii. 25, 26; *Lev.* xxv. 35–37; *Neh.* v. 1–13. If it had been in itself sinful under the gospel dispensation to exact interest, it is not likely that our Lord would, in his parables, have claimed the right of exacting it. *Matt.* xxv. 27; *Luke* xix. 23.

2. *Oppressors.* – There are various kinds of oppression. For instance, a man is guilty of oppression when he is hard and austere towards his dependents, when he exacts from them too much service, and compels them to pay more than a fair and moderate price for what he supplies them with, such as bread, clothing, land, or house. He is guilty of oppression when he covets houses, land, or business, to the injury of his poorer neighbours. In this selfish spirit some men 'Join house to house, and lay field to field, till there be no place.' In their oppressive eagerness they join small tenements to their large farms, and make it too difficult for their weaker neighbours to secure a few acres, from which to obtain food for their numerous families. Others oppress in trade, when they seek exorbitant profits, forestall the market in order unduly to raise the prices, and so destroy their neighbour's honest gains. 'They covet fields, and take them by violence; and houses and take them away: so they oppress a man and his house, even a man and his heritage.' *Mic.* ii. 2; *Isa.* v. 8; *Hab.* ii. 9–11.

3. *Misers.* – The Welsh words (*cybydd*, from *cwb*,) means 'One who closes upon or clutches something.' The Latin word (*avarus*) means 'one who is eager and rapacious for money.' There are two words in Greek which may be rendered by *miser*, the one signifying 'a lover of money,' and the other 'one who is eager for more.' Let us remember that covetousness is idolatry in the sight of God: Col. iii. 5. But, though this lust and all worldly lusts are exceeding sinful in the sight of God when they lurk unseen in the heart, they are not amenable to church discipline except in so far as they manifest themselves in men's lives in the form of deceit, violence, oppression, cruelty, or excessive and unseemly parsimony.

Document VI.9

Application to Join a Congregational Church, 1829

Membership of a gathered church was highly prized in the earlier years of the century. Application normally required some form of personal testimony of faith, either delivered orally to the church meeting or else, as here, in writing to the minister. The applicant in this case is Martha Tucker (1806–48), who was later to marry James Sherman (see DNB), minister of the Surrey Chapel, Blackfriars. She was applying to the Congregational church at Chase Side, Enfield, Middlesex.

The extract is taken from J. Sherman, *The Pastor's Wife*, 2nd edn, London, 1849, pp. 18–20.

Clay Hill, *July 28th*, 1829.

Reverend Sir,

In venturing to offer myself as a candidate for admission into the visible Church of Christ, under your care, I trust I am influenced by a deep conviction of sin, and an abandonment of all hope of salvation, on any other ground than the all-sufficient sacrifice of the blessed Redeemer, who died the just for the unjust, to reconcile us to God; and as an adequate return for such infinite love is wholly impossible, all I can do is to give myself to Him as my rightful owner. I therefore solemnly dedicate myself to Him, resolving that whatever others do, I will serve the Lord; I renounce the world and its proffered joys, and will seek my happiness in Him alone – by his help and the influences of his Holy Spirit, I resolve to forsake all sin, to do his will, and strive after conformity to his precepts and example. On his promises I rely, firmly convinced that not one of them can fail, for He is faithful that hath promised,

> 'Though cisterns be broken, and creatures all fail,
> The word he hath spoken shall surely prevail.'

To his faithful hand I commit my immortal soul, to be saved in his own appointed way, and though it may be by severe trials, I trust I shall be enabled to say, 'Thy will be done.' By obedience to the Divine command, and partaking of the symbols of the body and blood of Christ, broken and shed for the remission of sins, I hope to keep up a memorial deeply humbling, of his dying love, to feed upon it for my spiritual nourishment and growth in grace, holiness, and resemblance to him who first loved me. I hereby declare my entire dependence on the merits of his death and righteousness for my acceptance with God – my desire to participate of his fulness – that I am not ashamed to fight under his banner, and I trust the blessings resulting from a closer union to Christ, will be mine. I expect to be assailed by many temptations, but though, I hope, they will deeply humble and purify me, yet trusting to the great Captain of my salvation alone, I shall finally overcome – it is written, 'He will not suffer you to be tempted above that ye are able, but will, with the temptation also make a way to escape.' – 'We have not a High Priest, who cannot be touched with the feeling of our infirmities, but was in all points tempted like as we are.' Though blest from a child with every advantage from the pious instruction, example, and affectionate prayers of my beloved parents, it was not until death visited our family, in the removal of my dear and only sister, that I felt the emptiness of all worldly things, and their inability to console and support in affliction. To the free and unmerited grace of God, I am indebted, that I was thus led to seek Him, in whom alone true happiness is found; weak and cold as are my faith and love, (if, indeed, I have any) I would not part with that cheering hope of immortality which He has inspired in me, for all this world can promise. Oh! may each day witness in me a growth in grace, and in the knowledge of God, an increasing relish for spiritual things, greater love to the word, ordinances, day, and people of God; and, above all, to Him who has washed my soul in the fountain of his own precious blood. His be all the glory of my salvation, and if, indeed, it be my honour and felicity, to reach that blessed world where He is, with what joy shall I cast my crown at his feet, ascribing all my deliverance to his matchless love.

I am, Rev. Sir,
Yours respectfully,
Martha Tucker.

Document VI.10

Church Membership at the Metropolitan Tabernacle, 1860

The procedure for dealing with applications for membership at the Metropolitan Tabernacle, C. H. Spurgeon's huge and thriving church (see I.4), was more elaborate than at most: few churches had elders or more than one pastor. The desire, however, to confine membership to authentic believers who continued to show the reality of their conversion by their behaviour was general among gathered churches.

The extract is taken from an article by Spurgeon's brother James on 'Discipline of the Church at the Metropolitan Tabernacle', *The Sword and the Trowel*, February 1860, pp. 53–4.

All persons anxious to join our church are requested to apply personally upon any Wednesday evening, between six and nine o'clock, to the elders, two or more of whom attend in rotation every week for the purpose of seeing enquirers. When satisfied, the case is entered by the elder in one of a set of books provided for the purpose, and a card is given bearing a corresponding number to the page of the book in which particulars of the candidate's experience are recorded. Once a month, or oftener when required, the junior pastor appoints a day to see the persons thus approved of by the elders. If the pastor is satisfied, he nominates an elder or church member as visitor, and at the next church meeting asks the church to send him to enquire as to the moral character and repute of the candidate. If the visitor be satisfied he requests the candidate to attend with him at the following or next convenient church meeting, to come before the church and reply to such questions as may be put from the chair, mainly with a view to elicit expressions of his trust in the Lord Jesus, and hope of salvation through his blood, and any such facts of his spiritual history as may convince the church of the genuineness of the case. ... After the statement before the church, the candidate withdraws, the visitor gives in his report, and the vote of the church is taken; when the candidate has professed his faith by immersion, which is administered by the junior pastor after a week-day service, he is received by the pastor at the first monthly communion, when the right hand of fellowship is given to him in the name of the church, and his name is entered on the roll of members. A communion card is furnished, divided by perforation into twelve numbered parts, one of which is to be delivered every month at the communion, which is held every Lord's-day; the tickets are checked upon the register, and thus show the attendance of each member at the communion. If a member is absent more than three months without any known cause, the elder in whose district he resides is requested to visit him, and send in a report on a printed form which is given him; or if the residence be distant, a letter is written, a record of such visit or letter being retained. When a case for discipline presents itself, it is brought before the elders, who appoint one of their number to visit and report; if the matter demands action beyond caution and advice, we lay it before the church, and recommend the course of procedure to be adopted, whether censure or excommunication.

Document VI.11

Investigation into Bankruptcy of Sir Morton Peto at Bloomsbury Baptist Church, 1868

Sir Samuel Morton Peto (1809–89) was amongst the leading railway contractors of the 1850s and 1860s, both in Britain and overseas. His complex financial affairs (his financial liabilities in 1857 were £11 million) finally came to ruin with his bankruptcy in 1867, following the failure of the bankers Overend and Gurney, and that of the London, Chatham & Dover Railway Company. After his examination before the Bankruptcy Court, *The Economist*, 14 March 1868, concluded: 'what was being done was wrong, and all concerned were quite well aware of the fact'.

Peto had been an Independent from his school days, but in the 1840s switched to the Baptists. He used his vast resources to help missionary efforts, being treasurer of the Baptist Missionary Society 1846–67, and on a wider front was chairman of the Protestant Dissenting Deputies for many years. He paid for the building of Bloomsbury Chapel in 1848, and for many of its activities amongst the poor. The pain amongst the members of the Bloomsbury congregation at these events was very real, and two deacons, James Benham and G. Kinnear, conducted an investigation; the following comes from the church minutes for September 1868. See F. and B. Bowers, 'Bloomsbury Chapel and Mercantile Morality', *Baptist Quarterly*, 30 (1984), pp. 210–20.

We are strongly of opinion that Sir Morton Peto has not been guilty of any fraudulent or deceitful conduct whatever; that in all these unfortunate transactions he has conducted himself with perfect candour, openness, and integrity. We do not think that on any of the occasions stated he ever intended to do one thing while he professed to be doing another. In fact we do not think he has himself done anything inconsistent with the strictest honesty and integrity, and we consider his character as a man of honor is unimpeachable ...

Having acknowledged this we are quite aware that some of our brethren are of opinion that we ought to stop, and pass no censure whatever on Sir Morton Peto; and looking at it as a question of conventional morality alone they are probably right.

But we cannot forget that something more than conventional morality is demanded from followers of Christ, who says to each of us 'what do ye more than others'.

Those who have put on Christ are called on to live not only righteously but also soberly; to walk circumspectly, not to assume positions in which the duties are inconsistent one with the other; to maintain that moderation which should be apparent to all men; and to avoid the appearance of evil. In these respects we cannot declare our Brother to have been free from blame.

The amount of liability which a man may properly undertake depends of course on the amount of his means to meet it, and the firm of Peto & Co being in possession of so large a Capital (amounting probably to about Two Millions) it seems hard to make the magnitude of their transactions a source of blame. We must nevertheless hold that it is so. ...

Besides the unreasonable amount of his liabilities and responsibilities, we think Sir Morton is to be blamed for the nature of some of them. His position as Contractor for such extensive works was quite inconsistent with that of holding dictatorial power over the whole undertaking. His Contracts ought to have been performed under the Board of Directors, but it could not be so done while he held supreme power over them. ...

In the other transactions we have noticed we have acquitted him of any approach to dishonesty or deception, but we cannot say that he has avoided the appearance of evil; on the contrary he has mixed himself up with questionable matters, with which as a Christian he ought to have had nothing to do. In these respects Sir Morton did not exercise the Christian prudence and moderation which we should have expected from him. In doing so he has pierced himself through with many sorrows, he has brought discredit on our Church of which he is the ornament and the pride, and he has brought reproach on that holy name by which we are all alike called.

We must therefore say, although we do so with much grief, that our respected brother has justly exposed himself to the censure of the Church.

Document VI.12

Public Recognition of Wesleyan Members, 1878

The traditional basis for membership in Methodism was attendance at a class (see VI.17), but as the nineteenth century wore on meeting in class to air one's spiritual state became less congenial. Hence the new way of recognising additional members described below was recommended by the Wesleyan Conference in 1878. A form of service was to follow in 1894. The development, associated as it was with an insistence on the importance of the sacraments, was a symptom of the increasing churchliness of Wesleyanism. See H. D. Rack, 'The Decline of the Class-Meeting and the Problem of Church-Membership in Nineteenth-Century Wesleyanism', *Proceedings of the Wesley Historical Society*, 39 (1973), pp. 12–21.

The extract is taken from H. W. Williams, *The Constitution and Polity of Wesleyan Methodism*, London, n.d., pp. 9–10.

The Conference resolves:–

1. That it is very desirable to adopt some more public and formal mode of admitting new members into Society:–

(i.) Because such a practice is in accordance with early Methodist usage, and is, indeed, prescribed in our recognised 'Form of Discipline.'

(ii.) Because it is of the highest importance to give all possible impressiveness to a member's entrance into fellowship with the Church of Christ. A welcome thus given by the Society will, it is believed, tend to encourage the new members, whilst the public recognition will deepen their sense of responsibility.

(iii.) Because such a service, as is here contemplated, will certainly prove profitable and encouraging to older members, will give to the whole Society a stronger feeling of corporate existence, and may be made impressive and useful to the non-members who may be permitted to be present.

2. That, as the circumstances of different Circuits, in town and country, are very dissimilar, it is not expedient to lay down specific rules as to the exact nature of meetings to be held for the reception of new members, or as to the frequency with which such meetings should be held.

3. That, when practicable, these services may, with great advantage, be associated with the administration of the Lord's Supper.

4. That if, upon inquiry, it be found that any person, in other respects eligible for recognition, has not received Christian baptism, that Sacrament shall be administered before the recognition of that person, and, if not otherwise, in connection with the recognition service.

5. That in many places it will be found convenient to recognise new members at a Society-meeting after each visitation of the Classes, this meeting being held either on Sunday afternoon, or after the Sunday-evening service, or on the evening of a week-day; and that in country places such a meeting might well take the place of a week-evening service, and be announced in the Plan.

Document VI.13

R. W. Dale on Church Membership, 1881

R. W. Dale (see II.16) was the most lucid champion of Congregational polity in the late nineteenth century. His *Manual of Congregational Principles* (1884) was anticipated a few years earlier by an essay on Congregationalism in which he insists that the church must be a gathered community of believers. Growing laxity of practice meant that in some churches a roll of members' names was no longer maintained, but Dale calls for the drawing of a definite line between the church and the world. See J. W. Grant, *Free Churchmanship in England, 1870–1940*, London, n.d.

The extracts are taken from the essay by Dale, originally published in *The British Quarterly Review* for January 1881 and reissued as 'Congregationalism I' in Dale's *Essays and Addresses*, London, 1899, pp. 188–9 and 192–3.

By what methods any Christian Church should endeavour, in our own times, to assert the principle that the members of a Christian Church should be Christians, is a question which may be answered variously in various parts of the country, and by Churches surrounded by varying social conditions. It is not of the substance of Congregationalism that any particular set of rules should regulate the admission of members. If any Church is convinced that, without further inquiry, it can accept with unreserved confidence the expression of a desire for membership as a proof of living faith in Christ, that Church has a perfect right to receive all comers. If to another Church experience has made it certain that something more than this is necessary to prevent many persons from entering the Church, who have neither an intellectual nor a moral apprehension of what is meant by loyalty to Christ, some regulations become necessary to avert the peril. The principle is clear. Particular rules are not of the substance of the Congregational polity. Rules must change with changing circumstances. But the *Idea* is constant. Where it is forgotten or suppressed, Congregationalism is lost. A Christian Church should consist of Christians. Whatever really commands the confidence of generous and trustful men in a man's Christian integrity is a sufficient reason for admitting him to membership. What is not sufficient to command this confidence is not a sufficient reason for admitting him to membership. ...

In some congregations it has ceased to be customary to keep what is called a 'Church roll.' A 'Church roll' is not of the essence of Congregationalism. ... [But:] If no Church 'roll' is kept because it is not certain whether any particular person is in the Church or outside, and if the 'roll' is dispensed with because no one wishes to determine whether any person is in the Church or outside, then, as it seems to me, the Idea of the Church is imperilled, if it is not already lost. When a man is in the Church I take it for granted that he is my ally in the great endeavour to get the will of God done on earth as it is in heaven; I regard him with confidence and brotherly affection. But if Church membership is intentionally left vague and indefinite, so that I never know whether a man is in the Church or not, I am thrown back on my personal knowledge of individual men; and the large, free, and cordial sense of comradeship which ought to unite all who are in the same Church is paralyzed, and their mutual affection is checked and cooled.

Document VI.14

Articles of War for Salvation Army Soldiers, 1882

The Articles of War were a form of declaration introduced in 1882 to ensure wholehearted commitment to the Salvation Army by its members. They include, in clause 3, an unequivocal undertaking to observe total abstinence.

The extract is taken from R. Sandall, *The History of the Salvation Army*, vol. 2, London, 1950, pp. 312–13.

1. Having received with all my heart the salvation offered to me by the tender mercy of Jehovah, I do here and now publicly acknowledge God to be my Father and King, Jesus Christ to be my Saviour, and the Holy Spirit to be my Guide, Comforter, and Strength; and that I will, by His help, love, serve, worship, and obey this glorious God through all time and through all eternity.
2. Believing solemnly that The Salvation Army has been created by God, and is sustained and directed by Him, I do here declare my full determination, by God's help, to be a true Soldier of the Army till I die.
3. I do here, and now, and for ever, renounce the world with all its sinful pleasures, companionships, treasures, and objects, and declare my full

determination boldly to show myself a Soldier of Jesus Christ in all places and companies; no matter what I may have to suffer, do, or lose, by so doing.

4 I do here and now declare that I will abstain from the use of all intoxicating liquors, and also from the habitual use of opium, laudanum, morphia, and all other baneful drugs, except when in illness such drugs shall be ordered for me by a doctor.

5 I do here and now declare that I will abstain from the use of all low or profane language; from the taking of the name of God in vain; and from taking part in any unclean conversation or the reading of any obscene book or paper at any time, in any company, or in any place.

6 I do here declare that I will not allow in myself any falsehood, deceitfulness, misrepresentation, or dishonesty; neither will I practise any fraudulent conduct, either in my business, my home, or in any other relation in which I may stand to my fellow-men, but that I will deal truthfully, fairly, honourably, and kindly with all those who may employ me or whom I may myself employ.

7 I do here declare that I will never treat any woman, child, or other person, whose life, comfort, or happiness may be placed within my power, in an oppressive, cruel, or cowardly manner, but that I will protect such from evil and danger so far as I can, and promote, to the utmost of my ability, their present welfare and eternal salvation.

8 I do here declare that I will spend all the time, strength, money and influence I can in supporting and carrying on this war, and that I will endeavour to lead my family, friends, neighbours and all others whom I can influence, to do the same, believing that the sure and only way to remedy all the evils in the world is by bringing men to submit themselves to the government of the Lord Jesus Christ.

9 I do here declare that I will always obey the lawful orders of my Officers, and that I will carry out to the utmost of my power all the Orders and Regulations of the Army; and further, that I will be an example of faithfulness to its principles, advance to the utmost of my ability its operations, and never allow, where I can prevent it, any injury to its interests or hindrance to its success.

10 And I do here and now call upon all present to witness that I enter into this undertaking of my own free will, feeling that the love of Christ who died to save me requires from me this devotion of my life to His service for the salvation of the whole world.

Activities

Document VI.15

Wesleyan Conference Resolutions on Society Activities, 1821

The Wesleyan Conference of 1821 pinned on certain practices as specially calculated to promote the work of God. Most recommendations were designed to reinforce traditional Wesleyan methods – such as classes (see VI.17), bands (classes for those seeking entire sanctification) and the use of Wesley's *Twelve Rules of a Helper*.

The extract is taken from H. W. Williams, *The Constitution and Polity of Wesleyan Methodism*, London, n.d., pp. 310–12.

1. We resolve that there shall be a regular observance of the Quarterly Fasts in all our Circuits, as appointed by Mr. Wesley; which are, the first Fridays after Michaelmas-day, Christmas-day, Lady-day, and Midsummer-day; on which occasions, public Prayer Meetings shall be held in all our Chapels ...

2. We agree strongly to advise the members of our Society, especially in large towns, to meet in those Classes which are the nearest to their respective places of residence ...

3. We earnestly exhort all our Preachers to be increasingly diligent in Pastoral visits to the families of our people; endeavouring to render such visits eminently profitable to all present, by prayer, and by spiritual conversation.

4. We recommend to the Preachers, in all cases where it is practicable, the establishment and superintendence of Prayer Meetings in private houses ...

5. We strongly advise the Preachers in their respective Circuits, particularly in the more populous districts, and where there is a general neglect of the means of grace already established, to avail themselves of every opportunity to preach in private houses, especially in the cottages of the poor ...

6. The distribution of religious Tracts having, in many instances, been followed by the most beneficial results, the Conference recommends it to the Preachers, and to our people in general ...

7. We again exhort all our people, who have opportunity, to meet in Band, as an old established usage in our Connexion, and an important means of improvement in personal religion ...

8. For the spiritual benefit of our people, and in order that the blessing of God may rest upon their families, we earnestly press upon them the orderly and devout exercise of family-worship, accompanied by a deliberate reading of the Holy Scriptures. ...

9. We again solemnly resolve, after the example of our venerable Fathers in the Gospel, with all plainness and zeal to preach a free, present, and full salvation from sin ...

10. The Conference also requires, that in every Circuit the plans for the quarterly Visitation of the Societies shall be so arranged as not to crowd too many Classes together, but to afford proper time for a minute examination of the members, and for suitable advice, encouragement, and admonition.

11. We once more solemnly call upon the members of our Society conscientiously to sanctify the Sabbath-day, both individually and in their families; especially by a regular attendance upon the public worship of Almighty God in the *forenoon*, as well as on the subsequent services of that sacred day, and by suffering as few persons under their care as possible to be detained at home.

12. We also advise the Preachers occasionally to invite, after preaching on the Lord's day, such persons as may be seriously concerned for the salvation of their souls, to call upon them, and converse with them, on the following day, at an hour which they may appoint for this purpose.

13. The Conference directs, that the Twelve Rules of a Helper, and the Results of the Conversation on carrying on the Work of God, inserted in the Minutes of 1820, shall be annually read by the Chairman in every District Meeting, and proper time allowed for examination, and for useful conversation, on the several subjects to which they refer.

14. The Preachers are peremptorily required to read the Pastoral Address of the Conference to all the Societies in their respective Circuits.

Document VI.16

An Independent Sunday School Anniversary, c. 1825

Sunday schools were among the most flourishing of nineteenth-century institutions. Often attached to chapels, they inculcated basic reading skills until the growth of weekday education made that role redundant. Their anniversary services were among the high points of the chapel year, attracting large congregations to elaborate musical performances and raising substantial sums of money for the schools. See T. W. Laqueur, *Religion and Respectability: Sunday Schools and Working Class Culture, 1780–1850*, New Haven, 1976; P. B. Cliff, *The Rise and Development of the Sunday School Movement in England, 1780–1980*, Redhill, Surrey, 1986.

The extract describes the anniversaries at the Independent Chapel at Farnworth, Lancashire, and is taken from J. Dyson, *Rural Congregationalism*, Manchester, 1881, pp. 42–5.

The grand musical festival ... was always celebrated on Whit-Sunday in every year, when the Sunday-school sermons were preached, and a regular musical programme was gone through by some thirty to forty of the selected voices from the female scholars, assisted by a considerable number of instrumentalists who came from various parts of the surrounding district to assist on such grand occasions.

Organs were almost unknown in any Dissenters' place of worship in those days, and such a collection of musical instruments as was usually brought together on these special occasions would rather astonish any of our modern congregations.

The band generally consisted of six or eight violins, a viola, two or three violoncellos, one double bass, two or three clarionets, two flutes, two bassoons, a large bass serpent, (whose coarse rough tones could easily be heard above all the other instruments), and one trombone!

The girls selected as singers for what were then always styled, 'The Charity Sermons,' were dressed in white, and were arranged on a gallery stage which surrounded the pulpit, and entirely covered the large pew usually occupied by the singers. These girls were trained and rehearsed twice a week for some six or seven weeks before the grand event came off, and each service had, in addition to three special hymns, either a duet or trio, sung by two or three of the oldest and best girl singers, and then a good *crashing chorus* to follow, selected from one of Handel's or Haydn's Oratorios. If the performers kept tolerably good time, the more noise they made, and the better their performance was appreciated by the audience who invariably crowded the Old Chapel to suffocation on these occasions.

The large posters announcing these 'Charity Sermons' had a very prominent line at the bottom, informing the public that *'Silver would be expected from all who entered the gallery;'* and there being no threepenny or fourpenny coins in those days, there was a goodly number of sixpences paid for admission to the gallery, and the collection boxes were also passed round the pews in the gallery at the proper time, but these were usually found to contain nothing but copper coins!

I well remember the Rev. William Jones, minister of Mawdsley-street Chapel, Bolton, was the preacher on one of these Anniversaries, when, just before the sermon, was performed 'The Hailstone Chorus,' out of Handel's 'Israel in Egypt,' to which full justice was done, so far as plenty of rattle and noise could effect it; and after it was all over, Mr. Jones (who detested all instrumental music) got up and wiped the perspiration from his brow, and in a gruff and grumbling tone he said in his usual powerful and emphatic manner, *'Now, I will try to preach to you after this furious storm;'* and a most excellent sermon he delivered.

The principal trainer for these festivals was the leading singer, Mr. Nathaniel Topp, who had both an excellent voice and a thorough knowledge of music. He was assisted by his brothers Samuel and Hugh as singers, and his brother Robert who was an excellent player on the violoncello.

The last of these musical anniversaries was held on Whit-Sunday, 1830, and when they were abolished and a plain service substituted, the annual collections fell off considerably for a year or two, as the more commonplace services had not the same attraction for strangers.

Document VI.17

Hugh Bourne on Class Meetings and Love Feasts, 1829

The purpose of the weekly class meeting, the original core unit of Methodism, was to recount Christian experience and to receive guidance from the class leader. The love feast was an occasional common meal of bread and water at which members could give testimonies. Hugh Bourne (see IV.1) was converted through a love feast, which, like the class meeting, was taken over by the Primitive and other Methodists from the Wesleyans. See W. W. Dean, 'The Methodist Class Meeting: The Significance of its Decline', *Proceedings of the Wesley Historical Society*, 43 (1981), pp. 41–8; and F. Baker, *Methodism and the Love-Feast*, London, 1957.

The extract consists of Hugh Bourne's instructions for Primitive Methodist practice and is taken from the preface to the *Large Hymn Book for the Use of the Primitive Methodists*, Bemersley, near Tunstall, 1829.

Class Meetings.

1. Open with singing for about 4, 5, or 6 minutes.
2. Let 4 or 5 minutes be spent in prayer, ending with the Lord's prayer.
3. Sing about 2 or 3 minutes.
4. Leader speak about 1 or 2 minutes, chiefly his own experience.
5. Let 15, or from that to 20 minutes be spent in conversation of the leader with the members. And, to keep the attention alive, the leader, during the conversation, may, if he chooses, give out one or two verses, and sing.
6. If a class have 15 or 16 members, the average time of speaking should be about one minute with each member. If there be 20 or 30 members, the time should be less, because in speaking to one, the leader, in effect, speaks to all. In particular cases, more time may be spent with any member.
7. If any member have acquired or be acquiring a habit of long speaking, then the leader, after dropping a word or two, should immediately pass on to the next, and begin, at once, to speak to the next. If this be not attended to, the meeting will soon be injured.
8. When the speaking is concluded, sing for 2, 3, or 4 minutes.
9. Then let the members pray in quick succession, for about two or three minutes each. The leaders must take care that none of them trespass upon time. Also, one or two verses may be occasionally sung, to vary the exercises.
10. Be careful and exact in settling the class paper.
11. Conclude in an hour, or an hour and a quarter.
12. This outline may be judiciously varied in any point, as circumstances may require.
13. If a class be met by a preacher, after preaching, he may begin the conversation without previous singing and prayer, and go through this service in 15 minutes, or not exceed 20 minutes.

Lovefeasts.

Lovefeasts usually open with singing and prayer.* A piece is then sung by way of asking a blessing; after which the bread and water are served out, the Lovefeast collection is made, and a piece sung by way of returning thanks. The preacher makes a few remarks; the people rise in succession, and speak their own experience; and distant comers sometimes say a little about the works of God in other places. But none are allowed to run into useless exhortations, drag out to tedious lengths, or to speak unprofitably of others, and above all not to reflect upon or find fault, either with individuals or societies. And it is the preacher's painful duty to stop all who attempt to trespass. He has to preserve the Lovefeast in its clear and pure course, in order that the people may grow into faith, and that the Holy Ghost may descend.

Singing and prayer are occasionally introduced; and the Lovefeast finally closes with prayer.

*It has been a custom to have preaching before a Lovefeast; but this is very generally laid aside on account of its very great inconvenience.

Document VI.18

A Baptist on Church Meetings, 1835

The church meeting was the governing body of each congregation among the Congregationalists and Baptists. It was responsible, at least, for choosing ministers and deacons and for admitting and disciplining members. The right to attend was confined to members of the particular church, although this passage recommends that the meeting should be opened to attenders who had not become church members (a practice which became widespread among Congregationalists later in the century) and to members of sister churches.

The extract is taken from a letter from 'Urbane' to the editor of *The Baptist Magazine*, July 1835, pp. 264–6.

ON CHURCH MEETINGS.

Much of the comfort and prosperity of Christian churches consists in a proper management of these meetings. It is the only season when church members, *as such*, meet together; and is, from this circumstance, well adapted to call forth an energetic developement of the best feelings of the renewed heart. The precise method in which they should be conducted forms no part of the New Testament revelation; this is left to the wise and pious discretion of the members of which the church is composed. The circumstance of there being no authorized detail as to the orderly regulation of these meetings will account for the variety observable in the practice of different churches, and will justify a more frequent reference to it in the pages of a work designed for the benefit of the church at large, than it has already secured.

It must have been felt, by almost every church member of any standing and experience, that far too little importance is attached to these meetings. In many churches they have degenerated into the dry official discharge of duties, many of them of a mere secular character; and from the freedom of speech usually allowed, a frivolous and contentious spirit has, on many occsions, dissipated those holy sensibilities which the association ought to have enkindled. In one part of the country, we have been credibly informed, it was the invariable custom, after a short season spent in devotional exercises, to introduce the fumes of the tobacco pipe, and the appurtenances with which that instrument is associated. We trust, however, that in almost all cases this is now abandoned, and a more correct and spiritual character given to such assemblies. ...

Were the ministers of our churches, who usually preside at these meetings, aware how available they might be made to the peace and comfort of the church, they would strenuously endeavour to render them much more interesting and attractive. Instead of contenting themselves, when other business did not arise, with a few common-place prayers, suited to other and ordinary occasions, they would take this opportunity of drawing attention to an order of subjects not suitable to any other season. ...

It is the practice of some churches to leave their meetings open to the attendance of any thoughtful and inquiring persons belonging to the congregation; and especially to members of other churches to whom it may be convenient to attend. To this practice there can scarcely be the shadow of objection, except on special occasions, when it may be advisable to confine the attendance to church members, and of which due notice might easily be given. ...

In reference, likewise, to individuals wishing to become members, there is often an undefined awe and apprehension raised in the breast of the timid, which an occasional attendance on church meetings would very much allay. It would be no longer an ordeal formidable on account of its secrecy; but the kindness and complacency manifested by the church at large would exchange that which at a distance appeared repulsive into an engagement agreeable and inviting.

The opportunity afforded at our church meetings for indulging in a more free and unreserved intercourse with our Christian brethren ought on no occasion to be omitted. There is often a feeling of dissatisfaction cherished in the minds of the poorer members of our churches, on account of the apparent neglect with which they are treated, which, in the large assemblies convened on the sabbath, no opportunity is afforded of removing. The periodical meetings of the church, if judiciously conducted, will afford an occasion of obliterating any such impressions. It is then, in an emphatic sense, 'the rich and the poor meet together:' they stand upon equal ground; the artificial distinctions of society are melted away; and the relation which each sustains to the other, as brethren and sisters in Christ, is the only one recognized and acknowledged.

Document VI.19

Northamptonshire Baptist Association Circular Letter on Prayer Meetings, 1842

For an account of this association see T. S. H. Elwyn, *The Northamptonshire Baptist Association: A Short History, 1764–1964*, London, 1964. Circular letters were commisioned each year to bring matters of importance to the attention of each church in the association.

The circular letter *On Prayer Meetings* (Kettering, 1842) read at the association meetings in 1842 had been written by T. T. Gough, minister of the Clipstone church. Prayer meetings were commonly held on weekday evenings, and usually included a biblical exposition by the minister. The normal practice was for prayer to be offered only by individuals nominated by the minister. Gough stressed the importance of social prayer, and continued with some suitable directions (pp. 9–11).

Prayer Meetings demand suitable preparation. Notwithstanding all that we have advanced on the subject, it must be conceded that these religious services are often very dull and uninteresting. A manifest deficiency in the spirit of prayer is often felt and observed. There is neither method, design, copiousness, emotion, nor earnestness. A familiar round of commonplaces is strung together, in which it is but too evident that neither he who utters them, nor those who are expected to join in them, feel any suitable interest. If indeed we were to judge of the religious experience of some persons by the prayers they offer, we should conclude that it is fixed and invariable; that they always need precisely the same blessings; that they are at all times alike oppressed with guilt; that they perpetually feel thankful for the same class of blessings, and no others; and that they are always in possession of precisely the same amount of spiritual strength and consolation. Judging by the same rule, it might be supposed that in their estimation the circumstances of the church are of the same fixed character; since they ever request on its behalf similar divine communications. Persons to whom these remarks apply should be the last to object to set forms of prayer; and our Prayer Meetings in which the devotions are led by them, furnish no mean illustration of the objection usually and fitly alleged against forms of prayer in constant use, namely, that there can be no certain adaptation of the form to the circumstances of the worshippers. Hence arise listlessness, weariness, and formality, of which we are so ready to complain. The great remedy against all these evils is to be sought not merely in education, nor in intellectual endowment, which, could they answer the end, are not within the reach of the majority of our brethren; but in a previous religious preparation for our social exercises ... Let each christian, before he enters the house of prayer, ask himself, what is my errand to the throne of grace? What is the state of my heart? What blessings do the present circumstances of the Church render it especially fit to implore? What is the general condition of the congregation? What are the obstacles which hinder the progress of the gospel, or (in happier cases) what is necessary to its continued success? What particular lesson was inculcated by the word of God on the past Sabbath which I should now pray the Lord to write on my heart? Are there any instances of affliction, adversity, or religious concern which claim my intercession with God? What peculiar demands are now made on my gratitude? What is the general condition of the Church of Christ in the world, and what the present aspects of the missionary cause? If only a few of these, or similar enquiries, were by each of our brethren presented to his own mind, before he mingled with the social band, the most important and beneficial results would follow. If invited to lead the devotions of his brethren, he would be furnished with a subject on which to pray. Out of the abundance of the heart his mouth would speak. Instead of indulging in vague generalities he will have a definite object and aim. This will be perceived by others, some of whom at least, will sympathize with him, and mingling their devotions, will enkindle a flame, in which the incense of their desires and praises will ascend to the throne of God.

Document VI.20

William Gadsby on Sunday Schools, 1843

Unlike some high Calvinists, William Gadsby (see I.3), was an enthusiastic supporter of Sunday schools, and endeared himself to the 300 children in the school in his Manchester church. These paragraphs are taken from a letter on the utility of Sunday schools written in December 1843, a few months before his death, and printed in *The Sunday School Teacher's Magazine*, 1846, pp. 133–5.

Allow me to observe that I really do consider that, next to the preaching of the glorious gospel of the blessed God, and a spiritual attendance to the order and ordinances of God's house, Sunday schools are one of the best institutions in the kingdom; and I am sorry to see such a want of zeal for the promotion of them among some who profess to maintain the discriminating truths of God's grace. To me this appears highly wrong. I have heard some persons remark that too much education given to the poor raises them so far in life, that they become an injury to the middle class of society; and I have really felt shame when I have heard such remarks. Can any person, with the fear of God in his heart, believe that the laboring [*sic*] poor ought to be bond slaves to either the high class, or the middle class of society, and all means be kept from them of enabling them, if they are steady, industrious, and prudent, of raising themselves in society? Surely not. Some who are now in the highest ranks of society in the neighbourhood of Manchester, were once poor; and let them not now forget themselves, and think it wrong to try to be a means of raising others from their degradation ... For my own part, I feel persuaded that Sunday schools are of great benefit to civil society; and that those persons who engage themselves freely to teach in Sunday schools are useful members of society, and should be much esteemed as far as they fill that office well; for they are a means of raising the rising generation of poor children from that degradation into which they must otherwise have sunk ...

There are tens of thousands of poor children, in this day of vice and immorality, who were it not for Sunday schools, would be left to follow their own carnal inclinations, almost without any restraint; for it is a lamentable fact that, in too many instances, their own parents pay but little attention to them; and in a great many cases the parents have it not in their power to give them any education themselves. Perhaps, in the town of Manchester, where I now live there are not less than fifty thousand children who are kept under some restraint on the Lord's day at Sunday schools, and are taught to read; the greatest part of whom, but for this instruction, would be left to run at large ...

Children should also be taught their duty to their parents and the various branches of the family, and to their superiors in every station of life, yes, and to themselves, and to each other, and to their fellow-creatures at large, as members of the human race and of civil society. The evil nature of disobedience should be taught them, together with the awful nature and consequence of sin in all its bearing; and all proper means should be used to induce them to shun vice and immorality, and to regularly attend a place where God is worshipped, and his truth faithfully preached.

Document VI.21

A Congregational Funeral, c. 1850

Although, unless there was a chapel graveyard, Nonconformist burials normally took place in parish churchyards, where, until 1880, only an Anglican clergyman could officiate (see IX.9), the minister from the chapel would usually conduct a funeral service at the home of the deceased. Here Henry Garside Rhodes recalls such services taken by his father, minister for forty-six years from 1827, for members of Fulwood Chapel, near Sheffield, which had Presbyterian trustees but Congregational worshippers.

The extract is taken from *The Sheffield Congregational Year Book*, Sheffield, 1906, pp. 43–4.

But how I used to look forward to funerals! they were always interesting in our quiet village – they were generally saved for Sunday afternoon, and although the interment was in the Churchyard it was thought to be the correct thing to have the Dissenting Minister at the house, and so my father was asked. He was always invited to go up stairs to look at the corpse, which he politely declined. Then a table was brought outside the house, and a clean white cloth spread over it, and the coffin placed upon it. The friends and mourners stood round and a hymn was sung to a tune in a minor key, and then my father gave an address, and always finished up by saying: 'Be ye also ready, for in such an hour as ye think not the Son of Man cometh.' After he had prayed, the coffin was hoisted on the shoulders of the bearers (we had no hearses in those days), and carried through the country lanes to the churchyard. At the close a large square package in writing paper, sealed with black sealing wax, was handed to my father (it was his only fee), and I knew well that it contained a big sponge cake, and that my sisters and I would divide between us when we got home.

Document VI.22

A Brethren Bible Reading, c. 1850

Andrew Miller (1810–83) was a Scot who prospered as a London businessman. After pastoring a Baptist church for some time, he was attracted to the Brethren by a Bible reading, which he here recalls. Such occasions played a major role in the growth of the Brethren movement. For Miller, see H. Pickering, *Chief Men among the Brethren*, London, 1931, pp. 74–6.

The extract is taken from A. Miller, *"The Brethren" (commonly so-called)* [1879], revised G. C. Willis, Hong Kong, [1963], pp. 42–4.

We well remember the first, or one of the first, of such a class that we attended. Being invited by a Christian friend to meet a few Christians at his house for a social tea and reading, we accordingly went on the evening named. In observing the friends as they assembled, to the number of about thirty, we were struck with their plain appearance as to dress, and the absence of ornaments. The subjects of conversation before tea seemed only to concern themselves, or rather, the Lord's work in their different meetings. As for general news, nothing was said, and the mention of politics would have seemed sheer profanity. The Brethren, as a body, do not qualify, and they never vote at elections.

But the tea is ready; and the whole company drop into a profound silence. Some brother, after a short, but distinct pause, asked the Lord's blessing. All were very free and cheerful during tea; some were sitting and engaged in conversation, others were moving about for the purpose of speaking to as many as possible. This was a very happy part of the meeting, and lasted till about seven o'clock – fully an hour. When the tea was over and the time for edification had arrived, everyone found a seat, with Bible and hymn book in hand. All came provided with both. Again there was a pause, and perfect stillness. After a little waiting a hymn was sung, and prayer was offered for the Lord's presence in light and blessing.

The head of the house now stated, 'that if any brother had a portion of the word on his mind that he would like read, he was free to say so.' This seemed a very responsible part of the meeting, and there was a long pause. At length a chapter was named, and all turned to it. The portion was read, and a free interchange of thought as to its meaning, connection, and importance was kept up till about nine o'clock. Nearly all the brothers had something to say on some part of it: others contented themselves with asking questions; but it soon became apparent who was the most richly instructed in the Word, as the questions in time were addressed to him. After a hymn and prayer, the company dispersed about ten o'clock. But there was a distinct pause between each part of the service, leaving the Holy Spirit free to use whom He would, though it was not an assembly meeting.

From about half-past five till half-past nine, we seemed to be an atmosphere purely spiritual, which had a great effect on the mind. Whether all felt it to be so, we have no means of knowing, we only speak of what we experienced. The Bible from this time became like a new book, prayer like a fresh thing, nearness to God a reality more so than ever, though we had known the Lord more than twenty years, and been happy in Him and in His service all that time. There was no need of a president in such a meeting, the sense of the divine Presence was such that the least impropriety, or any appearance of the flesh, would have been intolerable. The spiritual sense of those so gathered would have marked its disapprobation in a way unmistakable to the intruder.

Document VI.23

Plans for a Wesleyan Sunday School, 1856

Elizabeth George (1831–56) lived with her mother and supported both of them by running a school in Welford-on-Avon, Gloucestershire. Having moved to Prestwich, Lancashire, she devised plans in 1856 for improving the efficiency of the Wesleyan Sunday school but did not live to put them into practice. The ideas recorded in her diary represent the latest techniques of the day.

The extract is taken from H. Pigott, *Memoir of Elizabeth George*, London, 1858, pp. 233–4.

That in the Sabbath-school, by conferring with the Superintendent and principal Teachers, I might, (1.) Get the 'Teachers' Magazine' circulated; (2.) Introduce the 'Sunday-School Union Lessons,' or those published by our Book-Committee in the 'Reporter;' (3.) Get the children throughout the school to learn texts of Scripture from the Lesson of the day; (4.) Introduce a system of rewards and punishments, the former chiefly in order to attract and encourage the children, and please the parents; (5.) Have the 'Child's own Hymn-Book' used in the school, and taught in the junior classes; (6.) Persuade the leader of the singing to introduce little pieces, as well as hymns, for the children to sing; (7.) Have little books, and the 'Band of Hope,' given as rewards.

All these things may, I think, be accomplished in time, if I propose them to the necessary parties in an unassuming way, so as that they shall forget or not notice who made the first proposition. I thought also, while on my knees, that I would present a copy of 'Rules for Holy Living' to each member, through the Leaders, privately; and try to get the friends of my day-pupils to take the 'British Messenger,' and to secure subscribers for the 'British Workman' and the 'Band of Hope.' O that these things may be done, and that the blessing of the Most High may rest upon them!

Document VI.24

Preparation for a Christmas Tea Party, c. 1890

This passage, though fictional, is based on accurate memories and captures the reality of social life in the late Victorian chapels, with its camaraderie and gossip. It is taken from the same source as III.22, W. H. Mills, *Grey Pastures*, London, 1924, pp. 63–4.

It was in preparation for the Christmas tea-party that in the Young Men's First Class Room they were 'cutting up.' I cannot but think that this process of 'cutting up' had got rather into the hands of a clique. It consisted merely in the reduction of loaves and tea-cakes and pounds of butter – heroic pounds of butter sprawling in soup plates – into the finished article of tea-parties – and yet a ritual with its appointed day and above all its priestess! To be 'asked to go and cut up' was to have an acknowledgment of some standing in the congregation; it was an admission into a subsection of the elect, and it slightly altered one's attitude to the tea-party, turning one's participation in the affair into an act of some self-sacrifice. There were other people to whom the tea-party was genuinely a treat. They sat passive, receptive, taking their fill. On the whole the tea-party was one of those functions in which it was socially preferable to stand and wait, to maintain one's reservations. At the entertainment which followed, those who had 'cut up' and turned the taps of the urns became definitely aloof, gregarious together at the back of the room. Composed and intimate talk of the Wright's dance, an approaching affair of some splendour, for which all the town cabs had been engaged, was general among them; the use of Christian names was a habit. The atmosphere around them was indeed bathed in the warm perfume of their common intimacies, and Gladys, leaning forward, would say something allusive, something cryptic, which was infallibly understood by Gertrude, four places from her along the form. They were unmistakably 'a set.'

PART VII

WOMEN

Introduction

There has recently been an explosion of interest in women's history, and, though lagging a little behind their work and education as foci of attention, their religious life has also become the subject of considerable research. It has become clear that, even if the gender balance was less skewed than in the Church of England, women outnumbered men in most congregations. In the membership of the chapels there was an even greater discrepancy in favour of women. In most chapels there were roughly two female members for every male member. The lack of alternative social outlets for women must be one explanation; so must the association of religion with childcare, a female province. Whatever the reason, the chapel pews were disproportionately filled with women.

It does not seem that religious experience was specially distinctive among women. An account of the urbane qualities of a Unitarian (VII.1) and a record of the stern self-discipline of a Wesleyan (VII.2) could equally apply to a man. Yet occasionally, as in the recollection of a striking incident in the spiritual life of the same Wesleyan (VII.3), there are phrases that could be uttered only by a woman. In an age when female education was the exception rather than the rule, women could sometimes pursue learning because of their Christian faith (VII.5). Nevertheless, their concerns often centred on family and home (VII.10). That was what some of the louder voices of the day claimed to be natural (VII.8), a view that persuaded some women to reject female suffrage (see IX.25). Although marriage could sometimes go wrong (VII.7), the more normal pattern in the chapels was for wives to concentrate on bringing up their children (VII.9) and then, when their offspring had grown to maturity, to have the latest sermon as a point of common interest (VII.4). The chapels, and especially the women in them, took pains to encourage family life in the broader society (VII.6).

The local Nonconformist community also provided an outlet for women to play a significant part. Mostly they could achieve prominence through regular activities such as tract distribution and collecting money (VII.13). But in some denominations they could go further. The extent to which the Quakers permitted gender equality can be exaggerated (VII.15), but, like the Primitive Methodists (VII.11), the Bible Christians (VII.12) and the Salvation Army (VII.14), they believed that the ministry should be open to women. Female preaching remained more common in the later part of the century than used to be supposed (VII.16) and by its end there were organised bodies of deaconesses (VII.17).

The proportion of women in Nonconformity is authoritatively discussed in C. D. Field, 'Adam and Eve: Gender in the English Free Church Constituency', *Journal of Ecclesiastical History*, 44 (1993), pp. 63–79. Two excellent sources of female experience are J. Lewis, ed., *The Secret Diary of Sarah Thomas, 1860–1865*, Moreton-in-Marsh, Gloucestershire, 1994 (on a rural Baptist); and H. G.

McKenny, *A City Road Diary, 1885–1888*, London, 1978 (on the daughter of a London Wesleyan minister). Experience is also the central theme of L. Wilson, *Constrained by Zeal: Female Spirituality amongst Nonconformists, 1825–1875*, Carlisle, 2000. The role of women as leaders in early nineteenth-century cottage religion is discussed in D. Valenze, *Prophetic Sons and Daughters: Female Preaching and Popular Religion in Industrial England*, Princeton, New Jersey, 1985. The theory and practice of Nonconformist attitudes to women are examined in L. Davidoff and C. Hall, *Family Fortunes: Men and Women of the English Middle Class, 1780–1850*, London, 1987. F. K. Prochaska, *Women and Philanthropy in Nineteenth-Century England*, Oxford, 1980, documents their charitable activities.

Female Experience

Document VII.1

A Unitarian's Life (died 1828)

> The benchmark for what was considered to be the exemplary life for Dissenting women for much of the nineteenth century was devotion to family, self-effacing good works and a strong adherence to a simple faith. Each denomination seemed to have its own formula to apply to its faithful followers; in the Unitarian case it was 'a firm believer in the strict and simple unity of God', as is shown in the following obituary from the *Monthly Repository*, June 1828, pp. 421–2. Variants of this phrase appeared in obituaries up until about 1850. It was unusual that no personal mention of Mrs Scott was made during the memorial service. For Russell Scott and family references see H. J. McLachlan, 'The Scott Collection', *Transactions of the Unitarian Historical Society*, 19 (1988), pp. 113–29.

April 24, at *Portsmouth*, where she has resided during a period of thirty-eight years, Sophia, wife of the Rev. Russell Scott.

Mrs. Scott was the eldest daughter of the late Dr. Hawes, of Spital Square, one of the founders of the Royal Humane Society, and was born in the year 1761. Few women have possessed a greater share of unpretending good sense, fewer still have so anxiously endeavoured to employ the means and opportunities afforded them by Providence in promoting the welfare and happiness of others. To do this in various ways, may be said to have been the occupation of her life; and with respect to those more especially with whom she was most closely connected, it was the result of an intensity of interest rarely indeed entertained, and certainly never exceeded; while oblivion of self, or rather a complete exemption from selfish feeling, was her yet more remarkable characteristic.

Mrs Scott was a firm believer in the strict and simple unity of God, and in those views of the Divine government which teach that he will pardon and accept all those 'who diligently seek him;' but her attachment to her religious principles was not founded on any narrow or exclusive feelings. She was herself possessed of too much genuine piety not to value all whom she found acting under its guidance, whatever the form of their religious creed; nor did she withhold the expression of her disapproval of whatever appeared to her to result from the absence of this principle. She considered the essence of religion to consist in the attainment of the spirit and temper of the gospel, and deemed purity of faith no justification of a love of disputation and controversy.

Her death was preceded by a very long illness, which she bore not merely with composure and resignation, but with a cheerfulness undisturbed by the consciousness which she fully entertained of the approaching termination of her earthly career. On Sunday, the 4th of May, a very impressive discourse was preached on the occasion of her decease, by the Rev. Michael Maurice, of Southampton. ... In compliance with her own particular request, all mention of herself was omitted; but the attendance of a numerous congregation attired in mourning, was one of many proofs most gratifying to the feelings of the surviving members of her family, that the sterling, though unobtrusive, excellencies of their departed relative had not been unappreciated.

Document VII.2

A Wesleyan's Resolutions, 1853

For Elizabeth George, the author of these resolutions, see VI.25. At the beginning of 1854 she recalled in her diary that she had made a set of decisions about how she would spend the previous year. They included intensive personal evangelism and solemn preparation for death, but were marked most of all by a rigorous self-discipline.

The extract is taken from H. Pigott, *Memoir of Elizabeth George*, London, 1858, pp. 141–3.

Last January I made several resolutions which the Lord has enabled me to keep in great measure. They were as follows:–
1. Never to go where I had no need.
2. To speak on personal religion to every individual with whom I should come into contact, if possible, to be instant 'out of season' as well as in season; to sow beside all waters.
3. To endeavour to spend the year 1853 as if I were sure it would be my last, and as I should wish I had done in the hour of death. That I might do this, I resolved to try to spend each day in the year as if my last; to do nothing I would fear to do on my dying day.
4. To ask every night whether I was as ready and willing to die as to sleep.
5. To live with death, and heaven, and the glorious realities of eternity, continually in my view.
6. Never to speak or hear evil of anybody, nor to engage in any unprofitable conversation.
7. To keep the strictest watch over my *thoughts*; never to allow myself to think on any subject that would draw my mind from Christ; especially never to day-dream, or dwell on the past, though ever so full of interest; never to look into the future, but to live *to-day*.
8. In all my visits among the sick and poor, to say what I had to say, and after prayer to leave; never to indulge a habit of trifling, but to speak to sinners as though I never should have another opportunity.
9. To do everything to the glory of God; to feel that I am the Lord's witness and disciple; and that all my work is to deny myself, and do His will.

10. To watch against, and, in the strength of God, to try to overcome, every known fault; that I may be blameless and harmless, the child of God without rebuke.

11. On no occasion whatsoever to attend any means of grace, or visit any person, (whether sick or well, rich or poor,) or read the Scriptures, without before and after imploring the blessing of God, as the case may require.

12. To write no *unnecessary* letter, none on which I cannot ask God's blessing; not to write for the praise of men, but in all things to seek the glory of God and the good of souls.

Document VII.3

A Wesleyan's Revelation, 1853

In the November of 1853, the year in which she adopted her stern spiritual regimen (VII.2), Elizabeth George had a vivid mystical experience. It was during a class meeting (see VI.17) and her aspiration was for entire sanctification (see II.14). The account is similar to equivalent male descriptions (usually of an earlier date), but Elizabeth is aware of being addressed as 'love', 'sister' and 'bride'.

The extract, which is taken from Elizabeth's diary for 11 November 1853, is printed in H. Pigott, *Memoir of Elizabeth George*, London, 1858, pp. 122–3.

Yesterday, after a day spent in one continual looking up to Jesus for richer blessing, I went to class. I felt the Lord drawing near, and was led to praise Him abundantly. I looked steadfastly unto Him, and while so doing the Leader addressed me. I expressed myself as 'having but one aim and one desire, to be made perfect and complete in all God's will.' Mr. H. said he 'hoped my faith would continue to increase, and that I should get into the holiest place, and ever keep there.' My eyes were closed, and my heart fixed, when I seemed to be taken into heaven, though I was perfectly conscious that I was in the chapel. This I know, that I was admitted into the immediate presence of God, the Father and the Son. I am at a loss how to express what I experienced so as to render it intelligible. I felt that I knew what Stephen meant when he said, 'I see the heavens opened, and the Son of Man standing on the right hand of God,' only that I was with Jesus, with God. I would have complained of weakness, imperfections, unworthiness, &c., but I could not. *A veil was thrown over them all*, and I was assured and re-assured that I was holy and without fault before God. This I was compelled to believe. I felt in an inexpressible manner that God Himself was as perfectly pleased with me as if I had never sinned at all; that He altogether forgot my sins, and admitted me to His friendship and communion as if I had been a holy being from the beginning. At length I was obliged to cease speaking, and passively to accept all God's love and favours. I simply said, though my lips never moved, 'Lord, why dost Thou thus condescend to bless and commune with me?' The reply was, 'It is no more condescension than it is to bless a glorified spirit: all is of mercy; and thou art as precious while on earth as thou wilt be when in heaven.' I can now understand the feeling of perfect complacency that saints enjoy in heaven. They are not suffered to feel shy distrust or backwardness, because they have been rebels: all are children, dearly beloved children. I am sure I enjoyed a foretaste of heaven, though I am at a loss how to describe it intelligibly. What I have written was not half that transpired. Jesus told me that heaven was mine, that He was mine, that the earth was mine, that all things were mine. He had purchased everything for me, and had appeared unto me to show me how I might obtain more and more holiness. I might have all that I needed; for everything was mine. I was His love, His sister, and His bride. He had pardoned me, sanctified me, and sealed me, and left me on earth to glorify Him. All that could give comfort and promote child-like confidence, my Saviour, whose love was unspeakable, said to me. He answered every question, met every excuse, told me never to doubt, but always to believe that He would ever be with me, and all that He had was mine. While in the chapel and walking home, I seemed to have every blessing I asked or needed. Glory be to God, this was no vision, but a reality – all of it! The blessedness has continued all this day. O that this delightful intercourse may ever be kept open! Surely it was talking with God as a man with his friend – face to face.

Document VII.4

A Strict Baptist's Letter to Her Son, 1858

Lady Hazlerigg was born in 1784, and believed her religion was merely formal until her sixty-fifth year, when the Lord began 'to work effectually upon her soul' (Obituary, *The Gospel Standard*, January 1869, p. 33). Letters to her son, Grey Hazlerigg, a Strict Baptist minister, and editor of *The Gospel Standard*, 1878–80, were published in 1874, under the title, *Sweet Memories*. Here is one from 1858 reflecting family concerns in a spiritual idiom (pp. 28–9).

I was rejoiced to hear from you on the Lord's-day, and you will be pleased to hear it was a good day for me. It began by the dear Lord's graciously giving me prayer for you. You will know what I mean. I do not call every time I kneel prayer. What a difference it seems when God the Holy Ghost inspires the cry. Then came your letter, which I took as a token for good, and I went to chapel rejoicing, and I really seemed melted to receive the word. Mr. Taylor was very nice; his text, John xi. 26. He opened up his text well, and I was not disappointed in the hope I formed that his sermon might cheer and comfort the poor mourners in Zion, for truly so began the day with your sister and Mrs. Coltman. But blessed be God for his all-enduring mercy, it did not so end. About 9 o'clock they both came with hearts almost too brimful for speech, and my heart felt so in union with them that it needed but few words to satisfy me that the Lord's name had been magnified in their experiences; that they had trusted in him, and he had not brought them to shame before the church. Bless his holy name, and may he make me more to see my nature's vileness, and his mercy and his goodness past my understanding, that I, so vile a sinner, should be so blessed. ... I had written my first sheet, not quite expecting the joy of a letter from you to-day. How wonderful are the ways of the Lord, who does all things well; and let us bless and praise his holy name that he was with us all conspicuously on the Lord's-day. The godly must have felt that all of this world was worthless when compared with the pearl of great price. O if I could always realise this precious pearl I should not so often groan, being burdened.

Document VII.5

A Primitive Methodist's Devotion and Culture (died 1891)

Jane Harvey, *née* Woolford (1815–91), was born in Childrey, Berkshire, where she was converted in 1831. Soon afterwards she became a Primitive Methodist itinerant until 1838, when she married William Harvey, himself a minister in the connexion. Thereafter she continued to preach and lead society classes. Her own spirituality was linked with a thirst for reading. See E. D. Graham, *Chosen by God: A List of the Female Travelling Preachers of Early Primitive Methodism*, Bunbury, Cheshire, 1989, p. 26.

The extract is taken from *The Primitive Methodist Magazine*, June 1894, pp. 469–70.

Her nature was intensely spiritual. She was acutely sensitive to everything divine and heavenly. God was not a mere abstraction or force to her, but a real, true, blessed personality – One whose presence flooded her being, and in whose conscious favour she delighted to live. She knew Him by constant and intimate communion. His indwelling she thoroughly understood and realised. 'Christ *in you*,' was a fact to her. Heaven was 'about her not merely in infancy,' but in maturity and age; she lived largely in the 'other world,' often thinking of those who had passed out of sight as being near her. This doubtless was chiefly the outcome of her devotional habit; part of each day she spent in private 'talk with God;' her custom of kneeling long in closet worship was not attended to as a penance, a task, or even a duty, but it was her time of spiritual recreation, when she bathed in the light and breathed in the atmosphere of heaven, and thence she would come forth recuperated in soul, and braced to do, and dare, and suffer for God. ...

Her native talents were above the average, and had she been thoroughly cultured she would have shone in literary circles, but her time in this life was otherwise employed; now she is being perfected. She read extensively, and not light trashy books; she had no taste for the sensational novel, the Bible she many times read from beginning to end, and in connection therewith she read every sentence in the Commentaries of M. Henry and A. Clarke, besides which she perused numberless sermons, biographies, and works on religious, social, and political subjects. She was an ardent admirer and follower of W. E. Gladstone, and often prayed God to spare his life.

Marriage, Home and Children

Document VII.6

Mothers' Meetings, 1841

In 1841 Martha Sherman, the wife of the minister of Surrey Chapel (see V.27), established a 'Maternal Association' connected with each of the Sunday schools run by the chapel. They were instances of the many mothers' meetings that were set up to encourage family responsibility among the poor.

The extract, an address to mothers associated with Surrey Chapel, is taken from J. Sherman, *The Pastor's Wife*, London, 1849, pp. 77–8.

TO THE MOTHERS ATTENDING AT SURREY CHAPEL.

My dear Friends ...

The anxious desire of a wife and a mother, is to see the circle, of which she forms the influential centre, happy, prosperous, and useful: and when her wishes have been mournfully disappointed, and she finds herself surrounded with discontent, discord, and many other evil dispositions, how often has conscience told her, that *her neglect* to check that *first* dissension with her husband, and to seek his comfort by the removal of the occasions of complaint; *her neglect* to check the rising corruptions in the *infant* minds of her children, and to lead them habitually, by example and effort, to the only true source of peace; nor less *her neglect* to watch over her *own* spirit and temper, have brought these evils into the family, which, but for *neglect* might have been a happy one.

The origin of half these sorrows is inconsideration. Among the large class of those who literally eat their bread by the sweat of their brow, little time can be spared for reading and reflection. To meet this difficulty, Societies have been formed for reading and conversation on the subject of maternal responsibility, and for prayer: and as many mothers have never devoted one quarter of an hour to serious and prayerful enquiry, 'How shall I make home the happy place it was designed to be? How shall I train my children to be blessings to their family and the world, and to be heirs of the heavenly inheritance?' the employment of one leisure hour once a fortnight in conversation on the subject, and in endeavouring to discover the right means to the desired end, has been found by many mothers the source of great benefit, both to themselves and their families; they have been led to the fountain of strength and wisdom for direction in their varied difficulties, and to their sympathising Friend, who has said, 'Cast thy burden on the Lord, and he shall sustain thee.'

These meetings are designed by no means to draw mothers *from home*, but to make that home an object of more intelligent interest; and to prevent the temptation to *waste* time in complaining of domestic trials, by employing it in the effort to remove them by the aid of that Divine Spirit, whose influence must bless as well as direct every plan.

Several of these associations have been formed in connexion with the Sabbath Schools at Surrey Chapel. I now affectionately invite the attendance of every mother in the congregation at that one which is situated nearest to her own abode.

Document VII.7

A Bad Marriage, 1840s

For Annie Auty, the writer of this account, see V.8. It describes the common phenomenon of a chapel-going wife married to an uncommitted husband who sometimes drank too much. In Annie's case the marriage nevertheless allowed her to travel as a preacher.

The extract is taken from A. Auty, *The Life and Labours of Mrs Auty*, Leeds, 1887, pp. 23–4 and 28–9.

I would say a word here to all my young Christian friends, into whose hands this book may fall. I hope you will avoid associating with all worldly young men and women, and be not unequally yoked together, or you may be led into a snare. I, myself, neglected closet prayer, the class-meeting was never attended, and the house of God was never visited. ...

So time passed on, until I formed an acquaintance with a young man, who is now my husband; he did not profess religion, nor yet teetotalism; notwithstanding all, he was called a good moral man; he had a good trade in his fingers; he proposed marriage to me while I was very young. I thought at that time if I got a home of my own I should be very happy, not having had one through the whole of my life that I could call one. I thought that when I got a husband to take my part that most of my trials would be over. Had I had any kind Christian friend to have consulted with, I might have seen with different eyes. I was not professing Christianity at that time, though I knew what it was; but I had to learn after my marriage, by bitter experience, the folly of marrying a man of the world. ...

I joined the church again, and commenced prayer meetings in my own neighbourhood. One night we had kept our meeting on rather late; we had had such a powerful meeting we forgot the time. I went home singing the praises of the Lord with my first child in my arms, then only three months old; it was about a quarter to ten o'clock; to my surprise my husband had come home the worse for drink, and he was so maddened with drink that when I entered the house he took me by the shoulders and put me out, locked and bolted the door. The weather was something similar to what it was when my father put me out – pouring with rain – which caused me to think of the hardships of my younger days. We were out the whole of the night. The next morning my husband went to his work and left the door open. When he came to himself he was sorry for what he had done. The baby caught cold, sickened, and died, which stroke I felt keenly, and repeatedly had to ask my God to help me under that severe trial – he heard my prayer.

Document VII.8

J. Angell James on Woman's Mission, 1852

John Angell James (see 2.28) wrote one of the most influential mid-century texts on the role of women: *Female Piety* (1852). Women, he argued, were primarily to be the helpers and comforters of men. That entailed endorsing what has been called the doctrine of separate spheres, the notion that whereas men should engage in business and politics, women should take the home for their province. James, however, is careful to insist that women are not to be degraded; nor does he attribute the doctrine of separate spheres to the positive teaching of Christianity. See L. Davidoff and C. Hall, *Family Fortunes: Men and Women of the English Middle Class, 1780–1850*, London, 1987.

The extract is taken from J. Angell James, *Female Piety*, 17th edn, London, 1881, pp. 59–72.

Here, then, is the design of God in creating woman, to be a suitable helpmate to man. Man needed a companion, and God gave him woman. And as there was no other man than Adam at that time in existence, Eve was designed exclusively for Adam's comfort: thus, teaching us from the beginning, that whatever mission woman may have to accomplish in reference to man, in a generic sense, her mission is to be, at least in wedded life, a suitable helpmate for that one man to whom she has united herself. It was declared from the beginning, that every other tie, though not severed by marriage, should be rendered subordinate to it, and a man should 'leave his father and mother and cleave unto his wife, and they two shall be one flesh.' If, then, woman's mission in Paradise was to be man's companion and joy, such must be the case still. ...

That woman is intended to occupy a position of subordination and dependence, is clear from every part of the word of God. This is declared in language already quoted, 'Thy desire shall be to thy husband, and he shall rule over thee.' This referred not only to Eve personally, but to Eve representatively. It is the Divine law of the relation of the sexes, then promulgated for all time. The preceding language placed woman as a punishment for her sin, in a state of sorrow; this places her in a state of subjection. Her husband was to be the centre of her earthly desires, and to a certain extent the regulator of them also: and she was to be in subjection to him. What was enacted in Paradise has been confirmed by every subsequent dispensation of grace. Judaism is full of it, in all its provisions. And Christianity equally establishes it. ...

If I am right as to the nature of woman's mission, I cannot err as to the proper sphere of it. If she was created for man, and not only for the race of man, but for one man, then the easy and necessary inference is, that home is the proper scene of woman's action and influence. ...

But it will, perhaps, be asked, whether I would shut up every married woman within the domestic circle and, with the jealousy and authority of an oriental despot, confine her to her own home; or whether I would condemn and degrade her to mere household drudgery. I have, I think, protected myself already from this imputation, by representing her as the companion, counsellor, and comforter of man. She shall, with my consent, never sink from the side of man, to be trampled under his feet. She shall not have one ray of her glory extinguished, nor be deprived of a single honour that belongs to her sex; but to be the instructress of her children, the companion of her husband, and the queen consort of the domestic state, is no degradation; and she only is degraded who thinks so. ...

But what shall I say of those women who claim on their own behalf, or of their advocates who claim for them, a participation in the labours, occupations, rights, and duties which have usually been considered as exclusively appertaining to men? ... Neither reason nor Christianity invites woman to the professor's chair, or conducts her to the bench, or makes her welcome to the pulpit, or admits her to the place of ordinary magistracy. Both exclude her, not indeed by positive and specific commands, but by general principles and spirit, alike from the violence and license of the camp, the debates of the senate, and the pleadings of the forum. And they bid her beware how she lays aside the delicacy of her sex, and listens to any doctrines which claim new rights for her, and becomes the dupe of those who have put themselves forward as her advocate only to gain notoriety, or perhaps bread. They forbid us to hear her gentle voice in the popular assembly; and do not even suffer her to speak in the Church of God. They claim not for her the right of suffrage, nor any prerogative by which she may 'usurp authority over the man.' The Bible gives her her place of majesty and dignity in the domestic circle; that is in the heart of her husband and the bosom of her family.

Document VII.9

Child Care, 1850s

The author, E. Macpherson (she does not give her first name), was employed as a servant in Bath, where she was baptised in 1850, joining the Baptists. Marrying a soldier, she had two sons, Jabez and Dougal, in 1855 and 1856. Bringing up the children prompted theological reflections centred on providence, sin and conversion.

The extract is taken from [E. Macpherson], *A Mother's Legacy to her Children*, Bristol, n.d., pp. 56–7.

At a very early age they showed a determination to be master (especially the first,) but they soon learned that would not do. I will only name one instance. Jabez, who was a chubby loving little fellow, often running to me and smoothing my hand with the back of his, and saying, 'I lub oo, mamma,' yet was self-willed and quick-tempered (faults I must confess he inherited from me.) On one occasion taking advantage of his loving grandmother being with us, he objected to go to bed; and, as I put his little bed-gown over his head, he tore it off, throwing it on the floor, and looking very defiant. I told him to pick it up; but he refused. I tried in vain to bend his stiff-back; then I whipped him smartly. My poor mother cried to see the darling whipped; but that one whipping saved him scores, as he never acted so again. Although I had had more experience with children than some, yet I never before felt such extreme need of Divine direction and support. Weak body, a bad memory, and not the sound mind and good understanding of many, which made me daily mourn my ignorance and foolishness. When one has the most to record, there is the least time to do so, but sometimes when the children were in bed I would note down – some of the exercises of my mind, from which I will now quote a few extracts.

1857, *Oct.* 11.   Lord, we would this day acknowledge thy kindness toward us as a God of Providence. Our two dear babes quite well in health, with all their faculties, but, alas! alas! being born of us, poor fallen creatures, they manifest too plainly their sad original. O put Thy hand upon them and bless them. May they be early born again of the Spirit. O keep them from the power of the devourer, from the snares and temptations of this deceitful wicked world, and from their nearest and most dangerous enemy, their own treacherous and deceitful hearts. Suffer us never to connive at their sins, to laugh at them, when we should be weeping and praying over them, but give us grace and wisdom to bring them up in the nurture and admonition of the Lord.

Document VII.10

A Woman Fulfilled (died 1892)

Ann Pennington (1821–92) was the daughter of weavers at Rainford near St Helens in Lancashire. She was converted, joined the Primitive Methodists and married. Her life was spent not in public work but in the private sphere. Nevertheless she supported her church through giving and hospitality; and she was notable for her philanthropy.

The extract is taken from *The Primitive Methodist Magazine*, October 1894, p. 792.

She was naturally of a retiring disposition, hence her most shining qualities were displayed in her home – a sphere where few could equal her. She lived for her family – ever sharing their joys and helping them to bear their sorrows. Though never taking such an active part as some in the church, she was ever anxious for its prosperity, contributing largely to its funds, entertaining its preachers and entering into and helping all schemes adopted for the success of our cause.

She was a true Christian. Christianity to her was a thing of reality, and as far as one could judge from observation, the whole of her character might be stated in the words of the Saviour in reference to Nathaniel, 'An Israelite indeed in whom there is no guile.'

Her sympathies were large, hence to her it was a real joy to minister to the needy poor. Her name and loving deeds are as 'ointment poured forth.'

Leadership in the Church

Document VII.11

Hugh Bourne on the Ministry of Women, 1808

Hugh Bourne (see IV.1) defended the ministry of women in a pamphlet of 1808 and female participation in preaching, the key issue, became the settled practice of the Primitive Methodists. Bourne's case is partly pragmatic, but he also cites the authority of Christ and the apostles before explaining the apparent Pauline prohibition of women preaching. The women concerned are individually identified in E. D. Graham, *Chosen by God: A List of the Female Travelling Preachers of Early Primitive Methodism*, Bunbury, Cheshire, 1989.

The extract is taken from Bourne's *Remarks on the Ministry of Women* reprinted in J. Walford, *Memoirs of the Life and Labours of the Late Venerable Hugh Bourne*, London, 1855, vol. 1, pp. 172–6.

Agreeably to my promise, I shall endeavour to give you a few remarks on the subject of women's ministry: though I have not been accustomed to study this controversy for the following reasons, which have been established among a few of us.

1. If persons who exercise in the ministry are of good report, and the Lord owns their labours by turning sinners to righteousness, we do not think it our duty to endeavour to hinder them; but we wish them success in the name of the Lord, without respect to persons.

2. We do not think it right to be the cause of any one's going to hell through a proud and fond desire of establishing our own (perhaps vain) opinions.

3. Instead of stopping to reason about various things, we find it best to be pressing on.

4. In general, instead of engaging in useless controversy, we find it more profitable to continue giving ourselves to God, and spending the time in prayer.

...

I shall now endeavour to follow your friend's propositions. The first of which may be compromised [*sic*] in the following words: – 'Is the preaching of women authorized by Jesus Christ?'

Answer. I think it is. I think he authorized Miriam, (Micah vi. 4,) Deborah, Huldah, and perhaps many others not recorded; and the gospel was preached in those days, (Heb. iv. 2,) and he is the same God now, and acts in the same way.

But, perhaps, you wish for an example when our Lord was upon earth. Well, besides the Virgin Mary and Elizabeth, you have Anna, the prophetess, who testified of Jesus in the temple; and this I take to be strong preaching. Well, but you say, whom did he authorize personally? Ans. The woman of Samaria. I believe she was commissioned by the Holy Ghost to preach Jesus, and she did preach him with extraordinary success; and he authorized her ministry, for he joined in with it, and acted accordingly.

But, perhaps, you want a personal commission, – very well, then you have Mary Magdalene. She was commissioned by an angel to preach, and then by Jesus Christ himself. It is said of Paul, in one place, that he preached Jesus and the resurrection, – so did Mary to the apostles themselves. Thus our Lord ordained her an apostle to the apostles, a preacher to the preachers, and an evangelist to the evangelists. ...

The fifth proposition may be stated thus: – 'Is not women's preaching interdicted by apostolic authority?' 1 Cor. xiv. 34. 1 Tim. ii. 11.

Answer.   It is rather harsh to suppose that an apostle interdicted what had been the practice of the church of God in all ages, what had been personally sanctioned by our Lord himself, and what even the same apostle had just been establishing, by giving rules for it. 1 Cor. xi. 5, 6, 7. The question, then, is, 'What are we to understand by these scriptures?' I shall not endeavour to give you on this any opinion as my own; for having never studied them very closely, I could not in conscience do it.

But I am told that these speak of church discipline, and of establishing church authority; and truly, if women must ordain or set apart the men for the ministry, it would be usurping authority, for the greater would be blessed of the less.

I have heard it stated further, that he there says, 'If they will learn any thing, let them ask their husbands at home.' This they say settles the meaning, for he must be speaking of something that the husbands can inform them of. This well applies to discipline, but if it extends to preaching also, then all who have ungodly husbands are inevitably bound over to eternal damnation, because they are restricted from learning any thing from any but their husbands.

If also this must be stretched out so as to exclude women from teaching men religion, it would reach too far, – it would break the order of God, – it would interdict mothers from teaching their sons; and I believe that I owe my salvation, under God, in a great degree, to a pious mother.

Document VII.12

William O'Bryan on the Punctuality of Female Preachers, 1822

> Female preaching was common among the early Bible Christians. See W. F. Swift, 'The Women Itinerant Preachers of Early Methodism', *Proceedings of the Wesley Historical Society*, 29 (1953), pp. 76–8. The Bible Christian leader, William O'Bryan (see X.8), in 'A Hint to Persons who come late to Worship', thought that timekeeping was a particular problem for his women preachers.
>
> The extract is taken from *The Arminian Magazine*, September 1822, pp. 298–9.

Coming late to places of worship, has a bad appearance as well as an evil tendency. ... But it may be objected that some of the female speakers have not watches and therefore do not know the time; for having sometimes to go a half-mile or mile from where they quarter, to the preaching-house, and perhaps the people where they quarter have no clock, they have to guess the time as well as they can; and the people may think they are in time, and tell the preacher so: and the preacher may very naturally think, that the people of the house who live in one place, and have an opportunity of observing the hour by the sun, or some other local mark which country people who have no clocks often have; but by mistaking the time the preacher may be too late as well as too soon. For this reason I think our friends should see that the female preacher has a watch as well as the man. If it was not given, a wealthy friend or two might lend one which they might have again on her quitting the circuit.

Document VII.13

A General Baptist's Role, 1840s

Maria Allen (1826–49) was the unmarried daughter of the lock-keeper at Red Hill Lock, near Sawley, Derbyshire, who served as a deacon in the General Baptist church in the village. Her activities included tract distribution, which is celebrated in an anecdote here, and collecting money for the chapel, a widespread aspect of female service that has hitherto received inadequate coverage in the secondary literature. In such work her zeal made her *prima inter pares*.

The extract is taken from *The General Baptist Repository*, April 1850, pp. 188–9.

To an agreeable person, M. A. united a popular address and pleasing manners. She always greeted her christian friends with a smile of cheerful urbanity, and evinced a lively interest in their welfare. These natural qualities burnished by divine grace, constituted her a fit agent for many departments of christian effort; consequently she was engaged by the church as one of its collectors, Sabbath school teachers, and tract distributors, and always manifested a ready mind to every good work. So great indeed was her ardour in the service of the Lord, that, had the finger of Providence pointed in that direction, she would have gladly joined the mission band. She was a great reader, and an intelligent christian; fond of retirement, and hailed the hour for domestic worship with holy rapture. She loved the house of God, and was not detained from its worship by trifles; as her frequent wet journeys of a mile and a half, over newly flooded fields, or on a rainy day, testify. She was a person of strong sense, a conscientious General Baptist, and could give an enlightened reason of her hope, and faith, and practice. She was a decided dissenter, and would earnestly contend for liberty of conscience, and for the maintenance of Christ's kingly character. She delighted to do good, and sought opportunities of usefulness, as the following incident attests, together with others that might be named. A short time ago three ungodly young men applied to her father, at a late hour on the Saturday evening, for admission through the lock, with a view, as she too truly suspected, of plying their boat on the approaching

Sabbath. Late, however, as it was, she selected three appropriate religious tracts and presented to them, at the same time requesting their careful perusal. They promised – left, performed their word, were diverted from their wicked purpose, and vowed henceforth to keep holy the Sabbath day. 'Blessed are they that sow beside all waters.'

Document VII.14

Catherine Booth on Female Ministry, 1859

Catherine Booth (1829–90), the 'Mother of the Salvation Army', was the wife of William Booth (see IX.18) when he was still a Methodist New Connexion minister stationed at Gateshead. In 1859 an Independent minister at Sunderland attacked Phoebe Palmer, a visiting American holiness teacher, for speaking in public. Catherine Booth leapt to her defence in a pamphlet, *Female Ministry*, which became the basis for the gender egalitarianism of the Salvation Army.

The extract is taken from the pamphlet as reprinted in F. de L. Booth-Tucker, *The Life of Catherine Booth*, 3rd edn, London, 1924, vol. 1, pp. 178–9.

Whether the Church will allow women to speak in *her* assemblies can only be a question of time; common sense, public opinion, and the blessed results of female agency will force her to give us an honest and impartial rendering of the solitary text on which she grounds her prohibitions. Then, when the true light shines, and God's words take the place of man's traditions, the Doctor of Divinity who shall teach that Paul commands women to be silent when God's Spirit urges her to speak, will be regarded much the same as we should regard an astronomer who should teach that the sun is the earth's satellite.

As to the obligation devolving on woman to labour for her Master, I presume there will be no controversy. The particular sphere in which each individual shall do this must be dictated by the teachings of the Holy Spirit and the gifts with which God has endowed her. If she have the necessary gifts, and feels herself called by the Spirit to preach, there is not a single word in the whole Book of God to restrain her, but many, very many, to urge and encourage her. God says she *shall* do so; and Paul prescribed the manner in which she shall do so; and Phebe, Junia, Philip's four daughters, and many other women actually did preach and speak in the primitive Churches. If this had not been the case, there would have been less freedom under the new than under the old dispensation; a greater paucity of gifts and agencies under the Spirit than under the law; fewer labourers when more work was to be done. Instead of the destruction of caste and division between the priesthood and the people, and the setting up of a spiritual kingdom in which all true believers were 'kings and priests unto God', the division would have been more stringent, and the disabilities of the common people greater. Whereas, we are told, again and again in effect, that in 'Christ Jesus there is neither bond nor free, male or female, but ye are all one in Christ Jesus'.

Document VII.15

Quaker Women's Meetings, 1861

Although women ministers, that is unpaid travelling speakers, were far more numerous than their male counterparts in the Society of Friends during the nineteenth century, women's business meetings were severely circumscribed in their work. It was not until 1896 that women were admitted on equal terms to the Quaker governing bodies. See E. Isichei, *Victorian Quakers*, Oxford, 1970, pp. 94–5, 107–9.

The extract is taken from *Christian Doctrine, Practice and Discipline*, London, 1861, pp. 169–71. Overseers existed to undertake pastoral work and enforce Quaker discipline (see X.5).

On considering the nature and extent of the discipline committed to women friends, it is our judgment, that its nature is, as expressed by the minutes of the Yearly Meeting, to come up to the help of their brethren in the discipline of the church.

As to its extent:

1. They are to inspect and, in their discretion, to relieve the wants of the poor of their own sex; and to apply to the men's meeting for the means, and for its concurrence, as cases shall require.

2. They are to take cognizance of proposals for marriage, conformably to the rules on that subject.

3. They are to join in certificates of removal for women friends, when about to be recommended with their husbands. ...

4. They are also, on receiving from the men's meeting certificates for women friends removed into the compass of the Monthly Meeting, to make appointments to visit them.

5. They are to have overseers; in order to which, when it is necessary that women overseers be appointed, the women's Monthly Meeting is to appoint a committee, which is to join a committee to be appointed by the men's Monthly Meeting. The joint committee is to nominate the overseers, and the names of the women then nominated are to be reported to the women's Monthly Meeting, and, if approved by that meeting, sent to the men's Meeting for confirmation.

6. The women's Monthly Meeting, at the desire of the men's Monthly Meeting, should make appointments to join the men in visiting such women as apply for admission, or reinstatement, into membership; and the report of the committee is to be made to the men's Monthly Meeting, which is to inform the women's meeting of the conclusion.

7. In cases of delinquency of women friends, when, after due exercise of private labour, the women's Monthly Meeting believes it necessary that any of its members be dealt with as delinquents, it is to inform the men's meeting thereof. That meeting may, if it think fit, request the women's meeting to proceed to deal with the delinquent, and report the result of their labours to the men's meeting; but, if the men's meeting should see it expedient to join them in the dealing, the

report of the joint committee is to be made to the men's meeting, which, in either case, is to inform the women's meeting of its determination. No proceedings of the women only, are to be a sufficient ground for a testimony of disownment; unless, after mature deliberation, and from any peculiar circumstances which may attach to the case, the men's meeting, feeling satisfied that the discipline has been fully exercised by the labour of the women friends, shall be convinced that it is not its place to make any appointment on the case of delinquency.

Document VII.16

Mission Preaching, 1875

Matilda Bass, born in 1831, was a Baptist who began to undertake preaching engagements from 1867 in the revivalist atmosphere that survived from the popular awakening of 1859. She went to preach the gospel on an undenominational basis in Leicester in February 1875, reporting on progress by letter to her husband. The atmosphere is very much that of the contemporary missions conducted by the American revivalists Moody and Sankey. On such female preachers, see O. Anderson, 'Women Preachers in Mid-Victorian Britain: Some Reflexions on Feminism, Popular Religion and Social Change', *Historical Journal*, 12 (1969), pp. 467–84; and J. Holmes, *Religious Revivals in Britain and Ireland, 1859–1905*, Dublin, 2000, chap. 4.

The extract is taken from J. V. B., *She Walked with God*, Bristol, n.d., pp. 62–3.

In the evening we had a good large meeting at the Gospel Hall, some said 1,600; some went away; they ought to have packed them in better. We had a good time, and some souls saved afterwards. We had a prayer meeting at noon to-day, at the Mission Church, and this will be every day, except to-morrow, when there is one at the Temperance Hall. It was good to be there. We are looking for much blessing. It was nice to greet at least two this morning at the Mission Church, brought to Jesus when we were here before, and now working for Jesus. Praise the Lord with us! We are expecting great things, – hundreds of souls. Stir them up to pray on Wednesday evening. ...

The Lord is blessing the Word here – souls are saved every night in varying numbers – Christians come and say what blessing they have received. We get warm sympathy in some quarters, and there seems a stir among Christians. To-day the noon-day prayer meeting was attended, I should say, by twice as many as last Tuesday. It is wonderful how the Lord gives us favour with the people, for His own purposes of grace, for I think I never felt so stupid and weak in myself; but they throng night after night, and so much blessing.

Document VII.17

Wesleyan Deaconesses, 1890

Thomas Bowman Stephenson (1839–1912) was a Wesleyan minister who from 1873 had full-time charge of what became the National Children's Home. In that capacity he recognised the desirability of trained female workers; the newly created city missions of Methodism were also beginning to appoint 'sisters of the people' to care for social needs; and Stephenson was aware of the German precedent for Protestant deaconesses. In 1890 he set out his scheme for a training institute for deaconesses, carefully guarding against any impression of Romanising by having vows. The project bore fruit as the Wesley Deaconess Order, which is the subject of E. D. Graham, *Saved to Serve: The Story of the Wesley Deaconess Order, 1890–1978*, Peterborough, 2002.

The extract is taken from a letter of 1890 to the religious press reprinted in W. Bradfield, *The Life of the Reverend Thomas Bowman Stephenson*, London, 1913, pp. 293–4.

A house will be taken within convenient reach of this spot, capable of accommodating ten or twelve Probationary Sisters. They must be women of good education as well as of fervent spirit. It is not intended, however, to exclude persons of exceptional force and spiritual gifts, even if they have not had the advantage of a complete early education. Applicants must be members of a Methodist Church, unless in exceptional cases. It is hoped that some will be able to pay their own expenses, but board and lodging will be provided. Three months' preliminary trial will be required; then a further period of nine months' training. The second year of probation will be spent in actual work. Instruction in Bible subjects will be given, also in such medical subjects as would be likely to be useful in the after work of the Sisters; and a portion of each day will be spent in practical work.

I need hardly say that no vow will be required or received of any Sister; but it is expected that candidates will be moved by a deep conviction that God has called them to their work, and that they will intend to spend at least a considerable number of years in it; otherwise the labour and expense of training would be thrown away.

Three great fields of usefulness lie before the Sisters.

1. Moral and spiritual education, in connexion with orphanages and industrial schools, both at home and in the missionary fields.

2. The ministry to the sick, especially the sick poor. The noble vocation of the nurse is not open, as it should be, to Nonconformist girls. It is hoped that, if not immediately, yet after a time, arrangements may be made for an Hospital Training Branch of the Institute.

3. Evangelistic visitation, in connexion with circuits, with congregations, perhaps with groups of village congregations, and certainly in connexion with mission centres.

PART VIII

MISSION

Introduction

Mission was the life-blood of Evangelical Nonconformists during the nineteenth century, and its pulse was also felt in other Dissenting denominations. Individual activities in the chapels were designed to spread the gospel and its influence in the vicinity and there were innumerable agencies for achieving the same goals on a broader scale. The example of the Methodists, with their vigorous itinerancy, induced other bodies to organise so as to take vital religion into remoter areas at home. Equally the Christian faith was propagated abroad through the foreign missionary movement. William Carey had gone to India for the Baptist Missionary Society in 1793, and the Missionary Society, primarily Congregational in support, had sent agents to the Pacific before the nineteenth century opened. The movement burgeoned during the century, encompassing the globe and having significant repercussions on Nonconformist life at home. Collections were made, deputations were heard and a window was opened on the world. What is more, the missionary impulse achieved its primary objective of planting Christianity in many parts of the earth where previously it was unknown.

The evangelistic efforts at home were at their most vigorous in the early years of the century. The vision of the Independents for gospel work in Lancashire, the most industrialised county, illustrates the enterprising spirit stemming from the Evangelical Revival of the previous century (VIII.1). The vibrancy of open-air evangelism among the Primitive Methodists (VIII.2) was reinforced by fresh influences from the United States (VIII.3). The growing cities were by no means neglected, as the achievements of Evangelicals in Manchester (VIII.4) and a programme of the Unitarians in London show (VIII.5). New methods were frequently adopted to reach the working people: lectures to mass audiences (VIII.6), for example, and free meals (VIII.7). Adaptation was exalted as a high principle by the Salvation Army late in the century (VIII.8) and its challenge to innovate was accepted by others (VIII.9). The extent to which Quakers, originally outside the Evangelical orbit, were drawn, with many others, into that world in the Victorian period is illustrated by their effective adoption of missionary methods in association with their adult schools (VIII.10).

The same spirit animated the overseas mission of the chapels. The Missionary Society, eager to follow the leadings of providence, organised efforts on the continent as well as in distant parts of the globe (VIII.11). The Jewish people were the special concern of some (VIII.13). The Bible, it was confidently believed, would win its own triumphs (VIII.12), but it was hoped that government colonial policy would put no obstacles in the path of mission (VIII.15). A wealth of literature publicised the work of the chapels at the ends of the earth (VIII.14); and once more the Quakers joined in the enterprise (VIII.16). The aim of some missions, by the second half of the century, was to establish free-standing indigenous churches (VIII.17), though certain observers saw an ominous gap looming between missionaries and the people they served (VIII.18).

The literature on home missionary activities includes D. W. Lovegrove, *Established Church, Sectarian People: Itinerancy and the Transformation of English Dissent, 1780–1830*, Cambridge, 1988; R. Carwardine, *Transatlantic Revivalism: Popular Evangelicalism in Britain and America, 1790–1865*, Westport, Connecticut, 1978; and J. Holmes, *Religious Revivals in Britain and Ireland, 1859–1905*, Dublin, 2000. J. Kent, *Holding the Fort: Studies in Victorian Revivalism*, London, 1978, is valuable, though its approach has been cogently criticised by J. Coffey, 'Democracy and Popular Religion: Moody and Sankey's Mission to Britain, 1873–1875', in E. F. Biagini, ed., *Citizenship and Community: Liberals, Radicals and Collective Identities in the British Isles, 1865–1931*, Cambridge, 1996.

Apart from the numerous studies of the impact of missions on particular parts of the world, there are histories of the main denominational societies: R. Lovett, *The History of the London Missionary Society, 1795–1895*, 2 vols, London, 1899; G. G. Findlay and W. W. Holdsworth, *The History of the Wesleyan Methodist Missionary Society*, 5 vols, London, 1921; and the more recent and excellent B. Stanley, *The History of the Baptist Missionary Society, 1792–1992*, Edinburgh, 1992. The same author has written on the relations of missions and empire in *The Bible and the Flag: Protestant Missions and British Imperialism in the Nineteenth and Twentieth Centuries*, Leicester, 1990. There is an attractive cameo from the end of the century in C. Binfield, '"The Church as by Grace Established": A Christian Imperialism', *So Down to Prayers: Studies in English Nonconformity, 1780–1920*, London, 1977.

Home Mission

Document VIII.1

Report of the Lancashire Independent Association, 1812

The Lancashire Independent Association, created in 1806, was one of the county organisations among Calvinistic Dissenters founded or revived around the opening of the nineteenth century primarily in order to promote itinerant evangelistic work. Its moving spirit was William Roby (1766–1830), the minister of Cannon Street Chapel, Manchester, whose zeal, kindled in the Countess of Huntingdon's Connexion, led to the huge expansion of Independency in the north-west of England. See W. G. Robinson, *William Roby (1766–1830) and the Revival of Independency in the North*, London, 1954; DNB; and, on the broader picture, D. W. Lovegrove, *Established Church, Sectarian People: Itinerancy and the Transformation of English Dissent, 1780–1830*, Cambridge, 1988.

The extract is taken from the *Fifth Annual Report of the Committee to the Independent Churches in Lancashire, associated for the Spread of the Gospel*, n.p., 1812, p. 2.

Multitudes, not only in the Heathen world, but among ourselves, deviate essentially, in principle or in practice, from 'the truth as it is in Jesus.' A sense of their deplorable condition should awaken our tenderest sympathies; and the hope of becoming the instruments of snatching their souls from impending destruction, and thus of preserving them from the dreadful consequences of their sins, should animate us to the use of all suitable means for their conversion to Christ. In this infinitely important service, not only the ministers of religion, but also private Christians in general may occupy their talents, and become 'fellow-helpers to the truth,' by the holy exemplariness of their conduct; – by their wise and affectionate counsels; – by the distribution of religious tracts; – by the circulation of the scriptures; – and by the liberal support of the various institutions established for the purpose of more widely extending the interests of revealed religion.

The preaching of the gospel is the principal mean [*sic*] which God has employed for this important end. Where Christian societies already exist, the ministry of the stated pastor is of essential importance; and numerous evils arise where this ordinance of God is not duly regarded. But the primitive churches not only supported their stated pastors, but also contributed jointly to the support of Evangelical Itinerants, who, like those whom Jehoshaphat sent forth, 'went about through all the cities of Judah, and taught the people.' You, the Churches and Congregations of the Independent denomination in Lancashire, have felt the same obligations, and have laudably united for this purpose. Besides aiding those ministers in the county, who have the opportunity and the disposition to itinerate, you have employed several, whose whole time and talents are devoted to this work; and whose success has afforded you, from time to time, the most enlivening satisfaction.

Document VIII.2

Hugh Bourne on Camp Meetings, 1829

Camp meetings were an import from the American frontier, where Methodist revivalists would preach to settlers who gathered from miles around. The first in England was held at Mow Cop, north of Stoke-on-Trent in Staffordshire, on 31 May 1807, and, despite the judgement of the Wesleyan Conference that 'even supposing such meetings to be allowable in America, they are highly improper in England', better planned events followed later in the year. Normally lasting only a day and not actually entailing any camp, they became a hallmark of early Primitive Methodism. See J. Kent, *Holding the Fort: Studies in Victorian Revivalism*, London, 1978, chap. 2. For Hugh Bourne and the style of preaching he recommended, see IV.1.

These guidelines are taken from the preface of his *Large Hymn Book for the Use of the Primitive Methodists*, Bemersley, near Tunstall, 1829. The 'mourners' were penitents convicted of sin and seeking salvation.

Camp Meetings.

Camp Meetings open at 9 o'clock in the morning, proceed with a variety of services, and close at 4 or 5 in the afternoon. Sometimes they stop an hour for dinner, and sometimes not. All the exercises in all the services must be short, as long exercises are peculiarly injurious at Camp Meetings.

They usually open with a praying service for about 30 minutes. At half-past 9, preaching service. At a quarter past 10, praying service in companies. At a quarter before 11, either a preaching or a reading service. At half-past 11, praying service in companies, and so on, varying the exercises, in order that the attention and energy of the people may keep rising and increasing to the last.

PREACHING Services open with singing and prayer, and close with sermon or discourse. Two preachers should always stand up in each service; and no preacher should, on any account, be allowed to speak for more than twenty minutes in any one service. And a preaching service should scarcely ever be allowed to continue for more than 45 minutes. The preachers should take a clear pure course, and not make any references to any preaching that has gone before or that is to follow after. Such references being most injurious.

READING services open with singing and prayer. One or two experiences are then read from the Magazines. The readers are allowed to comment a little as they go on. These services promote variety and are often very useful.

PRAYING services should be carefully supported. They are the chief strength of the Camp Meetings, and give energy and dignity to the whole. They are held in four different ways:

1. The general praying service at the opening.

2. About a quarter past ten in the forenoon, a praying service should open in companies; but no company should be allowed to fix near the stand. The movements in the service give variety, energy, and effect to the whole. If the congregation happen to be but small, they should nevertheless go out in companies, because the going out and coming in are a great relief both to body and mind; and are of great service to the people in other respects.

3. When a praying service, in companies, has gone on with energy, for half an hour, they are usually summoned to the preaching stand. But if the pious praying labourers happen to be engaged with mourners, then the next service must be deferred or put off as the case may require. Nevertheless, if circumstances render preaching necessary, then a permanent company is formed, and fixed at a suitable distance from the stand to pray for mourners: and this company does not break up for preaching. The permanent company is a relief to the whole; and all the other services proceed regularly as before.

4. Sometimes, when the work breaks out powerfully under preaching, it is found necessary to have a general praying service without going out in companies. In that case it is usual to make a ring or opening, and call up the mourners to be prayed for.

Document VIII.3

Charles Finney on Revivals, 1839

Charles Grandison Finney (1792–1875) was an American who, after training as a lawyer, became an immensely successful revivalist in upstate New York in the 1820s. His *Lectures on Revivals of Religion* (1835) publicised his mechanistic view of the universe in which, if human beings adopted certain techniques, conversions would automatically follow. First published in Britain in 1837, the *Lectures* achieved great popularity, especially in Wales. The Primitive Methodists distanced themselves a little from the views of a Presbyterian preacher, but were in general happy with his 'Arminianised Calvinism' and so reprinted his text in their magazine. See DEB; and R. Carwardine, *Transatlantic Revivalism: Popular Evangelicalism in Britain and America, 1790–1865*, Westport, Connecticut, 1978, chaps 2 and 3.

The extract is taken from *The Primitive Methodist Magazine*, January 1839, pp. 15, 18.

We take Mr. F. to be a divine of the Presbyterian persuasion. But still his lectures, with care, may be of service to religious societies in general; as they evidently contain many good and useful things; and of these we may avail ourselves; and matters not useful or not correctly understood, may be omitted with advantage. Also the lectures may occasionally be corrected or improved by suitable notes, and by a word or expression inclosed in crotchets, [ ]. Such words may vary the sense a little, in cases where there appears to be incorrectness, from haste or otherwise.

LECTURE 1

... I said that a revival is the result of the *right* use of the appropriate means. The means which God has enjoined for the production of a revival, doubtless have a natural tendency to produce a revival; otherwise God would not have enjoined them. But means will not produce a revival, we all know, without the blessing of God. No more will grain, when it is sowed, produce a crop without the blessing of God. It is impossible for us to say that there is not as direct an influence or agency from God, to produce a crop of grain, as there is to produce a revival. What are the laws of nature, according to which, it is supposed, that grain yields a crop? They are nothing but the constituted manner of the operations of God. In the Bible, the word of God is compared to grain, and preaching is compared to sowing seed, and the results to the springing up and growth of the crop. And the result is just as philosophical in the one case as in the other, and is as naturally connected with the cause.

I wish this idea to be impressed on all your minds, for there has long been an idea prevalent that promoting religion has something very peculiar in it, not to be judged of by the ordinary rules of cause and effect; in short, that there is no connexion of the means with the result, and no tendency in the means to produce the effect. No doctrine is more dangerous than this to the prosperity of the church, and nothing more absurd.

Suppose a man were to go and preach this doctrine among farmers, about their sowing grain. Let him tell them that God is a sovereign, and will give them a crop only when it pleases him, and that for them to plough and plant and labour as if they expected to raise a crop is very wrong, and taking the work out of the hands of God, that it interferes with his sovereignty, and is going on in their own strength; and that there is no connexion between the means and the result on which they can depend. And now, suppose the farmers should believe such doctrine. Why, they would starve the world to death.

Just such results will follow from the church's being persuaded that promoting religion is somehow so mysteriously a subject of Divine sovereignty, that there is no natural connexion between the means and the end. What *are* the results? Why, generation after generation have gone down to hell. No doubt more than five thousand millions have gone down to hell, while the church has been dreaming, and waiting for God to save them without the use of means. It has been the devil's most successful means of destroying souls. The connexion is as clear in religion as it is when the farmer sows his grain.

Document VIII.4

Manchester City Mission Operations, 1842–43

City missions were a means of evangelising the growing urban centres of the nineteenth century. Undenominational in organisation, they allocated a missionary

Mission

to each of several divisions of the city. The first was founded in Glasgow in 1826 by David Nasmith (see DNB), who subsequently persuaded other places to follow its example. See D. M. Lewis, *Lighten their Darkness: The Evangelical Mission to Working-Class London, 1828–1860*, Westport, Connecticut, 1986.

Manchester was the centre of the hugely prosperous cotton industry, but in 1842–43 was afflicted with acute labour tensions as a result of a downturn in trade. Its city mission employed thirty-five agents in those years. The list of their operations is taken from J. Campbell, *Memoirs of David Nasmith*, London, 1844, pp. 466–7.

Tracts distributed	802,424
Visits paid, including 26,311 to the sick and the dying	308,988
Meetings for reading the Scriptures, exhortation, and prayer	10,885
Average attendance at each meeting	28
Testaments and Psalms lent	1,047
Weekly average of persons who have had the Scriptures read in their houses	5,189
Persons induced to attend public worship	987
Children sent to Sunday-schools	1,293
Hopeful conversions	614
Persons who have become members of Christian churches, and are walking in the fellowship of the gospel	151
Infidels reclaimed	62
Drunkards reclaimed	214
Fallen women restored to their friends or to society	22
There are in the several districts occupied by the Missionaries persons who may be called inquirers, persons who are anxious to know the way of salvation, and who, from old age and poverty, are dependent on the Missionaries for religious instruction, to the number of	4,932

Document VIII.5

Unitarian Domestic Mission Station, 1859

The impetus for the creation in the 1830s of the Domestic Mission movement by Unitarians came from the earlier work done by Joseph Tuckerman in Boston, USA. The missions have been seen as the first recognisable social work agencies in Britain, though they learnt much from the example of Thomas Chalmers in Scotland. By the mid-century other Dissenting denominations were building on this pioneering activity by Unitarians in the poorest parts of English cities. By the 1850s the Domestic Missions had settled into a pattern and this extract from *The London Unitarian Register*, 2nd edn, London, 1859, p. 8, shows the nature and range of the work done in one of the key stations in London. See D. Steers, 'The Domestic Mission Movement: Liverpool and Manchester', and A. Ruston, 'London's East End Domestic Mission', *Transactions of the Unitarian Historical Society* (21 (1996), pp. 79–103, 117–35; and D Turley, 'The Anglo-American Unitarian Connexion and

Urban Poverty in the First Half of the Nineteenth Century', in J. Innes, ed., *Charity, Philanthropy and Reform*, Cambridge, 1998.

SPICER STREET (Domestic Mission Station).
Spicer Street, Brick Lane, Spitalfields.

SERVICE – Sunday Morning, quarter past 11 o'clock (for Children and Teachers); Evening, half-past 6 o'clock (Public).

SUNDAY-SCHOOL – Morning, half-past 9 o'clock; Afternoon, half-past 2.

Week-evening School, Tuesday and Thursday, half-past 7 o'clock.

Class for Junior Teachers, Wednesday Evening, half-past 8 o'clock.

Sunday-school Library and Savings' Bank.

Day-schools for Boys, Girls, and Infants.

Blanket and Clothing Club, Coal Club and Savings' Bank, Tuesday Evening, half-past 7 o'clock.

General Lending Library, Monday Evening, 8 o'clock.

Library Classes open to Male and Female Subscribers, Tuesday and Thursday Evenings, 8 o'clock.

Popular Lectures on Monday Evenings in November and December, and again in February and March.

Connected with the Congregation is a Benevolent Fund for the relief of Subscribers in sickness; the Subscription is 1d. weekly, or 1s. per quarter. There are a few Honorary Subscribers.

There is also a Burial Society containing above 50 members.

Other occasional Meetings are held, and the Poor visited at their homes.

Missionary. ... CHARLES L. CORKRAN, 65, Shepperton Cottages, New North Road, Hoxton, N.

Document VIII.6

Hugh Stowell Brown Lecturing to the Men of Liverpool, 1862

Hugh Stowell Brown (1828–86) was a Manxman who became minister of Myrtle Street Baptist Church in Liverpool in 1848. Six years later he began Sunday afternoon lectures to the working men of the city which attained great celebrity. They were widely imitated as a means of gaining a hearing from those who might be reluctant to attend ordinary services. The theme of this one is the characteristic high Victorian maxim, 'Cleanliness is next to Godliness'. For Brown, see W. S. Caine, ed., *Hugh Stowell Brown*, London, 1887; and DEB.

The extract is taken from H. S. Brown, *Lectures to the Men of Liverpool*, Liverpool, 1862, pp. 41–2.

I do not know to whom we are indebted for the saying, 'Cleanliness is next to godliness.' I have heard its origin ascribed to John Wesley. It is a maxim worthy of the sagacious founder of Methodism. I have no doubt that, in his continual intercourse with people, he found that, next to the devil, dirt was about the most formidable enemy to his great reformatory work. Drink and dirt are the devil's foremen; he pays them liberally, their wages are thousands of bodies and souls – men, women, and children; and they do their master's work diligently, faithfully, and effectively. They are at it night and day – these two demons of the pit; drink working in the beer-house and the gin-palace, dirt working in every narrow street, every dark alley, every ill-ventilated court, every badly-built house, every close, unwholesome workshop, every damp cellar, every open drain, every crowded graveyard. Ministers of religion, schoolmasters, town missionaries, and scripture readers are, with more or less of diligence and earnestness, trying to overthrow the devil's kingdom; but the devil points to his two foremen – drink and dirt – and laughs and snaps his fingers at all our efforts. I believe that the devil hates the gospel and dreads the gospel; I believe that he also hates and dreads soap and water. He is no great admirer of churches; as little does he admire public baths and wash-houses. *He* knows that 'cleanliness is next to godliness,' and that a plentiful supply and application of soap and water would do very much towards the overthrow of his dark and horrible dominion in the world. Last Sunday we had a look at the operations of one of the devil's foremen – drink; this afternoon I shall take a peep at that department of the devil's work of which dirt is the 'gaffer.' And here, at the outset, let me remark, that if you think it is too high praise to bestow upon cleanliness to say that it is next to godliness, you must remember that the word cleanliness has a moral, as well as a physical signification. This moral sense of cleanliness often comes out in our commonest forms of speech; as, for example, when we say that 'our hands are clean,' meaning that we are innocent of this or that sin; and when we say that such or such an act is a 'dirty trick;' and when we apply the term 'foul-mouthed' to a man who is in the habit of swearing and uttering obscene language. In all such cases, and in many more, we recognise the moral, and not merely physical, sense of cleanliness. In like manner the Scriptures often speak of sin as 'uncleanness;' of being freed from sin, as being 'washed;' the mercy of God, as communicated through the merit and suffering of Christ, is as 'a fountain opened for sin and for uncleanness;' all virtue is spoken of as 'purity;' and thus do the Scriptures continually indicate the moral meaning of this word 'cleanliness.' Take the word, then, in this its widest and highest signification; remember that it is a figurative expression, denoting all moral purity; and I think you cannot but admit that 'godliness and cleanliness' are very closely allied.

Document VIII.7

A Costermongers' Tea Meeting, 1863

William Carter, a man of Brethren sympathies, ran the Victoria Hall in South London on undenominational lines. In the autumn of 1863 he launched a series of evangelistic tea meetings that each targeted a section of the working classes. One aimed at the barrow-sellers of fruit and vegetables, putting up one of their number to give a testimony to a changed life.

The extract is taken from W. Carter, *The Power of Truth*, London, 1865, pp. 42–5.

We invited the costermongers on Monday. After issuing the tickets I feared we had made a mistake, for I found it was Croydon fair, where most of the costermongers of the South of London resort; this cast us more fully on God. We prayed that the feet of hundreds of these dear fellows might be turned away from the fair into the Victoria Hall. Our gracious God answered our prayers and exceeded our expectations, for upwards of four hundred came to tea instead of going to the fair, and nearly all that came were strangers who had never been in the Hall before, but they had all heard of the former meetings and were induced to come. We all rejoiced in spirit, because the Lord had triumphed gloriously. The dear converted costermongers waited on their mates, so that, on the whole, we had less confusion than at former meetings, but a stranger being present would have no doubt thought bad indeed was the best. It is astonishing with what rapidity the viands disappeared, they all seemed to have large mouths, sharp teeth, and enormous swallows, also good stow holes in their clothes. The heaps of bread and butter vanished like lightning. When I found that all the bread and butter was gone I gave orders to bring out the cake, and with great difficulty I got their attention, but not before I made them sensible that they should have no cake till they heard what I had to say. I said, 'My dear fellows, I can assure you that this cake is very good, and I advise you all not to put it in your pockets, for if you do you will lose it.' In a moment there was such lound hurrahs, stamping of feet, and rattling of cups and saucers, and then such laughter; the cake seemed to act like magic upon them. I believe these were the happiest moments they had spent in their lives. From the time the cups and saucers were given out till they were gathered up did not exceed twenty minutes. Where all the provisions had gone it would be impossible for any one to know, it seemed as though a band of locusts had passed through the hall and left not a crumb behind. While the cups and saucers were being gathered up we began the meeting by singing the twelfth hymn. (Order or ceremony is out of the question. We have to sing them quiet or holloa louder than they do, until they gradually settle down and pay attention. I pray and watch for this and then seize the opportunity to preach Jesus to them.) After we had sung, I introduced the 'king of the costermongers' to them, who had been converted at our first costermongers' tea meeting, (he was called the king of the costermongers because he used to sing a song called the 'Coster King,' and this he did sitting on a donkey, and riding to and fro on the stage of the Victoria Theatre before thousands of costermongers, hence he was called the king of the costers.) He spoke in a bold but touching manner to his mates, he said,

> 'You all know what I was before I was converted, and you all know what I have been since; I am a changed man, and you know it. You have sneered and jeered at me, and have said it is only a nine days' wonder, but you see it has lasted twelve months anyhow. The fact is I am converted and there's no gammon about it. I know some of you said, "stay till cherries comes in and then we shall

see whether you won't give threepence a pound for them and sell them for twopence." Did I not tell you that I should reckon cherries had not come in if I could not buy them to sell honestly? and you know I have not sold a cherry this season. And here I am to night with one shilling in my pocket, and you know I could cheat and steal with any of you, only I was lucky enough not to be caught. I should have had many pounds in my pocket to night if I acted as I used to do. Now, I challenge any of you to get up and contradict it at once, if what I say is not true. You know that you cannot; it is by the grace of God I am what I am; and when you come home drunk from your raffles, and get under my window and sing "The pearly gates are open, and H—— has entered in," I thank God I have entered in, and you too may enter in.'

Document VIII.8

Catherine Booth on Evangelistic Adaptability, 1883

Catherine Booth (see VII.14) provided an apologia for the unconventional methods of the Salvation Army in its enormously successful early days. She rejects the legitimacy of any exclusive claims about church order and commends the principle of cultural adaptation, so offering a rationale for the extraordinary inventiveness of the Army at this time. For Salvation Army methods, see G. K. Horridge, *The Salvation Army: Origins and Early Days, 1865–1900*, Godalming, 1993; and P. J. Walker, *Pulling the Devil's Kingdom Down: The Salvation Army in Victorian Britain*, Berkeley, California, 2001.

The extract is taken from [C.] Booth, *Papers on Aggressive Christianity*, London, 1883, pp. 10–12.

We have seen that it is clearly laid down in the texts I have read this afternoon that the law of adaptation is the only law laid down in the New Testament with respect to modes and measures. I challenge anybody to find me any other. While the Gospel message is laid down with unerring accuracy, we are left at perfect freedom to adapt our measures and modes of bringing it to bear upon men to the circumstances, times, and conditions in which we live – free as air. ...

People contend that we must have quiet, proper, decorous services. I say, WHERE IS YOUR AUTHORITY FOR THIS? Not here. I defy any man to show it. I have a great deal more authority in this book for such a lively, gushing, spontaneous, and what you call disorderly service, as our Army services sometimes are, in this 14th of Corinthians than you can find for yours. The best insight we get into the internal working of a religious service in Apostolic times is in this chapter, and I ask you – is it anything like the ordinary services of to-day? Can the utmost stretch of ingenuity make it into anything like them? But that even is not complete. We cannot get the order of a single service from the New Testament, nor can we get the form of a single church government. Hence one denomination think theirs is the best form, and another theirs; so Christendom has been divided into so many camps ever since; but this very quarrelling shows the impossibility of getting from the New Testament the routine, the order, and the fashion of mere modes. They cannot get it, because it is not there!! Do you think God had no purpose in this omission? The form, modes, and measures are not laid down as in the Old Testament dispensation. There is nothing of this stereotyped routinism in the whole of the New Testament. ... Here is the principles laid down that you are to adapt your measures to the necessity of the people to whom you minister; you are to take the Gospel to them in such modes and habitudes of thought and expression and circumstances as will gain for it from them a HEARING. You are to speak in other tongues – go and preach it to them in such a way as they will look at it and listen to it! Oh! in that lesson we read what beautiful scope and freedom from all set forms and formula there was. What freedom for the gushing freshness, enthusiasm, and love of those new converts. What scope for the different manifestations of the same spirit. Everything was not cut and dried. Everything was not pre-arranged. It was left to the operation of the spirit, and the argument that this has been abused is no argument against it, for then you might argue against every privilege. Here is abundant evidence that these new converts, each one had the opportunity to witness for Jesus, opportunity and scope to give forth the gushing utterance of his soul, and tell other people how he got saved, or the experience the Holy Ghost had wrought in him. And look at the result! 'If those that are unlearned, or unbelievers come in they are convinced of all, judged of all; and thus the secrets of their hearts are made manifest, and *falling down on their faces*, they will worship God, and report that God is in you of a truth.' What unkind things have been said of The Salvation Army because people have fallen on their faces under the convicting power of the Spirit at our meetings, but you see this is Apostolic!

Document VIII.9

Thomas Champness on Pioneer Evangelism, 1886

Thomas Champness (1832–1905) was a former missionary to West Africa who was probably the most venturesome evangelistic strategist in late Victorian Wesleyanism. In 1883 he launched a new popular weekly, *Joyful News*, and with the profits began to finance lay evangelists who would carry the gospel into fresh rural areas hitherto untouched by Methodism. The enterprise, as a passage here avows, was partly a response to the example of the Salvation Army. The colourful character 'Mo' Welsby, described here, was later to publish his autobiography, *From Coal-Pit to Joyful News Mission* (London, n.d.). There is discussion of Champness and his mission in J. Holmes, *Religious Revivals in Britain and Ireland, 1859–1905*, Dublin, 2000.

The extract is taken from Champness's address to the Wesleyan Home Missionary Committee on 'Village Methodism' in May 1886, published in Eliza M. Champness, *The Life-Story of Thomas Champness*, London, 1907, pp. 230–33.

I believe the task God has given me is to increase soon, and very largely, the number of hard-working agents on Methodist ground, and wherever it is possible to find a man fit for evangelistic work, to employ him, not as a minister, to administer Sacraments, not to meet classes, but to bring men to Christ. What is the reason why so many of our good men have gone into the Salvation Army? Some of the best men General Booth has, we ought to have had.

It is very plain to be seen that, if the villages are to be evangelized by us, we must largely increase the number of evangelists. We cannot increase the number of ministers. If we do, we shall not be able to pay our way; but, if the work is to be done, we must have pioneers, who will labour in the outlying villages according to their talents, and according to the circumstances of the place they visit. ...

... [W]e began, in August last, and I have now fifteen men, and some of them are very good men indeed. They are not parasites; they are men who can earn a living anywhere. If a man cannot get his living at his trade, whether he be a ploughman, a blacksmith, or a schoolmaster, it is no use his coming to me. I had a letter from one of that sort to-day, and if the gentleman is in this meeting, he may note what I say, and save me the expense of a postage-stamp. Do you think the Lord Jesus would have called Peter, James, and John to be fishers of men if they had not been good fishermen, and known how to catch fish? Not He! He knew better than that. And every one of my men is a real good man for the work. Of course they vary in many ways; they are not all alike. I have one man who is a very fine fellow; he has an impediment in his speech, but the Lord has wonderfully blessed him, and he is a fluent speaker, does not stammer in public, but preaches so that men and women are converted under the word. Then I have another who was a collier; was converted at Farnworth about five years ago. They call him 'Owd Mo' – he has been called that ever since he was a little child, because he was so knowing. He was a well-known character in all those parts – a dog-runner, a fighting, swearing, drinking, gambling man; but good Mr Crompton of Farnworth, and his helpers, led him to Jesus, persuaded him to go with them to chapel, and after a time of seeking, 'Mo' found the Saviour, and became a happy Christian. From his helping in evangelistic work now and then, I made his acquaintance, and we became interested in him. He used to work in the pit, and of course his life was in continual jeopardy; and though he was a very useful man in Christian work, he had to earn his living at winning coal. I had been wishing I could see my way, when one day my wife said to me, 'I cannot get Moses out of my mind. Supposing he was to get killed in the pit, we should never forgive ourselves that we hadn't employed him!' So I said we would try it, and took him; and I tell you, he can get hold of the rough Lancashire men as none of the rest can – you see he speaks their dialect, talks to them in their native Doric (oh, how I love it, and how I love to talk in it when I can find folk wise enough to understand it!). I tell Moses that when he can speak the English language I shall send him out of Lancashire. But he is doing good work, is a man of faith and prayer, and God is with him. ...

Document VIII.10

William White on Quaker Adult Schools, 1895

William White (1820–1900) was a convert to the Society of Friends from Wesleyanism, but brought his Methodist passion for souls with him. A bachelor bookseller and printer living in Birmingham, he took the initiative in making the Quaker First Day [Sunday] School there target adults. His example was widely followed, Mission Meetings with unQuakerly hymns and prepared addresses were established in the schools and their adherents soon outstripped Quaker membership. This paper by the patriarchal White wrestled with the problem of how to relate these largely working-class people to the largely middle-class meetings of the Society of Friends. See E. Isichei, *Victorian Quakers*, Oxford, 1970, chap. 9.

The extract is taken from White's paper on 'The Relations between Adult Schools and Mission Meetings and the Organisation of the Society of Friends' in *Report of the Proceedings of Members of the Society of Friends, held by direction of the Yearly Meeting in Manchester...1895*, 2nd edn, London, 1896, pp. 97–9.

The possibilities of reaching the masses may be said to have very much grown out of the work of our First-day Schools, commenced on a broader and more comprehensive basis, especially as regards Adult Schools, half a century ago. The teaching of reading and writing brought many of our members in friendly contact and sympathy with many men and women of the humbler classes, who were not slow in recognizing the useful services thus rendered to them. The addition in all these Schools of Bible-reading and teaching, formed, however, the closer bond between teacher and taught, helping, too, the spiritual life of the teacher, and leading many a scholar to a saving knowledge of the Truth as it is in Jesus. This loving service was not rendered in any mere proselyting spirit, and yet it was seen that some of our more thoughtful scholars were drawn nearer to Friends. Coming at first out of curiosity to our meetings, as the spiritual appetite grew, they settled down with us, and everywhere, of late years, our membership has been chiefly recruited from this class. ...

The inquiry naturally arises at this point, whether the Society as a body really desires a closer relationship with these institutions, and if it has elasticity enough, faith enough, self-sacrifice enough to enlarge its borders?

In the Schools men have heard some teachings as to peace, truthfulness and righteousness, as of more importance than mere doctrine and ritual. Christ and His office as the Great High Priest have been kept in view, and a loving and Christian brotherhood formed with lasting friendships and self-sacrificing service for each other; in short, in the best sense of the word, the School has become a Church to hundreds and thousands.

There was, however, something lacking; as religious convictions deepened the desire increased for a more definite mode of worship, in which for an hour on First-days wives and children might join with the scholars. Hence the establishment of those called Mission Meetings, commonly held in the evening; the name in most cases being a misnomer, as these gatherings are so much made up of those who have found good already in the School, and are thus only taking a step forward in the spiritual life.

These meetings ought therefore themselves to prove a valuable stepping-stone into full membership with the Society of Friends, and this might perhaps have been oftener the case if our members had had more faith in our principles and usages. In many instances the practices of other religious bodies have been needlessly imitated. The use of musical instruments, and frequent and untimely singing, too largely depended upon, as a means of attraction rather than a means of worship and thanksgiving. Indeed, it is no small matter for surprise that so many among us who have been trained above all things to reverence in worship, and in speaking of the things of God, should be able to bear with the irreverence and inanity of some of the singing practised in our mission meetings and elsewhere. The bustle and talking sometimes going on during these exercises is anything but conducive to that reverent waiting spirit, so needful for all who would profit in a meeting for Divine worship or for Scripture teaching. I have been thus emphatic on the subject of singing, not to discourage by any means its right use, and not from casual observation in one or two localities only, but from a very wide experience, extending over a long period of years.

Other hindrances to the fuller relationship of the School and the mission meeting with our own meetings may sometimes arise from the warmth of greeting and the home-feeling in the surroundings of the former, and the colder and apparently more constrained atmosphere of the latter. It is certain that in some of our meetings no arrangements seem to be made for the welcome of the strangers into our midst. There is no prayer-book, hymn-book, or Bible to be offered to our visitors as an outward and visible sign of such welcome, and the new-comer looks round on the assembled company sitting in silence, and wondering when something is going to be done. Help might sometimes be given to such by the kindly shake of the hand of the next sitter, to be repeated at the conclusion of meeting, and then by the offer of a suitable tract or book the stranger may feel that he is not regarded as an interloper, but that his presence is welcomed and his best interests cared for.

Overseas Mission

Document VIII.11

The Missionary Society Report, 1803

The modern missionary movement inaugurated by the foundation of the Baptist Missionary Society in 1792 gave rise three years later to the interdenominational Missionary Society. It was subsequently to become the London Missionary Society with largely Congregational support. The annual report of the directors for 1803 reveals their sense of being part of a cosmic plan for the conversion of the world. Following the Treaty of Amiens in 1802, there was opportunity to circulate the Bible, carrying a preface by David Bogue (see III.12), in France. The society also learned some of the vicissitudes of its first mission, the one in Tahiti. See R. Lovett, *The History of the London Missionary Society, 1795–1895*, 2 vols, London, 1899.

The extract is taken from *Four Sermons Preached in London at the Ninth General Meeting of the Missionary Society...*, London, 1803, pp. 1–9.

The communication of those occurrences which relate either to the introduction or revival of the gospel-dispensation among the nations of the earth, is a circumstance which strongly excites the attention, and engages the feelings of those who have a suitable concern for the honour of their Saviour. Whilst, as members of civil society, they are actuated by those benevolent principles which embrace with ardour the interests of the human race, their minds are engaged with others in the consideration of those momentous operations of Divine Providence, which are producing such important effects in the world: yet it is the connection of these with the spiritual dominion of Christ among men, and their influence in relation to that subject, which most strongly fixes their regards and interests their hearts.

Not only is this the evangelical medium through which the great arrangements of the Governor of the universe will be contemplated, by such as consider the triumphant reign of Christ over the nations to be the leading principle by which they are regulated, and the great result in which they will terminate; but these arrangements themselves will especially be regarded by those to whom the direction of Missionary institutions is committed, as containing those signals and intimations of the divine pleasure, respecting their plans and proceedings, which demand their particular attention.

When, therefore, those impediments are removed by the providence of God, which for ages have obstructed the progress of the gospel; when facilities are afforded for the circulation of the holy Scriptures, and the pure administration of its institutions, in countries where they have long been interdicted by the severest penalties, this state of things contains a providential voice, which instructs us in our duty, and invites us to improve it. On these grounds the Directors have proceeded, in their measures relating to the introduction of the unadulterated religion of Christ, into those nations on the Continent, which, for a series of ages, were so much under the controul of the Papacy, and more recently so overwhelmed with the principles of infidelity, as to be inaccessible to the exertions of Christians for this great purpose. As this is the most distinguishing measure of the Directors since the last Anniversary, they will introduce their Report with this subject.

For two preceding years, the Society has manifested the commendable desire of endeavouring to be instrumental in building, on the ruins of the Papacy, the divine edifice of pure Christianity; and as the most powerful means for that purpose, within their reach, was the circulation of the holy Scriptures, they determined to consecrate a part of their funds to this object. Reflecting also on the awful effects produced by the prevalence of infidelity, they judged it might be of great use to connect with the Scriptures, a vindication of their divine authority. This important service has been atchieved [sic] in the most satisfactory manner, by the superior talents of one of their highly respected members. ...

The Directors now proceed to give an account of the Missions already established, beginning, as usual, with that to Otaheite; which, as it engaged the first attention of the Society, has ever since been the subject of their particular care and solicitude. The arrival of the Royal Admiral, Captain Wilson, in July last, brought the intelligence, that the nine Missionaries, sent out by that vessel, had reached their destination in good health, and were cordially welcomed, both by their brethren and the heathen. It appeared that the outward tranquillity of the former had been preserved; and although they had not at that time acquired a sufficient acquaintance with the language to enable them to preach publicly to the natives, yet they were able to converse with them occasionally; and in this way scattered among them the precious seed of the gospel. The internal state of the Mission continued also to manifest, in a high degree, their devotedness to God, and their affectionate and peaceful conduct towards each other. They gave an intimation, that a general meeting of the chiefs was expected shortly to take place, when the question of peace or war would be decided; as it appeared that a spirit of disaffection had long prevailed in several of the Society Islands, which had caused much commotion, and threatened more. In their letter, dated July 8, 1802, very lately received, and which has been published for the information of the religious public in the Evangelical Magazine for the month of May, we are informed of a civil war having actually broken out in Otaheite, which had brought the brethren into a situation of great peril; from which they were delivered by the gracious and seasonable protection of God, through the means of the arrival of the Norfolk, Captain House, and the Venus, Captain Bishop; by whose assistance Pomarre was enabled to obtain very important advantages over the insurgents, after having previously been twice defeated by them, and brought nearly under the necessity of abandoning the island. ...

Altho' the Society acknowledge, with gratitude, the powerful and seasonable interposition of the providence of God in behalf of his servants, and with great confidence, in his continued goodness, commit these faithful brethren daily to his protection, – yet they anxiously wait the next information, in the hope that it will bring them the welcome account of the complete restoration of tranquillity, of their personal safety, and their useful labours among the heathen. In the mean time, it becomes us to acquiesce in this afflictive dispensation, which is the more painful to us, as it occurred at a season wherein our prospects were beginning to brighten, many difficulties had been surmounted, and the gospel-trumpet had been sounded in almost every district of the island. It is, however, the prerogative of God to determine the duration and degree of trial which shall exercise his people; and it is not unusual, in his wise and holy dispensations, that great spiritual success and prosperity succeed, and actually spring out of a series of preceding disaster and affliction.

Document VIII.12

Robert Hall on the British and Foreign Bible Society, 1810

The upsurge of missionary endeavour at the end of the eighteenth century bore fruit in the formation of numerous societies with evangelistic aims and objects. Among these was the British and Foreign Bible Society, formed in London in 1804 as a completely interdenominational society to distribute the scriptures without note or comment at home and overseas (see G. Browne, *The History of the British and Foreign Bible Society*, London, 1959). To encourage interest and support, local auxiliaries were formed throughout the country. This extract comes from an address given by Robert Hall (see I.1) at the inaugural meeting of the Leicester auxiliary in February 1810, and is taken from *The Works of Robert Hall, A.M.*, ed. O. Gregory, vol. 4, London, 1839, pp. 329–31.

We feel peculiar satisfaction in announcing to the public the formation of an Auxiliary Bible Society at Leicester, the object of which is, to co-operate with the Parent Society in London, in giving as extensive a circulation as possible to the Holy Scriptures. Notwithstanding the diversity of sentiment which unhappily prevails among christians, we may fairly presume on the concurrence of all parties and denominations in promoting a design so disinterested as that of diffusing the light of revelation. In the prosecution of this design, our party is the world; the only distinction we contemplate, is between the disciples of revelation, and the unhappy victims of superstition and idolatry; and as we propose to circulate the Bible without notes or comments, truth only can be a gainer by this measure. To those who confine their views to this country, the want of Bibles may not appear very urgent; but, without insisting on the many thousands even *here* who are destitute of them; it is certain, that in pagan, mahometan, and popish countries, they are extremely rare, and their number totally inadequate, not merely to supply the immense population in those parts, but even the increasing demand which a variety of circumstances have combined to produce. To supply this demand, to whatever extent it may be carried, is the aim of the society in London with which this is designed to co-operate. Their ambition, as far as it may please God to smile upon their efforts, is, by imparting the Holy Scriptures, to open the fountain of revelation to all nations. ...

In whatever light we consider the British and Foreign Bible Society, it appears to us replete with utility. Its formation will, we trust, constitute a new aera in the history of religion, which may be styled the aera of unanimity. It affords a rallying point for the piety of the age, an unsuspicious medium of communication between the good of all parties and nations, a centre of union and cooperation in the advancement of a common cause, which cannot fail to allay the heats, and smooth the asperities of discordant sentiment. By giving the most effectual aid to means already set on foot for the conversion of pagan nations, it also promises to accelerate the period when truth shall become victorious in the earth. When the pure light of revelation once shines amid the darkness of polytheism, we may venture to hope that the latter will be gradually expelled, that the contrast of truth and error, of sacred mysteries and preposterous fictions, they respectively display, will be deeply and extensively felt.

Document VIII.13

Ridley Herschell on the Jews, 1841

Ridley Haim Herschell (1807–64) came from a Polish rabbinical family, attended the University of Berlin, adopted Christianity through reading the New Testament, was baptised by the Bishop of London in 1830 and settled down as the minister of a London interdenominational chapel in 1838. He was a prime mover in the foundation of the Society for the Propagation of the Gospel among the Jews in 1842. His enduring love for the Jews and their ancient faith, Pauline in its intensity, is apparent from this passage from a work of the year before. See C. Binfield, 'Jews in Evangelical Dissent: the British Society, the Herschell connection and the pre-millenarian thread', in M. Wilks, ed., *Prophecy and Eschatology*, Studies in Church History Subsidia 10, Oxford, 1994, pp. 225–70.

The extract is taken from R. H. Herschell, *A Brief Sketch of the Present State and Future Expectations of the Jews*, London, 1841, pp. 124–8.

I have often felt hurt, at the way in which really pious persons have received information of the lives and writings of holy and spiritual Jews. Some have seemed to think such things hardly credible; while others have hinted that it is dangerous to speak of them, lest persons should imagine that Christianity is unnecessary; or rather, that Christ is not needed as the way of salvation. My dear Christian friends, I beseech you to consider that this is not exalting Christ; it is only degrading Christianity, by holding it up as a mere system of doctrines. Did Christ come to establish a religion altogether different from, and opposed to, that which God himself established at the beginning; or did He come to perfect that which had been formerly commenced? Was Judaism an ancient and foolish superstition He came to overturn; or was it a schoolmaster to lead men to Himself? If you admit that it was established by God, and that it was available for salvation, before Christ appeared, why deny that it may still be so to those who have never heard of any other way, and who seek God with a sincere and honest heart? I do not speak of those who wilfully refuse an offered Saviour, – who, hating the light, because their deeds are evil, reject it, and will not come unto it, – but of those who cannot believe in Him of whom they have never heard; of those who are as ignorant of Jesus, as the humblest peasant in this country is of Mahomet. I do not wish to enter into the details of this question; it is one that has been forced upon, not sought by me. I seek not to enquire whether there be many or few that shall be saved in this way, any more than I seek to enter into the kindred question of the salvability of some of the heathen, who have not heard either of a God or Saviour. I have only stated facts; and I do not feel answerable for the consequences to be deduced from these facts; I know that the God of Israel is a just God, hating iniquity; but I know that He is not a hard master, reaping where He has not sown, and gathering where he has not strawed.

But while I say these things, let it not for a moment be supposed that I am not sensible of the immense, the infinite difference there is, between knowing Christ Jesus our Lord, and being ignorant of Him; between the view of pardon held out in the ordinances of the law, and the full assurance of the pardoning mercy of God, sealed in the blood of His dear Son. I know well that the 'blood of bulls and of goats could not take away sin;' neither could they 'make him that did the service perfect as pertaining to the conscience;' it is only when we see the dismission of sin, as a barrier between us and God, through the one offering of Christ, that we can have our hearts 'sprinkled from an evil conscience,' that all doubts of God's forgiving love are taken away, and that we have thus 'boldness to enter into the holiest of all, by the new and living way' which our Saviour hath opened up for us. It is through Him alone we receive the full assurance of 'peace on earth, and goodwill towards men;' it is through Him alone that we see a reconciled God, beseeching sinful men to be reconciled to Him. O, my dear Christian friends, do not think that I am still clinging to what is commonly termed Judaism; or that I do not long earnestly that all my brethren may behold Jesus of Nazareth to be their Redeemer. Do not suppose that I am not acquainted with what a burdened conscience is, because of sin: I can joyfully say, 'Blessed be God who has opened my eyes to behold His great love in Christ Jesus,' O it is glorious and blessed to have that perfect love which casteth out fear. I know that we cannot without Christ have that liberty of soul, whereby we can cry, 'Abba, Father.' I know that we may serve God as servants, under the law; which is very much the state of those of my pious brethren to whom I have alluded; indeed all their illustrations of the relationship between man and God, are those of a master and a servant; but to be heirs of God and joint heirs with Christ, to be called the sons of God, we must behold God manifested in the flesh.

Document VIII.14

The Juvenile Missionary Magazine, 1844

In the proliferation of missionary literature during the nineteenth century, the magazines designed for children, with their stories and pictures of faraway places, held a prominent place. *The Juvenile Missionary Magazine*, begun in 1844, successfully promoted interest among the young in the work of the London Missionary Society. The 'missionary ship' mentioned in the editor's introductory address was the *John Williams*, named after the celebrated missionary murdered in the New Hebrides five years before, which many children had helped to buy.

The extract is taken from *The Juvenile Missionary Magazine*, June 1844, pp. 3–5.

TO THE YOUTHFUL FRIENDS OF CHRISTIAN MISSIONS THROUGHOUT THE EMPIRE, ESPECIALLY TO THOSE CONNECTED WITH THE LONDON MISSIONARY SOCIETY.

Beloved Young Friends,

It is your privilege to live in a period of great interest. These are wonderful times; they are the most wonderful of any that have happened since Jesus Christ was on the earth. 'Many prophets and kings have desired to see them.' Perhaps the years that are yet to come may prove more wonderful still. Of this, however, we cannot be quite certain, though it seems to be very probable. If you are spared to live twenty or thirty years longer, you will, very probably, see many things respecting the state of the world and the spread of the Gospel, that will make you 'tremble and rejoice.' Many countries that are now without the Gospel may by that time possess it, and become as much changed as Tahiti and Rarotonga have been. Perhaps thousands of the very people in India and China, who *now* worship only idols, may by that time cease to worship them altogether, and pray only to the True and Living God. Multitudes who have not yet even heard the name of Jesus the Saviour may be brought to know and love Him, as so many do in this favoured land of ours. In places where there is not a single school for children, we may hear of *many schools* well attended and very flourishing. Some that do *nothing* now to send abroad the Gospel may become very zealous in that delightful service. Some of *you* will perhaps be Missionaries yourselves, and *see* the very things about which you now only hear and read. And we may hope too that multitudes of the Jews, who do not at present believe that Jesus is the True Saviour, may lose their unbelief, and love Him as the 'Hope of Israel,' and become zealous Missionaries in His service, just as Paul was after the grace of God changed his heart.

Now this New Magazine is made on purpose to keep telling you of what is being done in the world to spread the Gospel. – No doubt you wish to hear respecting Missionary Societies, and Bible Societies, and Tract Societies, and Schools, and the Missionary Ship, and the Heathen and Children abroad, and as to what *you* can do to promote *their* happiness and *their* salvation. The solemn fact which we should all keep before our minds is, that *there are yet above* 600,000,000 *of souls in the world not converted to Jesus Christ.* If *we* are His disciples, we must do *all* we can towards their conversion.

Document VIII.15

Missionary Policy in India, 1858

In the wake of the Indian Mutiny, the London Missionary Society held a special meeting in the Exeter Hall under the chairmanship of Lord Shaftesbury on the future extension of its work in British India. It was the general Evangelical view that the military outbreak had been a judgement on previous neglect of the subcontinent and there were calls for a more ' Christian' public policy. William Baxter, a Dundee businessman and a United Presbyterian who represented Montrose in parliament (see DNB), shared the general Dissenting conviction that the state should have nothing to do with religion. Here he tries to reconcile this 'Voluntaryism' with the imperative to advance the gospel. Baxter's participation is a reminder of the close relations between Dissenters north and south of the border. See B. Stanley, 'Christian Responses to the Indian Mutiny of 1857', in W. J. Sheils, ed., *The Church and War*, Studies in Church History 20, Oxford, 1983, pp. 277–89.

The extract is taken from *The Evangelical Magazine and Missionary Chronicle*, March 1858, pp. 173–4.

Mr. Baxter, M.P., said: My Lord, I have to move the following resolution: –

> 'That, although this Meeting, in common with the friends of Christian Missions, would most seriously deprecate the employment of authority or patronage on the part of the British Government in India to induce its native subjects to embrace the Christian faith, it nevertheless most urgently appeals to the Government to withdraw its countenance from every form of idolatry, to withhold its sanction from the monstrous social evils connected with caste, while it secures to all classes, whether Christian, heathen, or Mohammedan, entire religious freedom, so far as is compatible with civil rights and public order.'

There are many reasons which should induce one who is jealous of his country's honour and of the honour of that religion to which his country owes all its greatness, to come forward on an occasion of this kind, to advocate the strengthening and extension of Christian missions at various stations in the Indian field which God has given to us. One inducement is the culpable neglect of times that are past. If I mistake not, my Lord, 200 years elapsed from the date of our first settlement in Hindostan before a single British Christian went thither to proclaim the Gospel of the grace of God. And even of late years, have we, I ask, made exertions at all commensurate with the magnitude of the responsibility imposed upon us by an overruling Providence? India has been given to England, as I believe, only in trust for the noblest of all purposes, and England has sent to India only some 400 missionaries to keep burning amid two hundred millions of idolaters the lamp of life. And not only have we sent but few missionaries to labour among the heathen, but, as a nation we have actually been ashamed of our faith; discountenancing the reading of the Bible; refusing to allow native converts to enter the ranks of the army; making grants to heathen temples; giving way to the most absurd prejudices and the most insolent demands of the Brahmins, and allowing the native courts to be degraded by the institutions of caste. By assuming an attitude, my Lord, of what I must call time-serving indifference, we have nearly lost the fairest gem in the diadem of our Sovereign, and the most glorious field of evangelisation that has ever been opened up to the Christian Church. Are these not sufficient inducements to us to put forth greater efforts? Then I will submit another. My Lord, I have a strong impression that, whether we put an end to the double Government or not; whether we restore, or reorganise, or altogether dispense with the native army; whether we leave the patronage in the hands of the East India Company, or give it to the proposed Indian Council; I have, I say, a strong impression that, whatever political or civil expedients may be adopted, India will, ere long, be severed from England, unless the tie that now binds the two countries together be cemented and strengthened by the bond of a common Christianity. I think what has recently taken place in that country is sufficient to convince every thoughtful man that the tenure of our power there must ever be frail and uncertain so long as Brahminism and Mohammedanism exercise a predominant influence over the public mind. When I see the Bible supplanting the Koran and Shastra, then I shall begin to think that we have some guarantee for the security of our empire in India; whereas, without that, there will always be a volcano ready to burst forth, and to pour a flood by insurrection and massacre over the land. It is something for us to know and feel that the people and the press of this country are nearly unanimous in their condemnation of our past faults and our temporizing policy, and in their conviction that the time has now arrived for emancipating India. But I have a firm belief that whatever our people, and whatever our press, may think, our rulers do not sufficiently realise and comprehend the exact position of affairs. Like your Lordship, I dread very much the hold which the ancient traditional policy has upon the minds of our statesmen. I fear lest the notions of the last century should be found powerful enough to present under an erroneous aspect the exigencies of the present century; in fact, I fear that if we do not make a bold and determined stand at this moment for what one might well be astonished that we should have to proclaim in the 19th century, namely, the great principle of religious freedom, the blood which has been spilt will have been shed in vain. And when we are about to send out more missionaries to India, let us see that they go forth under new and brighter auspices. Let us no longer have a Government that supports idolatry, and under which converts are exposed to civil disabilities. Let us have a bold and Christian policy; let a policy like that which has been announced by Sir John Lawrence in the Punjaub, he proclaimed in such a manner that if cannot be misunderstood, to all the natives, from Cashmere to Cape Comorin. ... We want no Government patronage; we expressly repudiate State endowment; we seek no Government support. We do not wish our religion to be extended by the military or the civil power in India; we simply ask that the Government should give up countenancing idolatry, that is should remove all the impediments which stand in the way of Christianity, that it should give us 'a fair field and no favour;' and, when we have once got that, I believe it will turn out that there is zeal enough among the British churches to enable us to go in and possess the land.

Document VIII.16

George Richardson Urging Quaker Missionary Work, 1859

George Richardson (1773–1862; see DNB) was an immensely travelled minister in the Society of Friends. In 1859 he wrote a letter, subsequently published, urging Quakers to join in the missionary movement of the age. It contributed significantly to the foundation of the Friends' Foreign Mission Association.

The extract is taken from *Journal of the Gospel Labours of George Richardson*, London, 1864, pp. 347–9.

My mind has long been burdened with an apprehension that our Religious Society is not coming forward as it ought to do, but has shrunk from its true line of service, in reference to an endeavour to promote the extension of the kingdom of our Lord Jesus Christ in heathen lands. In early times Friends went boldly forth, proclaiming the glad tidings of the Gospel of peace, but chiefly amongst professing Christians. ... But it is remarkable that a large proportion of the labours of Friends has been in the direction of serious inquirers amongst Christian professors, and very little among the heathen. ...

Within the last fifty years, the attention of the Christian community, in England and North America especially, has been powerfully and usefully awakened to a just sense of the sunk and degraded condition of the various heathen nations. ...

But have Friends, as a Religious Society, regarded these proceedings with that warm Christian interest which they might seem justly to claim from them? Have they not rather been looking askance at them? But why should it be so?

The Society of Friends have been occupying a useful position, both in England and America. They laboured long and hard for the benefit of the heathen population of Western Africa, that they might be relieved from the cruelties and miseries inflicted on them by the slave-trade, and successfully also for the abolition of West India slavery. They watched over the emancipated and their offspring, that the proper education of their children should not be wholly neglected. They also extended care, in this latter respect, to some on the coast of Western Africa. ...

Now we may observe that a large proportion of the labour of Friends has been directed to the improvement of the temporal condition of those who were the objects of solicitude; but surely we should go further, and seek to promote their spiritual and eternal welfare, and the diffusion of Gospel light amongst them. Christ's religion requires us to labour to turn the minds of men from darkness unto light, from the power of Satan unto God. 'Ye are the light of the world,' said our Lord; 'but men do not light a candle and put it under a bed, or under a bushel.' Are we coming up to the spirit of this injunction with regard to heathen nations? I feel the more solicitous on this subject from a persuasion that there is a door open into a field of good promise, in which Friends may usefully encourage and help those who are already engaged in the good work, and that they may do this without the abandonment of any of our main, characteristic principles or testimonies, which, we believe, were given us to bear before the world, by Him through whose Divine power we were gathered as a people.

Document VIII.17

Frederick Trestrail on Native Churches, 1860

Frederick Trestrail (1803–90) acted as Home Secretary of the Baptist Missionary Society from 1849 to 1870 and in 1880 was to be president of the Baptist Union. In 1860 he addressed the Liverpool Missionary Conference on 'Native Churches', enunciating the broad policy of his society on church planting. The speech is notable for its apostolic conception of the missionary, its pragmatic refusal to impose any particular polity on churches overseas and its belief in the encouragement of indigenous initiative. Self-help was for export. For Trestrail, see E. Trestrail, ed., *The Short Story of a Long Life*, London, 1892; and DEB. On missionary policy and ecclesiology, see B. Stanley, 'The Reshaping of Christian Tradition: Western Denominational Identity in a Non-Western Context', in R. N. Swanson, ed., *Unity and Diversity in the Church*, Studies in Church History 32, Oxford, 1996, pp. 399–421.

The document, quoted in full, is taken from *Conference on Missions held in 1860 at Liverpool*, London, 1860, pp. 279–83.

Some time ago, at the monthly meeting of the Secretaries of various Missionary Societies whose offices are in London, this question was proposed for discussion: 'What form of government is best for mission churches in heathen lands; Episcopalian, Presbyterian, or Congregational?'

In one thing all present were agreed, that Christian Churches in heathen lands should not be established by law; and they were pretty well agreed in another, that while the ecclesiastical form and polity of a Christian Church is of great importance, it is not so vital as the right of a Church to choose its own officers, and maintain its own discipline.

1. There is no exact *definition* of a Christian Church in the Scriptures. The one which is found in the Articles of the Church of England – 'a congregation of faithful men' – would doubtless be accepted by all here. But the Scriptures speak much about the Church of Christ, and of the individual churches which compose that grand whole. From these sayings we get the notion that a Christian Church is a congregation of believers in the Lord Jesus Christ, meeting in one place for the worship of Almighty God, and the observance of Christ's institutions; having its appointed officers of elders or pastors, and deacons.

2. Be it observed that these views are not incompatible with the adoption of any order of Church government existing among evangelical Christians; since the Scriptures, while laying down general laws, permit the exercise of a large discretion in working out details.

3. At the outset of the Christian dispensation, the first churches were evidently called into existence by the labours of the Apostles and Evangelists. They were *sent* forth to preach the gospel. Missionaries in these days are sent out to heathen lands to do precisely the same work. Very seldom are they natives of the lands in which they labour. Divest the Apostles of miraculous power, and the gift of inspiration, though perhaps not all even of them were thus endowed; and you have the *modern missionary*, a true successor of the Apostles.

4. When, by his labours in any given district, he gathers souls to Christ, it is for him to organise them; to teach them their duty to one another and to the world; to aid them to select those best suited to be office-bearers; and then to interfere as little as possible in their affairs. To visit them as often as practicable; to advise, to strengthen, correct; to set in order what may need rectification; appear to be some of the duties arising out of the relation which the missionary sustains to native churches.

5. Hence it follows that the missionary should not become a *pastor*. His position, habits of thought, education, his belonging, in many parts of the world, to the dominant race, place him too far apart from the mass of the people for him to exercise the pastoral function with success. His sphere is larger. He is, *or ought to be*, emphatically an overseer of others; his taking a pastorate should only be allowed on the ground of urgent necessity; and his continuance in that office should terminate, when the necessity which led to his taking it has ceased.

6. The pastorate is a grand difficulty in regard to Churches in heathen lands. Suitable men for this office are not abundant. This, indeed, can hardly be expected. Christianity and its institutions are new things, brought from afar, and by another race. But with great deference it is submitted that the want of men suitable for the pastoral office, which is so generally felt, may have arisen – first, from the too dependent state in which the Churches have been kept on the missionary, who has, therefore, almost inevitably united in himself the functions of every kind of office; and, secondly, from the want of sufficient confidence in the natives. The best use, with all the defects attached to it, is not made of the material at hand. Self-reliance, independence in thought and action, and administrative ability, cannot be developed and flourish in the face of this depressing influence. Perhaps we have not only expected too much from native Christians, but have too rigidly insisted on things being done according to the home type and formula.

7. The *status* of these pastors should be a real official one in the churches, and only fraternally, as far as practicable, with the Society at home. If pecuniary support be needed, it should be given, only as a supplement to what the church over which he presides gives; and that on the principle of the strong helping the weak. All sorts of difficulties arise when they are appointed and paid by a Society.

This system widely prevails. Wherever practicable it should be abolished; or vigorous, active, self-supporting churches can never grow and multiply.

8. The *titles* given to these pastors should harmonise with the customs, habits of thought and expression, regarding official persons, prevailing in their own country. To transfer to these regions our titles, and the style of behaviour and address connected with them, seems worse than absurd.

9. As far as possible, they should be kept from the English tongue. Much has been said about the advantages of English literature, especially biblical. In some few cases, confined mostly to Training-Schools, and perhaps rarely permitted even there, it may be of use. Besides the obvious remark that this literature is filled with strange idioms and illustrations – and its whole structure and style, are very different from the languages of the East, especially – it is not to be denied that the main body of native preachers are not prepared either to appreciate or use it. Let them have English, and they get English notions on all questions, and by so much are unfitted for their proper work. These observations are intended mainly to apply to India, and to those countries in which English influence largely prevails. Where our own language is in somewhat general use, a different course of observation would have to be taken; but this is a case which need hardly occupy the attention of this Conference.

10. The relation of native Churches to Home Societies naturally comes within the scope of these remarks. The policy of keeping churches that can support their own pastors associated with the home institution is most questionable. Societies don't like to diminish the number of churches in connexion with them, and churches deprecate a separation, as involving a loss of *status* and powerful influence. But if now and then the fact could be announced, that a few churches had taken all their responsibilities on themselves, some work would seem to have been done and completed; and in all future time such churches would supply a stronger motive for fresh exertion, and be a standing proof of success.

11. The practice of forming what are called Christian villages is open to serious objections. It withdraws native Christians from the mass of the people. it seems to be the design of our Divine Master that his people should be like leaven. *I pray not that thou shouldest take them out of the world, but keep them from the evil that is in it*, are words which bear this construction. This practice moreover creates a new caste, and raises up a secluded community, instead of a body of people who, in the world, fight the great battle of the Christian life, and exhibit the virtues of the Christian character.

12. Until the state of things here sketched out be brought to pass, native churches cannot be of much use in diffusing the gospel in the regions round about them. Injury has been inflicted on the great cause of Evangelisation, by the currency given to the idea that Missionary Societies are to enlighten the whole world. The men whom they send out are too often regarded as almost the sole instruments to accomplish this work. As a consequence, native churches in heathen lands have not been fully taught their duty in this respect; and it needs enforcement as much now as ever. Missionaries cannot be had in sufficient numbers to work out present plans; and if they could, the resources of the Societies do

not advance with sufficient rapidity. It may be questioned whether some of these Societies are not now too large, and getting unwieldy, and expanding beyond the natural limits of such institutions.

13. The state of dependency in which native churches mostly are, greatly affects the question of the property belonging to Missionary Societies. Chapels, school-houses, and residences, have been called *'the property of the Society.'* Hence the cumbrous machinery of trustees at home and abroad. In British colonies great difficulty has arisen from this practice; for when churches become independent, an extraneous control over property still exists, and it is difficult to get rid of it. In India matters are more simple; but even there the practice obtains. Doubtless there would be much risk in the contrary practice; but the risk would be amply compensated by the earlier freedom and stronger growth of native churches.

Moreover, as naturally connected with this subject, it may be questioned whether the style of building sometimes adopted is not too expensive and costly. As much as possible, edifices connected with missionary institutions should be conformed to the native idea of size, cost, and general structure. Large sums have been uselessly expended in many parts of the mission field, for want of a due regard to these principles.

14. The poverty of the people is unquestionably a great obstacle to the freedom and growth here contended for; severe persecution, and heavy loss of property, are often the consequence of a profession of Christianity. It is natural that the weak and feeble should fly for shelter to the missionary. But the history of our mission in Jamaica, with all the drawbacks that exist, shows that his presence and protection are not essential to the stability and growth of native churches. Recent intelligence in regard to the Sandwich Islands, and the present state of the native churches in Madagascar, afford still more striking examples; while over nearly all the isles of the Pacific, and the West Indies, the great majority of the churches is fast becoming self-supporting.

15. It would seem, therefore, but fair to conclude, that in the same measure as the principles here advocated are enforced and acted upon, the results so intensely longed for will be realised.

16. Finally, the question may be asked: Are these native churches as often remembered in prayer before God as they ought to be? The members composing them have been called out of a deplorable state of sin and degradation. They are exposed to terrible temptations. They are often tried and weak. Let us affectionately remember them at a throne of grace. It will quicken our own sympathies to do so. It will give greater breadth and power to our own views and feelings. Intercessory prayer has ever been honoured by God. May more earnest mutual prayer for each other ascend together from churches in heathendom and Christendom, to the throne of the heavenly grace.

Document VIII.18

Wesleyan Missionary Controversy, 1890

In 1889 the policy of the Wesleyan Methodist Missionary Society in India was arraigned in *The Methodist Times* (see III.17) as mistakenly reliant on higher education in English as a means of bringing about the conversion of the Hindu elite. The missionaries took particular exception to the charge that they were adopting an extravagant lifestyle that separated them from the Indian masses. Although major questions of evangelistic strategy were raised, a commission of enquiry, a section of whose proceedings are reproduced below, entirely exonerated the missionaries. W. C. Kendall, as he explains, was a former missionary; Dr Henry Lunn, an assistant to Hugh Price Hughes, was the original critic in the newspaper; H. Arthur Smith was a barrister; and the president of Conference was C. H. Kelly. See N. C. Sargant, 'The Missionary Controversy, 1889–1900', *London Quarterly and Holborn Review*, 190 (1965), pp. 304–10.

The extract is taken from *The Missionary Controversy*, London, 1890, pp. 205–7.

Rev. W. C. Kendall was next introduced to the Committee. He stated that he had spent five and a half years in the Calcutta district. He went out to Raniganj in 1877, married in 1880, and returned home in 1883.

In answer to questions put to him by Dr. Lunn, he said that when he was in the Calcutta district only one or two of the missionaries there preached in the vernacular. He spent more than two years in Calcutta with the English-speaking congregation; he was then appointed to Raniganj, where there were two stations for railway employees about 16 miles apart, and where he had a native girls' school and a catechist under his superintendency. At the end of five years he was set free entirely for native work; but at the end of three or four months he had to come home. The number of missionaries in the district was six or seven. He understood what was meant by what was called the native style of living, as compared with the English and the Eurasian style of living. Many of the Eurasians were better off than many of the English, and they lived quite as well. But there was a lower class of Eurasians, some of whom lived very nearly in the native style. As to attendance at Levées, he went once or twice to see the Viceroy. He believed the Chairman of the District used to go every year, as a matter of preference and duty. There were well-to-do Europeans in Calcutta who were not admitted into what was called 'society'; – tradespeople, for instance; but missionaries did not rank socially with tradespeople. Missionaries in India did not, because they could not, stand in exactly the same relation to their household servants as ministers did in England; they belonged to a different race, and *caste* in India was not the same in kind as *caste* in this country. That was a thing which English people did not understand. He did not think that he had ever dined *formally* with any native catechist. The catechist would sometimes come in and sit at his table, but not to take a formal meal. As to the cost of living, he thought that upon the whole it was cheaper in India than in England – at any rate he had found it easier to live within his income there than here. ...

Dr. LUNN: Do you remember the carriage that was driven by the Rev. ——? – (Answer: Yes.) Do you think there is any analogy between that and what in this country is known as a 'circuit gig'? – (Answer: There is more analogy in the purpose of it than in the carriage itself. – (Laughter.) You used to drive Burmah ponies – what was their cost as compared with the cost of country ponies? – (Answer: Two or three times that of country ponies.) In reply to other questions, Mr. Kendall said: With regard to the cost of living, Mrs. Kendall and himself spent in the bazaar about 1s. 8d. per day. But outside that they had to purchase other things, such as milk, tea, jams, bread, etc. The total amount spent in food of all kinds would be about £40 or £45 a year. On looking into his account-book he found that for two years the cost of this item was £40. His servants cost him about £30 a year. As to clothing, he and all the missionaries wore white drill. The cost was very light. He thought that £15 a year would cover everything for himself and wife. Something had been said about clothes being spoiled by insects, but he did not think that he had lost much in that way. With respect to charities, he did not think that any missionary in his district gave away so much as £20 a year, unless it was Mr. ——, who was liberally disposed. For a missionary to live in a large house surrounded by broad grounds was, in his opinion, detrimental to his influence – that style of living did not tend to promote a feeling of unity between natives and Europeans. At the same time he thought that there was a radical difference between the two races that would not be completely bridged over by the circumstance of a missionary going from a large house to a smaller one. He thought it would be possible to cultivate closer relations between the missionaries and the natives.

In reply to Mr. Fowler, Mr. Kendall said that the difference he had spoken of was a racial difference; a difference also such as naturally existed between a subject people and a ruling people; between the East and the West.

Mr. SMITH: I understand Mr. Kendall to estimate the cost of living to be £40 for food, £30 for servants, £15 for clothing, £10 for charities; thus making a total of £105. May I ask whether he managed to save the rest of his income?

Mr. KENDALL: No, I did not. There are many other ways in which money goes; but I am certain as to the matter of the bazaar account.

Mr. SMITH: It comes to this; we have, first of all, an estimate of total expenditure, presented to us under certain items; and then we are told that are there other sources of expenditure outside these items.

Mr. KENDALL: There are many expenses that come in, in addition to those connected with food, clothing, servants, and charities, such as postage, travelling from place to place, amusements, presents, the purchase of a piano, etc.

The PRESIDENT: I presume that you see the bearing of that statement. Now supposing that your estimate of total expenditure as given us a few minutes ago had gone forth to the world, the great unthinking part of the world would have concluded that missionaries were very much overpaid, because these other items had not been included. It is therefore a very unfair thing to suppose that the mere bazaar and other kindred expenses cover all that is involved in a missionary's outlay.

Mr. KENDALL: But surely nobody would suppose that that is what I meant?

The PRESIDENT: I am afraid that many would and that is precisely where the danger lies. What you have just stated qualifies very greatly your previous statements, and is a very important utterance.

PART IX

PUBLIC ISSUES

Introduction

Nonconformity played a part in the public affairs of the nineteenth century that no student of the period can ignore. Its traditional championship of civil and religious liberty gradually evolved into Gladstonian Liberalism. There were, of course, exceptions to this general pattern, but they were less marked than is often supposed. In particular, the Wesleyans are commonly thought to have been Tories in the early nineteenth century though Liberals at its end. Extracts in this part illustrate that, although strong Tory views were to be found (IX.12), there was a Liberal strain in mainstream Methodism throughout the century (IX.21, 22). The extent to which the Methodist laity were sympathetic to Liberalism is obscured by the 'no politics' rule that excluded the discussion of public affairs from connexional life. There were also those who repudiated all political concern as a diversion from the true work of the Christian. An extreme case is given here (IX.24). It was widely supposed, furthermore, that politics was not for women (IX.25 – by a woman). Yet public life was usually thought an honourable field of activity. It could even be considered an obligatory one (IX.27), though that view was subsequently modified (IX.28).

The main traditional reason for the Liberal proclivities of Nonconformity was the discrimination it suffered. Only progressive politicians would be likely to do away with the practical grievances under which Dissenters chafed. Unitarians were compelled to use a Trinitarian liturgy at their wedding services, which could take place only in the Church of England (IX.1); Quakers objected to paying tithes for the support of clergymen whose role they thought anti-Christian (IX.2); and Baptists could not obtain legal recognition of births in their families because the only official record was in the registers of infant baptisms of the established church (IX.3). All Dissenters were liable to local rates for the upkeep of the fabric of parish churches (IX.7); none of them could use their own forms of service for burials in parish churches (IX.9); their sons were unable to enter the University of Oxford or graduate at Cambridge (IX.10). A particular flashpoint was education. During the nineteenth century the state edged towards the creation of a national system of elementary schools. In 1843 in particular a Conservative government tried to give control of new schools to the established church, but was met by a cry of outrage from Nonconformity (IX.5, 23). A large number of Dissenters concluded that the only solution was the disestablishment of the Church of England (IX.11).

Several issues were the preoccupation of a single denomination. Unitarians pressed successfully for legislation to secure their legal possession of meeting houses originally occupied by their orthodox ancestors (IX.6). The highly unusual Catholic Apostolic Church expressed views closer to those of the Oxford Movement than to opinion in the rest of Nonconformity (IX.4). And the Society of

Friends maintained its traditional disapproval of warfare (IX.17). The Quakers were also in the van of international campaigns for religious liberty (IX.8) and an end to the slave trade (IX.13). Slavery was one of the questions that became the concern of Evangelicals in all denominations, rousing them to fierce denunciation of the institution in 1832 (IX.14). Other subjects taken up with Evangelical fervour included sabbath observance (IX.16) and temperance (IX.15, 19). Rural exploitation of working people induced some of their number, especially from Primitive Methodism, to band together in resistance, using the language of the gospel to express their aspirations (IX.26). The problems of an urban industrial society also stirred the conscience of many (IX.18), generating the social gospel illustrated elsewhere (II.39) and leading a few to socialist conclusions (IX.20).

The literature on Nonconformist attitudes and activities in public affairs is substantial. The extensive chapters 3 and 4 of M. R. Watts's *The Dissenters*, vol. 2, Oxford, 1995, cover the subject down to 1869. W. R. Ward, *Religion and Society in England, 1790–1850*, London, 1972, deals with the tensions, especially in Methodism, caused by its challenge to the established church, and D. Hempton, *Methodism and Politics in British Society, 1750–1850*, London, 1984, concentrates on Methodism itself. The campaign for the removal of grievances and for disestablishment is discussed by D. M. Thompson, 'The Liberation Society, 1844–1868', in P. Hollis, ed., *Pressure from Without in Early Victorian England*, London, 1974; W. H. Mackintosh, *Disestablishment and Liberation: The Movement for the Separation of the Anglican Church from State Control*, London, 1972; and J. P. Ellens, *Religious Routes to Gladstonian Liberalism: The Church Rate Conflict in England and Wales, 1832–1868*, University Park, Pennsylvania, 1994. G. I. T. Machin's two volumes, *Politics and the Churches in Great Britain, 1832 to 1868*, Oxford, 1977, and *Politics and the Churches in Great Britain, 1869 to 1921*, Oxford, 1987, cover the ground thoroughly. T. Larsen, *Friends of Religious Equality: Nonconformist Politics in Mid-Victorian England*, Woodbridge, Suffolk, 1999, deals authoritatively with the period 1847–67. The later years of the century are discussed in D. W. Bebbington, *The Nonconformist Conscience: Chapel and Politics, 1870–1914*, London, 1982; and J. Munson, *The Nonconformists: In Search of a Lost Culture*, London, 1991, chap. 8.

Ecclesiastical Issues

Document IX.1

Unitarian Marriage Grievance, 1817

Between 1815 and the 1830s Dissenters often made a protest to the vicar at being forced to marry in a parish church, a requirement under Hardwicke's Marriage Act of 1753. Unitarians were, for theological reasons, the most vocal, and became the main protagonists for civil registration (which came in 1837) amongst Dissenters. See M. J. Calle, 'The Making of the Civil Registration Act 1836', *Journal of Ecclesiastical History*, 25 (1974), pp. 39–59.

William Lawrence and Jane Clark were members of the Free Thinking Christian Church when they married at St Mildred's, Bread Street, in the City of London, on 21 September 1817. Their protest was published in the Unitarian journal, *The Monthly Repository*, 1817, pp. 570–71. William Lawrence (1789–1855), a building contractor, subsequently became a Unitarian, and in 1849 Sheriff of London. Three of his sons became knights and MPs, and two were also Lord Mayors of London; virtually the whole family were assertive Unitarians. A grandson was Lord Pethick-Lawrence, the suffragist and last Secretary of State for India. See A. Ruston, 'Unitarian Forsytes', *Transactions of the Unitarian Historical Society*, 20 (1992), pp. 126–36. The Mr Smith mentioned in the letter was William Smith (1756–1835), MP for Norwich, a Unitarian and the best known Dissenting MP of his day. The name of the clergyman, left out of the text in the magazine, has been reinserted.

Sir, – Your readers have doubtless heard with pleasure the intentions of Mr. Smith, of Norwich, that noble advocate of the rights of conscience, particularly as affecting Unitarians, to bring the marriage question under the consideration of the legislature. It is really a disgrace to our age and country that men, whatever may be their sentiments and religious opinions, should be called upon to bow at the altar of *any* mode of faith, established or otherwise. Marriage, in fact, is and should be *a civil contract*: it is a private agreement between the parties which is to be publicly sanctioned indeed by law, and which should be so sanctioned by the *magistrate*, not the *priest*. The sole object of the legislature in passing the marriage act, that act by which every one who marries is now compelled to visit the established church, the sole object I say, Sir, then in view was *publicity*, and to *prevent illicit and unadvised unions*; this should ever be kept in view in all our endeavours to obtain redress; till we obtain it, however, we must submit; though something may still be done in the way of bearing our testimony against this grievous imposition on the conscience of all Dissenters, Unitarians in particular. As a proof of this I enclose you the copy of the protest which, in a parish church in the city of London, was publicly delivered by two parties at the time of their marriage last Sunday; every effort was besides made by them to resist the performance of the ceremony, particularly by their refusing to kneel while the idolatrous and unchristian rite was performing.

Your giving publicity to their protest just at this particular moment, may essentially serve the cause of freedom of conscience in this instance. Requesting, therefore, your speedy attention to it. – I am, Sir,

London, Sept. 26th, 1817.   W.L.

To Mr. Crowther, commonly called the Rev. John Crowther, MA. The undersigned being Protestant Dissenters, present to you the following protest against the marriage ceremony, to which, according to the law of the land, they are compelled to subscribe. They disclaim all intention of acting disrespectfully to the legislature, or to its civil officer before whom they stand; they lament that they are placed in a situation so unnatural, as that even forbearance to what they consider established error, would be a formal recantation of opinions which they received on conviction, and which they will only renounce on similar grounds; against the marriage ceremony, then, they can but most solemnly *protest*.

Because it makes marriage a religious, instead of a civil act.

Because, as Christians and Protestant Dissenters, it is impossible we can allow of the interference of any human institution with matters which concern our faith and conscience.

Because, as knowing nothing of a priesthood in Christianity, the submission to a ceremony performed by a person 'in holy orders, or pretended holy orders,' is painful and humiliating to our feelings.

Because, as servants of Jesus, we worship the one living and true God, his God and our God, his Father and our Father, and disbelieve and abominate the doctrine of the Trinity, in whose name the marriage ceremony is performed.

(Signed),

WM. LAWRENCE,
JANE CLARK,

Members of the Church of God, meeting at the Crescent, Jewin Street, known by the name of 'Free Thinking Christians.'

Sept. 21, 1817

Document IX.2

Quaker Opposition to Tithes, 1832

Tithe was the payment, notionally a tenth of the value of agricultural produce, due to the Anglican incumbent of a parish. Quakers had traditionally refused to pay, as this statement from their Yearly Meeting explains, because of their fundamental religious principles. There was a risk, which the statement tries to combat, that their attitude could appear to be – or actually be – a political gesture. Refusal of tithe was associated with unwillingness to pay rates for the upkeep of parish churches. See E. Isichei, *Victorian Quakers*, Oxford, 1970, pp. 147–50.

The extract is taken from *A Brief Statement of the Reasons why the Religious Society of Friends object to the Payment of Tithes...*, n.p., 1832, pp. 1–3.

We have uniformly entertained the belief, on the authority of Holy Scripture, that when, in the fulness of time, according to the allwise purposes of God, our blessed Lord and Saviour appeared personally upon earth, He introduced a dispensation pure and spiritual in its character. He taught by his own holy example and divine precepts that the ministry of the Gospel is to be without pecuniary remuneration. As the gift is free, the exercise of it is to be free also: the office is to be filled by those only who are called of God by the power of the Holy Spirit; who, in their preaching, as well as in their circumspect lives and conversation, are giving proof of this call. The forced maintenance of the ministers of Religion is in our view, a violation of those great privileges which God, in his wisdom and goodness, bestowed upon the human race, when He sent his Son to redeem the world, and, by the power of the Holy Spirit, to lead and guide mankind into all truth.

Our blessed Lord put an end to that priesthood, and to all those ceremonial usages connected therewith, which were before divinely ordained under the Law of Moses. The present system of Tithes was not in any way instituted by Him, our Holy Head, and High Priest, the great Christian Law-giver. It had no existence in the purest and earliest ages of his Church, but was gradually introduced, as superstition and apostacy spread over professing Christendom, and was subsequently enforced by legal authority. And it further appears to us, that in thus enforcing as due 'to God and Holy Church,' a tithe upon the produce of the earth, and upon the increase of the herds of the field, an attempt was made to uphold and perpetuate a Divine institution, appointed only for a time, but which was abrogated by the coming in the flesh of the Lord Jesus Christ. The vesting of power by the laws of the land in the king, assisted by his council, whereby articles of belief have been framed for the adoption of his subjects, and under which the support of the teachers of these articles is enforced, is, in our judgment, a procedure at variance with the whole scope and design of the Gospel; and as it violates the rights of private judgment, so it interferes with that responsibility by which man is bound to his Creator.

In accordance with what has been already stated, we of course conscientiously object also to all demands made upon us in lieu of tithes. ... And we further consider, that to be compelled to unite in the support of buildings, where a mode a religious worship is observed in which we cannot conscientiously unite, and in paying for appurtenances attached to that mode of worship from which we alike dissent, is subversive of that freedom which the Gospel of Christ has conferred upon all.

Deeply impressed with a conviction of the truth of these considerations, we have felt it to be a religious duty to refuse active compliance with all Ecclesiastical demands which have been made upon us; or to be parties to any compromise whereby the payment of them is to be insured. That this conduct has not arisen from a contumacious spirit, we trust the general character of our proceedings will amply testify. And we trust also that it will be readily admitted, that political considerations have not governed our religious Society, but that we have been actuated by a sincere desire to maintain, in the sight of God and man, a conscientious testimony to the freedom and spirituality of the Gospel of Christ, and thus to promote the enlargement of his kingdom upon earth. ...

[W]e feel that there are laws still unrepealed, by which we might, in the support of these our Christian principles, be subjected to great loss of property, and to imprisonment for life; and in the execution of the law, as it now exists, much pecuniary suffering, and many oppressive proceedings, may be and are inflicted. And here we would observe, that each individual amongst us wholly sustains the amount of the distraint made upon him, and of all the consequent expenses: we have no fund out of which a reimbursement takes place, as some have erroneously supposed.

Seeing that we have as a Religious Society invariably made, on this subject, an open confession before men, we earnestly desire that we may all steadfastly adhere to the original grounds of our testimony; not allow ourselves to be led away by any feelings of a party spirit, or suffer any motives of an inferior character to take the place of those which are purely Christian. May none amongst us shrink from the faithful and upright support of our Christian belief, but through the Grace of our Lord Jesus Christ, seek after that meek disposition, in which our Society has uniformly thought it right to maintain this testimony, and which we desire may ever characterize us as a body. It becomes us all, when thus conscientiously refusing a compliance with the law of the land, to do it in that peaceable spirit of which our Lord has left us so blessed an example.

Document IX.3

Baptist Disabilities, 1833

In the wake of the Reform Act of 1832, Dissenters began to flex their political muscles. They demanded the redress of the civil disabilities from which they still suffered, notwithstanding the repeal, in 1828, of the Test and Corporation Acts that had branded them as second-class citizens. See D. Bebbington, 'The Dissenting Political Upsurge of 1833–34', in D. Bebbington and T. Larsen, eds, *Modern Christianity and Cultural Aspirations*, London, 2003. There were grievances common to all Nonconformists, but, as this petition to parliament from the Board of Baptist Ministers explains, the Baptists suffered from particularly invidious forms of discrimination. See D. W. Bebbington, 'The Baptist Conscience in the Nineteenth Century', *Baptist Quarterly*, 34 (1991), pp. 13–24, esp. p. 15.

The extract is taken from *The Baptist Magazine*, May 1833, p. 229.

Public Issues

COPY OF A PETITION TO PARLIAMENT FROM THE BOARD OF BAPTIST MINISTERS.

Fen Court, April 18, 1833.

The Rev. Dr. Newman, in the Chair.

Resolved unanimously, That the Petition now read be adopted, signed, and inserted in the next number of the Baptist magazine, and that the brethren, in the Churches throughout the country, be requested to present similar Petitions to both Houses of Parliament as soon as possible.

To the Honourable, &c. &c.

The Humble Petition of the undersigned

   Members of the Board of Baptist Ministers, assembling at Fen Court, London,

     Showeth,

That your Petitioners belong to the Denomination of Protestant Dissenters called Baptists, who conscientiously disapprove of infant Baptism, and which includes upwards of one thousand congregations in the united empire.

That they are the successors of devout and learned men, whose religious integrity and regard to the rights of conscience exposed them to many persecutions, which they meekly, but firmly endured; and that your Petitioners, embued with their principles and sentiments, cannot allow themselves to escape from social inconvenience and detriment, by abandoning the ordinances of their Lord, or by adopting those which he has not authorized; but that they are not inferior to any of their fellow-countrymen in their reverence for civil authority – their regard to constitutional freedom – their loyal and patriotic attachment to the sovereign and their country – nor in benevolent desires to promote the social happiness of the people, and the welfare of the state.

That, from their religious opinions, the Baptist Denomination are exposed to *peculiar evils*; since, even if public parochial registries were accessible to other Dissenters, they could not include the names of their children, since they are registries, not of births, but only of baptisms, which, as administered to infants, they cannot perform: and that, as by the regulations of the Established Church, the Clergy may withhold the burial service of the Church from persons who die unbaptized; the children of members of the Baptist Denomination may be excluded from interment in parochial church-yards, while any records of interment in private or congregational cemeteries, as well as any registers of births which they separately keep, are not received in evidence in the same manner with the parochial registers of the Established Church.

That, besides these especial grievances to which they are exposed, your petitioners and their Denomination, are subject, like the general body of Dissenters in England and Wales: – 1. To the annoyance of occasional demands of church and poor rates for places of religious worship which they rear at their own cost, and maintain without assistance from the state; – 2. To a conformity, for the solemnization of marriage, to the rites of that Established Church, from which they religiously and conscientiously dissent; – 3. To heavy charges on the renewal of the trust-deeds by which their chapels and meeting-houses are held; – 4. To the payment of church-rates, and mortuary and ecclesiastical dues, which they think the revenues of the Established Church alone should sustain, as well as to other local and general inconveniences, which they are compelled to endure.

And that, relying on the enlightened and liberal spirit of the government and legislature, and of many dignitaries and members of the Established Church, they hope for that redress which has long been needed, and so long withheld.

And your Petitioners, therefore, humbly pray your Honourable House candidly and carefully to consider their various complaints, and by the means your wisdom shall devise, to grant them early and ample relief. J. B. Shenston, Sec.

P. S. At the same time the Board renewed their Petitions to Parliament on the subject of Colonial Slavery, and hope that their brethren, in town and country, will not lose sight of *that object*, till the negroes' wrongs be full redressed.

Document IX.4

Catholic Apostolic Church Great Testimony, 1837

As in most other respects, the Catholic Apostolic Church (see IV.18) differed drastically from the rest of Nonconformity in its political attitudes. The great enemy of the faith, as J. H. Newman agreed, was liberalism – that is, the rejection of legitimate authority, whether in church or state, from below. Rulers received the commission to govern from above. Nations were to render corporate homage to the Almighty through established churches; the leaders of the churches of Christendom were to advise the civil power. These views were expounded in a document drawn up by the apostles of the church for transmission, in the first place, to the pope, and then to the European rulers. It was known as the Great or Catholic Testimony. See P. E. Shaw, *The Catholic Apostolic Church sometimes called Irvingite*, Morningside Heights, New York, 1946, pp. 92–4.

The extract, clauses 2, 72, and 93, is taken from the full text of the Great Testimony in E. Miller, *The History and Doctrines of Irvingism*, London, 1878, vol. 2, pp. 348, 410–11, 427–8.

§2. As the Church is the aggregate of the baptized, so Christendom is the community of those nations which, as national bodies, profess the faith of Christ's Church;– whose heads and rulers not only recognise that all their power is derived from God, but, being consecrated over their people in God's Church, have acknowledged themselves to be occupiers of their thrones from Christ, until He come and take the kingdom;– have, by receiving anointing from the hands of God's priests, also acknowledged that their ability to rule is by the grace of His Spirit, ministered unto them by His Church;– and, in that same holy act, have submitted, or professed to submit, themselves and their people to be instructed in God's ways from the lips of those, from whose hands they have received their anointing. Christendom is one corporate body;– separated from all other nations of the earth, in that they recognise the doctrines of Jesus Christ as the basis of their international law, and of their dealings one with another;– distinguishable from all other nations, in that, by their legitimate organs, they have been brought as nations into covenant with God, and thus entitled to all the blessings, responsible for all the duties, and exposed to all the judgments, attendant on, and involved in, such covenant;– and yet, as nations, distinguishable one from another, each governed by their legitimate rulers, whose authority is neither diminished nor increased, but sanctified, by their profession of the true faith, and by the anointing which they have received at the hands of the ministers of God.

§72. The civil and ecclesiastical rulers have, therefore, each their proper functions.– The office of the priesthood is to teach both kings and people their several duties, and to be channels for imparting to all and each the grace and blessing, without which they are unfurnished for discharging the same. Those are no sound politics which are not Christian politics; and the priesthood are the ordained teachers of principles, for the guidance of both rulers and ruled. But their duty is strictly a spiritual duty. Their words are addressed to the faith and conscience; their authority is spiritual: and as citizens they must obey. The duty of kings and rulers is to govern their people by the statutes and ordinances of God, which, in faith of Him, not of man, they receive from the lips of the priests;– as chief among the sons, to be the most obedient unto the Church, from whose womb all the baptized are born unto God, and from whose breasts they are nourished;– and to guard and shield her from every danger with filial care. Over the persons of all in their dominions they are to rule in righteousness; but dominion or jurisdiction in faith – authority internal or external in the Church – belongs not to them, and is an usurpation of the office of Christ, the true Melchisedec, who alone is both King of kings, and Priest of the most High God.

§93. The next step in this fearful descent is the principle, that the State shall consider and act towards all forms of religion on a footing of perfect equality, and either bestow on each sect a similar bounty in proportion to its numbers, or leave each to maintain its own Ministers. In either of these cases the State ceases to recognise the Church of God, but in the latter it ceases also to recognise either God or religion. In the former case the State ceases to be Christian, in any proper sense of the word; in the latter it proclaims a principle of Atheism, so far as the Government is concerned. God's truth is one; His salvation is one; and in the one Church of God alone are they to be found. They proceed *from* God to man, and must be received by man, or rejected at his eternal peril;– they never can be matter of human choice, nor be decided by mere human majorities: and therefore to place all classes of religionists on an equality, is a virtual denial of revelation on the part of the State; it is a betrayal of their trust wherever the Ministers of religion, who claim to be the Church of God, concur in it; it is a denial of their baptism in the people, to seek it. If the people are not kept conscious of their obligation, if the clergy do not assert for Christ their place, as His appointed channels of all God's blessings, and His Priests to bring the people up to God, they will but degrade themselves to a level with those self-elected pastors, those voluntary bishops, the birth of modern times, who neither have nor profess to have any Divine constitution or authority for their office; they will act either as if the pastoral work, and all ecclesiastical functions, required no gift or authority of God, no delegation from Christ; or as if their own standing were questionable, as the inheritors of that gift, authority, and delegation.

Document IX.5

Edward Baines on Education Policy, 1843

In 1843 the Conservative government introduced a Factory Bill containing educational clauses that would have given the Church of England a monopoly of the state-assisted schooling it proposed. Nonconformity, including the normally apolitical Wesleyans, was roused to strenuous protest that led to the dropping of the clauses. In the heat of the controversy many of the Nonconformists for the first time applied voluntaryism, the principle that the state should have nothing to do with religion, to schools, which, it was assumed, would teach the Christian faith. Edward Baines (see DNB) took the lead in this development, but here contents himself with objecting to the proposal on the broadest grounds. Baines was the proprietor of *The Leeds Mercury*, and, though Whiggish in his politics, the spokesman *par excellence* for provincial Dissent. See Derek Fraser, 'Edward Baines', in P. Hollis, ed., *Pressure from Without in Early Victorian England*, London, 1974, pp. 183–209, and C. Binfield, *So Down to Prayers*, London, 1977, chap. 4.

The extract is from Baines's *Letter to the Right Honourable Lord Wharncliffe, Chairman of the Committee of Council on Education, on Sir James Graham's Bill for establishing Exclusive Church Schools, built and supported out of the Poor's Rates, and discouraging British Schools and Sunday Schools*, London, 1843, pp. 6–8.

Now, my Lord, it is evident that these provisions have been studiously and carefully planned, for the purpose of *impairing* and ultimately *destroying* all *other* Schools for the operative children in manufacturing districts, and *drawing the whole rising generation into these Church Schools*, there to be educated under the *exclusive and irresponsible control of the Clergy*.

Such is the view entertained of them by *all* the religious bodies not connected with the Establishment, as your Lordship may see by the proceedings of the meeting at Leeds on Thursday, and by the resolutions of various bodies of Dissenters in London.

To make this more clear to your Lordship, who are not likely so soon to perceive the whole bearing of these provisions on the Dissenting communities as they themselves are, permit me to offer a few additional remarks. I request your Lordship to observe –

THAT Dissenters are to be compelled to pay towards the support of Schools, where religious doctrines are taught of which they disapprove, – Schools closely bound to an Establishment from which the Dissenters conscientiously separate themselves, Schools put under the absolute (I may almost say the *sole*) control of the *Clergy*, – in which no Dissenter can possibly be employed either as Master or Assistant, – and in which the children of Dissenters are to receive no religious instruction, unless they consent to receive that of the Clergyman, who would of course do his utmost to proselytize them.

THAT not only are Dissenters to be obliged to pay for these Church Schools, but those who belong to the operative classes will be *compelled*, in the vast majority of instances, *to send their children there*, however opposed to their inclination. It will be *unlawful* for them to *educate their own children in the schools of their own community!!!* That not only must they pay for exclusive Church schools, and send their children to them, but they are themselves debarred from receiving one farthing from the Poor's Rates towards their own schools. Nor is this all, but they must pay towards Schools which are manifestly designed and calculated to impoverish and undermine the Day Schools and Sunday Schools of their several religious communities. ...

THAT such being the natural and necessary effects of the Bill, it would be felt by every religious community, except the Church, to be an intolerable insult and injury; it would wound their consciences, exasperate their feelings, and stir up a religious strife which must either lead to the extermination of Dissent or the downfall of the Establishment.

Document IX.6

Dissenters' Chapels Act, 1844

Amongst the most dramatic events affecting Dissent in the early nineteenth century was one involving the old English Presbyterian chapels and trusts. Formed in the seventeenth and eighteenth centuries, these foundations had evolved gradually in their thinking so that by the early decades of the nineteenth century they had become Unitarian in theology. The passing of the Trinity Act (mentioned in the extract below) in 1813 was a watershed, and the increasing denominationalism in the following decades led to a series of legal cases. These sought to show that the Unitarians now in control of these foundations did not adhere to the theology of their founders, and so they should be removed as not fulfilling their trusteeship.

By the early 1840s the various court actions had gone against the Unitarian trustees, and they were about to be dispossessed of those chapels formed before 1813. In 1844 the government intervened with the Dissenters' Chapels Bill which would leave them in place. There was doubt it would pass, due mainly to fierce opposition from leading Independents and Baptists. However W. E. Gladstone's intervention on behalf of the Unitarians, on ethical rather than religious considerations, ensured its passage into law in July 1844. See four articles by A. Long, A. Ruston (2) and P. Tindall on the Dissenters' Chapels Act after 150 years, *Transactions of the Unitarian Historical Society*, 20 (1994), pp. 233–82 and F. Schulman, *'Blasphemous and Wicked': The Unitarian Struggle for Equality, 1813–1844*, Oxford, 1997.

The extract is taken from *A Collection of the Public General Statutes Passed in the Seventh and Eighth Years of the Reign of Her Majesty Queen Victoria*, London, 1844, pp. 421–3. The last section, not included here, put an end to any legal actions then before the courts.

An Act for the Regulation of Suits relating to Meeting Houses and other Property held for religious Purposes by Persons dissenting from the United Church of *England* and *Ireland*. 19th July 1844.

[W]hereas an Act was passed in the Fifty-third Year of the Reign of King *George* the Third, intituled *An Act to relieve Persons who impugn the Doctrine of the Holy Trinity from certain Penalties* ... And whereas prior to the passing of the said recited Acts respectively, as well as subsequently thereto, certain Meeting Houses for the Worship of God, and Sunday or Day Schools (not being Grammar Schools), and other charitable Foundations, were founded or used in *England* and *Wales* and *Ireland* respectively for Purposes beneficial to Persons dissenting from the Church of *England* and the Church of *Ireland* and the United Church of *England* and *Ireland* respectively, which were unlawful prior to the passing of those Acts respectively, but which by those Acts respectively were made no longer unlawful: Be it therefore enacted ... That with respect to the Meeting Houses, Schools, and other charitable Foundations so founded or used as aforesaid, and the Persons holding or enjoying the Benefit thereof respectively, such Acts, and all Deeds or Documents relating to such charitable Foundations, shall be construed as if the said Acts had been in force respectively at the respective Times of founding or using such Meeting Houses, Schools, and other charitable Foundations as aforesaid.

And be it enacted, That so far as no particular religious Doctrines or Opinions, or Mode of regulating Worship, shall on the Face of the Will, Deed, or other Instrument declaring the Trusts of any Meeting House for the Worship of God by Persons dissenting as aforesaid, either in express Terms, or by reference to some Book or other Document as containing such Doctrines or Opinions or Mode of regulating Worship, be required to be taught or observed or be forbidden to be taught or observed therein, the Usage for Twenty-five Years immediately preceding any Suit relating to such Meeting House of the Congregation frequenting the same shall be taken as conclusive Evidence that such religious Doctrines or Opinions or Mode of Worship as have for such Period been taught or observed in such Meeting House may properly be taught or observed in such Meeting House, and the Right or Title of the Congregation to hold such Meeting House, together with any Burial Ground, Sunday or Day School, or Minister's House attached thereto. ...

Document IX.7

Edward Miall on Church Rates, 1851

The campaign for the abolition of church rates, set locally for the upkeep of the fabric of the parish church whose doctrine, liturgy and establishment most Nonconformists rejected, took over thirty years from when it was first mooted in 1834 to their abolition as compulsory charges by Act of Parliament in 1868. Edward Miall (1809–81; see DNB) had suffered distraint on his goods for refusal to pay the rates. He was one the loudest supporters of the campaign, particularly in the columns of *The Nonconformist*, a weekly which he founded and edited from 1841. For the campaign, see J. P. Ellens, *Religious Routes to Gladstonian Liberalism*, University Park, Pennsylvannia, 1994.

This extract is from *The Nonconformist*, 3 December 1851, front page. The open letter is addressed to Daniel Wilson (1805–86), the Evangelical vicar of St Mary's, Islington.

Reverend Sir, – The law of the land, I believe, justifies you in regarding yourself as my spiritual pastor. Why it should do so, I attempt in vain to conjecture. I derive no benefit from your ministration, and I know not that I have ever been in the walls of the same building with you but once, when, as Chairman of a public meeting, you witnessed the perpetration, by two clergymen, of a gross outrage upon my person, without interference or protest.

This day, for the second time since I have resided in your parish, two silver spoons were taken from my house, by a rate-collector, acting under a legal warrant, for the payment of the sum of two shillings and threepence, charged to me on a 'rate for annuitants on chapel of ease, and interest on loan for building the new churches.' I will, therefore, make bold to offer you a few remarks, pertinent, as it seems to me, to the occasion.

I address myself to *you*, Reverend Sir, because I hold you to be a fitting representative of the congregations who assemble for Christian worship in the edifices thus compulsorily maintained; and I regard you as responsible for the act of flagrant injustice just done me, because I am convinced that were you and your subordinate clergy faithful to the obligations of your sacred office, in throwing the light of Christian principles upon a practice which the very genius of your religion condemns, and in inviting those of your parishioners who rejoice in your ministrations, and in those of your curates, to display the same honesty in regard to their religious, as to their worldly interests, the pillage of my property would have been rendered quite unnecessary, and gospel precepts would have been more strictly observed by those who are reported to cherish an ardent zeal for gospel doctrines.

You will probably absolve yourself from blame, in this matter, by attempting to throw it upon the law. Let me undeceive you – if, indeed, you are under any such delusion. The law is but an instrument. They who agree to put it in force are the responsible agents. The law, as such, possesses neither will nor power of action. It is a sword which cannot, in this instance, strike, until men are found sufficiently dead to the claims of Christianity to grasp and use it. The law has given you an unrighteous power, and you have not scrupled to resort to it. ... You are wicked to the full extent of your opportunity. Whether, if legally allowed to slay me, you would act up to your privilege, it is not for me to guess. This only I know, that being authorised by it to take from me that which is mine, you have done so, without the least regard to the eighth commandment of the Decalogue. And this you have done in the venerable name of Christianity!

I shall doubtless be reminded, Reverend Sir, that this is a debt for church building, incurred by the parishioners of St. Mary's, Islington, the interest on which common honesty binds them to pay. ... I repudiate the moral right of your congregations to render me liable for debts contracted for their comfort. Honesty, no doubt, prescribes the repayment of the loan. Decency points out that they who enjoy the benefits of it should take upon themselves the just responsibility. When *we*, Sir, the despised Nonconformists among your parishioners, erect places of worship, in which we may assemble to pay our homage to the common God and Father of us all, we feel ourselves bound, not only to make good our pecuniary obligations, but to do so without thrusting our hands into the pockets of our neighbours. We think that in acting thus we act in conformity with the mind of Christ. Do you wish, by seizing my silver spoons, to show your parishioners 'a more excellent way?'

Document IX.8

A Quaker Plea for Liberty of Conscience, 1856

The traditional testimony of Quakers was that the state had no right to intermeddle with spiritual matters. In the nineteenth century that stance turned into a staunch defence of rights of conscience at home and abroad. The Yearly Meeting issued this plea in 1856, directed to continental governments, and individual Quakers frequently carried messages to the crowned heads of Europe on behalf of the religious liberty of their subjects.

The extract is taken from *A Plea in Behalf of Liberty of Conscience*, London, 1856, pp. 3–7.

That conscience should be free, and that in matters of religious doctrine and worship man is accountable only to God, are truths which are plainly declared in the New Testament, and confirmed by the whole scope of the Gospel, and by the example of our Lord and his disciples. ...

How clear ... is the evidence ... that the kingdom of our Lord Jesus Christ is not of this world, and is not to be advanced by the sword; and that, in matters of faith, we are not to yield our convictions to political authority, nor to shape our conduct by the wisdom or decisions of the princes of this world; that we are even to suffer wrong and take it patiently; and that the blessing of Him whom we call Master and Lord rests not upon the persecutors, but upon those who are persecuted for righteousness' sake. Neither is there any authority whatever throughout the New Testament which justifies the Civil Government in inflicting temporal punishments on the professors of one particular creed, in respect only of their religious opinions, or in bestowing, on the like grounds, temporal emoluments on the professors of another. ...

We plead for no license to do wrong: we advocate no weak indulgence to the workings of unbridled imagination or passion: we plead for liberty of conscience toward God. To rule over the conscience, and to command the spiritual allegiance of his creatures, is his high and sacred prerogative. To prohibit by law the doing of that which conscience enjoins as a religious duty, and which in no wise interferes with the just requirements of civil order, is to assume a jurisdiction for which the Supreme Judge has given no warrant under the Gospel: whilst, to enforce the performance of services, under the plea of religion, upon those who believe such services to be uncalled for, or for them even positively sinful, must surely be highly offensive to a pure and holy God. In religion every act ought to be free: a forced worship is plainly a contradiction in terms under that dispensation under which, according to the declaration of our Lord himself, they that worship the Father 'must worship Him in spirit and in truth.' And in our apprehension every assembly which is held, with open doors, for the sole purpose of the public worship of God, ought to be free from all interruption or molestation, and is entitled to the protection of the civil power.

In that love which would embrace all who love our Lord Jesus Christ in sincerity, we cannot but mourn that there are any of our fellow Christians, of whatever denomination, who, though innocent of any crime and clear of all political movements and aims, are nevertheless still suffering for conscience sake, in different parts of Europe, simply because their religious faith differs from that of the State. In some instances they are members of Churches to which their ancestors have belonged for several successive generations; in others, they have been themselves brought, on conviction, to a change of religious profession, and to adopt views different from those of their education, but, as they believe, more in accordance with the revealed will of God. Our sympathy is awakened for many of these sincere-hearted believers in Christ, strangers to us and not connected with us in outward religious profession: we feel deeply for them, and for all who suffer persecution for the sake of Christ.

Document IX.9

Prosecution of Primitive Methodists for Singing at an Interment, 1861

Nonconformists enjoyed rights of burial in parish churchyards, but were compelled to observe the rites of the Church of England, which usually entailed payment to the clergyman. There were further annoyances, as this account of the burial of an infant by Primitive Methodists and its sequel illustrates. The legislation invoked against them had been designed to prevent anti-ritualist disturbances. The clerical Justices of the Peace at the original trial would have taken the part of the incumbent. The burials grievance was to be terminated in 1880, after which Dissenters were allowed to have their own forms of worship in parish graveyards. A similar episode from the 1870s is recounted in R. Fletcher, *The Akenham Burial Case*, London, 1974.

The extract is taken from *The Primitive Methodist Magazine*, February 1861, pp. 109–11.

A child died lately in the quiet parish of Horsey-next-the-sea, in the county of Norfolk. The dear babe who was not a year old, had not been baptized; and according to the rubric, a State clergyman cannot bury an unbaptized person, therefore, the little innocent must be consigned to the grave unceremoniously. This was to the parents very painful. In the parish we have a society of ten members. Joseph Fish, the leader, sympathised with the sorrowful mother of the child, and in great kindness, promised at her request, to accompany her to the grave, which he and several other members did. This aged man, of an eminently devout and christian character, walked in the funeral procession to the church gates where, on the road outside the churchyard, he and others knelt and offered an appropriate prayer, and then proceeded to bury the corpse, and the following lines were then sung at the grave:–

'Alas! how soon the body dies,
'Tis but an earthly clod;' &c.

The Rev Edward Pote Neale, vicar of Horsey, came into the churchyard in an agitated state of mind, and ordered the mourners to desist from singing, but no notice was then taken, nor a word of reply uttered. Then he said 'I will make an example of you, Fish.'

Joseph Fish and his friends quietly left the churchyard. But it must be observed that the singing was over the grave of an *unbaptized* child, and baptismal regeneration is the way to heaven, as taught by this minister, hence the child, according to his teaching, was in an unregenerate state at death; consequently he considered it outrageous, and *'indecent behaviour'* to sing over the grave. The Reverend gentleman probably thought that old Fish had no friends, and those poor Primitives could evoke no public feeling; so he obtained summonses to call to justice Joseph Fish and Ann Nockolds, and charged them with indecent behaviour in the churchyard, by singing a hymn over an unbaptized child.

The case was heard at Smallburgh Petty Sessions, on Tuesday, October 2nd, 1860. There was a full bench of magistrates. Sir Jacob Preston (chairman), Captain Cubitt; R. Rising Esq., Rev. E. Wilkins, and Rev. T. J. Blofeld. Several clergymen were present to witness the proceedings. Mr. Fisher (of London) appeared for the prosecution, and Mr. W. H. Tillett (Norwich) for the defence. The information was laid under an Act passed last session, 23rd and 24th Vict: Cap. 32. The Act was to meet the case of St. George's-in-the-East, and similar outrages. The case in question was essentially different. In Horsey churchyard there was no mob, no riot, no violence, no indecency, no personal disrespect. But the bench considered the rights of the vicar invaded, and after an hour's deliberation re-opened the court, and the chairman said, 'We consider an offence has been committed against the law by these parties in singing a hymn in the churchyard, and the fine we impose is merely nominal to show that it was an offence. We fine the defendants one shilling, and expenses thirteen shillings, in each case, or in default, three days imprisonment.' Mr. Tillett said 'he considered it his duty, under the 4th section of the Act, to appeal to the quarter sessions.' The room was again cleared for deliberation, and after a considerable interval, the bench announced that they required the parties to give sureties, themselves in £10, and two sureties each in £20 to prosecute the appeal. The sureties were then offered, and after a minute examination of the parties by the bench as to their worldly possessions, they were accepted, and the proceedings closed. During the interval, the press freely animadverted on the conduct of the minister, denouncing the prosecution as a monstrous perversion of a well intentioned Act of Parliament, the sole purpose of which according to its express terms, was to punish persons guilty of '*riotous, violent, or indecent behaviour.*'

The usual Michaelmas sessions were held on Wednesday, Oct. 17th, 1860, before Sir Willoughby Jones, Bart., and Edward Howes Esq., M.P. Mr Evans (instructed by Mr. Tillett) appeared for the appellants, and Mr. Bulwer (instructed by Messrs Kerrison and Preston) represented the respondent. Mr. Evans opened the case, and Mr. Bulwer in reply said, 'I am very happy to say that Mr. Neale has placed himself entirely and unreservedly in my hands, and acting upon the sentiment which he has himself expressed, I have great pleasure in saying that I think it my duty, with his entire concurrence to relieve the court from any further consideration of this matter, by consenting on the part of Mr. Neale to the quashing of the conviction.' Mr. Evans rose and said, 'My clients only desire to be vindicated from the charge on which they were convicted by the magistrates in petty sessions; and as my learned friend, acting I think most discreetly and properly, consents to the conviction being quashed, and has not raised the question of which I was prepared to fight the battle to day, I can only give my hearty concurrence in the course which has been taken.' The conviction was accordingly quashed. What were the feelings of the 'vexed and troubled vicar?' The Rev. Pote Neale's counsel read the conviction, and examined the Act of Parliament upon which the Smallburgh Justices had fined Fish and Nockolds, but counsellors, like other men, are in a fix sometimes, and the barrister hastily brought the business to an end. A fine piece of etiquette this to the Smallburgh Justices. We ask the rev. gentlemen, his advisers and friends, to take a retrospect of the whole affair from beginning to end, to ascertain what amount of comfort has been derived from the steps taken. Probably very little comfort, but possibly a good deal of instruction, at least we hope so. Joseph Fish, and the rest of the Primitives of Horsey are among his best friends after all, for they did not wish to further vex and trouble the already troubled minister, by charging him with the cost to which he had wantonly put them. It was rather a humbling time once in the vicar's life to have the tables turned upon him by a poor man. 'Now I have beaten you,' says pious old Joseph Fish, by his counsel, 'I will not triumph over you, I will not ask for costs!' In conclusion we say, thanks to the press, and those free-hearted public men, who step forward to defend the helpless poor when those in power treat them harshly. Persecutors of God-fearing people must now-a-days take heed lest in their folly they should step over the boundary of law and public opinion.

Document IX.10

Universities Tests Act, 1871

One of the key landmarks for Dissenters in the nineteenth century was the opening of Oxford, Cambridge and Durham Universities to those who dissented from the Church of England. It was now possible to take most degrees without a religious test. After 1871 Act the Dissenters felt that they had achieved parity in the field of higher education with the established church which had fought the opening up of the old universities for so long. The Universities Tests Act, which passed into law on 16 June 1871, is much cited but the actual text rarely quoted. For the background see W. R. Ward, *Victorian Oxford*, London, 1965.

This extract is taken from *The Congregational Year Book*, London, 1872, pp. 451–2.

From and after the passing of this Act, no person shall be required, upon taking, or to enable him to take, any degree (other than a degree in divinity) within the Universities of Oxford, Cambridge, and Durham, or any of them, or upon exercising, or to enable him to exercise, any of the rights and privileges which may heretofore have been or may hereafter be exercised, by graduates in the said universities, or any of them, or in any college subsisting at the time of the passing of this Act, in any of the said universities, or upon taking or holding, or to enable him to take or hold, any office in any of the said universities, or any such college as aforesaid, or upon teaching, or to enable him to teach within any of the said universities, or any such college as aforesaid, or upon opening, or to enable him to open, a private hall or hostel in any of the said universities, for the reception of students, to subscribe any article or formulary of faith, or to make any declaration, or take any oath respecting his religious belief or profession, or to conform to any religious observance, or to attend or abstain from attending any form of public worship, or to belong to any specified church, sect, or denomination; nor shall any person be compelled, in any of the said universities, or any such college as aforesaid, to attend the public worship of any church, sect, or denomination to which he does not belong: Provided that –

(1.) Nothing in this section shall render a layman, or a person not a member of the Church of England, eligible to any office, or capable of exercising any right or privilege in any of the said universities or colleges, which office, right, or privilege, under the authority of any Act of Parliament, or any statute or ordinance of such university or college, in force at the time of the passing of this Act, is restricted to persons in holy orders, or shall remove any obligation to enter into holy orders, which is by such authority attached to any office.

(2.) Nothing in this section shall open any office (not being an office mentioned in this section) to any person who is not a member of the Church of England, where such office is, at the passing of this Act, confined to members of the said Church by reason of any such degree as aforesaid being a qualification for holding that office.

Nothing in this Act shall interfere with or affect, any further or otherwise than is hereby expressly enacted, the system of religious instruction, worship, and discipline, which now is, or which may hereafter be lawfully established in the said universities respectively, or in the colleges thereof, or any of them, or the statutes and ordinances of the said universities and colleges respectively relating to such instruction, worship, and discipline.

Document IX.11

Case for Disestablishment, 1894

Disestablishment generally, and of the Church of England in particular, was a clarion call amongst many Dissenters during the middle decades of the century. It caused a great deal of heat on all sides, and the Liberation Society (founded in 1844 as the British Anti-State Church Association) did much to fuel the flames. However the issue had gone off the boil by the 1890s, enabling a more rational approach to be adopted, less based on extreme emotion, exemplified in this extract from *The Case for Disestablishment*, London, 1894, pp. 12–13. See W. H. Mackintosh, *Disestablishment and Liberation*, London, 1972, for a detailed account of the campaign.

Now that disestablishment has become a question of practical politics, it is inevitable that its political aspects should occupy the most prominent place in the public discussion of the subject. But as the movement against church establishments sprang from religious conviction, and is still largely, and in many cases almost exclusively, advocated on religious grounds, the religious argument against the Establishment system occupies the first place in this volume.

ARGUMENT FROM PRINCIPLE

The fundamental objection to Church establishments is one of principle, which underlies both the religious and political argument. ... The principle is that in matters of religion men are responsible to God alone, and that in founding or maintaining a Church establishment, the State steps beyond its proper province, and not only does violence to the rights of conscience, but invades the prerogative of God Himself.

It is not denied that in regard to the public exercise of their religious rights, by both individuals and communities, the State has a legitimate authority, and is bound to use it. It is bound, for example, so to frame its laws and exercise its authority as to secure to its subjects entire freedom of religious faith and worship; while carefully providing that the freedom so secured shall not be used by any to the detriment of the rights of others. But all that directly concerns religion itself lies between the individual conscience and God alone, and no secular authority is entitled to interfere. 'The whole jurisdiction of the magistrate,' says John Locke, 'relates only to civil concernments'; or as M. Guizot puts it, 'Temporal affairs are the State's domain – spiritual affairs do not belong to it. It has neither the mission nor the right to teach religion, or to cause religion to be taught in its name.' And the reason is obvious. The civil magistrate can have no proper authority in religion, because the only power which belongs to him is in its essence coercive, and coercion is inconsistent with the very nature of religion, and is really incapable of being exercised in its behalf.

Social Issues

Document IX.12

John Stephens on the Duties of the Poor, 1819

John Stephens (1772–1841; see DEB) was a Wesleyan preacher who totally endorsed the existing social order in the turbulent years following the Napoleonic Wars and went on to become president of the Wesleyan Conference in 1827. As superintendent minister at Manchester from 1818 to 1821 he enforced connexional discipline against political radicals according to the wishes of Jabez Bunting, the dominant figure in Wesleyan Methodism. This published sermon of 1819 refers to the recent events surrounding the Peterloo massacre and appeals to the loyalist teaching of John Wesley. It should be noted, however, that a balancing section on the paternalist duties of the rich to the poor follows.

The extract is taken from J. Stephens, *The Mutual Relations, Claims and Duties of the Rich and the Poor*, Manchester, 1819, pp. 36–8.

Let the Poor look up to the Rich as their natural and authorized Guardians, Benefactors, and Friends. I hope you poor people who now hear me, have not given heed to seducing spirits, and doctrines of devils: and I pray God you never may! Believe me, my poor brethren, your governors, your ministers, your masters, are your best, your only *real* friends. The infidel and seditious demagogues *could* do you no good if they *would*, for they have neither property nor influence; and they *would* not if they *could* for they are alike bankrupt in principle and character, as they are in property and influence; they mean only to use you as brands for the accomplishment of their own incendiary purposes: and should those purposes ever be accomplished, which God forbid, they will despise your memory and trample on your ashes. But your governors, your ministers, your masters, are not only possessed of power to do you good, but they have the inclination too, nay they have an interest in it; your interests and theirs are inseparable; your prosperity is their prosperity; your happiness is their happiness. To my certain knowledge, before the occurrence of late unhappy events, some respectable gentlemen had begun to take the state of the *poor weavers* into their most serious consideration, with a view to bring it before the parliament; and could the poor be taken out of the hands of the disturbers of the public peace, I doubt not but the subject might be resumed: and should it be laid before parliament by respectable men, I could almost venture to pledge myself that the parliament would under the paternal auspices of your benevolent Prince and his advisers afford to that meritorious class of our fellow countrymen, effectual relief, if it be only within the bounds of possibility. At all events, as Methodists, as Britons, and as Christians, 'Fear the Lord and the king; and meddle not with them that are given to change.' Avoid the factious, the seditious, the blasphemer, infringe not the laws; break not the peace; remember that good rule of the Methodist Society, 'Not to speak evil of Magistrates or Ministers;' honour the memory of your venerable found, the late Reverend John Wesley, who was always distinguished by his Loyalty; cast all your care upon God, for He careth for you; and anticipate, if you can, the happiness you will feel, on the return of better days, when you find you have passed through this hour and power of darkness, without having forsaken your God, violated your conscience, disturbed the peace of your mind, or stained the sanctity of your religious character. *Now* let your righteousness be as the waves of the sea, and *then* shall your peace flow as a river. If *now*, while the storm rages, while the billows are roaring and while so many are shipwrecked around you, you steadily fix your eye on your heavenly pilot, and strictly obey His commands, *then*, when you have escaped the perils of the voyage, and arrived safely in the peaceful harbour, you will rejoice with joy unspeakable and full of glory.

Document IX.13

Quaker Address on the Slave Trade, 1822

Although the British slave trade had been abolished in 1807, the transport of black people to the New World for sale to planters continued under the auspices of many other nations. Quakers, who had been the first to take up the cause of abolition in the mid-eighteenth century, maintained pressure for its universal termination. Their humanitarian appeal to continental powers in 1822 included the maxim that what is morally wrong cannot be politically right, a refrain in the social convictions of nineteenth-century Nonconformists. For the broad campaign, see S. Drescher, *Capitalism and Antislavery: British Mobilisation in Comparative Perspective*, London, 1986.

The extract is taken from *An Address to the Inhabitants of Europe on the Iniquity of the Slave Trade*, London, 1822, pp. 5–10.

In thus introducing ourselves to the notice of our Continental neighbours, we feel that we need not offer any apology, considering them as our brethren, as the children of one universal Parent, as fellow-professors of a belief in one and the same merciful Saviour. The same feelings which lead us to consider the natives of France, of Spain, of Holland, of Portugal, and of the other nations of Europe, as our brethren, induce us to extend this endearing appellation to the inhabitants of Africa. Our heavenly Father has made of one blood all nations of men that dwell upon the face of the earth; and we are all the objects of that great redemption, which comes by our Lord and Saviour Jesus Christ. And although the kindreds of the earth are divided into distinct communities and nations, we are all bound one unto another by the ties of love, of brotherly kindness, and compassion. ...

The arguments of the Christian, like the religion from which they are derived, are plain and simple, but they are in themselves invincible. The gospel of our Lord Jesus Christ is a system of peace, of love, of mercy, and of good-will. The Slave Trade is a system of fraud and rapine, of violence and cruelty. ... Our blessed Redeemer has taught us pure, impartial justice, in this plain but most important language, 'All things whatsoever ye would that men should do to you, do ye even so to them.' The Slave trader, in open violation of this injunction, acts towards others in a way which he would use every means in his power to resist, if it were practised upon him. He is indeed guilty of the greatest injustice: he deprives his fellow-men of their liberty, that gift of heaven which is estimated as the greatest of civil blessings; and which is the natural, and, (whilst we are not disturbing the peace and tranquillity of our neighbours,) the unalienable right of the whole human race. And here we would observe that as the practice itself is clearly unjust, it cannot be warranted by any *commercial* considerations. That which is morally wrong cannot be politically right. And our beneficent Creator has wisely ordered, that our duty and our interest should be intimately combined; and it is contrary to his gracious purpose, that gain and advantage should be sought by one part of his rational creation, from the distress and sufferings of another.

Document IX.14

William Knibb on Slavery, 1832

William Knibb (1803–45) was a Baptist missionary to Jamaica who determined, in the aftermath of the slave revolt there in 1831–32, that slavery must be put down. His tour of Britain holding meetings to denounce the institution in the colonies was largely responsible for the degree of feeling on the issue at the 1832 general election. That in turn led in the following year to legislation ending slavery in British dominions. See J. H. Hinton, *Memoir of William Knibb*, London, 1847; and DNB.

The extract is an account of Knibb's speech at Byrom Street Chapel, Liverpool, on 24 July 1832, as reported in *The Liverpool Mercury* and reproduced in Hinton's memoir, pp. 153–4.

He was fully aware of the use made of the decided part which he had taken, and which he intended still to take, on the question of British slavery as it existed in the West Indies; he was fully aware that selfish and interested motives were ascribed to him by those who knew none of a higher nature; he knew it would be said that his conduct in his native country proved that he was a most unfit person to be sent out to communicate knowledge to the slave. But his only answer to those imputations was – prove the fact. When in Jamaica he had a solemn duty to perform, that of teaching the slave obedience to his master and to his God; he had now returned to his native land, and he had another duty to perform, – to plead for his church and for his people, under all the horrors of British slavery as it existed in the West India islands. He stood there, in the land of liberty, in the land of light and knowledge; and to the utmost of his ability he would perform the duty which God had placed upon him, undismayed by the fears of lukewarm and timid friends, or the taunts and sarcasms of those who were interested in the continuance of slavery. With the political bearings of the question he had nothing to do; he had a church in Jamaica bought by the blood of the Redeemer; that church was exposed to all the horrors of slavery. He was sent as an advocate for the suffering, the degraded, the persecuted British slave, who had been robbed of everything which raised man above the brute creation, or gave him a title to rank himself in the human family, and had now been forbidden by men to seek consolation from the Father of mercies, who had made of one blood all the nations of the earth, who desired that every man should come to the knowledge of the truth, and who had commanded them to break the fetters of the slave, and bid the oppressed go free. In this godlike attempt to rescue the distressed from bondage, to break the fetters of the slave, and to bid the captive go free, all he asked for was justice, sympathy founded upon principle. Long had the politician and philanthropist exerted their energies in this noble cause, undismayed by the threats and the jeers of the interested dealers in human blood; while the Christian world (with the exception of those friends of liberty and humanity, the Quakers) had gazed upon the inhuman monster with almost profound indifference. It was true that they had sent out missionaries, and those missionaries, whilst they were permitted to preach the gospel on any terms, submitted to restrictions which sealed their lips to the sufferings of the slave, and entombed the manly affections of the soul, whilst they beheld their fellow-subjects and their fellow Christians exposed to every cruelty which uncontrolled power and unbridled licentiousness were sure to call forth. Even now, cautions as numerous as the sufferings of the Christian slave were presented to him who addressed them on the subject; but he was willing to stand or fall by the side, and to share the fate, of his brethren and sisters in slavery. He was the determined foe of slavery in all its modifications and branches, and the unbending advocate of the immediate emancipation of the slave, and the extirpation of slavery throughout the world. Slavery had thrown down the gauntlet; proud in its dying strength, it endeavoured to render unavailing the death of the Son of God. In Jamaica it had defied the living God, persecuting his ministers and pulling down his temples; but the stone cut out of the mountain would overthrow it; soon would it fall to rise no more; and then the earth would rejoice, and God would bless it.

Document IX.15

A Primitive Methodist on Total Abstinence, 1846

Primitive Methodism was the first religious body to show favour to the temperance movement. Its Conference recommended temperance societies as early as 1832, and in 1841 ordered unfermented wine to be used at communion. Here total abstinence is urged as a subject for Sunday school teachers on the grounds that drinking is detrimental to health and productive of sin. The scriptural justification is based on concern for the weaker brother. See B. Harrison, *Drink and the Victorians: The Temperance Question in England, 1815–1872*, London, 1971, chap. 8.

The extract is taken from J. Watson, *An Address to Sunday School Teachers on the Subject of Abstinence from Intoxicating Drinks*, Manchester, 1846, pp. 6–11.

In prosecuting the subject to which we have called your attention, we might expatiate upon the many physical evils which result, directly and indirectly, from the use of strong drink. We might shew you, that, in numerous instances, the seeds of disease are thus sown, and transmitted from parents to children, entailing debilitude, suffering, and premature death, throughout whole generations. And we cannot suppose, for a moment, that you would deem this view of the subject beneath your notice, or unworthy of your sympathies. But we wish you chiefly to look at the moral bearings of the the drinking usages of our country. You are engaged in promoting the moral and spiritual interests of your scholars. You are training them for eternity. You are striving to make them good citizens of this world, and fit for the 'habitation of the saints in light.' Every indication of success, as is becoming, you hail with delight, and the dangers of failure you tremble to contemplate. In the prevalent drinking usuages, we have a source more productive of immorality, crime, and death, than any other; they draught off annually, in this nation alone, fifty or sixty thousand into the drunkards' ranks; engulph, during the same period, an equal number in the drunkard's grave, and consume sixty millions sterling! Of these, not a few once occupied the benches of the Sunday school, and listened, sabbath after sabbath, to the instructions of the teacher and minister. ...

The Scriptures, we grant, nowhere command us to abstain from the use of intoxicating drinks, in so many words, but they instruct us 'not to make provision for the flesh to fulfil the lusts thereof,' and command us to 'cease to do evil.' We think you cannot fairly deny that the use of strong drink is a fearful evil. Ought you not then to abstain? But the Scriptures come closer still, and command us to 'abstain from every appearance of evil.' This, in our opinion, settles the case, and renders 'total abstinence' properly scriptural. We might further urge from scripture the principle of expediency. If Paul would abstain from 'eating flesh, or drinking wine, or doing any thing which caused his brother to stumble, or fall, or be made weak;' surely, the ravages of strong drink warrant, nay, demand, a much greater sacrifice than abstinence from that which the human economy can spare with advantage; and which has been pronounced by competent judges 'the most fruitful cause of poverty, lunacy, crime, and death.' Consider seriously, these matters, and ask yourself, if, whilst you countenance the drinking usuages of society you do not run the risk of destroying 'your brother for whom Christ died.' These arguments, with us, are conclusive in favour of 'total abstinence.'

Document IX.16

Peter M'Owan on the Sabbath, 1850

The observance of Sunday as a day of rest was virtually universal among Nonconformists, and it was a campaigning cause for many of them. The Wesleyans were particularly eager to see the sabbath enforced. One of their ministers, Peter M'Owan, contributed an essay to a collection on the subject at mid-century. After condemning Sunday work, he went on to specify more subtle forms of desecration that might infringe the sabbath ideal. See J. Wigley, *The Rise and Fall of the Victorian Sunday*, Manchester, 1980.

The extract is taken from P. M'Owan, 'Several Prevailing Forms of Sabbath Desecration Exposed', in *The Christian Sabbath*, Edinburgh, 1850, pp. 165–7.

Sunday ought to be a privileged day in food, in clothes, and in family fellowship, as far as its sanctity and the discharge of its appropriate duties will permit. All Christians ought to salute its dawn with songs, and Christian parents should endeavour to make their households happy when they meet at the family board. The trials and crosses of the past week should, as far as possible, be forgotten and banished. The grace of redemption, the care and kind interpositions of Providence, the progress of the work of God, the virtues and self-denying labours of the Lord's people, the wonders of creation, and the felicities of the heavenly rest, should be the themes of our Sabbath-day discourse. Shy distrust and lofty reserve ought to be banished from the family circle on this day especially; and all should be encouraged to join in spiritual conversation, in singing psalms and hymns, and in offering up prayer. At such a time, and in such circumstances, the parent and master, who is himself in the Spirit on the Lord's day, will feel his heart warmed and enlarged; and, anxious to diffuse the peace and joy which animate his own bosom, he will delight to bless his household, saying, 'The Lord bless thee and keep thee; the Lord make his face to shine upon thee; the Lord lift up the light of his countenance upon thee, and give thee peace.'

This would be to call the Sabbath 'a delight.' But we regret to say, that in many families in which God is not wholly forgotten, the evening of the day is spent in a very different manner. Relatives and near neighbours regularly congregate: and, after a few pious preliminary topics have been touched, they slide by degrees into a free conversation about politics, prices of grain, growing crops, and passing events: and ere they break up they fix the times of projected journeys, repeat the scandal of the week, and discuss the characters of magistrates and ministers, to the infinite damage of the religious interests of their children and servants. This is a soul-destroying and a God-dishonouring custom. It has indeed an air of friendship to man, but it betokens enmity to God. If any of our readers have opened their houses for such gatherings, or have mingled in them, we entreat them, as they regard the favour of God, the credit of religion, and the salvation of their families, to give them up at once, and for ever. It matters not whom you offend, or what reproach you incur, the practice must be renounced, or the curse of God will rest on your souls, and abide in your houses.

Document IX.17

Quaker Appeal against the Crimean War, 1854

The Society of Friends believed all war to be contrary to the will of God. Accordingly its members took the leading part, in 1816, in the foundation of the Peace Society, a pressure group aiming for the elimination of warfare. The chief figure in the peace movement by mid-century was Joseph Sturge, who in early 1854 led a quixotic delegation to the Tsar to try to avert conflict between Britain and Russia. He failed, the Crimean War broke out and it was left for the Quakers, in December 1854, to restate their opposition to war. See E. Isichei, *Victorian Quakers*, Oxford, 1970, pp. 219–27; A. Tyrrell, *Joseph Sturge and the Moral Reform Movement in Early Victorian Britain*, London, 1987, chap. 18.

The extract is taken from *A Christian Appeal from the Society of Friends to their Fellow-Countrymen on the Present War*, n.p., 1854, pp. 1–3.

We would respectfully bespeak the serious attention of our fellow-countrymen, whilst we earnestly plead with them, on behalf of the claims of religion and humanity, in reference to the sanguinary conflict now raging in the East.

It is, we reverently trust, in the love of Christ, and it is in the spirit of true patriotism, that we make this appeal. Our country is dear to us; we honour our Sovereign, and prize our free institutions; and we can but desire that our national policy may accord with the spirit and precepts of that Redeemer who came 'not to destroy men's lives but to save them.' We feel it to be a solemn thing thus to stand forth as the advocates of inviolable peace; and the events which are passing around us, and the warlike spirit which meets us in every direction, have led us very seriously to review the grounds of our Christian testimony in this matter. But this review has only confirmed the conviction, which we dare not shrink from avowing, however unpopular at a crisis like the present, that all War, on whatever plea of policy or of necessity, is unlawful under the Gospel Dispensation.

It will be admitted as a truth, applicable alike to individuals and to nations, that it is only in the use of those means which are sanctioned by the law of Christ, that we can expect the Divine blessing upon our efforts. When these means are exhausted, it becomes man, as a dependent being, to commit all results unto God – a trust which will never be confounded.

Can it then be that War, with all its attendant misery and crime, is a means the employment of which is sanctioned by Christianity? We unreservedly make our appeal to those inspired Records, which, as Christians, we all profess to accept as a revelation from Heaven. True it is, that in the Old Testament we find not only war, but retaliation also, permitted and, under certain circumstances, even commanded. As regards the command, we presume that no such commission to wage war against the Lord's enemies, as that given to his chosen people formerly, is claimed, or even expected, now. And in regard to the permission, it is sufficient to say, that the provisions of the Old Covenant, as to the return of evil for evil, like those bearing upon the conjugal relation, are expressly contrasted by our Lord himself with his own precepts, for the purpose of showing that that which, in both these cases, was allowed to them of old time, by reason of the hardness of their hearts, is prohibited by the higher and holier morality of the New Covenant. To the Gospel standard, therefore, whether exhibited by prophecy, or more fully developed by Christ himself and his Apostles, must his disciples resort for their practical guidance. In the face then of all the glorious anticipations of prophecy in regard to the peaceable reign of the Messiah, and of the deep significance of that name by which He is called, 'The Prince of Peace;' – in the face of the annunciation of the Heavenly Host which characterised the new dispensation, as that which was to bring 'Glory to God in the highest, and on earth peace, goodwill towards men;' – in the face of the express commands of our Redeemer himself, 'Love your enemies, bless them that curse you, do good to them that hate you, and pray for them that despitefully use you and persecute you;' – who will venture to say that Christianity affords any authority or justification for war? ...

To the members of the Government of our beloved Sovereign, in the first place, would we address our earnest but respectful appeal, imploring them to use every Christian effort for the restoration of peace. We are not insensible to the difficulties of their position in this momentous crisis, in having to deal with a powerful enemy, and at the same time, to stem the mighty torrent of martial excitement in the public mind, or to satisfy its exaggerated expectations with reference both to the war itself, and to the results to be obtained by it. Yet we believe, that trust in God, combined with humbling views of our national sins and a temperate estimate of our own position, even when convinced that we have clearly the right on our side, will be found at all times, and especially in the present peculiar and critical circumstances of the country, the best preparation for obtaining peace.

Document IX.18

William Booth on the Way Out of Darkest England, 1890

William Booth (1829–1912) was a minister of the Methodist New Connexion who in 1861 left to become an independent evangelist. In 1878 he founded the Salvation Army, with himself as General. Its military style gave him autocratic powers that he used to develop the body into a worldwide organisation within his lifetime. Confronted by the challenge of urban destitution, in 1890 he projected a scheme for rescuing the 'submerged tenth' of the population. As a result a 'farm colony' was established at Hadleigh in Essex, and the enduring commitment of the Salvation Army to social work was begun. See H. Begbie, *William Booth: The Founder of the*

Salvation Army, 2 vols, London, 1920; DNB; P. J. Walker, *Pulling the Devil's Kingdom Down: The Salvation Army in Victorian Britain*, Berkeley, California, 2001; and, for the context of the scheme, D. W. Bebbington, 'The City, the Countryside and the Social Gospel in Late Victorian Nonconformity', in D. Baker, ed., *The Church in Town and Countryside*, Studies in Church History 16, Oxford, 1979, pp. 415–26.

The extract is taken from [W.] Booth, *In Darkest England and the Way Out*, London, 1890, pp. 91–3.

The Scheme I have to offer consists in the formation of these people into self-helping and self-sustaining communities, each being a kind of co-operative society, or patriarchal family, governed and disciplined on the principles which have already proved so effective in the Salvation Army.

These communities we will call, for want of a better term, Colonies. There will be–

(1) The City Colony.
(2) The Farm Colony.
(3) The Over-Sea Colony.

THE CITY COLONY

By the City Colony is meant the establishment, in the very centre of the ocean of misery of which we have been speaking, of a number of Institutions to act as Harbours of Refuge for all and any who have been shipwrecked in life, character, or circumstances. These Harbours will gather up the poor destitute creatures, supply their immediate pressing necessities, furnish temporary employment, inspire them with hope for the future, and commence at once a course of regeneration by moral and religious influences.

From these Institutions, which are hereafter described, numbers would, after a short time, be floated off to permanent employment, or sent home to friends happy to receive them on hearing of their reformation. All who remain on our hands would, by varied means, be tested as to their sincerity, industry, and honesty, and as soon as satisfaction was created, be passed on to the Colony of the second class.

THE FARM COLONY

This would consist of a settlement of the Colonists on an estate in the provinces, in the culture of which they would find employment and obtain support. As the race from the Country to the City has been the cause of much of the distress we have to battle with, we propose to find a substantial part of our remedy by transferring these same people back to the country, that is back again to 'the Garden!'

Here the process of reformation of character would be carried forward by the same industrial, moral, and religious methods as have already been commenced in the City, especially including those forms of labour and that knowledge of agriculture which, should the Colonist not obtain employment in this country, will qualify him for pursuing his fortunes under more favourable circumstances in some other land.

From the Farm, as from the City, there can be no question that large numbers, resuscitated in health and character, would be restored to friends up and down the country. Some would find employment in their own callings, others would settle in cottages on a small piece of land that we should provide, or on Co-operative Farms which we intend to promote; while the great bulk, after trial and training, would be passed on to the Foreign Settlement, which would constitute our third class, namely The Over-Sea Colony.

THE OVER-SEA COLONY.

All who have given attention to the subject are agreed that in our Colonies in South Africa, Canada, Western Australia and elsewhere, there are millions of acres of useful land to be obtained almost for the asking, capable of supporting our surplus population in health and comfort, were it a thousand times greater than it is. We propose to secure a tract of land in one of these countries, prepare it for settlement, establish in it authority, govern it by equitable laws, assist it in times of necessity, settling it gradually with a prepared people, and so create a home for these destitute multitudes.

The Scheme, in its entirety, may aptly be compared to A Great Machine, foundationed in the lowest slums and purlieus of our great towns and cities, drawing up into its embrace the depraved and destitute of all classes; receiving thieves, harlots, paupers, drunkards, prodigals, all alike, on the simple conditions of their being willing to work and to conform to discipline. Drawing up these poor outcasts, reforming them, and creating in them habits of industry, honesty, and truth; teaching them methods by which alike the bread that perishes and that which endures to Everlasting Life can be won. Forwarding them from the City to the Country, and there continuing the process of regeneration, and then pouring them forth on to the virgin soils that await their coming in other lands, keeping hold of them with a strong government, and yet making them free men and women; and so laying the foundations, perchance, of another Empire to swell to vast proportions in later times.   Why not?

Document IX.19

The Methodist Temperance Manual, 1895

The Wesleyans, who in the 1840s had been the least enthusiastic of the Nonconformist denominations about the temperance movement, were mostly becoming its keen advocates half a century later. They issued an official 'handbook for temperance workers and Band of Hope conductors'. The Bands of Hope, usually attached to particular chapels, were enormously popular classes for the young that concentrated on the evils of drink. See G. T. Brake, *Drink: Ups and Downs of Methodist*

Attitudes to Temperance, London, 1974; and, on Bands of Hope, L. L. Shiman, *Crusade against Drink in Victorian England*, London, 1988, chap. 6.

The extract is taken from W. Spiers, *The Methodist Temperance Manual*, London, 1895, pp. 219–21.

The whole teaching of Jesus Christ and the very spirit of the Gospel are, in effect, a rebuke against indulgence in that which works so much harm to our fellow-creatures. I will not say we cannot be Christians without being abstainers, but we can certainly be better Christians, more useful, more successful in finding our way into the hearts of the tempted and the fallen, by showing them an example of self-sacrifice – if indeed it *is* a sacrifice to give up a drink that, on all grounds, we are better without. We may contend for our Christian liberty, but the truest, noblest freedom is that of the man who voluntarily denies himself for the good of others and for the sake of Christ. It is by Christian influence that the abominations of the drink traffic are most likely to be destroyed, and every Christian must settle for himself whether he will do his best to bring this about, or by a weak indulgence deprive himself of all power to help in a Holy Crusade. If our Lord had seen what we see, would He not have spoken as indignantly against the sellers of drink as He did against the hypocrisies and sins of His day? Would He not have pronounced woe on the blind leaders of the blind, who, to enrich themselves, are causing so many hapless ones to fall into the ditch? If St. Paul had witnessed the debaucheries of our large towns, the pauperised crowds, the embruted sots, and the neglected, starving children that swarm around us, the sad fruits of the unwieldy liquor traffic which has fastened upon the very vitals of our domestic happiness and our national prosperity, would he not have burned within him, and counted all things but loss that the might throw down this formidable obstacle to the salvation of mankind? He could eat meat offered to an idol without defiling his conscience; but the lawfulness of enjoyment influenced him far less than the expediency of self-denial for the good of others. Self-gratification weighed less than a feather with him where the welfare of others' souls was in the balance. 'If meat make my brother to offend, I will eat no flesh while the world standeth, lest I make my brother to offend.' 'It is good neither to eat flesh, nor to drink wine, nor anything whereby thy brother stumbleth, or is offended, or is made weak.' These were the magnificent principles that guided St. Paul in all things. They express the spirit of Christ who 'pleased not Himself'; and they must enter into and control the lives of all who claim to be imitators of Christ. Our own safety, the well-being of our children, the strength and success of the Church, the good of society, the elevation of our perishing fellow-creatures, the salvation of the world – all are dependent on the measure in which these principles actuate our lives and determine our habits and conduct. While the Christian is confronted with the fact that more than three millions of paupers are dragging out their miserable existence among us, of whom the vast majority are crushed into the gutter and kept there by the giant Alcohol; while he is conscious that nearly a million drunkards are reeling and staggering through our streets, that the goals and asylums are filled with recruits from this appalling army, and that through England's pernicious example whole nations are being corrupted and decimated; can he remain unmoved, or refuse to take his part in so tremendous a conflict as that which is being waged with drink? These are questions which every Christian must answer for himself. May God help us all to give a true answer, one that will satisfy our own consciences and retain for us our self-respect and the favour and blessing of our God!

Document IX.20

Samuel Keeble on Christian Socialism, 1896

Samuel Keeble (1853–1946) was a Wesleyan minister who was to become in 1905 the founder of the Wesleyan Methodist Union of Social Service, the leading Christian socialist organisation in Nonconformity. He read Marx carefully, but distinguished a Christian socialist position sharply from the Marxian standpoint, which he called 'economic socialism'. His *Industrial Daydreams* was a landmark in the evolution of Nonconformist sympathy for socialism, opening the way for a younger generation to identify intellectually with the Labour Party. See M. S. Edwards, *S. E. Keeble: The Rejected Prophet*, Broxton, Chester, 1977.

The extract is taken from S. E. Keeble, *Industrial Daydreams*, London, 1896, pp. 60–63.

Christian Socialism is most obnoxious to the Socialist proper. To him it is 'bastard' Socialism – a misnomer and a fraud, he cannot away with it. This is singular, inasmuch as both kinds of Socialism agree in their diagnosis of the social disease. Both declare that modern society is suffering from a bad industrial system, based upon fundamental economic errors, and ruled by an anti-social motive and spirit. They agree that the labourer is at a disadvantage in the higgling of the market, and is thereby defrauded of his full share of the product, that we are suffering not so much from over-production as from under-consumption, and that whether or not there be levelling-down, there must be levelling-up. Both declare that political economy has, by its science falsely so called, made the depression of labour a fine art, and that the possession of political power by the employing class has assisted in the process. Both seek a more equitable distribution of the products or profits of Labour and Capital, and both have one ultimate object – the elevation of the working classes by putting them in full possession of the product of their labours, and therefore of themselves. Nevertheless, the stanch Socialist will have none of the Christian Socialist. He may, if he be a Fabian, use him for his purposes, but he does not believe in him; and if he be a Social Democrat, he regards him as a heathen man and a publican with whom he cannot company.

The reasons for this probably are, that most Christian Socialists do not see their way to accept the basis of economic Socialism – that labour is the source of all value – with its logical corollaries, that profit, rent and interest are therefore robberies; nor are they prepared to advocate the transfer to the State of *all* the instruments of production and distribution – land, mines, machinery, tools, roads, railways, trams, ships, telegraphs, and suchlike. They see great economic, administrative, and moral difficulties in the way of this. They are not convinced that society is fundamentally wrong, and needs upturning and revolutionizing. They do not believe it to be essentially unjust, as do the Socialists, but that injustice has arisen through greed, selfishness, and a false political economy; if these be eliminated, they have hope of the present body politic. In addition to this economic difference between Socialists and Christian Socialists, there is also a moral and religious difference. Socialism threatens the family and the Church, and through them morality and religion. Christian Socialism cleaves close to both. This largely accounts for the antipathy between the two. Socialism is nothing if not anti-religious, although perhaps the theory does not necessitate this; Christian Socialism is nothing if not religious and Christian. The former puts material readjustments in the very forefront, the latter puts moral. The Socialist expects most from material, the Christian Socialist most from moral, changes. The latter is not indifferent to material changes – it is part of his policy to demand them – but he aims at the Christianization of industry, and that not in the interests of Christianity, but in the interests of humanity. The Socialist really suspects the Christian Socialist of being a wolf in sheep's clothing, of caring not so much for the people as for his sect or his Church, and of engaging in the social struggle in order to make religious capital out of it. He gives him credit only for religious propagandism. The Christian Socialist has to bear all this meekly, knowing that the Christian Church has given only too much ground for this hostility and suspicion. ... He offends the Socialist by not going far enough, and the Christian Individualist by going too far – he is therefore eschewed by both. Against Christian Individualism, which demands 'the simple Gospel,' Christian Socialism maintains that the Christian Gospel is twofold – individual and social – that the former never has been, and never can be, neglected, but that the latter both has been and is grossly neglected. The social Gospel is as sacred and as indispensable as the individual Gospel – the two are complementary, and the neglect of either always brings its penalties. An impartial study of the Scriptures reveals the fact that in both Testaments the social Gospel is, if anything, the most prominent, and that to ignore the material and social life of men, and the moral condition of classes, communities and states, is the most utter unfaithfulness to the precepts and teachings of the Word of God and the examples of priests, prophets, apostles, evangelists, and the Lord Jesus Christ Himself. A Christianity, 'spiritual' in the sense of not being ethical and social, and 'other-worldly' in the sense of not being this-worldly, is really travestying the good Gospel of God. That Gospel, contends Christian Socialism, is far from being 'simple' – it is profound and manifold – and is bent upon saving, not only the individual, but also society; upon setting up in the earth the Kingdom of Heaven.

Public Life

Document IX.21

Adam Clarke on Civil Government, 1830

The Toryism of the Wesleyan leadership in the early nineteenth century has so often been insisted on that the political convictions of prominent members of the connexion who were by no means Tories have sometimes slipped from view. Adam Clarke (see I.2), the leading scholar in Methodism, naturally analysed politics from the standpoint of a classicist and so decided that the British constitution was a salutary mixture of the monarchical, the aristocratic and the democratic. That was to align him with mainstream Whig opinion.

The extract is taken from A. Clarke, 'Thr Origin and End of Civil Government', *Discourses on Various Subjects*, vol. 3, London, 1830, p. 358.

DEMOCRACY *aims well*; but is *violent, indecisive,* and *fickle*; often enacts without wisdom, and executes without foresight; and is generally *hasty* in all its measures.

MONARCHY (*absolute*) keeps especially in view the prerogatives and glory of the crown; independently of all other considerations.

ARISTOCRACY keeps in view the honour and independence of the *nobility*, being often regardless of the people.

DEMOCRACY labours to bring all to a level, and keep it there; and frequently destroys emulation, because, through its jealousy of power and influence, it, in effect, discountenances profound knowledge, and high achievement.

Neither of these forms, simply considered, is much to be preferred. The British government, though called a *monarchy*, differs from them all; and yet embraces them all. It is *monarchical*, and it is not. It is *aristocratical*, and it is not. It is *democratical*, and it is not. It consists of the *three estates*. It is monarchical, because it acknowledges a *King* as the supreme head; it is *aristocratical* in its *House of Lords*, where the nobles possess a legislative capacity; it is *democratical* in its *House of Commons*, where representatives chosen by the people possess the same power. These three estates are perfectly *mixed* by the constitution; they counterbalance each other, each having an equal legislative authority; and this government possesses in itself all the excellencies of the three *forms*. It can become *corrupt*, only when any of the three estates *preponderates* over the rest. In its nature and regular operation, it secures the *prerogative* of the *nobility*; it respects and secures the *rights* of the *people*; it is, in a word, a *limited monarchy*, a *popular aristocracy*, and an *ennobled democracy*. God grant it permanence; and constitutional administration! Amen.

Document IX.22

G. B. Browne on Parliamentary Reform, 1832

G. B. Browne (1787–1839) was a civil engineer who became local preachers' secretary for the Halifax Wesleyan circuit in 1815 and secretary of the Wesleyan prayer leaders' meeting three years later. In 1832 he travelled as part of a Halifax deputation to London to urge Earl Grey to keep up the struggle for parliamentary reform and on his return moved the first resolution, which was to the same effect, at a public meeting in the town. Browne illustrates the rising tide of Liberal opinion within Wesleyan Methodism at a time when, according to many historians, the connexion was polarised between Tories and radicals. The Liberal voting pattern is noted in D. Hempton, *Methodism and Politics in British Society, 1750–1850*, London, 1984, chap. 7.

The extract is taken from *The Halifax and Huddersfield Express*, 19 May 1832.

G. B. Browne, Esq. begged leave to move the first resolution, which he read. ... He must acknowledge that he could not do justice to the merits of the resolution, which had his most cordial approbation. They were all aware of the primary importance of the measure. It was a most vital question to themselves as men and Christians. Nothing could so much promote the spread of true Christianity, as a proper enlargement of the civil liberties of mankind; and therefore, based as this measure was on that principle, he most sincerely regretted its rejection by the House of Lords. When we consider the amazing pains taken in the business, – how many years the question of reform had been pleaded, we found that it had grown up, and overcome prejudices; and from a small company, it advocates had become the majority of the nation. It was not now a question of a few, poor and discontented, but of persons of property and understanding, of sound and honest principles, who would not do wrong to any man. When they talked of reform, they did not mean revolution; their object was not to unsettle property, but to establish the liberties of Englishmen on the surest and firmest foundation. As science and literature became diffused, for the schoolmaster was abroad, and the march of intellect was making way; what had we to expect, but that all dilapidations and corruptions that had crept into the system should be removed? Our constitutional system, King, Lords, and Commons, was a sound system, and thoroughly good; the only mistake was in its present practical working. The three orders should be perfectly independent of each other. The House of Commons should be perfectly independent of the King and the nobles. That there were many of the lordly house in the House of Commons was notorious. That there was a vast deal of impropriety in the representation, was notorious. [The proceedings were here briefly interrupted by the appearance of a large white banner. On one side was a sailor, with a crown on his head, and his breeches' pockets turned inside out. The inscription was 'No Supplies;' and the effect on his Majesty's countenance seemed most disastrous. On the reverse was a crown almost covered by a large blue petticoat. The inscription was,

May the petticoat over the crown
Soon fall off or soon fall down.

The device was received with cheers.] The importance of reforms in that House, had been, for many years, gaining ground in the estimation of the people; and he sincerely regretted the virtual rejection of the measure. When he considered the rise of the bill, it was in consequence of the absolute refusal of Lord Wellington to give any kind of reform; he resigned office, and a ministry came in, pledged to reform. The king sanctioned it, but it was thrown out by the Lords; his Majesty dissolved the parliament, and the country responded to the call. A new bill was prepared, and taken into the Upper House, where it was virtually accepted as to its principle: but they began at the wrong end of the details. There was not a countryman, a mechanic, or an apprentice boy, but had more sense that Lord Lyndhurst. (cheers) He put it to their common sense whether an artizan would not, in repairing any thing that was old, take away the old, before he put in the new stuff. Did ever any joiner say he could not take the old timber away, until he had put in the new? With all their talking and elocution, it was a virtual rejection, and we were not such fools as to be turned round by such a political cabal. It was an insult to them, as Britons; and he hoped they would this day shew that they were indignant at the dishonour cast on their rights. He most sincerely regretted that when it was impossible to be carried without making Peers, his Majesty should have shrunk from what he was bound to do, by his having begun it. (Cheers.) He had told them, on a former occasion, that he was a loyal man; he loved his king, and his country also; and he would not now lose his loyalty. He sincerely respected the constitution of his country; and considered it our bounden duty to obtain such a measure as would secure our rights. Giving the House of Commons a pure and independent character, was the only way to secure the real liberties of Englishmen; and they must never allow any infringement on that bill. They must take nothing less. (More.) It was a matter of some consequence, whether they must not ask for more. (Cheers.) 'We now,' said Mr. B. 'are brought to a point. The House of Lords is standing on its prerogative of saying, "No;" and we must take up our prerogative and say, "We will have it."' (Cheers.)

Document IX.23

West Riding Baptists on Civil Rights, 1843

Francis Clowes (1805–73), the author of this letter to the editor of *The Baptist Magazine*, was the classical tutor at Horton Baptist Academy, Bradford, and acted as secretary of the Yorkshire West Riding Baptist Association. The Conservative government of Sir Robert Peel had just proposed to put the Church of England in charge of popular education (see IX.5), and so Clowes calls on Baptists to be the champions of liberty. Twelve years later he was to be the founding editor of *The Freeman*, the first Baptist denominational newspaper. See DEB.

The extract is taken from *The Baptist Magazine*, May 1843, pp. 271–2.

The Yorkshire West Riding Association has for several years appointed, at its annual meeting, a small committee to watch over the civil interests of the denomination, whose duty it has been to correspond with the churches, prepare petitions, &c., if any measures of government threatened our religious liberties. We have found it of great service. It has several times given promptitude and energy to the movements of our churches.

The committee itself has, however, by recent government proceedings, been taught the importance of a still better arrangement for *systematic* and *instantaneous* opposition to the numerous attacks, which they must now expect, upon our dearest Christian and civil liberties.

Sir Robert Peel now proposes to *endow* new churches; and, while the present ministry is in power, we may be sure of insidious, or open legislative hostility. The utmost will be done, so to fetter our liberties that before another election not 'a dog will dare to wag his tongue' against the hierarchy or the aristocracy. The audacity which could coolly propose to put the education of the multitude in the hands of the opponents of education, and take it out of those of its friends, will not hesitate soon to invade the ministry of the word and the freedom of [the] press. Baptist churches are, in God's providence, the chosen nurseries of freedom. They emancipated the negro – they have been the core of the liberal cause. Baptists are the only body, who, as a body, care neither for the traditions of the elders, nor the adherence of wealthy trimmers. Our denomination must, then, gird itself to its duty. If we lose a few wealthy, we shall gain the many. We shall be the body to convince them that the Bible is the book of the people, and, however the interested of all parties may scorn, that Bible Christians contend equally and honestly for the rights of all.

The plan we have resolved to suggest to our churches, and which I have been requested to communicate to you, in the hope of stirring up other associations, is this – To appoint in each church a small committee, whose business it shall be to act on the first appearance of any aggression. They must understand the case, prepare a petition, and correspond with members of the house of commons. Let it not be objected that we shall make our churches too political. Political duties is only a Greek phrase for citizen duties – (oh deliver us from these transferred, and not translated Greek words!) – and what member of a baptist church will contend that we ought not to attend earnestly to our citizen duties? We are never told to prefer the condition of wealth or aristocratic rank; but says an apostle, who himself never gave way 'by subjection, no, not for an hour,' 'If thou mayest be *free*, use it the rather.'

Baptists stand in the Thermopylæ of English liberties. If we do our duty, Independents, perhaps even Methodists, must follow. Large classes of the empire – Roman catholics, non-intrusionists, chartists, free-traders – are all finding out the great truth, that government has no right to interfere with trade, or education, and, least of all, with religion; in short, that *protection of life and property* is its one duty.

Document IX.24

J. N. Darby against Voting, 1848

John Nelson Darby (1800–82) was a clergyman of the Church of Ireland who gradually separated from it to become a prominent figure among the Brethren – the so-called 'Plymouth Brethren'. From 1847 he was the leader of the Exclusive section who refused fellowship with any who had a connection with the more open-minded Brethren. Darby was the progenitor of the system of biblical interpretation known as dispensationalism, a species of premillennialism (see II.29) that was to become enormously influential, especially in the United States. It led him to reject voting as a form of identification with the current world-system that stood under the judgement of God, a view that became common among Brethren. See M. S. Weremchuk, *John Nelson Darby*, Neptune, New Jersey, 1992; J. D. Burnham, *A Story of Conflict: The Controversial Relationship between Benjamin Wills Newton and John Nelson Darby*, Carlisle, 2004; and DNB.

The extract is taken from a letter to an anonymous correspondent from Montpellier dated 24 March 1848, during the year of revolutions on the continent, in *Letters of J. N. D.*, vol. 1, London, n.d., pp. 129–30.

It seems to me so simple that the Christian, not being at all of this world, but united to Him who died and rose again, has no business to mix himself up with the most declared activity of the world, by an act which affirms his existence as belonging to the world, and his identification with the entire system which the Lord is about to judge; that I think the truth has only to be presented in order to be acknowledged by those who have understood their position; so much the more that these events place the world more manifestly (not more really) on its own ground, but more really near the great catastrophe which is about to fall upon those who rise up against God. Oh how my soul longs that His people should be separated to Him, and even with understanding of what is awaiting the world, and still more of what they ought continually to await themselves! May God give the grace to be faithful in bearing this testimony, and everywhere, according to the door that He will open, in season and out of season; for His own, so dear to Him, need it.

Events are hastening on, dear brother, and yet as to us we are waiting for but one, that our Beloved, our Saviour should come. His coming becomes a resource, as it has long been a joy to us, and a reality still more precious, and more near. May we expect it continually; God alone knows the moment. The Christian takes cognizance of the events which are taking place, as a testimony to the one who understands; but his thought, his desire, his portion, is much more within the sanctuary than all that. But is it not true that this voting, as an act of identification with the world (in the very forms which it assumes in the last days), ought to be avoided as a snare by all Christians who understood the will of God and their position in Christ? Always true (I have been acting upon it for twenty years), it is doubly true now.

Document IX.25

Ann Gilbert against Women's Suffrage, 1849

Ann Gilbert (see V.13) had received a letter from a friend, Ann Knight, urging the cause of votes for women. In February 1849 she replied, expounding standard contemporary objections based on the theory that a woman's place was in the home. Later in the century, however, Nonconformists such as Handel Cossham, MP, were to be early advocates of female suffrage. For the arguments against, see B. Harrison, *Separate Spheres: The Opposition to Women's Suffrage in Britain*, London, 1978.

The extract is taken from J. Gilbert, ed., *Autobiography and Other Memorials of Mrs Gilbert*, 3rd edn, London, 1878, pp. 373–5.

I believe that if half every family – observe, not half the *community* (and there perhaps lies the practical mistake), for that might be a *class* only; but that, if *half of every family* is honestly represented, the rights of the whole will be, in fact, as well secured as by any other arrangement. There will be, I think, as much justice, with perhaps less dissension – dissension which might affect domestic happiness – together with a much less cumbrous machine to manage.

Nature seems to have settled the question *a priori*. We have not lungs; we have not courage; we have not time for it (to say nothing of interruptions which might happen inconveniently during the sittings of Parliament!). And modern science says, further, that the *division of labour* is the great secret of order and progress. So long as houses have insides as well as outsides, I think that the female head will have enough to do, even, I might almost say, irrespective of the numerous demands now making upon her by benevolent and religious societies. To these she does feel it her duty to attend, but they make a large addition to 'woman's work' as understood by our grandmothers; still, with a warm heart and managing head, much of this sort may be accomplished, but it seems to me to form the boundary line of her out-of-doors business. Indoors she may do much, even politically – that is, I should say, it is her duty to instil *principles* into her children – principles affecting all the great questions – Freedom; Slavery; Justice; Humanity; War; Monopoly; Private Judgment; Voluntaryism, with as many more as may be thought of – and, supposing she do all this well, wisely, effectively, and see to it at the same time that dinners come *secundum artem*, that shirts have buttons (and buttons shirts) – that everything, in short, within the homestead is 'done decently and in order' – she will have, to my thinking at least, enough to do!

You adduce scripture, and, suitably applied, we all bow to its authority, but not misapplied. 'The righteous is bold as a lion,' – certainly, and as a general truth, has no need 'to fear what man can do unto him;' but if applied to women as women, it would be plainly confronted by other passages especially intended for our own guidance, in which 'shamefacedness,' 'subjection,' 'a meek and quiet spirit,' the 'inquiring of husbands at home,' and many such like are enumerated, as *their* virtues; and in describing their *sphere*, a very different course is assigned to them – 'To guide the house;' 'to bring up children;' 'to entertain strangers;' to descend to the humblest kindnesses – are marked out for them by apostolic authority. It appears to me, therefore, that whenever Scripture legislates for *us* specially, it speaks in direct opposition to the views you advocate. I do not think they would comport with the design of our creation, or with actual, undeniable, unevadeable duties; I think they would subvert the wise result of experience in the division of labour, so necessary to the working of all great machineries; and I think after all, that we should not be a whit the better for woman's interference!

Of course, I believe that there are both wise women and foolish men, but these terms do not divide the sexes. Generally speaking, if wise, we are not the *wisest* – on a large scale especially, – though perhaps on a small one. But 'the hand cannot say to the foot, I have no need of thee,' each is best about its own business; and unless we could regard ourselves as likely to make, not only able statesmen, but the *ablest* of the two, all we could plead for would be an admission into their councils, and then, large committees are always, I believe, less effective than small ones. The fewer that *can* manage a business the better; and as Government do not take upon them to make laws for us *as women*, but only as 'all one concern' with the men, we may, I think, without anxiety, consent to 'share and share alike' with the law makers.

Document IX.26

Agricultural Trade Unionists, 1872

In 1872 there took place 'the Revolt of the Field', the first large-scale organisation of agricultural labourers for collective bargaining. Its leader was Joseph Arch (1826–1919; see DNB), a Primitive Methodist local preacher who went on to enter parliament. As this account of the formation of the National Union of Agricultural Workers in that year shows, it was suffused with the sentiments of Evangelical Nonconformity. See N. Scotland, *Methodism and the Revolt of the Field: A Study of the Methodist Contribution to Agricultural Trade Unionism in East Anglia, 1872–96*, Gloucester, 1981.

The extract is taken from *The Congregationalist*, July 1872, pp. 420–23.

On Wednesday morning, May 29th, a number of Warwickshire men met in the Circus at Leamington, and were shortly joined by delegates – chiefly labourers – from most of the English counties. George Dixon, Esq., M.P. for Birmingham, took the chair, and formally constituted the assembly 'The National Congress of Agricultural Labourers.'

After the transaction of some preliminary business, Dr. Langford submitted the report of 'The Warwickshire Executive,' and Mr. T. Strange, 'The leader of the Herefordshire Hinds,' moved – 'That a National Union of Agricultural Labourers be formed, having district Unions throughout the Kingdom, and its centre of management at Leamington.' A brief discussion ensued on one or two minor points, and then the resolution was passed, – passed by men whose honest faces shone with a new hope, whose stooping forms seemed to rise into erection as they passed it, and whose ringing cheers were followed from some of the older men by devout utterances of 'Amen,' and 'Praise Him.' Said an ancient labourer to the write of this paper, 'Sir, this be a blessed day; this ere Union be the Moses to lead us poor men up out o' Egypt.' Nearly a score of resolutions followed, bearing upon the constitution and management of the new Union, all of which were intelligently discussed, and unanimously carried. ... One delegate, a broad shouldered, open-faced, mirthful soul, commenced his speech with the explanation, given in a confidential tone, 'Genelmen and b'luv'd Chrissen frends, I's a man, I is, hes goes about wi' a oss.' A second informed the assembly that 'King Dâávid sed as how "the usbanman as labours must be fust partaker o' the fruit"' – adding, 'and now he's mo'astly th' last, and loike enuff gets none at all.' Another, descanting on the ways of Divine Providence, remarked that 'little things wus often chuz te du grâât ones, and when e sa' the pôôr labrin' man comin' forrud in this ere movement, and a bringin' o' the fâârmers to terms, he wer remôinded o' many things in the' Scripters, more perticler o' th' ram's horns what blew down th' walls o' Jericho, and frightened Pharaoh, King of Egypt.' ...

Repeated reference was made during the session to the moderate language employed by the delegates. They case few, if any, reflections, repudiated all idea of coercing, or 'serving the masters out,' declared their willingness to let bygones be bygones, and sternly called to order one or two men from the towns, who could not resist the temptation of a fling at 'our upstart aristocrats.' Bearing upon this fact was another. Numbers of the speakers used phrases redolent of the village pulpit. 'My Christian friends,' 'Beloved brethren,' 'Dear fellow Christians,' slipped out incessantly, and taken in connection with the studiously moderate bearing of the men generally, led the writer of this paper to the discovery that three-fourths of the delegates were members of Christian Churches, and half of them local preachers. In the hands of such men the movement is safe. They are men of character and conscience. The fear of God is before their eyes. They will neither overstate their case, nor countenance extreme measures for securing their rights, and we may safely dismiss the anxieties which we might have to entertain were the matter in passionate and unscrupulous hands.

Document IX.27

R. W. Dale on Political and Municipal Duty, 1884

R. W. Dale (see II.16) was a powerful exponent of the Christian obligation to participate in public life, a duty grounded in the doctrine of the incarnation. As befitted a man who co-operated with Joseph Chamberlain in the urban regeneration of Birmingham, he laid particular emphasis on the responsibility to use municipal powers for good. This 'civic gospel' is discussed in E. P. Hennock, *Fit and Proper Persons: Ideal and Reality in Nineteenth-Century Urban Government*, London, 1973, part II.

The extract is taken from R. W. Dale, 'Political and Municipal Duty', in *The Laws of Christ for Common Life*, London, n.d., pp. 187–99.

When the Son of God became flesh, He revealed the sacredness of human life; its sacredness, not merely in its direct relations to God, but in its relations to that natural order and social environment by which it is disciplined and developed, and in which it exercises its affections and virtues. In translating us into the kingdom of heaven, He does not separate children from parents, husbands from wives. He takes up the Family into the diviner order, and so consecrates it. He does the same for industry and commerce, for literature, and science, and art. Christ does not pronounce them common and unclean; He makes them His own and transfigures them, by declaring that in all these pursuits men are to do the will of God. Nor does He call us out of that social and political order which is necessary, not only to the prosperity, but to the existence of nations. On the contrary He affirms the sacredness of civil authority, and enforces civil duties with new and Divine sanctions. As there is no conflict between the Divine Kingdom and the Family, neither is there any conflict between the Divine Kingdom and the State. Christ does not suppress the Family, but purifies and ennobles it. Christ does not suppress the State, but inspires political life with a more generous temper, and directs it to higher ends; He makes loyalty the religious duty of subjects, and under penalty of the Divine displeasure requires rules to be just. ...

Civil authority – this is the main point I want to assert – is a Divine institution. The man who holds municipal or political office is a 'minister of God.' One man may, therefore, have just as real a Divine vocation to become a town councillor or a Member of Parliament as another to become a missionary to the heathen. In either case it is at a man's peril that he is 'disobedient to the heavenly vision.' The Divine right of kings was a base corruption of a most noble truth; so was the fanatical dream about 'the reign of the saints.' We shall never approach the Christian ideal of civil society, until all who hold municipal, judicial, and political offices, recognise the social and political order of the nation as a Divine institution, and discharge their official duties as ministers of God.

But in this country the responsibilities of government are shared by the people. The great outlines of national legislation and policy are laid down, not in Parliament, not in the Cabinet, but at the polling-booths. It is the electors who make war or maintain peace, who repeal old laws and pass new ones, who interfere, justly or unjustly, between landlords and tenants, masters and servants, parents and children. Those who abstain from voting, determine the national policy as truly as those who vote. The responsibility of the Parliamentary franchise cannot be evaded.

I sometimes think that municipalities can do more for the people than Parliament. Their powers will probably be enlarged; but under the powers which they possess already they can greatly diminish the amount of sickness in the community, and can prolong human life. They can prevent – they have prevented – tens of thousands of wives from becoming widows, tens of thousands of children from becoming orphans. They can do very much to improve those miserable homes which are fatal not only to health, but to decency and morality. They can give to the poor the enjoyment of pleasant parks and gardens, and the intellectual cultivation and refinement of public libraries and galleries of art. They can redress in many ways the inequalities of human conditions. The gracious words of Christ, 'Inasmuch as ye did it unto one of these My brethren, even these least, ye did it unto Me,' will be addressed not only to those who with their own hands fed the hungry, and clothed the naked, and cared for the sick, but to those who supported a municipal policy which lessened the miseries of the wretched, and added brightness to the lives of the desolate. And the terrible rebuke, 'Inasmuch as ye did it not unto one of these least, ye did it not unto Me,' will condemn the selfishness of those who refused to make municipal government the instrument of a policy of justice and humanity.

Document IX.28

R. W. Dale on Christ and the State, 1891

R. W. Dale (see II.16) developed a more chastened view of political affairs after he had diverged from the Liberal Party in 1886 over home rule for Ireland. He retained a high estimate of the state, which he here attributes to the combined influence of Mill, Burke and Maurice, but he was now less sanguine about the potential for remoulding society through political means. The primary role of the church was to preach the gospel so that human beings were transformed in their hearts.

The extract is taken from the annual sermon for the Baptist Union Home Missions delivered by Dale in 1891 and published as 'Christ and the State' in R. W. Dale, *Fellowship with Christ*, London, 1892, pp. 200–13.

I suppose that we should all agree that during the present generation there has been a gradual change among Evangelical Nonconformists in their conception of the State and of the functions of the State. Half a century ago there was a very general acceptance among us of the theory that the whole business of the secular Government is to repress force and fraud. The State was even regarded by many of us as founded on a kind of mutual contract for the purpose of protecting life and property – a Limited Liability Company, with its objects and powers strictly defined in the articles of association. To restrict its action within the narrowest possible area was supposed to be the first duty of a wise and liberal politician. Many of us, I suppose, owed our emancipation from that theory, partly to Mr. John Stuart Mill, whose authority was at its zenith in 1850; partly to Edmund Burke, who taught us that the State is a great historical growth, not an artificial creation, and that instead of having any analogy to a voluntary association with limited liability, it is a 'partnership in all science, in all art, in every virtue, in all perfection.'

To Mr. Frederick Denison Maurice, probably more than to any other man, many of us owe the original impulse which started us on another line of thought. I think that I am not in error when I say that many Evangelical Nonconformists had come to have a vague impression – it was not inherited from their greatest ecclesiastical ancestors – but they had come to have a vague impression that political activity lies beyond the true province of the Christian life. When I was a young man I believe that that impression was a very general one. Mr. Edward Miall had already done something to dissipate it, but it had not disappeared. The State, with all its affairs, was regarded by large numbers of Christian people as belonging in an evil sense to this world, and to be political was to be worldly. They went to the polling booth, many of them, no doubt; but they went, as many Christian people now go to the theatre, feeling that they were hardly in their right place. Mr. Maurice insisted that the State is a Divine institution – like the Family, like the Church; many of us, I say, probably owe to him more than to any other man the original impulse which started our thought in that direction. But as soon as we began to look seriously into the New Testament we found it there, and we were astonished that we had not found it before. ...

It is our belief that the Church and the State, though both of them are Divine institutions, are Divine institutions of such a different description, and with such different immediate objects, that any organic alliance between them is certain in the long run to be injurious to both. The State is primarily the visible representative and defender of the Divine justice in the temporal order; the Church is primarily the visible representative of the Divine mercy and the Divine redemption in the eternal order. The State has other functions; the Church has other functions; but there is that deep distinction between them. When listening to Christ in the Church, and learning His conception of what our life should be, we hear Him say, 'Resist not him that is evil, but whosoever smiteth thee on thy right cheek turn to him the other also; and if any man would go to law with thee and take away thy coat, let him have thy cloak also.' But when we want to learn the Christian conception of the function of the civil ruler, we discover that if any man does evil he is not to expect the ruler to treat him after that manner; and that it is not the will of God that the ruler should treat him after that manner. 'If thou do that which is evil be afraid, for he beareth not the sword in vain; for he is a minister of God, an avenger for wrath to him that doeth evil.' ...

We ought to take our full share, we Christian people, in every movement for the practical amelioration of the condition of our fellow-countrymen. But speaking as one who for many years took an active part among the obscurer members of a great political party, I think that we must often be doubtful whether political and social schemes which are full of promise may not, from causes which human sagacity is unable to anticipate, turn out mischievous. In endeavouring to draw individual men to Christ – in disciplining to Christian intelligence, to righteousness and sanctity, those who already acknowledge His authority – we cannot go wrong. Every man that has received the Spirit of Christ, and is eager to do the will of Christ, is a new power for bringing in more just and more gracious conditions of economic and social life. John Wesley and George Whitefield did more for the social redemption of England than all the politicians of this century and the last, whose names are associated with great reforms;

under God, they created those moral and spiritual forces which have rendered all reforms possible.

In this work, I say again, we cannot go wrong. We trust that future generations of men, inheriting our name, speaking our tongue, living on English soil, will achieve an organization of life so just and so beautiful, that the poverty, the crime, the ignorance, the social strife of our own days shall seem to them an evil dream. But the great harvests of the world ripen slowly. We rejoice that while they are ripening it is possible, through God's grace, for God's lost children to be found and brought home to their Father. Their life in this world is brief at the longest. They are destined by the thought and purpose of God to an endless life of righteousness and wisdom, of joy and glory. That thought and purpose are not to be defeated by the inequalities and confusions of their earthly condition. The Apostles did not wait till slavery was abolished before they preached the Christian Gospel to slaves; slaves received the Gospel, and, remaining slaves, became children of the Eternal and heirs of the glory of God. Nor need *we* wait till the social miseries of many of our own countrymen disappear before we endeavour to make clear to them that they are born to an inheritance in the infinite love of God, and in the redemption which has been achieved for the human race by Christ. To those who are suffering from these miseries in their intenser form we should carry material relief, which, thank God, the Church has always been eager to give to the wretched. But with the material relief we should also carry the animating and glorious hope of a larger, freer, and nobler life when their earthly troubles are over. But the immense majority of our people are not worn with anxiety, wasted with hunger, crushed by despair; and among these there are millions who know nothing of the power and blessedness of the Christian Redemption. To these we have free access; there is nothing in their circumstances and condition to prevent them from receiving the Gospel of Christ, and from living according to His will. Let *them* learn to acknowledge Him as the true King of men, and within a generation the whole life of the country would be changed. Have courage, have faith. In the power of Christ, and in the power of the truth of Christ, we may confidently hope to recover our country both from its sorrows and its sins.

PART X

DENOMINATIONS

Introduction

The sheer variety of Nonconformity is evident in the bewildering range of denominations falling under its umbrella. The contrast between the centralised and the decentralised bodies was fundamental. The Quakers had an elaborate and long established system of decision-making organisations (X.5), while the Wesleyans developed their equivalent (X.2, 6), but not without protest and secession (X.9, 12). Congregationalists and Baptists, on the other hand, left decisions to local churches. They were joined in their principled opposition to central control by the Churches of Christ, who, like the Brethren, would not even accept a denominational designation (X.14). Nevertheless the trend during the nineteenth century was towards the creation of national organisations to co-ordinate and speak on behalf of the historically decentralised communities. The Unitarians, whose original inter-congregational links had long ago withered, set up a representative organisation (X.1); the Congregationalists (X.3) and Baptists followed. The same imperative to develop structures marked the Primitive Methodists, though they were suspicious of undue centralisation (X.13), and the Presbyterians, who had no reservations on that score (X.11). By the end of the century there was a trend to create institutions to represent the whole of Nonconformity (X.4).

Developments in the provinces led to the creation of movements with a distinctly local flavour. In Lancashire there were the Methodist Unitarians (X.7) and in Devon and Cornwall the Bible Christians (X.8). Some tiny groups were even more localised: the Cokelers lived only along a stretch of the Sussex/Surrey boundary (X.16), and the Fritchley Friends were limited almost exclusively to that village in Derbyshire (X.17). Other bodies, however, had larger claims. The Free Church of England aspired to being a shadow of the established church, a refuge for Evangelicals distressed by the advance of ritualism (X.15). The Catholic Apostolic Church had the grandest ambitions of all, for it believed that it held a commission to the whole of Christendom (X.10).

Some in the Church of England looked with jaundiced eye on the diverse mosaic of Nonconformity. Newman dismissed it (X.20); other Anglicans longed to assimilate the serviceable portions of it (X.23). Dissenters could give cogent traditional reasons for remaining outside the established church (X.18), and some erstwhile Anglicans concluded that its structures were incompatible with the implications of the gospel (X.19). Nonconformists were on the whole wary of the Church of England during the nineteenth century, whether they were Presbyterian (X.21), Congregationalist (X.22) or Wesleyan Methodist (X.24). It was left to a man of great learning and sagacity, P. T. Forsyth, to take a more balanced view at the end of the century (X.25).

The increasing bureaucracy of Nonconformity is discussed in D. M. Thompson, *Denominationalism and Dissent, 1795–1835*, London, 1985. The structures of

Methodism form the central theme of R. Currie, *Methodism Divided: A Study in the Sociology of Ecumenicalism*, London, 1968; and the transition to denominationalism is analysed in J. M. Turner, *Conflict and Reconciliation: Studies in Methodism and Ecumenism in England, 1740–1982*, London, 1985, chap. 5. The problems of creating a representative body in denominations upholding a congregational polity are considered in A. Peel, *These Hundred Years: A History of the Congregational Union of England and Wales, 1831–1931*, London, 1931, and E. A. Payne, *The Baptist Union*, London, 1959. Other denominational histories touch on organisational issues. Developments at the end of the century are discussed in J. W. Grant, *Free Churchmanship in England, 1870–1940*, London, n.d.; and in E. K. H. Jordan, *Free Church Unity: History of the Free Church Council Movement, 1896–1941*, London, 1956.

Structures

Document X.1

The British and Foreign Unitarian Association, 1825

The Association was formed to foster the interests of Unitarians and their congregations, but was not intended to adopt a supervisory or controlling role. The emphasis was on spreading Unitarian ideas and expanding and preserving the rights of individuals. It was purely by chance formed on exactly the same day – 26 May 1825 – as the American Unitarian Association. The constitution made no mention of theological beliefs and did not attempt to define Unitarianism, in contrast to the founding instruments of national associations in many other denominations.

District associations of Unitarian churches were formed from about 1800 as communities of the very independent churches, and Fellowship Funds were congregational organisations that raised money to create new causes. This extract is taken from the Second Annual Report of the Association, published in 1827. See H. L. Short, 'The Founding of the British and Foreign Unitarian Association', *Transactions of the Unitarian Historical Society*, 16 (1975), Supplement.

Rules of the Association

1. The Association is formed for the promotion of the principles of Unitarian Christianity at home and abroad – the support of its worship – the diffusion of biblical, theological, and literary knowledge on topics connected with it – and the maintenance of the civil rights and interests of its professors. ...

3. It shall consist of District Associations communicating with the central body and sending representatives thereto – of Congregations or Fellowship Funds communicating in like manner – of individual subscribers – and of Honorary Members. ...

5. Until otherwise resolved, the following shall be considered as the leading divisions of its objects:–

I. The promotion of Unitarian worship in Great Britain, by assisting poor congregations, and sending out or giving assistance to Missionary Preachers.

II. The publication and distribution of books and tracts, controversial and practical, – principally in a cheap and popular form.

III. The pursuit of the two last-mentioned objects (as opportunity and the means of the Association may afford) in foreign countries, and the maintenance, in the mean time, of correspondence and general co-operation.

IV. The protection and extension of the civil rights of Unitarians.

Document X.2

Wesleyan Conference against Agitation, 1835

The first half of the nineteenth century was marked by periodic unrest within Wesleyan Methodism against the central authority of the Conference and of Jabez Bunting (1779–1858), its mastermind. Bunting dominated the connexion from about 1812 to 1851, imposing administrative efficiency on the growing organisation. When his leadership was challenged in 1835 (see X.9), Conference responded by insisting on the unity and order of Wesley's Methodism and the corresponding illegitimacy of the opposition under Samuel Warren that, as the Grand Central Association, was evolving into the Wesleyan Methodist Association. See D. A. Gowland, *Methodist Secessions: The Origins of Free Methodism in Three Lancashire Towns: Manchester, Rochdale, Liverpool*, Manchester, 1979; and, on Bunting, T. P. Bunting, *The Life of Jabez Bunting, D.D.*, London, 1859–87; W. R. Ward, ed., *The Early Correspondence of Jabez Bunting, 1820–29*, Camden 4th series, 11, London, 1972; W. R. Ward, ed., *Early Victorian Methodism: The Correspondence of Jabez Bunting, 1830–1858*, Oxford, 1976; and DNB.

The passage is taken from *Official Documents: extracted from the Minutes of the Wesleyan-Methodist Conference*, London, 1835, pp. 59–61.

All the leading features of those agitations which have disturbed our societies in the course of the past year are gross violations of our rules and economy. The Wesleyan Methodists are not a number of isolated and independent societies or churches, but of societies united in one body; and from their commencement they have existed under one common system of government. Every person who chooses to unite himself to these societies is bound, as the condition of his fellowship, to abstain from violating the laws of the union, to live peaceably, and by all the means in his power to promote the piety, prosperity, and establishment of the community. The late attempts to subvert the Connexion have therefore been a violation of faith on the part of the agitators. And it must be obvious to all, that, as a community subsisting for no purposes but those which are religious and spiritual, it is impossible that we can maintain such simple conditions of admission into our societies, without this understanding, that though all may retain their peculiar opinions on minor points, yet all must consent to live in peace, and abide by the objects and conditions of their union; pursuing, in their connexion with the body, the only purposes of their religious fellowship.

The first great violation of the principles of our compact during the past year, and the occasion of the confusion which has resulted, was the refusal of the leader of the opposition to submit to the well-considered decision of his brethren; and then his appeal against them to the societies at large, and to the world. Having thus commenced a series of acts, independent of the jurisdiction of the Connexion, and set up the standard of revolt, in palpable contradiction to all his engagements, tacit and avowed, he proceeded so far as to make an appeal to the Courts of Chancery, and by various violent proceedings to lead on the people to overthrow the institutions of the Connexion. Nothing therefore remained to us, but, by a final sentence, to confirm the virtual separation of the several Preachers who had thus combined with him to produce a 'schism in the body.'

The formation of what has been called 'the Grand Central Association,' with its various branches, is equally an outrage on the peace and union, as well as on the rules, of the Connexion. No community, whether civil or religious, can long exist, if a large combination of its members be allowed to control its administration, and violently to beat down its constitutional barriers: the very existence of such a combination within the body must, in the nature of things, if tolerated, overthrow its whole economy. The officers of society, who have united in the Association, have done so in direct violation of their engagements and obligations. When Leaders and Local Preachers are admitted to their respective trusts, they assent to the discipline of the Connexion, place themselves under its authority, and bind themselves to a strict and conscientious observance of all its rules. No injury had been done to the men who have thus betrayed the trust reposed in them; no invasion of their rights and liberties is alleged; the economy remained as it was when they entered upon their respective offices; and yet, in a moment of temptation, many were induced to place themselves in hostility to the system they were pledged to obey and support. Not only is the Association illegal in principle, but its acts have also been opposed to the principles of Christian philanthropy, duty, and piety, and are acts of hostility against the kingdom of Christ.

We are thankful to God, that the greater number of our beloved people have proved themselves faithful in their opposition to this unhallowed combination; and, instead of uniting in 'stopping the supplies,' have, by their increased liberality, preserved the Connexion from the embarrassment into which the agitators designed to plunge it. Indeed we never could imagine that any great number, instructed in the doctrines, and devoted to the noble designs, of Mr. Wesley, would entertain sentiments so opposed to every thing that bears his name. As these confederates stood pledged to their principles, and avowed, through their leader, in the presence of the Conference, their determination to adhere to their revolutionary designs, you will see that it was impossible to hold any fellowship with them without compromising the constitution and interests of Wesleyan Methodism.

Document X.3

Henry Allon on the Congregational Union, 1881

Henry Allon (see IV.24) delivered an address on the Congregational Union as chairman in its jubilee year, 1881. He reasserted the central principle of Congregationalism, that each church was independent of all external authority, suggesting that criticism of the Union as having ambitions to control the churches was a healthy check. Affiliation to the Congregational Union, as to its sister Baptist Union, remained entirely voluntary.

The address is taken from A. Peel, *These Hundred Years: A History of the Congregational Union of England and Wales, 1831–1931*, London, 1931, pp. 320–22.

The union of churches is for the benefit of the individual churches that constitute it. It is their creation, and is subordinate to them. It is accidental; they are inviolable. It can be justified only by its practical recognition of their inviolability. Each Church has an indefeasible right to stand aloof from the Union or to withdraw from it, and every Church joining it is, in virtue of the cardinal principle of Independency, inviolable in its autonomy. All association involves compromise; some exercises of individual liberty are surrendered for the sake of concerted action, but the surrender of Church autonomy is impossible without the surrender of Congregationalism itself.

So long as the Union maintains its character as a voluntary confederation for fellowship and work of independent Churches, it is both unimpeachable and invaluable. Let it in any way put disability upon Churches not belonging to it, impose conditions of Church life and work, assume that membership with it is the criterion of orthodoxy or of moral worth – and these are the natural tendencies of association – and it will invert the true order of its relationship, and become a legislative synod, and that of the worst type, because without its carefully devised safeguards.

Hitherto, the Union has not interfered with Congregational principles. In no way intended to discredit their intrinsic truth, excellency, or sufficiency, it is simply a concert for their broader and more efficient application. It has neither power nor right to put its imprimatur upon either church or minister. A jealous maintenance of individual liberty is really the essential condition of both order and strength.

It is easy, then, to see how the organization of Congregational Churches, constituted upon a theory of individual independence, necessarily involves some of the gravest of ecclesiastical questions. No problem of social life is greater than exactly to adjust the balance of liberty and order, individualism and co-operation, the independence of each and the legitimate subordination of each to the whole.

When, after some tentative and local experiments, the Congregational Union was projected, these problems presented themselves to its projectors with special gravity. They were largely discussed; they are not solved yet; probably they never will be; they are of a character that admits only of empirical, not of scientific, solution.

With the ecclesiastical history of Christendom as a warning, and considering the insidious tendency of association to emasculate and destroy liberty, there was a natural and wholesome jealousy lest the projected fellowship should encroach upon indefeasible rights of independent churches; lest, following the precedents of ecclesiastical history, the Association should become a synod, the synod a legislature, the legislature an autocracy, and thus, by gradual and unintentional encroachments, the parent principle of liberty should be devoured by its own offspring.

Under the influence of the apprehension, some of our wisest and strongest men regarded the projected Union with misgivings; by some it was formally and strenuously opposed. This gospel also was preached 'with much contention'.

So far from this being cause for regret, it was in every way most wholesome. For the incipient Union itself it was beneficial that it should be subject to the keen scrutiny and criticism of men jealous for the liberties of the churches, and justly deeming no possible precision of action a compensation for any compromise of these. To this wholesome criticism the Union has been subjected ever since – its principles tested, its methods questioned, and its own spirit of freedom kept quick and vigilant.

It will be a disastrous day for our churches when this spirit relaxes. There is nothing that should be more assiduously cherished by us than the spirit of independence – the robust and wholesome integrity of individual responsibility. It is more than a compensation for a hundred practical defects. The most disorderly exercise of liberty were better than its negation. The suppression of liberty is not peace. Maintain a true principle of life, it will be a corrective of all practical defect; surrender the principle and virtue itself is deprived of nobility.

Whatever, therefore, our Congregationalism may lose in precision and force through morbid jealousies of exaggerated individualism, its privation of the responsibilities of individual life would be incomparably more disastrous. Better that our churches were resolved into their primitive constituents than their association should develop legislative authority or even irresistible moral constraint.

These early fears were gradually dissipated, and the Union won the suffrages of its most vigilant critics. From that time to this it has incurred no tangible blame, and has excited only vague and evanescent suspicions. Churches still stand aloof from it. Some, probably, in the mere wantonness of independency; others with unallayed fears concerning the natural tendencies of confederation; but their moral right to do this is fully recognized. They suffer no disability, they are held in unimpaired esteem, save as one judgment necessarily thinks itself superior to another.

It is, I think, in every way advantageous that there should be churches maintaining this witness. The misgivings do not respect Congregationalism itself, but the integrity of it as imperilled by such associations.

Document X.4

J. Guinness Rogers on a Congress of the Free Churches, 1890

James Guinness Rogers (1822–1911) was minister of the well-to-do Grafton Square Congregational Church, Clapham (1865–1900), chairman of the Congregational Union in 1874 and joint editor of *The Congregationalist* (1879–86) and *The Congregational Review* (1887–91). In addition he was a prolific contributor to other periodicals, supplying influential commentary on Liberal politics as well as on Nonconformist affairs. In this article he mooted the creation of an annual congress, modelled on that of the Church of England, to articulate the interests of all the bodies that he was one of the first to call the Free Churches. Such a congress was inaugurated in 1892 and during the following decade local Free Church Councils sprang up in most parts of the country, vindicating Rogers's contention that there was a sense of common purpose among Evangelical Nonconformists. See E. K. H. Jordan, *Free Church Unity: History of the Free Church Council Movement, 1896–1941*, London, 1956; and, for Rogers, J. G. Rogers, *An Autobiography*, London, 1903; and DNB.

The extract is taken from *The Methodist Times*, 20 February 1890, pp. 173–4.

Has not the time come when the true unity which, I believe, undoubtedly exists between the different Evangelical and Nonconformist churches of the country should be made more distinctly visible? That there has been a softening of the old asperities of centuries, the growth of a more true and generous appreciation of each other's work, an increasing desire for the cultivation of more close and friendly relations – in short, that a more Christian sentiment of brotherhood has been growing up among the several Free Churches, is patent to every careful observer. I was very much struck in reading the life of Dr. Bunting, to find how strained (to use a common phrase of the times, but one which is the mildest that can be employed here with truth) were the relations between the Wesleyan and Congregational ministers when he travelled for the first time in a London circuit; how much there was of mutual distrust, growing largely out of a common ignorance; how little intercourse there was between the two classes; how much afraid each seemed to be of approaching the other. There is a marked contrast in the state of feeling to-day, which indicates a happy advance.

The change is not due to the surrender of any theological position on either side, and even if there has been a distinct approximation on the part of both, the improved relations are due rather to the development of a spirit of true tolerance, which is one of the happiest signs of the times. God has been teaching us great lessons, which some of us have been very slow to learn, of the same kind as He taught the church as Jerusalem in the conversion of Cornelius and in the gathering of the Church at Antioch. We have learned that true godliness may have many varieties of manifestation and many different forms of service, and that we are warring against God when we refuse to acknowledge a work which is evidently of Him, because it does not conform to all our ideas and is carried out on lines far removed from those which we have been accustomed to regard as decorous. The result has been a more intelligent recognition of a truth, alas! too continually overlooked in the heated feeling of sectarian controversy, that there will always be diversities of operation and differences of administration, though there is but one Lord and though it is the same God who worketh all things in all. In this is the true secret of spiritual unity. This spirit, which is much more than a 'sweet reasonableness,' which carries on controversy without passion and with a scrupulous endeavour to weight truly the arguments on both sides, which is a frank and thorough admission that truth does not belong to any one system nor has any church a monopoly of goodness, has been gaining strength. The question which I desire to raise is as to the wisdom of giving it such expression as shall make it manifest that the Evangelical Nonconformity of England is a compact and united force, welded together by Christian principle for the advancement of spiritual truth and the extension of Christ's kingdom.

A Church Congress meets year by year for the purpose of strengthening the Establishment in the work it has to do in the nation. It is impossible to deny that the influence which it has exerted has been considerable. Why should not Nonconformists profit by the example and have a similar gathering of their own? It is true that the Congress includes the members of one Church only, whereas we are divided into several communities. But, as a matter of fact, the theological differences which separate the various bodies of Nonconformists from one another are neither so extreme nor so vital as those which divide the parties which meet under the shelter of the Established Church. It is true that they are united by a common desire to preserve the Establishment, but does not this zeal of theirs, in defence of the National Church, expose us to a serious danger which we should unite to repel. Despite the generous and liberal sentiments of a certain number of the clergy, among whom some of the Deans are conspicuous, there is a manifest determination to spare no effort for the suppression of Dissent. Abundant evidence of this may be found in the proceedings of the Cardiff Congress. So deep is the impression produced on Welsh Nonconformists, that earnest efforts are now being made for a federation of Nonconformity in the Principality. Such steps are not taken a day too soon. What I desire is that a movement should be made in a similar direction in this country. Formal organisation is neither desirable, possible, nor necessary. But opportunities for conference on topics of common interest, such as a Congress would afford, would be invaluable. Such an assembly could have no more authority than is possessed by the Congregational or Baptist Union, or by the Church Congress, but its moral influence would necessarily be great.

It is not suggested that such a Congress should assume a hostile attitude towards the Established Church. It is quite possible that occasion may arise when the voice of united Nonconformity should be raised in protest against an aggressive clerical policy, full of menace to some of its vital interests. An example of this is before us at this moment in the shameless violation of the Education Act in the action of the Department at Salisbury and York. Whatever be our differences on various educational questions, Nonconformists must surely be agreed that School Boards are not to be superseded by Kilburn Sisterhoods, and the schools of the nation converted into happy hunting grounds for the clergy. The protests of Nonconformists on such a subject could not but be effective. Apart even from incidental action of this kind, the mere demonstration of the unity of Evangelical denominations would exercise a power which it is not easy to measure. It would be a public development of a Church idea which at present is hardly realised. Wesleyans, Presbyterians, Baptists, Congregationalists meeting on the same platform, not for an interchange of compliments and courtesies, but for true Christian fellowship in devotional service, and for counsel on common Christian work, would be a striking illustration of a Catholic Church, including various sections, each with its own form of development, and with its distinctive features of doctrine and ritual, but all one in Christ Jesus. To me it seems that there could be no counteractive of the false ideas of the 'Holy Catholic Church,' so sedulously propagated and so seductive to many, as such a manifestation of true Christian unity. The spirit of such a fellowship should not be polemical, its attitude antagonistic, nor its action controversial, except when controversy is forced upon it. Its power will be found in this practical exhibition of a positive truth. But I must pause, and ask for another opportunity of presenting my idea more in detail.

Document X.5

Quaker Organisation, 1891

Caroline Stephen (see IV.12) describes the tight-knit, multi-layered structure of the Society of Friends, similar in many respects to Presbyterianism. She expounds the distinctive manner of reaching decisions by trying to discern the will of God. The relaxation of discipline in 1861 was crucial: no longer were Friends excluded from the Society for marrying non-Quakers. See E. Isichei, *Victorian Quakers*, Oxford, 1970, chap. 3.

The extract is taken from C. Stephen, *Quaker Strongholds*, 3rd edn, London, 1891, pp. 14–20.

Every 'particular meeting,' that is, every congregation meeting habitually for worship on the first (and generally also on one other) day of the week, is one of a group of meetings for worship (usually about five or six) which meet together once a month, for the transaction of business and of discipline, and which together form what is therefore called a Monthly Meeting. Each Monthly Meeting, again, is one of group of probably four or five Monthly Meetings, which in like manner unite to form a Quarterly Meeting, at whose quarterly sittings matters of larger importance are considered; and the eighteen Quarterly Meetings of Great Britain form in their turn the London Yearly Meeting, which is the supreme authority in the Society. It may in a certain sense be said indeed, that it *is* the Society of Friends of Great Britain, for every Friend is a member of the Monthly, Quarterly, and Yearly Meetings to which he or she belongs, and is entitled to a voice in all their deliberations. The Yearly Meeting assembles in May, and its sittings, which are held, as they have been from the first, in Devonshire House, Bishopsgate Street, last generally about a fortnight. The actual attendance, is, of course, small in comparison with the number of members. At the present time the Society in Great Britain consists of about fifteen thousand members, and the annual gatherings in Bishopsgate Street number perhaps from twelve to fifteen hundred.

The men and women sit separately, or rather to speak quite correctly the men and the women Friends have each a separate Yearly Meeting; the women's Yearly Meeting being of considerably later date than the men's. It was established in 1790, and it deals in general with matters of less importance, or at any rate of more restricted scope, than the men's meeting. It is, however, not unusual for men

Friends, 'under religious concern,' to visit the women's meeting, nor for women Friends on a similar ground to visit that of the men.

'Joint sittings' – meetings, that is, of men and women Friends in one body – are also held occasionally, when any question of special interest to all the members is to be considered, and on these occasions the women are free to take their full share in the discussions. These occasional combinations are the more easily practicable, because, strange as it may seem to most people, no question is ever put to the vote. From the earliest times, all decisions have been arrived at by what may be called a practical unanimity. The Yearly Meeting, like every other meeting for 'business' or 'discipline,' has its clerk, who, with one or more assistants, performs the combined functions of chairman and secretary. When any question has been fully considered, it is the duty of the clerk to interpret the sense of the meeting, and to prepare a minute accordingly; which minute, being read to the meeting, often receives a certain amount of verbal, or even of substantial modification, in accordance with the suggestions of individual Friends; but, when entered upon the books, is accepted as embodying the decision of the meeting. Should there be any considerable division of judgment upon any important question, it is usually, if possible, adjourned till the next Yearly Meeting; and this plan has, I believe, been almost invariably found sufficient to bring about the practical unanimity required for a final settlement of the question. It is certainly a very remarkable fact that so large a body should transact all its affairs without ever voting, to the full satisfaction of the great majority of those concerned.

The Quarterly and Monthly Meetings are, in most respects, repetitions on a smaller scale of the Yearly Meeting. The business of all these subordinate meetings is transacted, like that of the Yearly Meeting, without voting, and settled similarly through the action of the clerk when a practical unanimity is arrived at. Each Monthly Meeting appoints 'representatives' to the next Quarterly Meeting, and the Quarterly Meetings in like manner appoint 'representatives' to the next Yearly Meeting. These Friends have no very definite function to perform, but their names are called over, and their presence or absence noted at the opening of each meeting to which they are sent; and they are expected to serve in a general way as a special medium of communication between the larger and the smaller meetings to which they belong.

In like manner, upon any subject affecting the Society at large, the Yearly Meeting communicates with the Quarterly Meetings, who in their turn diffuse the impulse through their own Monthly and particular meetings, till it reaches every individual member; and, in return, information respecting every meeting for worship is from time to time given to the Monthly Meetings, to be by them in a condensed form reported to the Quarterly Meetings, and so eventually presented to the Yearly Meeting in London. All these ascending and descending processes are carried on with minute accuracy and regularity, and are duly recorded at every stage in the books of each meeting. There is thus a complete system of circulation, as of veins and arteries, by which every individual member is brought within reach of the Society at large, and through which information, influence, and discipline are carried to and from the centre and the extremities.

The 'discipline' of the Society is a matter of extreme interest, as to which I cannot venture to say with any confidence how far our recognised ideal is actually carried out in practice. There is no doubt that of late years considerable changes have taken place, mainly in the direction of a relaxation of discipline with regard to comparatively trivial matters. Certain 'queries' have from the earliest times been appointed by the authority of the Yearly Meeting, to be read and considered at certain seasons in the subordinate meetings and to most of these queries (some relating to various branches of Christian morality, and some to regularity in attendance at meetings and conformity to established standards of simplicity in dress and language) it was formerly the practice to require detailed answers from each particular meeting, to be in due course transmitted in a summarized form to the Yearly Meeting itself. In 1861, however, the Yearly Meeting issued directions that a certain number of these queries should be merely 'considered,' but not answered. In 1875 this method was adopted with regard to nearly all the queries, and at present those only which relate to the regularity of attendance at meetings for worship and business are answered. This change has a very obvious significance, and I believe that its effect is even more marked than would be understood by any one not accustomed to the extreme care and gravity with which these matters were formerly pondered and reported upon in each 'preparative meeting' (*i.e.* each particular meeting sitting specially with a view to preparing the business to be transacted at any approaching Monthly Meeting), and again at each stage of the progress of the report towards its final presentation by the Quarterly to the Yearly Meeting. Dress and language and other external matters are now practically left entirely to the individual conscience, as is surely wisest. With regard to weightier matters, such as strict integrity in business, sobriety, and correctness of moral conduct, etc., there is still, I hope and believe, a considerable reality of watchful care exercised through specially appointed members. In every Monthly Meeting there are Friends holding the offices of elder and overseer. The business of the elders is to watch over the ministers in the exercise of their gift; that of the overseers to see to the relief of the poorer members, the care of the sick, and other such matters; to watch over the members generally with regard to their Christian conduct, to warn privately any who may be giving cause of offence or scandal, and in case of need to bring the matter before the Monthly Meeting to be dealt with as it may require. Should the Monthly Meeting think it necessary to disown a member for persisting in conduct not consistent with our Christian profession, or for any other reason, the member in question may appeal to the Quarterly Meeting, and from its decision to that of the Yearly Meeting, which is in all cases final.

The London Yearly Meeting has two standing committees for the transaction of such of its affairs as need attention more frequently than once a year. One of these represents the Yearly Meeting at large, and has charge of its money matters and other general business; it bears the curious and suggestive title of the 'Meeting for Sufferings,' from having been originally occupied mainly in relieving Friends under persecution. The other is a committee of the Yearly Meeting on Ministry and Oversight, and is called the 'Morning Meeting.'

Meetings on Ministry and Oversight are held in every Quarterly and Monthly Meeting as well as at the Yearly Meeting. They are composed of all the recorded ministers, the elders and overseers of each meeting, together with (in some Quarterly Meetings) some Friends described as 'associate members,' who attend them as it were not officially, but by a standing invitation. These meetings are concerned, of course, with questions relating to the special offices exercised by their members.

Document X.6

J. H. Rigg on Wesleyan Organisation, 1897

James Harrison Rigg (1821–1909) was a Wesleyan minister from 1849 who became principal of the connexion's Westminster Training College for teachers (1868–1903). He was a member of the London School Board (1870–76) and of the Royal Commission on Elementary Education (1886–88), president of Conference (1878 and 1892) and editor of *The London Quarterly Review* (1886–98). He provided the official justification for Wesleyan practices in the work quoted here. Like the early church, he contended, the connexion had evolved a pragmatic species of Presbyterianism. The arrangement for laymen to attend the middle week of Conference, a solution to the perennial problem of clerical-lay relationships in Wesleyanism, was Rigg's own idea. See J. Telford, *The Life of James Harrison Rigg, D.D.*, London, 1909; and J. T. Smith, *Methodism and Education, 1849–1902: J. H. Rigg, Romanism and Wesleyan Schools*, Oxford, 1998.

The extract is taken from J. H. Rigg, *A Comparative View of Church Organisations, Primitive and Protestant*, 3rd edn, London, 1897, pp. 222–8.

The connexional union of Methodism is closer and more complete than could be the union of the Churches of distant regions in the apostolic ages. But such union is in strictest harmony with the spirit of primitive Christianity. So also the responsibility and power, with which Methodism invests its ministers, to take the lead in all evangelistic enterprise, to initiate Christian missionary effort wherever it is possible to make advances from the ground already occupied, is a point of organisation and discipline in which Methodism is in the strictest harmony with apostolic Christianity. The close mutual brotherhood, again, of the ministers, and their common responsibility for the appointment of their colleagues and successors, and for the exercise of moral and spiritual discipline over their fellows – these are points in which Methodism, more completely than any other form of Presbyterianism, carries out the original principles of apostolic Christianity.

In respect of the manner in which the laity are associated with the ministers of Methodism in administrative and in disciplinary functions, it is sufficient to claim that the spirit of the apostolic precedents is well observed in Methodism. The precise mode in which this point is kept in view and carried out has been determined by the growth and history of the Methodist Connexion. The manner of the growth and the facts of the history determined the law of the organisation. As in the primitive Church, so in Methodism, need and aptitude were the two factors which, from time to time, governed the steps of development and adaptation in the organic growth of the united community. The distinction between clergy and laity is one which had no application, no meaning, in relation to Methodism in the earliest stages of its history. Methodism was at first merely a Society, a sort of extended spiritual guild. As such, it was most effectively managed and governed. There were classes and class-leaders for spiritual fellowship; each local Society had its stewards, who took charge of the moneys contributed in the classes and congregations, and who saw to their proper distribution. When in the course of time the preachers, who had at first been merely lay helpers of the Wesleys, grew into the character of pastors, and when the aggregate Society or union of Societies developed into a Church, the leaders and stewards became the local Church council of each Society. The whole guild-system was, in fact, gradually transmuted into a Church organisation. The leaders and stewards were invested with disciplinary functions; they became a sort of diaconate, the stewards being godly men whose attention was mainly devoted to the secular business and responsibilities of the Church, the leaders being the class of deacons who, as assistants of the ministers, the 'pastors and teachers,' the 'elders,' were placed in charge chiefly, but not exclusively, of the spiritual character and condition of the members. Official authority and position were thus founded on appropriate gifts and on service rendered to the Church; gifts and service were the qualification for official status and rights of government (1 Cor. xvi. 15–18).

Another sort of office in our Methodist Church – which some have regarded as a branch of the diaconal service, and others as the modern equivalent to the office of prophet in the early Churches – is that of lay or local preacher. There is in Wesleyan Methodism a distinct local preachers' Quarterly Meeting, over which the superintendent minister of each 'circuit' presides. There are also for the 'circuit' generally officers called originally 'general stewards,' – now called 'circuit stewards,' – who receive the moneys from the stewards of the various Societies. There are trustees of the chapels, and trustees' meetings; trustees, who are members of the Society, being also members of the Circuit Quarterly Meeting. All the Society and circuit officers are, according to the practice of the early Church, approved and appointed to office by the ministers, but approved and chosen also by the members of the meeting into which they are to be introduced; the ministers, on the one hand, and lay members of the meeting, on the other hand, possessing thus a separate power of veto, as well as the right of joint approval, in regard to every appointment. The administration of the spiritual affairs of each Society, or local Church, is vested in the leaders' meeting, and those of the general business of the circuit in the Quarterly Meeting, or collective assembly of the lay officers of the circuit. A circuit of a thousand members may be estimated, on an average, to have a Quarterly Meeting of not less than a hundred and twenty members. These powerful bodies invite the ministers, determine and raise their 'allowances' (*i.e.* money payments), review all the interests of the circuit, and send resolutions to the District Synod or memorials to Conference. They have also the right to appoint a circuit jury of appeal from the findings and verdict of a leaders' meeting in certain cases of discipline. Moreover, in case of the enactment by the Conference of a new law, intended to be binding on the circuits and Societies, each Quarterly Meeting has the right of suspending, if it so determine, the operation of the law for one year, until it shall have been reconsidered by the Conference.

The Conference itself – that is, the Annual Assembly which governs the whole Connexion – has, like the local organisations of the Connexion, grown into its present form and functions according to the suggestions of necessity or pressing convenience. The Conference cannot alter the 'Rules of the Society,' or the settlement of the chapels, or the provisions of the Deed of Declaration by which, in 1784, it was legally constituted and defined by John Wesley. Before that date, the Conference was the annual assembly of such of Wesley's preachers as he called together to take counsel with himself. In 1784 he gave it a legal constitution, and certain authority and rights in regard to the chapels of the Connexion and the appointment and disciplinary control of the preachers. These rights, and others with which the Conference has in various ways been invested, have received the fullest and most explicit recognition from the highest legal tribunals of the country. The Conference, at the present time, combines two functions: it is, in part, an assembly of co-pastors, annually meeting to exercise mutual discipline and to take mutual counsel in regard to such questions as are specifically pastoral subjects; and, in part, it is a conjoint assembly of ministers and lay brethren convened to receive reports and to deliberate and determine in regard to the general interests of the Connexion. All the points as to its order and method of procedure, and the classes of questions to be dealt with respectively in the two distinct but correlated sessions, are exactly defined. In the first capacity – as the assembly of co-pastors – it sits for about ten days, in the second – as the assembly of representative ministers and representative laymen – for a week; the Conference being, throughout both terms of session, regarded as one continuous assembly. Between 1878 and 1890 (inclusive) the two sessions were consecutive. Now the representative mixed assembly occupies the intermediate week, the co-pastoral session meeting in the first and third week. The legal body which gives unity, and, in a sense, identity, to the Conference in both its sessions, is what is called the 'Legal Conference,' a body of one hundred ministers, constituted and perpetuated in virtue of the provisions of the 'Deed of Declaration' already referred to, and which, as a matter of necessary legal form and solemnity, endorses and adopts what has been done in the sessions of the General Conference.

Intermediate between the Conference and the circuits of Methodism are the District Meetings, which are in effect provincial synods. These assemblies, which have been officially described and known as Synods since the Conference of 1893, were originally organised as Committees of the Conference, and, like the Conference, are, during the transaction of certain business, – what has been defined as properly pastoral business, – purely pastoral assemblies; while for all other business, and during its consecutive transaction, they are mixed assemblies; the circuit stewards, and, besides the circuit stewards, the specially elected representatives of the circuit quarterly meetings, the District treasurers of Connexional funds, and the lay members of District committees which have charge respectively of Chapel Affairs, of Sunday and Day School Affairs, of Home Mission Affairs, of Temperance, and of the District organisation of the Foreign Missionary Society, being members of the meeting for the transaction of all such business. At the pastoral sessions of the Synods the ministers exercise mutual discipline, including a strict enquiry into character and administration; they take counsel in regard to their common and also their respective pastoral responsibilities and duties, and the spiritual interests of their work; they conduct theological and pastoral examinations in regard to candidates for the ministry and probationers for the ministry provisionally accepted by the Conference. These are their pastoral responsibilities. In regard to other points of administration, the ministers and laity deliberate and act in common. The general religious interests of the work of the Church, including both the condition, spiritual and financial, of the circuits, and collective action on the part of the District as a whole, so far as that may be practicable, are considered in the full District Synod. These meetings are accustomed to send suggestions or recommendations to the Conference on the points which come under review. The Conference also is accustomed to remit questions for consideration to the Synods, nor can any legislation adopted by the Conference become binding law for the Connexion till it has been ratified by the majority of the Synods. The Synods are also courts of appeal from the circuits. To the pastoral session of the Synod appeals lie on questions of ministerial character or of discipline. The co-pastoral business of the Synod precedes and follows the financial and general business, which occupies in the largest Districts two intermediate days, but in small Districts only one.

New Denominations

Document X.7

Methodist Unitarians, c. 1817

Joseph Cooke (1775–1811) was expelled by the Methodist Conference in 1806 for propounding heretical views, and formed a new movement centred at Rochdale. This grew slowly, and the members were known as 'Cookites' even after his early death. His followers, led by John Ashworth (1781–1852), found their views evolving into Unitarianism, and this close association of churches in Lancashire consisting of poor working men and their families became known as the Methodist Unitarians. John Ashworth, in *An Account of the Rise and Progress of the Unitarian Doctrine in the Societies at Rochdale, Newchurch in Rossendale, and other places, formerly in Connexion with the late Rev Joseph Cooke: in ten letters to a friend*, London, 1817, sets out their story. The extract is from Letter 10, pages 64 and 69, and the reference to 'those friends who have given ... towards assisting us' is to Unitarians in other parts of the country who gave financial support.

See H. McLachlan, *The Methodist Unitarian Movement, 1806–1857*, Manchester, 1919; A. Ruston, 'New Light on Joseph Cooke', *Transactions of the Unitarian Historical Society*, Vol. 21 (1997), pp. 205–12.

Since we gave up the doctrine of the proper deity of Christ, we have seen translations of this passage (Isaiah 9: 6, 7) which in our opinion divest it of all its supposed force, in proof that the child born was also the uncreated Jehovah; and there are sufficient reasons to prove that such translations are right. But, among those who are as ignorant of the original language of the Scripture as ourselves, such an answer has been treated with contempt. And really I cannot help thinking it a great pity that the unlearned, which constitute the great mass of mankind, should be considered as dependent on the learning of the few, who differ as much in their translations of the Scriptures as the unlearned do in their opinion of them when translated. And, without depreciating learning, surely we may say there is, or ought to be, some other criterion of truth, than that which depends upon learned criticism. ...

It will be natural for our friends who have done so much towards assisting us, to look for, and expect, our further progress. And those who have the oversight of us are anxious that our increase and growth in virtue and piety should be such as not to disappoint them. From the time of forming ourselves into Christian churches under the care of Mr. Cooke, we have not only had regular services on the Lord's day at Rochdale and Newchurch, and at Padiham as oft as we had opportunity, but we have also had private social meetings on the week day, where those who fear the Lord converse together, pray with one another, and sing hymns of praise to God. By this, a more intimate acquaintance and fellow-feeling have been produced among us, which have provoked one another to love and good works. But, should these means be neglected (and with much pain we have seen them too much neglected), the social religious affections, like the scattered embers, will die away; and as on this account there will be less union, so there will be less strength, and consequently less progress will be made.

Document X.8

William O'Bryan on the Bible Christian Schism, 1815

William O'Bryan (1778–1868) was an energetic but angular Cornish farmer who served as a Methodist local preacher. Rejected as a candidate for the ministry in 1810, he was expelled from the connexion and organised his own groups of followers. After rejoining the Methodists in 1814, he was again expelled in the following year for persisting in acting as a roving evangelist. He therefore set up his own connexion, the Arminian Bible Christians. In 1829 he was to be forced out of this body because of his domineering ways, and he soon emigrated to North America. See T. Shaw, *The Bible Christians, 1815–1907*, London, 1965.

O'Bryan's own narrative of the schism is taken from his account of 'The Rise and Progress of the Connexion of People called Arminian Bible Christians' in *The Arminian Magazine* (which he edited), August 1823, pp. 254–61. The issue came to a head at a quarterly meeting of the Stratton Mission on the Cornwall/Devon boundary held on 27 September 1815. Richard Spettigue was a circuit steward; George Banwell was the superintendent minister.

One of the principal speakers, gave his vote for me to take a plan in common with the local preachers of the mission, on the Lord's-days; and on the week days go as a missionary where I thought proper; and offered on these conditions to support my interest. Brother Spettigue observed, that he thought this might be inconvenient for me to attend a local preacher's plan on the Lord's-day, as I might be at a great distance the day before, yet, as he was delegated to go to the quarterly meeting, and had from me liberty to do his best to promote peace, he engaged that I would submit to this inconvenience rather than separate from the Methodist church. When G.B[anwe]ll the travelling preacher came into the room, the conditions of reconciliation were stated to him. To which he positively objected, declaring that he would have nothing to do with me, and that if I would preach, I should return to the circuit from whence I came, &c. – and that he himself would preach in no house where I did. Brother S. answered, I did not intend to preach on their side of the circuit, where he did, except at Mary-Week, and that house being taken for me, I would not give it up. All overtures being rejected, and seeing that it appeared impossible to unite, unless I would consent to comparative silence, contrary to my conscience; and by this time also, contrary to the sufferance of scores, if not hundreds of hearers; so having no alternative, we became decided;

and in four days I found myself in a circuit of my own, containing a fortnight's plan, calculated to supply eighteen places, once a fortnight at each place. ...

[Later Banwell sent instructions by messengers from Stratton that O'Bryan was not to be welcomed to the Methodist society at Northlew.] My *Stratton friends* looked rather confounded, when they saw one of the principal preachers lead me by the arm and put me up in the pulpit; and after preaching lead me into the house, and place me at the head of the table; and the friends at the meeting kind and loving. Illwill deserves to be mortified. If it be not in this world, it will in the next. May God grant that my enemies may have all their punishment in this world.

Document X.9

Propositions Leading to the Wesleyan Methodist Association, 1835

When Jabez Bunting (see X.2) was nominated as president of the new Wesleyan Theological Institution, an agitation against his domination of the connexion sprang up in the north of England. The leader was Samuel Warren (1781–1862; see DNB), a preacher since 1802 and a man whose scholarship earned him the Glasgow D.D. Warren encouraged criticism of connexional policy along the lines of these resolutions of a meeting held in Manchester from 20 to 23 April 1835. The agitators went on to create the Wesleyan Methodist Association, asserting lay rights, local freedoms and majority rule, but Warren left in 1838 to become an Anglican clergyman. See D. A. Gowland, *Methodist Secessions: The Origins of Free Methodism in Three Lancashire Towns: Manchester, Rochdale, Liverpool*, Manchester, 1979.

The extract is taken from *Propositions and Resolutions of a Provisional Meeting of Delegates from Various Parts of the Kingdom*, Manchester, 1835, pp. 11–13.

RESOLVED, GENERAL PRINCIPLE.

That the basis of a plan for a reformation of existing abuses in Methodism, shall be the principle of the right of interference on the part of the members of the church, in the regulation of all its affairs.

PROPOSITION I.

That leaders' meetings be composed, as usual, of the stewards and leaders of each separate society; local preachers' meetings, of all the local preachers of the circuit; quarterly meetings, of the stewards, leaders, local preachers, and trustees of the Circuit; the itinerant preachers having a voice in all such meetings, and the superintendent preacher be *ex officio* president of the same; but should any superintendent refuse to put to the vote any resolutions regularly proposed, then the meeting shall have the authority to appoint another person to be, for that time, the chairman of the meeting.

PROPOSITION II.

That leaders' meetings have authority to transact all business connected with the societies to which they belong; local preachers' meetings to manage, as usual, all matters relating immediately to the work and office of local preachers; and quarterly meetings to have the control of all the affairs of the circuit.

PROPOSITION III.

That all our rules be based upon the principle that we exist as a Connexion for purposes purely religious; that they be published for the information of the whole body, their meaning being first unequivocally defined; and that no rule or regulation be considered binding upon the Connexion until it have received the approbation of a majority of the societies, through the medium of their respective quarterly meetings.

PROPOSITION IV.

That the discipline of each circuit be administered by its own local authorities; an appeal lying from the leaders' and local preachers' meetings to the quarterly meetings, whose decision, without the interference of either district meeting or Conference, shall be final.

PROPOSITION V.

That unrestricted discussion on all subjects affecting the interests of the body be allowed in all our official meetings, every question being decided by the majority.

PROPOSITION VI.

That the members of society by means of the leaders, in conjunction with the other officers of the circuit, be represented in all district meetings, and in Conference, according to some equitable plan of lay delegation to be adjusted between the preachers and the delegates at the approaching Conference to be held in Sheffield.

PROPOSITION VII.

That the management of the financial affairs of the Connexion be placed exclusively in the hands of laymen, so as to disencumber the ministerial office from the burthen of secular matters.

PROPOSITION VIII.

That as there are many members of society sincerely attached to Methodism, who most decidedly object to the establishment of the Theological Institution, and who, from the opinions they entertain thereon, conceive that the character of our ministry will thereby be injuriously altered, and the pecuniary resources of the Connexion diminished; and as it is obvious from the past prosperity of Methodism,

Denominations

without such an institution, that it is not indispensable; the Conference should therefore consent, rather than hazard a division of the Connexion, to give up the Theological Institution forthwith.

PROPOSITION IX.

That the Rev. Dr. Warren, and the various officers and members who have been suspended, or expelled for their conscientious opposition to the Theological Institution, or have left the Society in consequence of the unjust and unconstitutional treatment they, or their brethren, have received since the Conference of 1827, be reinstated in the respective situations which they had previously occupied.

Document X.10

Catholic Apostolic Catechism, 1843

The Catholic Apostolic Church (see IV.18) was a strange blend of the charismatic and the catholic. In its catechism there is stress on the prophetic word preceding ordination (q. 11) and the gifts of the Holy Ghost (qq. 17–19); but equally all is to be done under the authority of bishops ('angels'), priests and deacons (qq. 10, 12–15). The supreme power is vested in the apostles (qq. 5–7). See C. G. Flegg, *'Gathered under Apostles': A Study of the Catholic Apostolic Church*, Oxford, 1992, sect. 3.

The extract is taken from *The Liturgy and Other Divine Offices of the Church* [1843], London, n.d., pp. 546–9.

1. *Q.* You have said that you believe the 'Holy Catholic Church:' What is the Church?
A. The Church is the congregation of all who believe in the Lord Jesus Christ, and are baptized according to His commandment. It is the Household of God, the Body of Christ, the Temple of the Holy Ghost.

2. *Q.* How doth God make known His will in the Church?
A. Holy men of old were moved by the Holy Ghost to declare the will of God; and the words of God delivered by them, and contained in the Scriptures of the Old Testament, were committed to the Jews. These, together with the writings of the evangelists and apostles of the New Testament, have been preserved in the Christian Church, and handed down to us: and Christ hath set in His Church ministries for the guidance of His people, in accordance with His written word. And to all men God bears witness by the Church, proclaiming His salvation, and blessing the works of His hands.

3. *Q.* What ministries hath our Lord Jesus Christ given to His Church?
A. When He ascended up on high, He received gifts for men: and He gave some men, apostles; and some, prophets; and some, evangelists; and some, pastors and teachers.

4. *Q.* For what ends were these ministries given?
A. They were given for the perfecting of the saints, for the work of the ministry, for the edifying of the Body of Christ; till we all come unto the unity of the faith and of the knowledge of the Son of God, unto a perfect man, unto the measure of the stature of the fulness of Christ.

5. *Q.* What is the meaning of the word *Apostle*?
A. *Apostle* is 'one sent forth.'

6. *Q.* How are apostles distinguished from all other ministers?
A. Apostles are neither of men, nor by man; but by Jesus Christ and God the Father, sent forth immediately and directly.

7. *Q.* How are all other ministers set in the Church?
A. They are set in the Church by our Lord Jesus Christ, not immediately, but through ordination by apostles, or by those whom they have delegated for that purpose.

8. *Q.* What do you mean by *Ordination*?
A. *Ordination* is the means appointed by God for admitting those who are to serve in the ministry to some *order* or degree therein.

9. *Q.* How is Ordination conferred?
A. Ordination is conferred by the laying on of hands with prayer: and therein God bestows the gift of His Holy Spirit, for enabling him that is ordained to fulfil, in spirit and in truth, the work of the ministry, in the order to which he is admitted.

10. *Q.* Which are the principal orders in the ministry?
A. These three; namely, the order of the Angel, or Bishop, the order of Presbyter or Priest, and the order of Deacon.

11. *Q.* You have now told me in what way men are ordained to, and set in, the priesthood and all the higher ministries of the Church; doth not God previously call them to these holy ministries.
A. Yes; God calleth those whom He purposes to employ by the word of the Holy Ghost, through the prophet.

12. *Q.* How are deacons chosen?
A. Deacons are chosen by the congregation, or with their concurrence. The seven deacons of each church are elected by the congregation among whom they are to minister; and they become their representatives, when confirmed in their places by the apostles. Other deacons are chosen to the work of the ministry by the apostles, or by some angel having their authority, after due notice and inquiry.

13. *Q.* How are we to regard the angel of the church?
A. We should honour the angel as the chief minister and pastor, to whom God has committed the charge of the whole flock, including the priests and the deacons; and who is appointed to offer in the congregation the intercession of the Church.

14. *Q.* How are we to regard the priests?
A. We should honour the priests as those appointed, under the angel, to minister the word of God and the sacraments; to watch over our souls as good shepherds of the sheep; and to offer in the congregation the prayers of the Church.

15. *Q.* How are we to regard the deacons?
A. We should honour the deacons as the ministers of God appointed to guide us, both by word and example, in the paths of righteousness; to assist the priests in the ministry of the Church; to help those who seek to them, in the managements of their secular affairs; and to relieve the poor and afflicted.

16. *Q.* What is the rite of the Laying on of apostles' hands on the members of the Church?
A. It is a sacrament or rite in which is bestowed the Gift of the Holy Ghost, the Comforter, upon those who have been baptized and are come to full age.

17. *Q.* What benefits are conferred upon them in this rite?
A. They are established and confirmed, sealed and anointed: and therein the Holy Ghost divides His gifts to each one severally, as He will.

18. *Q.* What is meant by speaking of the Gift of the Holy Ghost as sevenfold?
A. The prophet Isaiah foretold that the Spirit which was to rest upon Christ should be the spirit of wisdom and understanding, the spirit of counsel and might, the spirit of knowledge and of the fear of the Lord, and should make him to be of quick understanding in the fear of the Lord.

19. *Q.* What is the manifestation of the Spirit, which is given to each, for the profit of all?
A. The Holy Ghost, in coming down upon them that are sealed, gives to one the word of wisdom, to another the word of knowledge, to another faith, to another the gifts of healing, to another the working of miracles, to another prophecy, to another discerning of spirits, to another divers kinds of tongues, to another the interpretation of tongues. All these worketh that one and the self same Spirit, dividing to every man severally as He will.

Document X.11

Presbyterian Church in England Overture on Independence, 1844

The evolution of the old English Presbyterians into Unitarians meant that orthodox Presbyterians, especially Scottish immigrants, needed to establish their own separate existence. Gradually the various groups consolidated, creating a synod in 1836. In the wake of the 1843 Disruption of the Church of Scotland, when the majority of the Evangelical section left because the state did not allow the church to abolish patronage, most of the Presbyterians in England sympathised with the new Free Church of Scotland. They therefore broke the nominal link with the Church of Scotland by means of this overture on independence. See D. Cornick, *Under God's Good Hand: A History of the Traditions which have come together in the United Reformed Church in the United Kingdom*, London, 1998, pp. 127–8; and idem, 'The Disruption in London: English Presbyterians and the Scottish Disruption of 1843', in D. Bebbington and T. Larsen, eds, *Modern Christianity and Cultural Aspirations*, London, 2003.

The extract is taken from L. Levi, *Digest of the Actings and Proceedings of the Synod of the Presbyterian Church in England, 1836–1876*, n.p., 1877, pp. 27–30.

Whereas, according to the Word of God, and the constitutional principles of Presbyterianism, every orderly-constituted and regularly-organised branch of the Church catholic – that is, in other words, every competent number of Sessions and Presbyteries professing and adhering to the same doctrines, discipline, government, and mode of worship, founded upon and agreeable to the Word of God, and associated together in the unity of a general Synod or Assembly – is a particular Church of Christ upon earth, and, as such, is authorised and empowered by Him, its only King and Head, to administer all the ordinances of His appointment; to make and execute such regulations and orders, in accordance with, and in subordination to, His Holy Word, as may be required for the ordering and government of that portion of His spiritual kingdom on earth which such particular Church constitutes; is invested with all requisite powers and jurisdiction spiritual to administer its own ecclesiastical economy, and is, in short, an independent province in the kingdom of Christ upon earth, holding only of Him, and subject only to Him, in all matters spiritual, and consequently subordinate to, and dependent upon, no other particular branch of the Church catholic, but possessing exclusive jurisdiction and supreme authority, subject only to Christ, in all its own spiritual affairs. And whereas the Presbyterian Church in England, in connection with the Church of Scotland, is such an orderly-constituted and regularly-organised branch of the Church of Christ, in all matters according to the premises, –

It is therefore hereby resolved, decreed, and declared by the foresaid Presbyterian Church in England, in Synod assembled:

First. That this Synod having been originally formed and constituted by the voluntary association or union of the several Presbyteries that composed it, each Presbytery acting in the forming and constituting of such Association, or Union, or Synod, by and in virtue of those powers spiritual which Christ Jesus has conferred upon associated Church officers for the good and government of His Church; and having for some years existed as a Synod, without assuming to itself any denominational title or designation, did, in the year of our Lord one thousand eight hundred and thirty-nine, in the free exercise of its own heaven-derived authority, assume to itself the designation or title of 'The Synod of the Presbyterian Church in England in connection with the Church of Scotland;' that at the time when this designation or title was assumed there existed no Synodical connection whatsoever between this Church and the Church of Scotland as by law established, and that no jurisdiction was exercised or even claimed by the latter Church over the former; that the latter clause of the forecited title or designation of this Church, viz., 'in connection with the Church of Scotland,' therefore, neither was nor could be intended or understood to indicate a connection between the two Churches which involved a right of jurisdiction on the one part, or an acknowledgment of submission on the other, seeing the Church of Scotland, in General Assembly convened, solemnly declared, in the year of our Lord one thousand eight hundred and thirty-four, that being an Established Church, she neither did possess legally, nor could constitutionally exercise, ecclesiastical jurisdiction in England; seeing also that, since the forecited title or designation was assumed, this Church has, in all matters pertaining to its own economy and the administration thereof, acted in the most entire independence of the Church of Scotland, nor was its right so to do ever so much as called in question, even when certain ministers of this Church who had received their orders in the Church of Scotland were deposed from the holy ministry by sentence of Presbyteries of this Church, acting by warrant from this Synod; that consequently the forecited clause in the title or designation of this Church was assumed only in order to distinguish this Church from another denomination, viz., Socinians or Unitarians, who, without having any right whatever to the name, call themselves, and are called by others, 'English Presbyterians,' and also from certain denominations of orthodox Presbyterians resident in England, viz., those connected with the Scottish United Secession and Relief Churches; but the forecited clause, viz., 'in connection with the Church of Scotland,' having led to various misapprehensions, as if a connection involving a right of jurisdiction on the one side, and an acknowledgment of submission on the other, did exist between the Church of Scotland as by law established and this Church; and various other sufficient reasons having arisen to render it expedient that the present designation of this Church should be altered; wherefore the associated Presbyteries constituting this Church in Synod assembled, acting upon their own authority, as set down in the premises, and possessing the same right and power now to alter, as at the first to assume, their present designation, hereby resolve, decree, and declare that the designation of this Church shall, from this time forth, be 'The Presbyterian Church in England;' as also this Synod further resolves and declares that, being and continuing the same corporate body as it has hitherto been, unchanged in doctrine, discipline, government, or mode of worship (in respect of all which each member of this Synod solemnly adheres to his ordination vows, and will continue, through grace, stedfastly to maintain and adhere to the same), the Presbyterian Church in England will continue to assert all its lawful claims, and to maintain all its lawful possessions, rights, and privileges, of what sort soever they be, as the same have been hitherto claimed or possessed by this Church.

Second. That this Church shall, through the grace of Almighty God, as an independent branch of the Church of Christ, and in virtue of its own inherent powers of self-government and jurisdiction, administer its religious ordinances, make its disciplinary and ritual regulations, and exercise its spiritual jurisdiction; and, further, maintain inviolate all the rights, powers, and privileges wherewith Christ has invested it, in all matters, according to the premises.

Third. That in all acts of intercourse with another branch or other branches of the Church of Christ, or in forming or maintaining a friendly relation or relations with such branch or branches of the Church of Christ, this Church shall assert, provide for, and maintain its own freedom and independence, in all matters spiritual, according to the premises.

Document X.12

Wesleyan Reformers' Resolutions, 1850

The greatest convulsion in Wesleyan Methodism took place in the years around the middle of the century. Three men, Samuel Dunn, James Everett and William Griffith, were expelled from the ministry for advocating reforms that would restrict the arbitrary rule of Jabez Bunting and his associates. Resolutions adopted at a reform meeting in London on 12 March 1850 are reminiscent of the demands made in 1835 (see X.9). The bulk of the dissidents eventually coalesced with the Wesleyan Methodist Association to form the United Methodist Free Churches, though some remained independent as the Wesleyan Reformers. Both bodies, though loyal to Methodism, upheld the anti-centralising principles embodied in these resolutions. See O. A. Beckerlegge, *The United Methodist Free Churches*, London, 1957.

The extract is taken from *Wesleyan Delegate Takings...together with an Exposition and Defence*, Manchester, 1850, pp. 123–6.

I. – That we cordially approve of the doctrines of John Wesley, as laid down in his standard writings, believing them to be scriptural; and our object is to make Wesleyan Methodism more efficient, by the removal of such laws and usages as are unscriptural, or unfriendly to the civil and religious interests of the body, and by rendering its constitution and laws conformable to New Testament principles; and we declare that the Wesleyan Conference has no just or scriptural ground for constituting itself the sole legislative body of the Connexion.

II. – That the impropriety and evil of such assumption of power, is abundantly manifested by the oppressive character and injurious tendency of some of the enactments of the Conference, so likely to irritate and destroy the peace of the Connexion, and especially the declaratory resolutions of 1835, and *others* which infringe upon the liberties of the people.

III. – That we disapprove of all the regulations which prevent the Members of Office-bearers from holding meetings, or memorialising the Conference *on any subject whatever*, and are of opinion that they should be at once repealed.

IV. – That we are of opinion that if the Conference be confined to the assemblage of the legally constituted 100 members who compose it, and to the exclusive discharge of the duties and requirements of the 'Deed Poll,' then the introduction of laymen to participate in its proceedings may be rendered unnecessary.

V. – That all Leaders and Office-bearers should be chosen by the vote of the church, and thus the people be represented in the Quarterly and other official meetings.

VI. – That all disciplinary acts, admission into and expulsion from the church, should be determined by the Leaders' meeting, subject to an appeal to the Quarterly meeting, whose decision shall be final.

VII. – That the Quarterly meeting consist of all the Travelling and Local Preachers, Leaders, Trustees (being Members of Society), and Stewards, in the Circuit, with power to appoint, out of their own number, Secretaries or Auditors.

VIII. – That the District meeting consist of the Travelling Preachers stationed in the District, and an equal number of Lay Representatives, to be chosen at the March Quarterly meeting; each Circuit in the District choosing as many Lay Representatives as there are Preachers entitled to vote in that Circuit.

IX. – That the Superintendent Preacher be the chairman at all meetings of the church; but his absence or refusal to act, should not prevent or invalidate the proceedings of such meetings. The meeting, in such case, should be at liberty to elect one of its members to that office; the Chairman should have the casting vote only.

X. – That the Connexional Committees should consist equally of Preachers and Laymen, the latter to be chosen by the Lay members of the District meeting; and that the Treasurers of the Funds should invariably be laymen, and also the Secretaries, if practicable.

XI. – That a Committee of Laymen be appointed, in the first instance by the Delegate meeting, [*who were named accordingly*,] for guarding the rights and privileges of the people; and that such Committee revise the whole of the Methodistic laws, and shall be empowered to act in conjunction with the Conference or their Committee, and to agree upon and settle such a Code as shall tend to promote the peace and prosperity of the Connexion; and that in future two members of Committee be appointed annually by the Laymen assembled in every District meeting; and that the aggregate number so chosen, shall constitute the Committee for the privileges of the people.

XII. – That we, strongly condemning the acts of discipline upon the Rev. Messrs. Everett, Dunn, and Griffith, believing them to be directly opposed to the spirit and genius of British law, Methodist usage, and the common interpretation of Scripture, which require the production of evidence, before infliction or penalty, urge that these decisions should be re-considered by the Conference; and, further, that the recent disciplinary acts upon Laymen, (resulting from the above,) be deemed null and void, as founded upon laws so generally condemned.

We the undersigned, are of opinion that the adoption of the principles contained in the foregoing Resolutions would be the most effectual way to preserve and strengthen every thing that is valuable in our beloved Methodism, remove the causes of agitation, and restore peace and harmony throughout the Connexion.

Document X.13

Primitive Methodist Organisation, 1864

The Primitive Methodists gradually turned their revivalist movement into a church similar in structure to that of the Wesleyans. Yet their more democratic ethos was reflected in their institutions. Laymen enjoyed greater prominence, especially on the Circuit Committees and in Conference, where they outnumbered the ministers by a ratio of two to one. District Meetings, furthermore, enjoyed a far higher degree of autonomy from Conference because they were largely responsible for the stationing of ministers. For class meetings, see VI.17. Primitive Methodist organisation is discussed in relation to other non-Wesleyan versions in R. Currie, *Methodism Divided: A Study in the Sociology of Ecumenicalism*, London, 1968, chap. 5.

The extract is taken from J. Parrott, *A Digest of the History, Polity & Doctrines of the Primitive Methodists*, London, 1864, pp. 38–43.

For the most efficient working of all its parts and institutions, the Community is divided into Classes, Societies, Circuits or Stations, and Districts. A society includes all the members within a given locality, having one or more classes in which those members statedly meet. A circuit or station, includes all the societies within prescribed limits; a district includes all the circuits or stations within defined boundaries; and all the districts are embraced in the word Connexion, which is a Christian Commonwealth, voluntarily united for mutual counsel, aid, and supervision, most efficiently to promote the good of every part, the salvation of immortal souls, and the extension of the Kingdom of Jesus Christ upon earth.

A Class is a company of believers, varying in numbers according to circumstances, who meet weekly for spiritual worship and mutual improvement in Christian knowledge and holiness. One of their number is denominated 'Leader,' and when practicable he has an assistant. These are officially set apart to take oversight of the class, to conduct its meetings, keeping a steady eye on the spiritual welfare and moral conduct of each member, counselling and encouraging them as their varied cases may require, visiting the sick and absent ones, marking their attendance in a specially prepared book, and recording their offerings for the cause of God. A Leader is expected to be a pattern of consistent piety to his little flock, capable of sympathy with, and being a helper of, his members in their Christian warfare. A good efficient Leader becomes a kind of moral signet, and stamps his own spirit and the measure of his own attainment in holiness to a considerable and observable extent, on those with whom he so frequently meets in audience with Deity. Societies generally prosper in proportion as their Class

Leaders are up to the mark in spirituality, practical godliness, and orderly discipline. Good Leaders are of incalculable assistance to their pastors in feeding the church of God. The Primitives, like John Wesley and the Methodists of that day, consider these means, when properly attended and conducted, as contributing very largely to the growth in grace of the individual members, and to the life and power of God in the church. They do not consider meeting in class indispensable to salvation, yet they hold class meetings to be strictly scriptural in principle, and that avoidable neglect of them has ever given evidence of a declining and low state of spirituality, and *vice versa*, in general. Holding these views, meeting in class is a condition of membership with the Primitives, where health and circumstances allow of it. They believe the *principle* of class meetings runs through the Old and New Testament Scriptures, of which the following passages are a sample. – Psalm lxvi. 16; Mal. iii. 16, 17; James v. 16.

Society Stewards is a modern name for 'deacons,' and when their duties are properly discharged, they are of great service to a congregation and society. They should see that the chapel or place or worship is kept properly cleaned and lighted, its doors open in due time for service, that the pulpit is supplied with correct notices for announcements, provide all requisites for baptisms, love-feasts, and sacraments; make or see that all orderly collections are made according to public announcement; attend Leaders' meetings, receive all society moneys thereat, and after paying legitimate costs, hand the balance to the station treasurer, keeping an orderly debtor and creditor account, presenting the same for examination and audit at the Leaders' meeting; and in conjunction with the leaders and ministers, aid in promoting the general order and weal of the society, according to the connexional rules. A Society Steward may be nominated by a society, but his legal appointment is with the quarterly meeting.

Leaders' Meetings are composed of the travelling preachers of the station, the class leaders, the society stewards, and the station steward, when he can attend. A society with only one class may have a steward, and then its business can be done uniformly on the connexional principle, and not by a travelling preacher and the leader only. No leaders' meeting is legal unless a travelling preacher be present, extraordinary cases excepted, the meeting being judge of what cases are extraordinary, and leaving its judgment for the approval or disapproval of its station committee or quarterly meeting. In the unavoidable absence of a leader, his assistant must attend and act in his stead. He may also attend with his leader, but without voice or vote in his leader's presence, unless called upon by the meeting to speak. The business of the leaders' meeting is to examine all the class books, to ascertain the attendance of the members, receive from the leaders and pay over to the treasurer all class moneys received, take due cognizance of the conduct of the members, and settle any difference that may have arisen between them, receive new members on trial, or dismember any whose moral conduct requires it, see that the absent and sick are visited, and propose such measures as it deems requisite the better to promote the spiritual and temporal advancement of the society and station, and forward the same to the quarterly meeting. The leader is amenable to this meeting, and any difficult case touching conduct or discipline may be taken to the station committee or quarterly meeting, which is the highest court of appeal for private members, in whose case its decision is final.

The Station or Circuit Committee. At an early period when the circuits were very large and the duties of the superintendent preachers particularly heavy and important, the superintendent of the Nottingham circuit, invited a selection of his official brethren whom he deemed most judicious, to aid him by their counsel, in managing the general affairs of the circuit between the quarterly meetings. This was found to work so well that the plan was connexionally adopted, and this committee is now one of its legal courts, whose members are elected by each quarterly meeting, and its duties are defined in the connexional rules, pages 34–35. The itinerant preachers, the station steward, and any other *official* whom the quarterly board may elect, not fewer than four in number, form this committee; *private* members and *assistant* leaders cannot be legal members of it. *Assistant* leadership *alone* does not constitute any one an *official* in this connexion.

The Meetings of this Committee are regular and special, the former held at stated periods, the latter are convened by a travelling preacher or a station steward, who personally, in writing, by public announcement from any one of the pulpits, or in such a way as may have been appointed by a quarterly meeting, desires its members to meet at a given place and time, to attend to business which requires attention, prior to the regular meeting. And this committee being an auxiliary and subordinate to the quarterly meeting, a *judicious selection* of officials only, should be elected to serve on it, and they, as far as practicable, from each society on the Station, the largest number residing nearest the usual place of meeting, to secure a better attendance and a special meeting when needful.

Quarterly Meetings are so called because held four times a year, usually in March, June, September, and December. The first part is termed *the preachers' meeting*, whose business is to inquire into the doctrinal views, pulpit capabilities, moral and official conduct of all who on the station's plan are recognized as preachers and exhorters, and no one but themselves and the station steward has a legal seat in this meeting; but by the vote of a majority of those present, any doubtful or difficult case may be transferred to the second part called 'the full board.' This is composed of all the members of the former meeting, with the addition of the class leaders, society stewards, the first superintendent of each sabbath school, or when he cannot attend his assistant may take his place, if a member in society; also such *other* persons as *the meeting chooses* to admit, they being *members in society*. This is the highest official meeting or church court in a circuit or station, and the acts of all minor courts are subject to it. It inquires into the spiritual and temporal state of all the societies, schools, chapels, and preaching rooms; makes or sanctions needful provision for the whole, for the ensuing quarter, determines the case of any one recommended by a leaders' meeting to become an exhorter on the preachers' plan, or which, if any, of its local preachers shall be recommended for the reserve list, as itinerant preachers, settles, as far as it can, any case of misunderstanding among its officials when properly brought before it, and enters the minutes of its proceedings, and the numerical and financial accounts of the whole station in suitable books. 'The meeting must *close* by 9 o'clock p.m. of the day on which it commences but if necessary must *previously* (to 9 p.m.) appoint an adjourned meeting to *complete* the *unfinished* business. The adjournment, however, must *not undo* what *was done* at the *principal* meeting.' This clause was *specially* enacted to prevent late meetings, and to guard against any falling into the temptation of *reversing* or *neutralizing* what the fuller or more sober meeting might have carefully decided on. Honor and justice to the majority who form the principal meeting are thus guarded, and some of the selfish and mischievous vagaries of human nature are *legally* and *clearly* provided against. – Rule 4, p. 22, Con. Sol. Mins. 1860.

District Committees are composed of itinerant preachers, and lay officials, and are elected by each Annual District Meeting, for Conference to confirm or vary. These form courts of appeal to the lower courts and officials in their family of stations, when cases may have been decided in them contrary to the views of those possessed of the right of appeal. They also give advice in prescribed cases, when properly asked by official meetings or their members; and they present their Report of the year's proceedings to their respective District meetings for approval or otherwise.

District Meetings are held annually, in the month of May; when each station in their jurisdiction, the district committee, and the general committee send one delegate thereto. The March Quarterly Meeting elects its own delegate, and sends with him two reports which describe the numerical, temporal, and spiritual condition of the station for the past year. These are carefully read by the meeting, which records one or more minutes on each for conference, and if deemed needful, a letter is sent to the station, expressive of the meeting's views or desires on any statement or omission found in the reports. Each station has the right to propose any legislation, and send it with its report. The meeting reads the whole, and forwards its views thereon to Conference. After examining all candidates, and deciding all matters affecting any of its itinerant preachers, it stations all the eligible ones for the ensuing year, within its jurisdiction, paying regard to the requests of the various stations. It adjusts as far as possible, all matters legally sent to it for adjustment, for any of its stations – elects the proper number of delegates to represent the district in the ensuing Conference, from those present, or from eligible ones not present. It also elects the District committee for the ensuing year, and its general committee delegate to attend its next yearly meeting, and provisionally does any other legal business for the district. A duplicate report is returned to each station, being first duly signed by the meeting, and the others are bound together in one volume, and with its minute book and all other documents, forwarded through the general committee to Conference, where the delegates meet the whole properly arranged for examination, etc.

The General Committee is the highest connexional court of appeal while Conference is not actually sitting. It is composed of itinerant preachers and lay officials, in the proportion of two of the latter to one of the former, who are elected by the annual Conference out of the various districts, its executive residing in or near London, where they meet weekly for business. It keeps its eyes on every part of the community, and renders assistance by advice to all its stations, courts, and officials, in cases of difficulty, adjusts differences when legally applied to by the lower courts and parties, leaving its acts for the approval or disapproval of Conference to which it submits its Report for the year.

Conference. – Each Annual British Conference is composed of delegates elected thereto by the District Meetings, one-third of whom are itinerant preachers and the other two-thirds laymen, filling the office of local preacher, class leader, or Station Steward, the twelve Deed Poll members, and not more than four other persons whom the preceding Conference appointed to represent the Book Room, and other important Connexional Establishments. Its business is to examine the state and affairs of the whole Connexion as sent to it by the District Meetings, the General Committee, the General Missionary Committee, and its Foreign Conferences; and, as the highest Court of appeal, it decides cases which may have been forwarded to it for that object. It confirms or varies the decisions of its District Meetings and Foreign Conferences, endeavouring to promote the weal of every part of the United family. And, after carefully examining and recording its numerical, temporal, and spiritual state for the past year, with its prospects for future, it directs for their publication with such minutes of its proceedings as it deems advisable.

Thus federating, the strong aid the weak, financially, spiritually, by counsel and by labor, demonstrating that a united and well-governed body acts with greater force, securing much greater success than were it dissolved into fractions, each trying to stand and act alone, repudiating any other supervision and control than its own.

Document X.14

Churches of Christ Principles, 1873

Gilbert Tickle (1819–88), a Liverpool merchant, was chairman of the Annual Meeting of the Churches of Christ six times and editor of their *Christian Advocate* from 1879 to 1888. In this address at the stone-laying of a new church at Windsor Street, Liverpool, in 1873 he expounds the leading principles of his body. They agreed with the Baptists in upholding the independence of each congregation and with the Scotch Baptists, from whom they derived, in rejecting a separated ministry. They held, however, that the baptism of believers was for the remission of sins, and so conveyed the assurance of pardon (as Archibald McLean and Charles Stovel taught; see DEB). They also laid emphasis on the unity of all believers and on the weekly observance of the Lord's Supper on the Lord's Day. See D. M. Thompson, *Let Sects and Parties Fall: A Short History of the Association of Churches of Christ in the Great Britain and Ireland*, Birmingham, 1980.

The extract is taken from *The Christian Advocate*, 1873, pp. 289–92.

Other religious bodies may consider themselves at liberty to adopt names drawn from this or the other part of the Christian system, or called after this or the other great leader of religious thought; reserving nevertheless, always and by all means, the right and privilege of calling themselves 'Christians,' and ready to resent as an injury every expression of doubt as to their title to bear that ever-glorious name. We prefer to take that 'one name,' and to bear it, exclusive of every other. We have had our great leaders of religious thought – men who have fought, in the face of day, for every inch of Christian ground, wielding Christ's own pure weapons against His most insidious foes with the rarest sagacity and with consummate power; but, as we do not take their names, neither do we take anything they have written as authoritative and binding. Purely and simply do we cleave to the apostolic writings as a divine system of doctrine and rule of life, to the exclusion of every other creed or confession whatsoever. To this position we have unreservedly committed ourselves as a Church of Christ ever since we had an existence. ... In choosing to rest their faith in the pure Word of God in preference to an extracted formulary, professing, through the filter of the human brain, to clarify and prepare for use a form of doctrine which comes to us fresh and pure and living from the spirit of truth and holiness, we believe they [the early leaders] made a wise and happy choice, even though the sanctities of age and the authority of an eldership stood in the way. If they had utterly failed in their life's work from that moment, and never been more heard of, yet the course they took in obeying the calls of truth and conscience was the right one, and commends itself still to our best judgment. But God has owned and blessed the deed by raising up around the standard then erected a loving, devoted brotherhood, whose constant prayer is for the unity of all believers on the platform of a pure, uncorrupted Christianity, and whose constant aim is to maintain the unity of the spirit unbroken in their own church life and experience. What, then, are our objects in thus standing more prominently before the public? Briefly, evangelisation, edification, the bringing of men into the fold of Christ, the building them up unto life eternal. For the salvation of the world we preach and teach that 'God so loved the world, that He gave His only begotten Son, that whosoever believeth on Him might not perish, but have everlasting life.' We baptise believers on a personal confession of their faith, but we are not 'Baptists.' We cannot consent to be called after that or any other institution. Yet we desire to lay hold of the true meaning and purpose of every divine appointment. We believe baptism to be an institution in which the believer may and ought to receive, on the testimony and authority of Christ Himself, the assurance of pardon, as promised by Him in the commission He gave to His apostles, and which was realised by the first disciples on the day of Pentecost, and during the apostolic age. Mr M'Lean among the Scotch Baptists, and Mr Stovel among the English Baptists, have laid down this, the great design of baptism, very clearly; but it has been practically ignored by both the parties to which they belonged, and stands as a mere mark of the denominations. It is, we conceive, to the barren and meaningless holding of this great institution of Christ on the part of the Baptists on the one hand, and the utter perversion of it in its application to infants by Pædobaptists on the other, that may be traced to a very large extent the power which the Ritualist now wields over the public mind in his liberal application of Scriptural teaching, as embodied in the Prayer Book, to those for whom the institution and the solemn promises connected with it were never intended. In like manner the Lord's Supper, whose observance in Apostolic days was the very object for which Christians came together, is by evangelical bodies of the present day so indifferently regarded that the Ritualist has an advantage, a hold upon the public mind, in lifting the ordinance out of the dusty corner, and setting it before men not only as a commemoration, but as a communion – and more. As a communion we regard it, but no more. A fellowship in all the blessings it symbolises – no more. A fellowship in which we receive Christ, not into our mouths but into our hearts, which is far more. The time is coming when the true-hearted of all denominations will have to fall back, in sheer self-defence, on original foundations. The tide of infidelity, will worship, priestly domination, and fleshly Ritualism is rolling in and can never be stemmed or resisted with footholds less firm than those afforded by the eternal truth of God. Human names and human devices will all have to be abandoned in that day of fiery trial, when we must either relinquish any act involving complicity with the enemies of truth or sink in the general corruption that surrounds us. The nearer and the sooner, therefore, we seek after and lay hold of the primitive truth in its purity and simplicity, the better for ourselves, the better for the Church, the better for the world.

Document X.15

Free Church of England Declaration, 1876

The Free Church of England was created by Evangelical Anglicans who separated from the established church. The first congregation, at Bridgetown, Totnes, in Devon, left the Church of England in 1845 as the result of the harassing of its clergyman, James Shore, by the High Church Bishop of Exeter. It grew as others became dismayed by the advance of ritualism. In 1876 its first bishop was consecrated by a bishop of the Reformed Episcopal Church from North America, with which it eventually united in 1927. The anti-ritualist stance of the church was embodied in its constitution, which also laid down lay participation in its government. See F. Vaughan, *A History of the Free Church of England otherwise called the Reformed Episcopal Church*, London, 1936; and for the Shore case, G. Carter, *Anglican Evangelicals: Protestant Secessions from the* Via Media, *c. 1800–1850*, Oxford, 2001, chap. 9.

The extract is taken from A. E. Price, *The Organization of the Free Church of England*, Ilfracombe, 1908, pp. 15–16.

A DECLARATION EXPLANATORY OF THE CONSTITUTION OF THE
FREE CHURCH OF ENGLAND.

Made by and with the Authority of the Convocation, assembled in London, June, 1876.

GOVERNMENT. – The governing body of this Church shall be called Convocation, and shall assemble in the month of June every year; and Special Meetings may be called at other times in the manner hereafter provided for. Twelve members shall form a quorum.

Convocation shall consist of all the Bishops or Presbyters, and Deacons or Wardens of this Church, with two Lay Deputies from each Congregation, and the Members of Council *ex-officio*.

PRESIDENT OF CONVOCATION. – The President of Convocation shall be chosen by ballot from among the Bishops, to serve for one year; *provided* that such annual election shall not preclude his re-election.

ORDERS. – Guided by the New Testament and by the ecclesiastical polity of the Primitive Church, this Church recognises only two orders of Ministers – viz., Presbyters and Deacons. Nevertheless, the first order is divided into two distinct offices – viz., Bishops and Presbyters.

This Church maintains the ecclesiastical parity of Presbyters, whether episcopally or otherwise ordained, as a fundamental principle of its Constitution.

But for the due and solemn setting apart or consecration of Presbyters to the office of Bishop, the Free Church of England adopts the form used in the Consecration of Bishops, as revised and set forth by the Second General Council of the Reformed Episcopal Church.

The title of Deacon shall include licensed Evangelists and Probationers for the office of Presbyter; and such Probationers may be made Deacons of the Church according to the Form set forth in the Second General Council of the Reformed Episcopal Church.

RITUAL. – Every officiating Presbyter or Deacon of this Church, at the time of the Communion, and at all other times of liturgical worship or ministration, shall wear a plain white surplice and plain black scarf. The black gown shall be used in preaching.

No Church decorations, ornaments, vestments, postures, or ceremonies, calculated to teach either directly or symbolically, that the Christian Ministry possesses a sacerdotal character, or that the Lord's Supper is a sacrifice, shall ever be allowed in the worship of this Church; nor shall any Communion Table be constructed in the form of an Altar.

APPOINTMENT OF MINISTERS. – Every Congregation shall be at liberty to choose its own Minister, subject to the regulations laid down in the Canons of this Church.

BASIS OF RELIGIOUS BELIEF. – The Free Church of England holding 'the faith once delivered to the saints,' declares its belief in the Holy Scriptures of the Old and New Testaments as the Word of God, and the sole rule of faith and practice; in the Creed 'commonly called the Apostles' Creed;' in the divine institution of the Sacraments of Baptism and the Lord's Supper; and in the doctrines of grace substantially as they are set forth in the Thirty-nine Articles of Religion.

FORM OF SUBSCRIPTION. – The Form of Subscription for the Ministers and other Office bearers of the Free Church of England, until and unless altered by

Convocation, shall be as follows: (that is to say) 'I do believe the Holy Scriptures of the Old and New Testaments to be the Word of God, and to contain all things necessary to salvation; and I do sincerely engage to conform to the Doctrine, Discipline, Worship and Government of the Free Church of England.'

THE PRAYER BOOK. – This Church, retaining a Liturgy which shall not be repressive of freedom in prayer, accepts the Book of Common Prayer as revised or recommended for use by the Convocation of the Free Church of England.

Document X.16

The Cokelers, 1879

The Cokelers, or Dependant Brethren, were established by John Sirgood (1820–85), originally a Gloucestershire bootmaker, on the northern edge of Sussex from 1850. They believed, with other holiness groups, that the power of God could preserve them from sin; they were teetotallers, pacifists and wearers of traditional clothing. Their most distinctive views, however, were discouragement of bringing children into the world and encouragement of trading at the village stores that they set up on the co-operative principle. Both these attitudes are explained by Benjamin Piper (b. 1868) in a manuscript written in 1936. Benjamin was a son of Henry Piper (d. 1921), an agricultural labourer and one of the early leaders of the Cokelers' chapel at Warnham, near Horsham. See P. Jerrome, *John Sirgood's Way: The Story of the Loxwood Dependants*, Petworth, West Sussex, 1998; R. Homan, 'The Society of Dependents: A Case Study in the Rise and Fall of Rural Peculiars', *Sussex Archaeological Collections*, 119 (1981), pp. 195–204.

The extract is taken from a transcription of Benjamin Piper's manuscript in the West Sussex County Record Office, MP.1994, pp. 8–10. The original spelling and punctuation have been preserved. The permission of West Sussex County Record Office to reproduce this document is gratefully acknowledged.

I should like to go back now to what I have heard my Father say, that when He was coming home from work one night, God taught Him what a deal more liberty and freedom both himself and dear Mother would have for Christ sake if them remained as they were and not bring Souls into the world, which if not born again is very sad. Now the very next Sunday Brother John Sirgood came down from London and taught the very same that how much more useful we could be for Christs sake by keeping free from entanglements, which by the grace of God could be avaided. This very much strengthened their faith in God and in each other. For at this time unknown to my Father Br John Sirgood had met with very much opposition about this line of things. Therefore they were able to strengthen each others hands in God. This line as always been taught at Warnham that the more free we are the more useful we can be for Gods work. Now in the 1st Corinthians 7th Chapter verse 20th. Let every man abide in the calling He was called verse 24th. There in abide with God verse 27th Art thou bound unto a wife seek not to be loosed Art thou loosed from a wife seek not a wife. but if thou marry, thou has not sinned, never the less such shall have trouble in the flesh. Verse 29th But this I say Brethren the time is short, it remaineth that both they that have wives be as though they had none verse 32nd. But I would have you without carefulness. He that is unmarried cares for the things that belong to the Lord how he may Please the Lord verse 33rd. But He that is married careth for the things that are of the world, how He may please His Wife verse 34th.: There is a difference also between a wife and a virgin. The unmarried woman careth for the things of the Lord, that she may be Holy both in Body and Spirit. But she that is married careth for the things of the world, how she may please her Husband verse 38th. So then He that giveth her in Marriage doeth well, but He that giveth her not in Marriage <u>doeth</u> <u>better</u>. This has been lived out both by Brothers and Sisters, they Choose to keep free for Christs sake. There was a good number of Sisters in saervice who were serving Worldly Masters and Mistresses, therefore they had no much liberty to be at the Meetings: There was such a desire in Br John Sirgood, for the Sisters Souls welfare that He wanted them to have their liberty to be at the house of God to all be able to worship together so He began to work on their berhalf. He spoke to my Father Henry Piper what He had in his mind to be able to free the Sisters and they both helped ewach othe in this wonderful work of Love and God also worked with them and many Brethren also. This was the starting of our Stores which now is. Note there was also much opposition but that could not stop God from working. There were many very earnest Prayers offered to God to Bless and Prosper the labour of the Saints hands. This God answered and worked on behalf of the Saints. Satan worked against it but God turned all his working into profit for His Saints who were striving together in love for each other and although this was started in the year 1879 it is still going on the same love ruling which is the love of Jesus that will last for ever.

Document X.17

Fritchley Monthly Meeting of Friends Minute, 1881

John Sargeant (d. 1883) founded an unofficial meeting of Quakers in the Derbyshire village of Fritchley in 1864. Six years later it established a new General Meeting there, so breaking entirely with the Society of Friends. The Fritchley secession, however, considered itself to be maintaining the true Quaker witness to the inward light, against Evangelical innovations in theology, and the traditional distinctives, against recent laxities in discipline. A Monthly Meeting minute of 1881, printed in 1885, justifies their secession.

The minute is taken from the authority on the subject, W. Lowndes, *The Quakers of Fritchley*, London, 1981, pp. 31–2.

We feel it to be duty incumbent upon us at this time, for the information of those who may come after us and the satisfaction of serious inquirers, to place on record a brief statement of the grounds or reasons which induced us to withdraw from the larger body of professing Friends in this land, and to meet together for Worship and Discipline apart from its control.

We maintain that we are Friends, members of the Society, attached to the true, ancient and original principles of our profession, and desirous of maintaining all those testimonies to the pure and spiritual nature of the Christian religion, which our forefathers in the Truth upheld before the world. We claim no new discoveries, no other light in Divine things than such as was vouchsafed to our honoured predecessors; we profess to be actuated by no desire for change, either in doctrine or church government, our object being if so permitted, to continue or sustain the Society upon its original basis, as it had existed from its rise until the early part of the present century.

On this ground we are opposed to those changes in Doctrine and Discipline, that have been so largely introduced into the body, which were partially incorporated with the Discipline in 1834 and to a still greater extent at its revision in 1861. We believe that they are the out-come of grave departures from the fundamental principles of the Society, which departures have been encouraged and connived at, and in a great degree sanctioned by a succession of Yearly Meetings held in London during the last half century, so that it cannot be denied, but that the body at large has been a consenting and acquiescing party thereto.

The compact being broken, the constitution of the Society violated, our course was clear. We had to withdraw from a body which we felt was no longer the (true) Society of Friends, and to endeavour, through much weakness and poverty, to sustain the Society in this land on the ancient foundation. In so doing we have felt that we were but following the example of our worthy predecessors, and of the faithful in all ages, who, when convinced of the Truth, believed that they must no longer consort with their former associates, but 'come out from amongst them, be separate and touch not the unclean thing': and we have in our measure found His promise – ['and I will receive you and will be a father unto you and ye shall be my sons and daughters, saith the Lord Almighty' – 2 Cor. vi. 17, 18] – to be true, as of old, and now, in this the twelfth year of our existence [1881] as a distinct religious Society from the larger body of professing Friends in this land, we feel constrained to acknowledge that we have been mercifully helped in our endeavour to be found faithful.

These departures are so clear and obvious, and have been so often shown to be so, to the convincement of candid and impartial minds, that we do not think it necessary, on the present occasion, to particularize them. Great efforts were made by truly-concerned Friends from time to time within the body, to resist and keep back the tide of innovation that has set in, and had the Society been in a healthy condition and the good order of the Discipline impartially adhered to, all those who busied themselves in laying waste the precious principles of Truth, would, after due labour had been bestowed for their restoration to unity, have been disowned. This is in accordance with the principles of Friends.

Meanwhile, the ancient Discipline of the Society, established as we believe in the ordering of Divine Wisdom as a wall of preservation to the Church, became the object of attack: the barriers raised by the faithful of a former age, for the defence of Truth and its testimonies were thrown down, and a new Discipline was gradually set up, which we could not recognize or make use of, or even handle, inasmuch at it was seen that it was the growth of an apostacy at enmity with the Truth.

Neither could meetings for Worship held under the control of London Yearly Meeting be longer recognized as meetings of Friends, for, having once departed from the fundamental principle of our profession, – the immediate teaching and guidance of the Holy Spirit in the heart of man, the unerring Guide and Leader into all Truth, – it was impossible but that great changes would take place in Friends mode of Worship and in the character of the Ministry. This was pointed out as one of the practical consequences of letting fall this precious distinguishing doctrine. What was predicted has most surely come to pass; nor have we seen the end yet, for more changes must follow; one departure prepares the way for another; unless it shall please Infinite Goodness to interpose and stop the Society in its downward course. We should have rejoiced had we seen, and should rejoice did we now see, any prospect of its being arrested in its career, induced to return heartily to those paths from which it has so far strayed, and to condemn its wanderings from the true fold, but we fail to do so.

Relations with the Church of England

Document X.18

Dan Taylor's Reasons for Dissenting from the Church of England, 1805

Dan Taylor, the General Baptist leader (see II.2), here explains the biblical grounds for Dissent. The Church of England, he holds, is not under the headship of Christ, a view also expressed in III.12.

The extract is from D. Taylor, *A Catechism*, 6th edn, London, 1805, pp. 25–7, and was freshly added to this edition.

SECT. XIX.
Reasons of dissenting from established Churches.

Q. 1. What is meant by a gospel church?

A. A society of persons professing faith in Jesus Christ, and love to him; and usually meeting together, for divine worship. This appears from the following passages of scripture: Gal. i. 22. Acts viii. 1. ix. 31. xiii. 1. Rom. xvi. 5. 1 Cor. xiv. 23. 33. Rev. i. 11. and many others.

Q. 2. Who is the head of the church?

A. Jesus Christ is the head of his body, the church; and the head over all things to the church. Col. i. 18. Ephes. i. 22.

Q. 3. Does Jesus Christ, as our Lord and Master, require cheerful and uniform obedience?

A. Yes; he says, Why call ye me Lord, Lord, and do not the things which I say? Luke vi. 46.

Q. 4 Does he require that his disciples, in matters of religion, submit to no other authority besides his own?

A. Yes; he says, You have one master, even Christ, and all ye are brethren. Matt. xxiii. 8. 10.

Q. 5. Are national churches established by civil laws, which are enforced by human penalties, under the direction and government of Jesus Christ alone?

A. No; they are under the direction and government of men. Hence their creeds, and their rites and ceremonies, are different in different countries, and in different ages.

Q. 6. Are these sufficient reasons for dissenting and separating from national churches?

A. Yes; for no man can serve two masters; and *we* must serve the Lord Christ. Matt. v. 24. Col. iii. 24.

Denominations

Q. 7. Did Christ and his apostles, and the first christians, dissent and separate from all national churches?

A. Yes; it is evident that they did, from the whole New Testament, and the history of the following ages.

Q. 8. How did they vindicate themselves, when called to account for their conduct?

A. They said, We ought to obey God, rather than men. Acts v. 29.

Q. 9. But ought you not to obey all the civil laws of the country in which you live?

A. Yes; civil laws are the ordinances of men; and we are commanded to submit ourselves to every ordinance of man for the Lord's sake. 1 Pet. ii. 13.

Q. 10. Is the church of Christ, then, distinct from all civil governments?

A. Yes; the kingdom of Christ is not of this world. John xviii. 36.

Q. 11. But are the members of christian churches allowed to rebel against civil authority?

A. No; they ought to be the best subjects under every government; and, if real, well-instructed christians, they are the best in reality: for they fear God, and honour the king. They are subject to civil rulers, not only for wrath, but also for conscience' sake. 1 Pet. ii. 17. Rom. xiii. 5.

Q. 12. Is the scripture a sufficient guide for man in every branch of faith and practice, without any human additions?

A. Yes; all scripture is given by inspiration of God, and is profitable for doctrine, for reproof, for correction, for instruction in righteousness; that the Man of God may be perfect, thoroughly furnished unto all good works. 2 Tim. iii. 16, 17.

Q. 13. Has every man a right to judge of the scriptures for himself, and to act according to that judgment?

A. Yes; even our Lord himself appeals to the scriptures, and exhorts the Jews to search them. John v. 39. And the Bereans are commended because they searched the scriptures, to see if these things were so. Acts xvii. 11.

Q. 14. Is this a duty of sacred and awful importance?

A. Yes; for we must all appear before the judgment seat of Christ, that every one may receive the things done in his body, according to that he hath done, whether it be good or bad. 2 Cor. v. 10.

Document X.19

J. C. Philpot's Resignation from Worcester College, Oxford, 1835

J. C. Philpot (1802–69) graduated with first class honours in classics at Worcester College, Oxford, in 1824. He was appointed to the perpetual curacy in the Oxfordshire parishes of Stadhampton and Chislehampton in 1828. After his secession from the Church of England in 1835 he joined the Strict Communion Particular Baptists, and ministered jointly to congregations at Stamford and Oakham. See DEB.

These paragraphs from his 1835 letter of resignation are taken from a reprint in J. H. Philpot, ed., *The Seceders*, vol. 1, London, 1930, pp. 276–9, which explains the context. His central concern was the impossibility in the Church of England of assembling a gathered church of believers.

Mr. Provost, – I beg leave to resign the Fellowship of Worcester College, to which I was elected in the year 1826. This step I am compelled to take because I can no longer with a good conscience continue a Minister or a Member of the Established Church.

After great and numerous trials of mind, I am, as I trust, led by the hand of God thus to separate myself from the corrupt and worldly system, called the Church of England. Her errors and corruptions, as well as her utter contrariety to a Gospel Church as revealed in the New Testament, have been for two or three years gradually opening upon my mind. But though I have thus slowly and by degrees obtained light from above to see the Established Church somewhat in her true colours, it is, I confess, only but very lately that the sin of remaining in her has been forcibly laid upon my conscience. I have felt of late that, by continuing one of her ministers, I was upholding what in the sight of the holy JEHOVAH is hateful and loathsome. I have felt that, by standing up in her pulpit, I was sanctioning a system in principle and practice, in root and branches, corrupt before God. I have felt that I was keeping those children of God who sat under my ministry in total darkness as to the nature of a true Gospel Church. I have felt that both I myself, and the spiritual people that attended my ministry, were, in principle and system, mixed up with the ungodly, the Pharisee, the formalist, the worldling, and the hypocrite. And thus, whilst I remained in the Church of England, my principles and my practice, my profession and my conduct, my preaching and my acting, were inconsistent with each other. I was building up with the right hand what I was pulling down with the left. I was contending for the power, whilst the Church of England was maintaining the form. I was, by my preaching, separating the people of God from 'the world lying in wickedness,' and the Church of England, in her Liturgy and Offices, was huddling together the spiritual and the carnal, the regenerate and the unregenerate, the sheep and the goats. I was contending for regeneration as a supernatural act wrought upon the souls of the elect alone by the Eternal Spirit, and the Church of England was thanking God for regenerating every child that was sprinkled with a little water. ...

But though I felt, and at time could groan beneath the wretched formality of the Church of England, I was from two motives chiefly kept within her. One was, that I desired to be useful to the children of God in a dark neighbourhood, with whom I had been connected for nearly seven years, and of whom some professed to derive profit from my ministry. The other was altogether carnal ... This was the desire of retaining that independence which my Fellowship secured ... Lately, however, I have been brought to see 'that I must not do evil that good may come,' and that if my conscience was fully convinced of the sin of remaining in the Church of England, no clearer or more direct intimation of the will of God was needed. Thus have I laid open the inward workings of my heart, and the experience through which I have been led, in order to show that the resignation of my Fellowship and Curacy, and secession from the Church of England, is no sudden and hasty step, but the gradual and deliberate conviction of my soul.

Document X.20

J. H. Newman on Dissent, 1836

John Henry Newman (1801–90), the leader of the Oxford Movement and later cardinal in the Roman Catholic Church, saw Dissent as an evil – the equivalent of the Donatists whom Augustine condemned. The passage is from one of his sermons as an Anglican, 'Religious Worship a Remedy for Excitements', on James 5: 13. In superb melodious prose he pours contempt on those who separate from the Church of England. On Newman, see I. T. Ker, *John Henry Newman: A Biography*, Oxford, 1988.

The extract is taken from J. H. Newman, *Parochial and Plain Sermons*, London, 1907, vol. 3, pp. 342–6.

Now, this advice is often given: – 'Indulge the excitement; when you flag, seek for another; live upon the thought of God; go about doing good; let your light shine before men; tell them what God has done for your soul;' – by all which is meant, when we go into particulars, that they ought to fancy that they have something above all other men; ought to neglect their worldly calling, or at best only bear it as a cross; to join themselves to some particular set of religionists; to take part in this or that religious society; go to hear strange preachers, and obtrude their new feelings and new opinions upon others, at times proper and improper. I am speaking now of the temper, not of those who profess adherence to the Church, but of such as detach themselves, more or less, from its discipline; and the reason I allude to them is this. It is often said, that schism and dissent are but accidents of a religious temper; that they who fall into them, if pious, are the same in heart as Churchmen, only are divided by some outward difference of forms and circumstances. Not so; the mind of dissent, viewed in itself, is far other than the mind of Christ and His Holy Church Catholic; in whatever proportion it may or may not be realized in individuals. It is full of self-importance, irreverence, censoriousness, display, and tumult. It is right, therefore, ever to insist that it is different, lest men should be seduced into it, by being assured that it is not different. ...

To go into details. It often happens that in a family who have been brought up together, one suddenly takes what is called a religious turn. Such a person wishes to be more religious than the rest, wishes to do something more than ordinary, but does not know exactly what to do. You will find, generally, that he joins himself to some dissenting party, mainly for this reason, to evidence to himself greater strictness. His mind is under excitement; he seems to say with St. Paul, 'Lord, what wilt Thou have me to do?' This is the cause, again and again, of persons falling from the Church. And hence, a notion has got abroad that dissenting bodies have more of true religion within them than the Church; I say, for this reason, because earnest men, awaking to a sense of religion, wish to do something more than usual, and join sects and heresies as a relief to their minds, by way of ridding themselves of strong feelings, which, pent up within them, distress them. And I cannot deny, that in this way those bodies do gain, and the Church does lose, earnestly religious people, or rather those who would have been such in time; for it is, I fear, too true that, while the sects in question are in this way recruited and improved from the Church, the persons themselves, who join them, are injured. They lose the greater part of that religious light and warmth which hung about them, even though they have been hitherto careless, and but partially availed themselves of it. It is as if a living hand were to touch cold iron; the iron is somewhat warmed, but the hand is chilled. And thus the blossom of truth, the promise of real religion, is lost to the Church. Men begin well, but being seduced by their own waywardness fall away.

Document X.21

James Hamilton on the Need for English Presbyterianism, 1850

James Hamilton (1814–67) was a Scottish minister who in 1841 was appointed to the National Scotch Church in Regent Square, London. In 1843 he led it into separation from the Church of Scotland at the time of the Disruption and subsequently became an architect of the Presbyterian Church in England. In 1850 he addressed the General Assembly of the Free Church of Scotland on the mission of his own body in England. Apart from serving Scots, it was to provide an alternative to the Church of England and to administer a tonic to English theology. See W. Arnot, *The Life of James Hamilton*, London, 1870; DNB; and R. B. Knox, 'James Hamilton and English Presbyterianism', *Journal of the United Reformed Church History Society*, 2 (1982), pp. 286–307.

The extract is taken from *The English Presbyterian Messenger*, July 1850, pp. 401–2.

There was a threefold function for an orthodox Presbyterianism in England. It should, first of all, be a home for expatriated Scotchmen, – a nursing mother for your Church's orphan children. For remember, how many Scotchmen are located in England. Why, Sir, in a single large town of England you will find as many Scotchmen as in some of our northern counties. There are nearly as many Scotchmen in London as in Edinburgh. And what becomes of them? In the absence of Presbyterian ordinances, what is the fate of these northern immigrants? In Clifton, and Cheltenham, and Brighton, and Hastings, and such places, where our refined and wealthy countrymen go to live for the sake of their far-famed salubrity, they join the Church of England, and the pious parents become the right arm of the Evangelical clergyman; but their children, – M. and N. – who received a Christian name in their baptismal regeneration, – turn out Puseyites, – the girls embroidering altar-cloths and fald-stool covers, and the boys making High-Church speeches in Parliament. (Laughter.) And then the pious tradesman or steady artisan from your Lowlands, who settles in a provincial town, – finding no Presbyterian Church, as the next best joins the Baptist or Independent Chapel, and soon, by dint of superior intelligence and sound theology, backed by his manly bearing, or his *canny conveyance*, you will find him in a few years the principal deacon, the chief supporter, of a congregation which, however, excellent, is not Presbyterian. (Hear, hear.) Whilst a much larger class, – many of the artisans and clever operatives, breaking loose from the religious restraint of their fatherland, sit down in the seat of the scorner: become libertines and lawless livers; and in workshops and factories, as the apostles of Socialism, and the champions of Infidelity, pervert their good education to the perdition of their hapless companions, and bring a stigma on the land whose faith they have renounced, and from whose virtues they have apostatized. But besides proving a timely home for these wanderers, an effective Presbyterian Church might be an asylum to many refugees from the Church of England. (Hear.) At this moment there are doubtless many who, in the event of coming calamity, are marvelling into what community to convey themselves and their children. Would that our Church were so fully equipped and so conspicuous, that in its sound doctrine and scriptural organization they saw a ready ark against the coming deluge! And this leads me to add, as a third good service which our Church might render – it might serve as a tonic to English theology. My friend, Mr. M'Gillivray, remarked to me last night that England is not the land for testimonies. The reason is, that England is not the land for theology. As you are aware, theology is scarcely taught at all in the English Universities; and though the Dissenters are very anxious to provide theological training for their ministers, many of their pastors never pass through their colleges. The consequence is, that the usual ministrations of English pulpits are in doctrine very meagre and jejune; and consequently English piety, even when most fervent, is ill able to give a reason for its faith. In fact, English piety is too molluscous. (Laughter.) It is sadly in want of vertebrae. It needs a back-bone. (Laughter.) And nowhere would the food convenient be better bestowed, which within its soft frame would go to form the bones and the cartilage. (Hear, and laughter.) And with the orthodox osteology of their own English Confession and Catechisms (for the Westminster Standards are English) with the firm substructure of a sound and Puritan Evangelism, covered over with the flesh and sinews and mantling life's-blood of English virtues and English graces, southern piety would stand on its feet exceeding strong and exceeding fair, withal able to 'testify' and to adorn its testimony. (Cheers.)

Document X.22

Joshua Wilson on the Forthcoming Bicentenary of the Great Ejection, 1861

Joshua Wilson (1795–1874; see DNB), though trained as a barrister, enjoyed sufficient means to be a man of leisure. He collected works on Nonconformist history and spent time trying to enhance the denominational consciousness of Congregationalism. The imminence of the bicentenary of the Great Ejection of 1662, when some two thousand ministers had been expelled from their livings for refusing to accept Restoration uniformity, gave him an opportunity to propose a series of measures to mark the event. One that came to fruition was the building of the Memorial Hall, which became the headquarters of Congregationalism. Despite Wilson's caution to remember the faith held in common with Evangelical Anglicans, the bicentenary was to do permanent damage to relations with the Church of England. See T. Larsen, 'Victorian Nonconformity and the Memory of the Ejected Ministers: The Impact of the Bicentennial Commemorations of 1862', in R. N. Swanson, ed., *The Church Retrospective*, Studies in Church History 33, Woodbridge, Suffolk, 1997.

The extract from Wilson's paper to the autumn meeting of the Congregational Union on 9 October 1861 is taken from *The Second Centenary, &c.&c.*, n.p., n.d., pp. 3–12.

The recurrence during the year 1862 of the second centenary of the ever-memorable day, the 24th of August, known among contemporary Nonconformists as the Black Bartholomew, and which Locke says was 'fatal to the English church,' will afford a most favourable opportunity – one, indeed, which it would be a sin in these times to let pass unimproved – for recalling and recording the noble principles, the heroic darings, and the admirable doings of these excellent men. ...

To the Puritans of the Separatist class, who quitted their native land and all the endearments of home, and withdrew to a foreign land, or transported themselves by voluntary exile to a remote and inhospitable clime, that they might find in another country, or in the far-off wilderness, what was denied to them by intolerant prelates at home – 'freedom to worship God,' without the observance of human rites and ceremonies – to these self-banished Puritans we are indebted for the noble practical testimony borne amid perils of all kinds to the great principle, that full liberty of conscience, – the privilege of rendering religious homage to his Maker in a form and manner agreeable to the dictates of his own conscience, without molestation or disturbance from any authority, civil or ecclesiastical, – is the native birthright and indefeasible inheritance of every human being. To those less rigid, and, it must be added, less consistent Puritans, who remaining in their own country, and even retaining their connexion with its Established Church, although refusing submission to some of its ritual injunctions (deemed by them superstitious), we are deeply indebted as a body of English Nonconformists, and our country is deeply indebted as a constitutional monarchy. These men well understood the intimate and inseparable connexion which subsists between civil freedom and religious liberty. To the firm resistance which they made to the arbitrary encroachments of the royal prerogative during the reign of Elizabeth and those of the early Stuarts, and to the arrogant assumptions of the priestly faction led on first by Whitgift and then by Laud, and their associate prelates, our nation owes its civil liberties. ...

To the illustrious band of confessors, who, on the 24th of August, 1662, resigned their earthly all, along with their public ministerial status, that they might preserve ' a conscience void of offence toward God and toward man,' we owe our present position as a religious body, having a legally recognised right of meeting for worship in buildings of our own, and protected in the exercise of that right by law. For although this right was not obtained till the glorious revolution in 1688, we may properly regard the ejected ministers, who survived that event, as the founders of our churches in the cities and principal towns of England, in many of which congregations had been gathered previously to that auspicious era. It may also be mentioned that their numerous, and in some cases voluminous, writings, have greatly contributed to enrich and vitalise our English theology; while some of the productions of their pens, after they were silenced, have been blessed by God to the conversion and salvation of multitudes, as well as to the instruction, comfort, and edification of tens of thousands. ...

Let the people of England know on what an antichristian and sectarian foundation the Ecclesiastical Establishment in this country was re-constructed in 1662; and that it still rests on the same basis, – an Act of Parliament, and *such an* Act! Let the infamous character of this Act, the base spirit in which it was framed, the base arts by which it was carried, the base purpose for which it was intended, be exposed to the public gaze in all their hideous deformity. Many, I am persuaded, of the more thoughtful and candid adherents of that Establishment will be led by such an exposure to see and acknowledge the dishonourable origin and shameful character of an Act which can only be regarded as a blot and a disgrace to our English statute-book. ...

Before concluding this paper, I shall be excused for subjoining a word of brotherly admonition. We are about to contend earnestly for great ecclesiastical principles; let us take heed to our spirit, and see that we 'strive lawfully,' in a truly Christian temper, 'with meekness of wisdom.' Nor let us forget that there are yet more important matters on which we are at one with many from whom we differ widely upon these; and that our first duty, in a time of much declension and indifference to doctrinal truth, is to 'strive together for the faith of the Gospel,' to 'contend earnestly for the faith once for all delivered to the saints,' the faith of Christ crucified, well knowing that other safe and abiding foundation can no man lay than that which has already been laid by the hands of apostles and prophets, even Jesus Christ.

Document X.23

J. H. Blunt on the Future of Methodism, 1886

Victorians loved religious dictionaries, and read those which allowed them to pursue 'gainful knowledge' at home, and which agreed with their religious presuppositions. Most dictionaries were written by Anglicans, enabling them to score points over Nonconformists, and reveal (to later generations at least) their presuppositions. One of the best known writers of these works was Dr John Henry Blunt (1823–84), vicar of Kennington from 1868, and Beverston, Glos, 1874–84 (see DNB). He was mainly known for his annotations of the Prayer Book and the Bible.

A Dictionary of Sects, Heresies, Ecclesiastical Parties and Schools of Religious Thought, edited by J. H. Blunt, was first published in 1874 and remains valuable for the range of subjects covered, including descriptions of long disappeared groups and the then latest sects found in America. This extract comes from the edition published after his death, near the end of his long account of Methodism (London, 1886; republished 1891, p. 322). It shows a width of mind remarkable in its time; it is likely to have been written by Blunt, but this is not certain as he is just described in each edition as 'editor' and no further clue as to the writer of each article is given.

In conclusion it may be said that there is nothing which really differences the Methodist community from the Church of England, except the assumption of the sacerdotal office and sacerdotal functions by its ministers. This is an error of a very grave character, but is one which has partly resulted from the incomplete manner in which the nature of the priest's office was set forth by theologians of a past day; and it is, therefore, one for which much excuse may be made. The day may come when the better instructed Methodist preachers may seek and obtain episcopal ordination, and when the less educated class may also have work assigned to them analogous to their present work, but not sacerdotal, under similar authority. A general movement of this kind would go far towards ending the sectarian position of the Methodist body and restoring it to the position which it was intended by its founder to occupy. The two streams of practical godliness which now flow in the two separate channels of the Church of England and Methodist community, might then combine to form one great river whose broad expanse would represent a unity consistent with the varieties of English character and habit, and whose almost irresistible force would mould the religion of English-speaking people throughout the world.

Document X.24

J. H. Rigg on the Oxford Movement, 1895

J. H. Rigg (see X.6) wrote trenchantly on the influence of the Oxford Movement, which he called 'Puseyism' after E. B. Pusey, the Professor of Hebrew who consolidated the ranks of the Anglo-Catholic clergy after the departure of Newman to Rome. The hostility of Newman to Dissent (see X.20) found a counterpart in the views of Rigg, who, like most other Nonconformists, could see no difference between the theology of the Oxford Movement and the Roman Catholic position.

The extract is taken from J. H. Rigg, *Oxford High Anglicanism*, London, 1895, pp. 298-9.

Let us clearly understand that Puseyism, indeed, is essentially Popery; not, like the Laudian Movement, Popery revived from its embers in a nation of which the great mass of the people had never really embraced the Reformation, but Popery revived after ages intervening in which England, through all its ranks and classes, had ceased to be Popish, and, with whatever shortcomings, had yet been an enlightened and Protestant nation, delivered alike from the gross superstitions and the spiritual despotism of Rome. The two plague-spots of Puseyism – of High Church Catholicism – are its sacramental perversions, whereby the holy seals of the Christian faith and profession are turned into superstitions; and its dehumanising doctrine of the confessional. And these two roots of error being once accepted, there is no tenet either of Tridentine or of modern Popery which may not be received. Those who have learned to regard the priest-confessor as the searcher of hearts, and the healer and absolver of the soul, gifted for his office with corresponding attributes and authority from God, need find no difficulty in addressing prayers to the Virgin Mary, or to perfected saints, and can surely find nothing too hard for them in the doctrine of the Pope's infallibility, when speaking *ex cathdrâ*, as the 'Vicar of Christ.'

The papal infallibility is, in reality, a less revolting tenet than that which invests the parish priest with the prerogative of confessor. And yet if the priest by his consecrating act can bring to pass the sacramental miracles, what wonder if attributes are imputed to him which are much more than merely superhuman? All the landmarks of truth are confused in such a system; all the perspective of things human and divine is lost and confounded; men are no longer to be sanctified through God's word, which is 'the truth,' but by participation in theurgic mysteries, wrought by the hands of priests. He who has accepted the main roots of the whole system of error in the sacramental and confessional doctrines, need not stumble even at the doctrine of the Immaculate Conception of the Virgin. Pusey said that, if the Gorham controversy had turned against his party, he should have gone over and accepted Popery whole. He need have found no difficulty in doing this at any time. Nor was it at any time a real revulsion from the doctrines of Popery which retained him within the Church of England.

Document X.25

P. T. Forsyth on Established and Free Churches, 1896

P. T. Forsyth (see II.19) was keenly aware of the differences that separated the established church from the Free Churches, and yet he wanted to pursue the debate on the question of establishment with a suitable respect for the Church of England. At the same time he wished to assert the claim of the Free Churches, as much as the Church of England, to represent the authentic tradition of Western Christendom.

The extract is taken from P. T. Forsyth, *The Charter of the Church*, London, 1896, pp. 9-11.

This issue of Church and State will soon grow more keen. Let us enter it as fellow Christians, fellow believers, with our true opponents. Let us think often of the names that have made and do make the Established Church lovely and mighty in the service of God's Kingdom. Do not let the pusillanimity of some village cleric, the bigotry of some civic priest (say, on a School Board), or the dull worldliness of churchly fashion irritate the whole of your judgment on a question so great, an institution so venerable, a principle so solemn, as is here involved. Do not descend below the level of a great principle in discussing the matter. There are as good, holy, and devoted consciences on the one side as on the other. There is an immense amount of common tradition, common faith, common brotherhood on both sides. We have common enemies much more deadly to humanity than any issue which parts us. We have a common Lord Who is much more vital to the race than any name or cause that can unite men outside of Him and us. We have a common text-book which we regard with a common reverence, which we study together and adopt as containing our common standard of faith and morals. We have for many centuries a common history. The whole history of the Church up to the Reformation at least is as much ours as theirs. We believe in a church, and in one common inheritance in the historic Church of the West. But do we not agree, further, that there ought to be a national recognition and establishment of Christianity?

Everything turns here on what is meant by establishment. We recognise that the nation is a unity. It is a moral unity. It has a sanctity. It cannot dispense with a religion. No moral unity can. A nation ought to have a religion, and to give that religion expression. We begin to differ about that expression. Our opponents say it should be the establishment of a church by the State authority. What we say is that that has just been one of the chief causes why the nation has so much less real religion than it should, and so little practical expression of it. It was a national church that slew the universal Christ. You will note that it is one thing to have a church established in law, and another thing to have religion established in a nation's heart and life. The Church would have been a mother to more if it had not been so imperious to all. You will also note that the State authority has no faculty to decide on the form of religion to be established as a church, because it is not a religious body. It has no religious insight, no discrimination of religious truth. We say that the State is not the organ of the nation's religion, but only of the righteousness which is the true political expression of religion. We say the State recognition and establishment of religion should be the practical expression of the spiritual principles prescribed by that religion in social and international affairs. It is national Christian conduct. We say the destruction of war and of social injustice would be a greater, truer State recognition of Christianity than all the established churches that ever were damaged with public property and prestige. The establishment of religion by the State sinks it to the region of the State, the region of social and political relations, of laws, and the spirit of laws, a region only secondarily connected with spiritual life and freedom. We admit the ideal sanctity of the nation, and we assert that the only way to it is religious equality, which makes national righteousness the equal duty and result of all the religious communities, and not the charge of one alone. ...

So we have some agreement with our opponents on the principle that religion should be established in the public affairs of a nation. We differ when we urge the establishment of Christian righteousness and not of the Christian Church. We claim that the Free Churches have done at least as much, and probably more, for the English State of to-day than the Church which Establishment has, for the greater part of its history, secularised and paralysed. And we claim, as I have said, that the whole history of the Western Church, up to the Reformation at least, is as much ours as our opponents', if we were not so often too ill-informed and narrow in our views to realise the fact.

Select Bibliography

This list contains a number of works covering broad developments, whether in particular denominations or in Nonconformity as a whole. More specialised books and articles are mentioned in the introductions to the parts and in the notes on the documents to which they apply.

Bassett, T. M., *The Welsh Baptists*, Swansea, 1977.
Bebbington, D. W., *Evangelicalism in Modern Britain: A History from the 1730s to the 1980s*, London, 1989.
Bebbington, D. W., *The Nonconformist Conscience: Chapel and Politics, 1870–1914*, London, 1982.
Bebbington, D. W., *Victorian Nonconformity*, Bangor, Gwynedd, 1992.
Beckerlegge, O. A., *The United Methodist Free Churches*, London, 1957.
Binfield, J. C. G., *So Down to Prayers: Studies in English Nonconformity, 1780–1920*, London, 1977.
Binfield, J. C. G., *Pastors and People: The Biography of a Baptist Church: Queen's Road, Coventry*, Coventry, 1984.
Bolam, C. G., et al., *The English Presbyterians: From Elizabethan Puritanism to Modern Unitarianism*, London, 1968.
Briggs, J. H. Y., *The English Baptists of the Nineteenth Century*, Didcot, Oxfordshire, 1994.
Brown, K. D., *A Social History of the Nonconformist Ministry in England and Wales, 1800–1930*, Oxford, 1988.
Carruthers, S. W., *Fifty Years, 1876–1926*, London, 1926 [on orthodox Presbyterianism].
Carwardine, R., *Transatlantic Revivalism: Popular Evangelicalism in Britain and America, 1790–1865*, Westport, Connecticut, 1978.
Cashdollar, C. D., *A Spiritual Home: Life in British and American Reformed Congregations, 1830–1915*, University Park, Pennsylvania, 2000.
Coad, F. R., *A History of the Brethren Movement*, Exeter, 1968.
Cornick, D., *Under God's Good Hand: A History of the Traditions which have come together in the United Reformed Church in the United Kingdom*, London, 1998.
Cox, J., *The English Churches in a Secular Society: Lambeth, 1870–1930*, New York, 1982.
Davies, R., et al., ed., *A History of the Methodist Church in Great Britain*, vols 2–4, London, 1978–88.
Dix, K., *Strict and Particular: English Strict and Particular Baptists in the Nineteenth Century*, Didcot, Oxfordshire, 2001.
Drysdale, A. H., *History of the Presbyterians in England*, London, 1889.

Select Bibliography

Everitt, A., *The Pattern of Rural Dissent: The Nineteenth Century*, Leicester, 1972.
Glover, W. B., *Evangelical Nonconformists and Higher Criticism in the Nineteenth Century*, London, 1954.
Gowland, D. A., *Methodist Secessions: The Origins of Free Methodism in Three Lancashire Towns: Manchester, Rochdale, Liverpool*, Manchester, 1979.
Grant, J. W., *Free Churchmanship in England, 1870–1940*, London, n.d.
Green, S. J. D., *Religion in the Age of Decline: Organisation and Experience in Industrial Yorkshire, 1870–1920*, Cambridge, 1996.
Hempton, D., *Methodism and Politics in British Society, 1750–1850*, London, 1984.
Hempton, D., *The Religion of the People: Methodism and Popular Religion, c. 1750–1900*, London, 1996.
Hilton, B., *The Age of Atonement: The Influence of Evangelicalism on Social and Economic Thought, 1785–1865*, Oxford, 1988.
Hopkins, M., *Nonconformity's Romantic Generation: Evangelical and Liberal Theologies in Victorian England*, Carlisle, 2004.
Isichei, E., *Victorian Quakers*, Oxford, 1970.
Johnson, D. A., *The Changing Shape of English Nonconformity, 1825–1925*, New York, 1999.
Jones, R. T., *Congregationalism in England, 1662–1962*, London, 1962.
Jones, R. T., *Congregationalim in Wales*, ed. R. Pope, Cardiff, 2004.
Jones, R. T., *Faith and the Crisis of a Nation: Wales, 1890–1914*, ed. R. Pope, Cardiff, 2004.
Kent, J., *Holding the Fort: Studies in Victorian Revivalism*, London, 1978.
Larsen, T., *Friends of Religious Equality: Nonconformist Politics in Mid-Victorian England*, Woodbridge, Suffolk, 1999.
Lovegrove, D. W., *Established Church, Sectarian People: Itinerancy and the Transformation of English Dissent, 1780–1830*, Cambridge, 1988.
Machin, G. I. T., *Politics and the Churches in Great Britain, 1832–1868*, Oxford, 1977.
Machin, G. I. T., *Politics and the Churches in Great Britain, 1869–1921*, Oxford, 1987.
Madden, L., ed., *Methodism in Wales: A Short History of the Wesley Tradition*, Llandudno, 2003.
McLeod, H., *Class and Religion in the Late Victorian City*, London, 1974.
McLeod, H., *Religion and Society in England, 1850–1914*, Basingstoke, Hampshire, 1996.
Munson, J., *The Nonconformists: In Search of a Lost Culture*, London, 1991.
Obelkevich, J., *Religion and Rural Society: South Lindsey, 1825–1875*, Oxford, 1976.
Payne, E. A., *The Baptist Union*, London, 1959.
Peel, A., *These Hundred Years: A History of the Congregational Union of England and Wales, 1831–1931*, London, 1931.
Roberts, J., *The Calvinistic Methodism of Wales*, Caernarfon, 1934.

Select Bibliography

Rosman, D., *The Evolution of the English Churches, 1500–2000*, Cambridge, 2003.

Rowdon, H. H., *The Origins of the Brethren, 1825–1850*, London, 1967.

Sell, A. P. F., *Philosophy, Dissent and Nonconformity*, Cambridge, 2004.

Sellers, I., *Nineteenth-Century Nonconformity*, London, 1977.

Shaw, I. J., *High Calvinists in Action: Calvinism and the City: Manchester and London, c. 1810–1860*, Oxford, 2002.

Shaw, P. E., *The Catholic Apostolic Church sometimes called Irvingite*, Morningside Heights, New York, 1946.

Shaw, T., *The Bible Christians, 1815–1907*, London, 1965.

Smith, M., *Religion in Industrial Society: Oldham and Saddleworth, 1740–1865*, Oxford, 1994.

Thompson, D. M., *Let Sects and Parties Fall: A Short History of the Association of Churches of Christ in Great Britain and Ireland*, Birmingham, 1980.

Thompson, D. M., *Nonconformity in the Nineteenth Century*, London 1972.

Vickers, J. A., ed., *A Dictionary of Methodism in Britain and Ireland*, Peterborough, 2000.

Walker, P. J., *Pulling the Devil's Kingdom Down: The Salvation Army in Victorian Britain*, Berkeley, California, 2001.

Watts, M. R., *The Dissenters*, vol. 2, Oxford, 1995.

Werner, J., *The Primitive Methodist Connexion: Its Background and Early History*, Madison, Wisconsin, 1984.

Index of Persons

Adamson, W. 22
Allen, M. 249
Allon, H. 86, 102, 151, 343
Anderson, O. 252
Andrews, S. 109
Arch, J. 330
Armitage, J. 165
Arnot, W. 382
Arthur, W. 63, 180
Ashworth, J. 355
Auty, A. 171, 242

Baines, E. 300
Baker, D. 319
Baker, F. 221
Banks, C. W. 85, 135
Banwell, G. 356
Banyard, J. 177
Barton, D. A. 158
Bass, M. 252
Batty, M. 198, 204
Baxter, W. 278
Beard, C. 89
Beard, J. R. 47
Bebbington, D. W. 9, 31, 63, 82, 106, 164, 202, 292, 296, 319, 362
Beckerlegge, O. A. 364
Begbie, H. 318
Benham, J. 213
Bennett, G. V. 26
Bennett, J. 111
Biagini, E. F. 9, 258
Bidder, W. 85
Binfield, C. 65, 121, 126, 140, 156, 181, 198, 258, 275, 300
Binney, T. 181
Blackburn, J. 156
Bloxham, V. B. 9
Blunt, J. H. 386
Bogue, D. 111
Booth, C. 3, 250, 267
Booth, W. 5, 50, 250, 269, 318, 319
Booth, W. B. 154

Booth-Tucker, F. de L. 250
Bourne, H. 127, 149, 220, 221, 247, 260
Bowers, B. 213
Bowers, F. 213
Bowmer, J. C. 126, 201
Bradfield, W. 253
Bradley, W. L. 69
Brailsford, E. J. 62
Brake, G. T. 320
Briggs, J. H. Y. 7, 32
Brook, W. 191
Brooke, J. H. 97
Brown, E. B. 84
Brown, H. S. 264
Brown, J. 192, 193
Brown, J. B. 84
Brown, K. D. 198
Browne, G. 274
Browne, G. B. 325
Budgett, S. 180
Bunting, J. 311, 342, 346, 357, 364
Bunting, T. P. 342
Burnham, J. D. 328

Caine, W. S. 264
Calle, M. J. 293
Campbell, J. 263
Capper, E. N. 169
Cardale, J. B. 145
Carey, W. 257
Carter, G. 372
Carter, W. 265, 266
Carwardine, R. 258, 261
Cashdollar, C. D. 126, 198
Chalmers, T. 98, 263
Champness, E. M. 14, 268
Champness, T. 14, 268
Chandler, J. 182
Channing, W. E. 23, 87
Charles, D. 36
Charnock, S. 165
Chichester, J. L. 191

Index of Persons

Chilcote, P. W. 117
Clark, D. 8
Clark, J. 293, 294
Clarke, A. 16, 99, 129, 142, 324
Clarke, J. B. B. 129
Clemenson, R. 187
Cliff, P. B. 219
Clifford, J. 92, 108
Clipsham, E. F. 59
Clowes, Francis 326
Coffey, J. 258
Coghill, H. 118
Cooke, J. 355
Cooper, T. 102, 103
Cornick, D. 362
Cox, F. E. 150
Cox, J. 9
Cox, S. 87, 88
Crewdson, I. 77
Crowther, J. 294
Cunningham, V. 97
Currie, R. 340, 366

Dale, A. W. W. 65
Dale, R. W. 32, 39, 65, 66, 80, 100, 134, 164, 215, 331, 332, 333
Dallinger, W. H. 109
Darby, J. N. 328
Darlow, T. H. 139, 140
Davidoff, L. 234, 243
Davidson, S. 79
Davies, D. 137
Davies, E. 137, 206
Davies, H. 14, 126, 132
Davies, R. 7, 32, 126, 137
Davies, R. E. 70
Davis, V. D. 23
Dean, W. W. 221
Dick, T. 106
Dickson, N. 131
Dix, K. 85, 135
Dixon, G. 330
Drescher, S. 312
Drew, J. 192
Drummond, J. 64
Dudley, E. 188
Dudley, M. 188
Dunn, S. 364
Dykes, O. 52

Dyson, J. 219

Edwards, M. S. 322
Ellens, J. P. 292, 303
Eliot, G. 117
Elwyn, T. S. H. 223
Evans, E. 117
Evans, W. 32
Everett, J. 364
Everitt, A. 2, 8

Fairbairn, A. M. 68, 104
Farningham, M. 115
Field, C. D. 9, 233
Findlay, G. G. 258
Finney, C. G. 261
Flegg, C. G. 145, 359
Fletcher, J. 60
Fletcher, M. 117
Fletcher, R. 306
Forrester, D. 152
Forsyth, P. T. 31, 69, 339, 388
Foster, J. 111
Fox, G. 77
Franks, R. S. 68
Fraser, D. 300
Fuller, A. 19, 33, 59, 60, 84

Gadsby, W. 17, 59, 148, 166, 175, 225
George, E. 228, 236, 237
Gilbert, A. 176, 329
Gilbert, A. D. 8
Gilbert, J. 176, 329
Gilley, K. 114
Gladstone, W. E. 64, 301
Glover, W. B. 31, 91
Goldhawk, N. P. 126
Gordon, J. M. 164
Gosse, E. 183
Gosse, P. H. 183
Gough, T. T. 224
Gowland, D. A. 342, 357
Grace, J. 182
Graham, E. D. 239, 247, 253
Grant, J. W. 198, 215, 340
Green, S. J. D. 9
Gregory, O. 14, 128, 274
Griffith, W. 364
Grubb, M. 77

396

Index of Persons

Hall, C. 234, 243
Hall, R. 14, 74, 128, 274
Hamilton, J. 382
Harris, J. 82
Harrison, B. 315, 329
Harrison, F. M. W. 33
Hart, D. G. 202
Hart, T. 69
Harvey, Jane 239
Harvey, John 126, 206
Harvey, W. 239
Harwood, W. H. 151
Hazlerig, G. 238
Hazlerig, Lady 238
Hearn, M. A. (Marianne Farningham) 115
Helmstadter, R. J. 5, 6, 9, 107
Hempton, D. 292, 325
Hennock, E. P. 331
Herschell, H. 180, 181
Herschell, R. H. 275
Hewitson, A. 133
Hicks, E. 77
Hill, E. 114
Hilton, B. 5, 9
Hincks, W. 114
Hindmarsh, R. 9
Hinton, J. H. 84
Hirst, J. 166
Holdsworth, W. W. 258
Hollis, P. 292, 300
Holmes, J. 252, 258, 268
Homan, R. 374
Hopkins, M. 19, 31, 65, 84, 86, 90
Horne, C. S. 140
Horridge, G. K. 267
Horton, R. F. 27, 91
Hughes, D. P. 26, 52
Hughes, G. W. 14
Hughes, H. P. 26, 52, 92, 105, 116, 285
Hunter, C. 168
Hunter, J. 140
Huntington, W. 72, 175, 191
Huntsman, J. 189
Hutton, J. E. 9

Inglis, K. S. 9
Innes, J. 264
Irving, E. 144
Isichei, E. 44, 251, 270, 295, 317, 348

Jackson, T. 62
Jacob, W. M. 63
James, J. A. 80, 170, 243
James, S. 73
Jenkins, J. 191
Jerrome, P. 374
Johnson, D. A. 32, 117
Johnson, M. D. 86
Jones, A. 126
Jones, R. T. 32
Jordan, E. K. H. 52, 340, 346

Kaye, E. 104
Keeble, S. E. 322
Kelly, C. H. 285
Kendall, W. C. 285
Kenrick, J. 113
Kent, J. 26, 258, 260
Ker, I. T. 381
Kershaw, J. 166
Kessler, J. B. A. 49
Kidd, B. 105
King, D. 49
Kinnear, G. 213
Klaiber, A. J. 75
Knibb, W. 313
Knox, R. B. 382
Kreider, A. 9
Kruppa, P. S. 19

Laqueur, T. W. 219
Larsen, T. 103, 292, 296, 362, 384
Lawrence, W. 293, 294
Levi, L. 152, 362
Lewis, D. M. 263
Lewis, J. 233
Lidgett, J. S. 70
Lightfoot, J. 174
Lincoln, J. 72
Lindley, K. 126
Livingstone, D. N. 106, 108
Long, A. 301
Lovegrove, D. W. 258, 259
Lovett, R. 258, 272
Lowndes, W. 375
Lumpkin, W. L. 33
Lunn, H. 285
Lynch, T. T. 83

Index of Persons

McCurdy, L. 69
MacDonald, F. W. 21
Machin, G. I. T. 292
McKenny, H. G. 234
Mackintosh, W. H. 292, 309
McLachlan, H. J. 235, 355
MacLaren, A. 24
McLaren, E. T. 24
McLean, A. 370
Maclean, C. M. 120
McLeod, H. 9
M'Owan, P. 316
Macpherson, E. 244
Madeley, E. 9
Manley, K. R. 165
Marchant, J. 92
Marriott, J. A. R. 27
Martineau, J. 23, 64, 87, 132
Maurice, F. D. 70
May, E. 179
May, J. H. 179
Medway, J. 107
Miall, E. 130, 303
Milburn, G. 198, 204
Mill, J. S. 102
Miller, A. 227
Miller, E. 298
Mills, W. H. 121, 229
Mohler, R. A. 202
Moore, J. R. 108
Moore, R. 198
Morden, P. J. 59
Morris, J. W. 59
Moss, R. W. 67
Müller, G. 184
Munson, J. 198, 292
Murray, D. 152

Newman, F. W. 100
Newman, J. H. 298, 381, 387
Newton, B. W. 81
Newton, J. 176
Nicoll, W. R. 139
Noel, B. W. 144

Obelkevich, J. 8
O'Bryan, W. 248, 356
Oldstone-Moore, C. 26
Oliphant, M. 118

Owen, R. 103
Owen, W. T. 60

Paley, W. 106
Palmer, P. 250
Parker, J. 22
Parrott, J. 366
Parsons, G. 8
Paterson, A. T. 193
Payne, E. A. 51, 90, 93, 340
Payne, G. 98
Pearse, M. G. 119
Peel, A. 27, 39, 83, 340, 344
Pennington, A. 245
Pethick-Lawrence, Lord 293
Peto, S. M. 213
Phillips, P. T. 23, 32
Philpot, J. C. 85, 150, 182, 379
Philpot, J. H. 17, 380
Pickering, H. 131, 227
Pigott, H. 228, 236, 237
Piper, B. 374
Piper, H. 374
Pope, R. 32
Pope, W. B. 67
Porteus, M. 174
Powicke, F. J. 93
Price, A. E. 372
Priestley, J. 23, 60
Prochaska, F. K. 121, 234
Punshon, W. M. 21
Pusey, E. B. 386

Rack, H. D. 164, 214
Raleigh, A. 13
Raleigh, M. 14
Ramsbottom, B. A. 17
Redford, G. 39
Reid, T. 97
Reynolds, H. R. 102
Rhodes, H. G. 226
Richardson, G. 280
Rigg, J. H. 351, 386, 387
Rippon, J. 148, 165
Robinson, W. G. 259
Robjent, R. D. 136
Roby, W. 259
Rogers, H. 100
Rogers, J. G. 345, 346

Index of Persons

Rowdon, H. H. 81, 131
Rowell, G. 87
Ruston, A. 114, 263, 293, 301, 355
Ryland, J. E. 112

Sambell, P. 157
Sandall, R. 50, 154, 216
Sargant, N. C. 285
Sargeant, J. 375
Schulman, F. 301
Scotland, N. 330
Scott, R. 235
Scott, T. 176
Selbie, W. B. 68, 140
Sell, A. P. F. 97, 100
Sellers, I. 7, 16, 84, 149
Sharman, C. 184
Shaw, J. 9
Shaw, P. E. 145, 298
Shaw, T. 356
Sheils, W. J. 49, 278
Sherman, J. 190, 210, 241
Sherman, M. 190, 241
Shiman, L. L. 321
Shore, J. 372
Short, H. L. 341
Simon, D. W. 31, 93
Sirgood, J. 374
Smith, B. 32, 64
Smith, D. 130
Smith, H. A. 285
Smith, J. P. 93, 107
Smith, J. T. 351
Smith, M. 8
Smith, W. 293
Smith, W. S. 9
Sorrell, M. 177
Spettigue, R. 356
Spiers, W. 321
Spinks, B. D. 126
Spurgeon, C. H. 8, 19, 31, 90, 119, 147, 164, 202, 212
Spurgeon, J. 212
Stanley, B. 258, 278, 281
Steadman, T. 73
Steadman, W. 73
Steers, D. 263
Stephen, C. A. 138, 348
Stephen, L. 138

Stephens, J. 311
Stephenson, T. B. 253
Stevens, J. 59
Stewart, D. 97
Stocks, R. 169
Stoughton, J. 181
Stovel, C. 370
Strawson, W. 32
Sturge, J. 317
Swanson, R. N. 131, 281, 384
Swift, W. F. 248

Taggart, N. W. 63
Tarrant, W. G. 155
Tayler, J. J. 23, 87
Taylor, A. 35
Taylor, D. 35, 378
Telford, J. 119, 351
Thom, J. H. 23
Thompson, D. M. 7, 92, 292, 339, 370
Thwaite, A. 183
Tickle, G. 370
Tindall, P. 301
Tolson, A. 170
Trestrail, F. 281
Trotter, W. 131
Tucker, M. 210, 211
Tuckerman, J. 263
Turberfield, A. F. 70
Turley, D. 263
Turner, J. M. 340
Turner, W. 47
Tyrrell, A. 317

Unwin, G. 119
Upton, C. B. 64

Valenze, D. 234
Vaughan, F. 372
Vaughan, R. 102, 200

Wakefield, G. S. 164
Walford, J. 127, 247
Walker, B. G. 135
Walker, M. 126, 147
Walker, P. J. 267, 319
Waller, R. 32, 64
Walsh, J. D. 26
Ward, W. R. 292, 307, 342

Index of Persons

Warren, S. 342, 357
Watson, J. 315
Watson, J. R. 126
Watson, R. 62
Watts, I. 148
Watts, M. R. 1, 8, 9, 113, 164, 292
Waugh, T. 172, 177
Webb, R. K. 23, 32
Wells, J. 85
Welsby, M. 268
Weremchuk, M. S. 328
White, W. 83, 270
White, W. H. 120
Wickham, E. R. 1, 8
Wigley, J. 316
Wilkinson, J. T. 127
Wilks, M. 275
Williams, E. 60, 93
Williams, H. W. 214, 218

Williams, M. 184
Williams, S. C. 8
Williams, W. 150
Williamson, D. 25
Wills, J. 158, 159
Wilson, B. R. 9
Wilson, D. 303
Wilson, J. 384
Wilson, L. 164, 234
Wolffe, J. R. 49
Wood, D. 49
Wood, E. 167
Wood, J. 86
Wood, P. 107
Wright, T. 72

Yates, N. 63
Young, K. 198

www.ingramcontent.com/pod-product-compliance
Lightning Source LLC
Chambersburg PA
CBHW081147290426
44108CB00018B/2466